OXFORD HISTORICAL MONOGRAPHS

Editors

PACIFISM IN BRITAIN
1914 - 1945:
THE DEFINING OF A FAITH

by

MARTIN CEADEL

CLARENDON PRESS · OXFORD
1980

Oxford University Press, Walton Street, Oxford OX2 6DP

OXFORD LONDON GLASGOW
NEW YORK TORONTO MELBOURNE WELLINGTON
KUALA LUMPUR SINGAPORE JAKARTA HONG KONG TOKYO
DELHI BOMBAY CALCUTTA MADRAS KARACHI
NAIROBI DAR ES SALAAM CAPE TOWN

*Published in the United States
by Oxford University Press, New York*

British Library Cataloguing in Publication Data

Ceadel, Martin
    Pacifism in Britain, 1914–1945: The defining of
    a faith — (Oxford historical monographs).
    1. Peace — Societies, etc. — History — 20th century
    2. Great Britain — Politics and government —
    20th century
    I. Title   II Series
    327'.172'0941   JX1908.G7   79-41540
    ISBN 0-19-821882-6

*Set by Hope Services, Abingdon
Printed in Great Britain by
Billing & Sons Ltd.,
Guildford, Worcester & London*

TO MY MOTHER
AND THE MEMORY OF MY
FATHER

ACKNOWLEDGEMENTS

In the course of research I have accumulated many obliga-
tions: to two outstanding tutors, Brian Harrison and John
Walsh, for their stimulus and encouragement; to Nuffield
College for providing so congenial a launching-pad; to Martin
Gilbert for his kindnesses as supervisor of the thesis on which
this book is based; to A. J. P. Taylor and James Joll for
examining it and recommending its publication; to David
Butler, J. R. Milton, Maurice Shock, A. F. Thompson, Roy
Walker, and Philip Williams for advice and comments; and to
the librarians and staff of the Bodleian Library, the British
Library Reference Division, the British Library of Political
and Economic Science, the National Library of Wales, and
the libraries of Cambridge, Hull, and Sussex Universities,
Friends' House, Nuffield College, and University College,
London for their courtesy and co-operation.

In locating source material I have been aided by L. R.
Bisceglia (who with the altruism of the true scholar has made
available his findings through the National Register of Ar-
chives), John Ramsden, Carolyn Scott, Richard Storey, and
Daniel Waley; and also by friends expert in tracing private
papers: Chris Cook and his colleagues—Philip Jones, Jo
Sinclair, and Jeffrey Weeks—on the S.S.R.C. Political Archives
Investigation, and Christine Woodland.

A pleasure of studying this particular subject has been
the helpfulness of the societies and individuals I have
approached for information about or access to their papers:
the Friends' Peace Committee, the National Peace Council,
the Peace Pledge Union, the United Nations Association, Mrs
Elizabeth Bing, Mrs Olwen Bridgeman, Lady Cobbold, John
Freeman, Frank Hardie, the Hon. Mrs J. C. Hogg, Edward
Milligan, Mrs Mabel Eyles Monk, Mrs Pamela Parkin, and
Myrtle Solomon. In addition the following have been generous
in talking or writing to me about their pacifism: the late
Gerald Bailey, Ruth Baker, Lord Brockway, Ronald Duncan,
Frank Hardie, Margaret Storm Jameson, the late Frank Lea,
Ethel Mannin, the late Leah Manning, Mrs Lucy Middleton
(*née* Cox), Mrs Mabel Eyles Monk, Mrs Hilda Morris, Sybil

Morrison, Mrs Mary Middleton Murry (*née* Gamble), Henry
Pelling, Lord Soper, Nigel Spottiswoode, David Spreckley,
Roy Walker, John Wanstall, and Roger Wilson. A number of
others have assisted me with topics for which space has not
been found in this book: I hope to have the pleasure of
acknowledging their help in due course. For any inadvertent
omissions in the above lists I apologize.

I have left my greatest debt till last. Deborah Ceadel has
been the final arbiter of each draft of this book: her pene-
trating criticisms have condemned numerous pages to the
waste-paper basket; but her comradeship and inspiration have
frequently saved the whole text from ending up there.

April 1979

ABBREVIATIONS

(i) Text:

B.A.-W.M.	British Anti-War Movement
C.C.P.G.	Council of Christian Pacifist Groups
C.O.	conscientious objector
F.o.R.	Fellowship of Reconciliation
League	League of Nations
L.N.U.	League of Nations Union
N.-C.F.	No-Conscription Fellowship
N.M.W.M.	No More War Movement
N.P.C.	National Peace Council
P.P.U.	Peace Pledge Union
U.D.C.	Union of Democratic Control
W.I.L.	Women's International League
W.R.I.	War Resisters' International

(ii) Footnotes:

A.P.	(Arthur Ponsonby) Ponsonby Papers.
Co.	Council Minutes
D.D.	(David Davies) Davies of Llandinam Papers.
E.C.	Executive Committee Minutes.
F.H.	Frank Hardie Papers.
F.P.C.	Friends' Peace Committee Minutes.
G.C.	General Committee Minutes.
G.M.	Gilbert Murray Papers.
M.P.	Max Plowman Papers.
N.C.	National Committee Minutes.
NMW	*No More War*
NS	*New Statesman*
NW	*New World.*
P	*Peace*
PN	*Peace News.*
R.C.	(Robert Cecil) Cecil of Chelwood Papers.
Rec.	*Reconciliation.*
Sponsors	Sponsors' Meetings Minutes

(Note. All works were published in London unless otherwise stated.)

CONTENTS

x CONTENTS

PART ONE:

BEFORE THE 1930s: IN THE SHADOW OF *PACIFICISM.*

1

PACIFISM AND *PACIFICISM.*

This book has two aims: to tell the story of the most interesting and influential pacifist movement in modern times, that
of Britain in the era of the two world wars: and, in so doing,
to develop a means of analysis that can be applied to pacifist
movements in other countries and at other times.

The first aim is prompted by the relative historical neglect of
the inter-war peace movement, a neglect which is surprising
in view of the attention lavished on most other aspects of
a period which was not only bounded and defined by two
world wars, but also strongly conditioned by memories of the
one and gloomy forebodings of the other. Moreover, when the
peace movement and public attitudes to war have been alluded
to in passing they have been the subject of frequent and fundamental errors even by distinguished writers. Michael
Howard, for example, seems to believe that Canon Dick Sheppard's peace pledge was a petition or plebiscite organized in
'spring 1938',[1] whereas in fact it originated in October 1934
as an appeal for postcard declarations of support for pacifist
principles and became after May 1936 the membership basis of
the Peace Pledge Union (P.P.U.), Britain's leading pacifist
society, which is still in existence today. Similarly, the crucial
distinction between this pledge and the Peace Ballot (a private
referendum organized in 1934-5 by the League of Nations
Union, a body which, albeit equivocally at times, opposed
pacifism and endorsed the use of sanctions against an aggressor)
has frequently been missed—not merely by recent scholars,[2]

---

[1] Michael Howard, *War and tne Liberal Conscience* (1977), p. 87 n.

[2] See e.g. Stephen Roskill, *Hankey: Man of Secrets*, iii (1974), p. 175; Samuel
Hynes, *The Auden Generation* (1976), p. 194; T. E. B. Howarth, *Cambridge
Between The Wars* (1978), p. 220; Julian Symons, *The Thirties; A Dream
Revolved* (1960), p. 42.

but also by those who themselves worked for these causes during the thirties.[1]

A major reason for the confusion, and for the fact that ex-participants have been among the worst offenders, has been the tendency to view the inter-war years from the perspective of the Second World War, when the aggressiveness of Germany's international policy could no longer be denied. In consequence, memoir-writers have tended to forget how slow they themselves were to abandon their optimistic expectations that the Great War had ushered in a new international morality. To take an extreme example, even Hugh Dalton, who has gained deserved credit for steering the Labour Party away from outright opposition to rearmament in the second half of the thirties, was in the late twenties a declared sympathizer of the absolute pacifist No More War Movement,[2] a fact of which his autobiography understandably makes no mention.

A tendency towards *ex post facto* rationalization is present, of course, in many historical contexts; but it is particularly prevalent among those who lived through the inter-war years because of the unprecedented rapidity with which international circumstances then changed. Attitudes and ideas which had seemed enlightened and even practical in the aftermath of the Great War, one of the most reviled wars in human history, were suddenly rendered obsolete and ludicrous by Hitler, whose behaviour rehabilitated warfare and ensured that the Second World War's credentials as a just war were almost unimpeachable. The speed and shock of this fundamental change of expectations generated self-deception and also genuine confusion about how this process had occurred, both of which still distort our historical picture of thinking about war and international affairs in the twenties and thirties.

There is a need, therefore, for a reliable history of the

---

[1] e.g. Edward Hyams (who in 1937 had published a P.P.U. pamphlet *Few Men Are Liars*), *The New Statesman: The History of its First Fifty Years* (1963), p. 149; and Lord Eustace Percy (a member of the L.N.U. Executive Committee at the time of the Peace Ballot), *Some Memories* (1958), p. 171.

[2] 'Why I Believe in the No More War Movement', Appendix to W. J. Chamberlain, *Fighting for Peace: The Story of the War Resistance Movement* (n.d. [1928]).

peace movement and attitudes to war to set the record straight. One of its major tasks would be to distinguish once and for all between two often confused but essentially different anti-war viewpoints: the belief that all war is *always wrong* and should never be resorted to, whatever the consequences of abstaining from fighting; and the assumption that war, though *sometimes necessary*, is always an irrational and inhumane way to solve disputes, and that its prevention should always be an over-riding political priority. Both these positions were called 'pacifism' during the inter-war period— an additional cause of the historical confusion already noted. In this study, however, only the former position will be given this label; the latter will be described, following A. J. P. Taylor's usage, as *pacificism*.[1]

Etymologically, it must be admitted, this distinction is somewhat contrived. Strictly, 'pacificism' and 'pacifism' are not different words: the former is simply the original and correct form of the word which right from the start was sometimes—and is now invariably—contracted to the latter. The justification for here employing the longer, less euphonious, and now archaic form (pacificism) as if it were a distinct word is twofold. Firstly, there is no other term that can more conveniently be used to describe the non-pacifist strand within the peace movement. Secondly, the pristine meaning of the word pacificism (variant: pacifism) was not what is now understood as pacifism but what is here analysed as *pacificism*: when coined in the first decade of the twentieth century,[2] pacificism meant no more than being in favour of peace and arbitration and opposed to militarism and settling disputes by war; and, on its first appearance in any of the Oxford dictionaries, in the addenda dated September 1914 of the *Concise Oxford Dictionary*, it was defined as 'the doctrine that the abolition of war is both desirable and possible'. (Absolute pacifism tended to be described, on the rare occasions the distinction was perceived, as 'extreme'

[1] A. J. P. Taylor, *The Trouble Makers* (1957), p. 51 n.
[2] According to Elie Halévy, writing in the mid-1920s, the word was first coined in French in 1901, becoming common French usage after 1905 and current in English soon after that: *Imperialism and the Rise of Labour* (1951 edn.), p. 66 n. See also A. J. A. Morris, *Radicalism Against War 1906–14* (1972), pp. 198–9 n.

pacificism—or 'extreme' pacifism—or as the doctrine of non-resistance.) The Great War brought the word into prominence and reinforced it with emotive and derogatory connotations, but failed to give it any more precise meaning. It was used simply for someone who opposed the war; and since it was possible to oppose a war of such tragedy and horror for a wide range of reasons, the word remained vague even despite the success of the conscientious objectors in dramatizing a stricter, absolutist meaning. This is confirmed by its first appearance in the *Oxford English Dictionary* itself: in the 1933 Supplement (it had been too new a word for the original edition of 1905), which gave its meaning as 'The policy of avoiding or abolishing war by the use of arbitration in settling international disputes; advocacy or support of this policy, or belief in its practicability; often with depreciatory implications the advocacy of peace at any price.' Similarly, and also in 1933, the first edition of the *Shorter Oxford English Dictionary* defined it as 'The doctrine or belief that it is desirable and possible to settle international disputes by peaceful means.' Even allowing for linguistic conservatism on the *O.E.D.*'s part these definitions show that the original usage was still common in the early thirties; but other sources indicate that its modern (absolute pacifist) meaning was already gaining ground. At the same time its shorter form (pacifism) was becoming increasingly usual and the longer form increasingly pedantic. Thus by the late 1930s what is now regarded as correct usage had established itself. Since then, however, the English language has been bereft of an authentic term to signify the original meaning: hence the resort in this study to *pacificism* (which is italicized both in recognition of the fact that its usage is artificial and to avoid visual confusion with pacifism).

Though obliged to share the same verbal identity for several decades, pacifism and *pacificism* are fundamentally different ideas. Pacifism is the personal conviction that it is wrong to take part in war or even, in an extreme version, to resist evil in any way. It thus has perfectionist implications for politics, since only a national policy of total (and, if necessary, unilateral) disarmament can prevent a sharp conflict arising between the pacifist's conscience and his duty as a citizen. Yet, it will here be argued, it is not primarily a political idea but, rather, a moral creed.

Where pacifism must thus be seen, in Weber's celebrated distinction, as an 'ethic of ultimate ends', *pacificism* is close to being an 'ethic of responsibility'. It sees the prevention of war as its main duty and accepts that, however upsetting to the purist's conscience, the controlled use of armed force may be necessary to achieve this. Essentially, it is a political idea since it believes that implementing reforms at the political level—rather than waiting for profound changes to occur in men's consciences offers the only realistic chance of limiting the use of force and of curbing warfare as a human institution. The nature of the reforms contemplated has depended on the political philosophy of the *pacificist*. The most common, the range of proposals here categorized under the heading 'internationalism', derive from the liberal belief in a latent harmony of real interests between nations; they envisage that this harmony will be actualized either through improved international contact or, if economic and cultural influences prove insufficient to overcome irrational national prejudices, through more positive measures to diminish the sovereignty of the individual state such as the transfer of certain powers to specially established confederal or federal institutions. The main rival to internationalism has been the minority view that the economic drives of capitalism and imperialism are the basic and inexorable causes of war and that the only real solution lies in striving for world socialism—although in the short term the workers should adopt a policy of 'war resistance', normally in the form of a general strike against any warmongering Government. A third *pacificist* strand, developed initially by late-Victorian and Edwardian radicals, attempts to reconcile these liberal and socialist traditions: while accepting the liberal idea that there can be no rational economic reason for war, it attributes to certain vested interests—arms manufacturers, international financiers, the 'jingo' press, the officer class and diplomats—rational motives for overlooking this fact and indulging in power politics based on rearmament and the threat of war.

In order to take root, *pacificist* ideas require a symbiosis of optimism and pessimism: optimism, because they offer a prospect of the withering away of war; pessimism, because they will only attract support when there is a widespread fear of war. *Pacificism* flourished in inter-war Britain because of the prevailing blend of nineteenth-century optimism and twentieth-century pessimism. Internationalist, socialist, and radical critiques—and, indeed, the peace movement itself— were products of Victorian Britain's strategic security and confidence in human progress, rather than of fear of war. It was the Great War, involving as it did both conscription and the first bombing raids on British cities, which generated this fear on a significant scale for the first time in Britain. Even though its prospects of success had been undermined by growing international instability, the peace movement attracted unprecedented support after 1918 on the grounds that the need for it to succeed was greater than ever. A traditional expectation of human progress, tempered by experience of total war, had thus produced a mood of despairing hope ideally suited to *pacificism*.

Pacifism and *pacificism* each deserve serious historical study in their own right and this book was intended to cover both. However, after much of the material had been collected, it became clear that justice could not be done to both within the space available. The latter has, therefore, been reserved for a separate book; which means that general attitudes to war, non-pacifist ideas for preserving peace, and the role of both in British political life have reluctantly but necessarily been excluded from this one. Pacifism alone is tackled here: in part because it has always been the peace movement's inner core and focal point, but also because it offers, in addition of the challenge of historical analysis, an opportunity to consider a moral problem illustrating in acute form the tension between the demands of conscience and those of political action. Since it is a moral and philosophical issue, the approach adopted, while aspiring to provide a rounded treatment of pacifism including both its composition and its tactics as a movement, is designed primarily to explore pacifism as an idea.

On purely historical grounds, moreover, this approach is more justified than other possible biases. Even at their inter-war peak pacifist societies were too small (and tactically stereotyped) for an approach aiming mainly to evaluate their performance as pressure groups to be a rewarding one. It was, after all, fear of the Germans and of their bombers which dictated the major changes in public thinking on the peace question; the peace movement merely responded to these changes and there is no evidence that the particular response of the pacifists (whatever may have been the case with the *pacificists*) was ever of the slightest concern to the Government. Similarly, although Frank Parkin's excellent analysis of the sociological and attitudinal characteristics of the Campaign for Nuclear Disarmament might be thought to provide a model for a work such as this, systematic evidence of the sort which Parkin derived from his questionnaires is lacking for the pacifist rank and file of half a century ago; and even if it could be retrieved it would only illuminate one dimension of its subject. It is revealing, moreover, that Parkin does not claim his book to be primarily about C.N.D. but a case study in sociological method.[1]

This book assumes that analysis of such impact as the pacifist movement did have and of the type of support it attracted cannot be attempted without first understanding its ideas and expectations, since these largely determined the quantity and quality of its support. The movement's influence was greatest and most broadly diffused when it could present itself as a distinct position in its own right (rather than merely as an extreme tendency within *pacificism*) and one which offered a practical strategy for preventing war. It lost influence, and contracted into a minority movement of committed and homogeneous activists, when its limitations as a practical strategy could not be overlooked. For this reason—and also in view of the *ex post facto* rationalizations and semantic confusion already mentioned—this book will give priority to expounding the content of pacifist ideas and explaining the changes which took place.

The extent to which this intellectual clarification is needed may not be self-evident: at first glance pacifism seems one of the least complicated of social beliefs. But close examination

---

[1] Frank Parkin, *Middle Class Radicalism: The Social Bases of the British Campaign for Nuclear Disarmament* (1968), pp. 2–3.

of how pacifists justify it, what they expect to achieve, and how they perceive their obligations to the society in which they live, reveals within pacifism a number of distinct positions. Just as the study of socialist movements could never have made progress without an understanding of, say, the distinction between collectivism and libertarianism, or that between Marxist notions of class conflict and Christian-inspired ideals of brotherhood, so the analysis of pacifist movements cannot proceed without establishing its own analytical categories. The appropriate conceptual tools for pacifism have, it is here argued, yet to be forged—hence the second aim of this book, which will begin by introducing a new typology, of, it is hoped, general applicability to pacifist movements. Once this has been done, briefly in the following chapter, a coherent pattern to the modern history of pacifism can be discerned: as a debate between a limited number of conceptions of pacifism, progressing under the stimulus of a deteriorating twentieth-century international situation towards a mature understanding of the idea, not as a political strategy, but as a moral faith—'The Faith Called Pacifism', to quote the title of a leading pacifist work of the second half of the thirties.[1]

[1] By Max Plowman (1936)

2

INSPIRATIONS AND ORIENTATIONS

A major obstacle to the analysis of pacifism has been an insufficiently precise definition of its scope: this has often resulted from an implicit equation of the pacifist with the conscientious objector. It should be recognized, however, that even the most 'sincere' and courageous refusal to fight need not be prompted by pacifism; and that, in addition, the granting of conscientious objection by the state has always had a pragmatic justification: ridding the military authorities of those certain to be more trouble than they are worth. In constructing a typology, therefore, two categories of objector will be excluded which have commonly but erroneously been accorded the status of pacifist because they are commonly found among C.O.s.

The first category, the selective objector (i.e. to certain wars only), is logically *pacificist*. His explicit or implicit criterion for deciding whether or not to support a particular war is whether or not the war advances the political cause (normally, as already noted, internationalism or socialism) which he favours. A particularly clear illustration of the distinction between selective objection and true pacifism was provided by those who opposed the Second World War because their fascist principles made them object to fighting against a fascist state. Where the main risk of war is from a conflict with a fascist state, a fascist movement can fulfil a *pacificist* function; but, depending as it does on values such as nationalism and self-fulfilment through physical struggle—which cannot be claimed to be incompatible with war—fascism can never be an inspiration for pacifism.

The second category, the objector to military service for reasons which are not *pacificist* but which fall short, nevertheless, of a universalizeable, principled objection to all war, is here described as quasi-pacifist. His reasons, which usually amount to a claim for special treatment on account of his particular characteristics as an individual, or those of the group to which he belongs, can be classified into two main sub-varieties. One, here characterized as 'esoteric', is based on unorthodox religious tenets, such as certain idiosyncratic interpretations of the biblical attitude to killing or to war, or convictions which indirectly lead to non-combatancy such as refusal to take uncongenial military oaths or to serve alongside non-believers. The other, in certain respects its secular counterpart, and here described as 'élitist', is based on the assumption that certain gifted individuals should, on account of their personal qualities, be excused from having to fight. Both types of quasi-pacifist seem to regard exemption from combatant service as a privilege of the elect or the élite, and they often imply that ordinary citizens should be left to get on with the fighting—and should even be encouraged to do so in order to prevent national collapse. In contrast, a true pacifist feels that though he must respect the conscientious right of his fellow citizens to disagree with him, there is no reason in principle why all of them should not come to share his beliefs. Indeed, he would ideally like them to do so, whatever the immediate military consequences, for he regards his pacifism not as a means of personal or group exculpation but as a contribution to the moral welfare of his society and of mankind in general. Although neither selective objection nor these two brands of quasi-pacifism are recognized in this study as pacifist, they will be further discussed in due course and the importance of their historical contribution to the pacifist tradition fully acknowledged.

Simply by being thus based on a more rigorous definition of pacifism, the typology to be introduced in this chapter differs from those already offered by pacifism's leading academic students, David Martin and Peter Brock. Martin's failure, in applying a distinction derived from the sociology of religion, to distingush in certain circumstances between pacifism and *pacificism* will be discussed in the following chapter;[1] the objection to the typology drawn up by Brock at the conclusion of his invaluably comprehensive historical survey of European and American

[1] See below, pp. 25-6; see also David A. Martin, *Pacifism: An Historical and Sociological Study* (1965).

pacifism requires, however, immediate explanation because it also introduces a second, more important, difference of approach. The six types of pacifism listed by Brock,[1] as well as including those more properly classed as quasi-pacifism, fail to embody a distinction vital to the analysis of pacifism: that between its *inspiration* or basis; and its *orientation* or attitude towards society and the problem of war prevention. The priority of this brief chapter will thus be to differentiate these two dimensions of pacifism, beginning with the question of inspiration.

What do pacifists object to in war? This question is surprisingly difficult to answer in the case of the very many pacifists whose objection to war is not derived from an absolute refusal to take life or to employ force and who, therefore, not only accept their local police force but also support the death penalty, or even euthanasia.[2] Two separate (but in practice normally intertwined) arguments are commonly advanced for singling out warfare from other applications of force: first, that war is an *illegitimate* use of force; second, that it is a *qualitatively* worse form of force. The illegitimacy argument against war is as follows: man has not introduced sufficient order into his international relationships to be permitted to use those same measures which nation states, by civilizing their domestic behaviour, have earned the right to employ as a punishment of last resort. It follows that if a proper world state existed, its judicial

---

[1] Peter Brock, *Pacifism in Europe to 1914* (Princeton, 1972), pp. 472-6; these pages draw together the threads of his previous works, including *Pacifism in the United States from the Colonial Era to the First World War* (Princeton, 1968), and *Twentieth-Century Pacifism* (New York, 1970). The six types of pacifism he puts forward are each recognized by this study but are classified either as belonging to the category of quasi-pacifism or as orientations (rather than inspirations). His first three types are thus here interpreted as sub-categories of quasi-pacifism: (i) 'Vocational' is what is here called elitist quasi-pacifism; (ii) 'Soteriological', 'an objection to shedding human blood (and sometimes animals' as well) because it leads to ritual impurity', and (iii) 'Eschatological', 'a kind of non-violent interim ethic', are both varieties of the esoteric sub-category of quasi-pacifism. His last three categories accord exactly with what this study will call orientations: (iv) 'Separational' is what will be analysed as sectarian; (v) 'Integrational' is collaborative; and (vi) 'Goal-directed' is the same as non-violence. His typology thus says nothing about what are here called the *inspirations* for pacifism, except for the quasi-pacifist ones.

[2] e.g. Frances Partridge, *A Pacifist's War* (1977), p. 205.

penalties would be as legitimate and, therefore, as acceptable to pacifists as those of any well-ordered polity. But how does this view differ from the internationalist (i.e. *pacificist*) belief that measures which when used by a nation state would be dismissed as warlike are transmuted into acceptable 'military sanctions' by being authorized by an international organisation? The answer is that pacifists have in practice refused to accept that the modest developments in international law and judicial machinery which have been achieved by bodies such as the League of Nations are sufficient to render killing and force legitimate. In particular, whereas internationalists have implied that the legitimacy of coercion arises from the (international) quality of the authority applying it, pacifists have implied that it arises from the (judicial) quality of the coercive process itself. In a true world state offending citizens would be brought to law and punished as individuals. But in any merely confederal system which retained the identity of the nation state or any intermediate political unit the process of retribution might have to be directed indiscriminately against a whole country for collective offences of which the citizens could not in the normal judicial sense be shown to be individually guilty. And to many pacifists indiscriminate coercion of whole nations makes war illegitimate. However, during the inter-war period in particular, many pacifists were prepared to advocate economic and other forms of non-military coercion against whole nations, suggesting that it was the nature of the force employed (rather than its legitimacy) which was the more salient factor in their thinking. At all times, moreover, pacifist propaganda has dwelt on the qualitatively greater horror of the military variety of force; and the technological advances this century have turned this into the main objection to war.

Even non-pacifists have come to accept that war is the least legitimate and qualitatively the worst application of force. Yet they do not regard force of whatever kind as the greatest evil imaginable: they are convinced that in certain circumstances justice, liberty, or even honour, is worth going to war for. The pacifist, in contrast, regards all war as wrong whatever the practical consequences of fighting or not fighting. So absolute a belief is, it will here be argued, a value judgement which is susceptible of neither proof nor disproof; it is, in other words, a dogma or creed. (Alternatively, as in the case of pacifism based on the wrongness of killing or of employing force, it is itself a deduction from another such dogma.) Normally, of course, the pacifist does not rest content with his dogmatic assertion that all war is always wrong. He attempts to argue that this belief is itself inspired by and represents the correct deduction from a generally respected religious, ethical, or philosophical position. Three types of position have been appealed to as justifications—or, in the terminology to be used in this study, inspirations—for pacifism. The oldest and most durable inspiration has been religion: in Britain, almost exclusively Christianity. To this has been added, from the late nineteenth century, pacifism derived from political creeds such as socialism or anarchism. Finally, starting in the inter-war period, attempts began to be made to justify pacifism not on the basis of any religious faith or secular equivalent but on the basis of war's effects on net human happiness and suffering.

The first two inspirations are, in philosophical terms, deontological. Whether or not Christian theology or socialist principles do lead to pacifist conclusions is a matter of doctrinal interpretation, and a significant portion of this study will be devoted to historical debates on these very points. But even religious and political pacifists frequently resort, as a clinching argument, to the third inspiration, a 'utilitarian'[1] calculation of the results of war. This, in philosophical language a consequentialist position, professes to offer a justification of pacifism independent of prior assumptions, and must be seen as inter-war pacifism's most ambitious and important intellectual development.

In fact, however, as many pacifists came to realize during the later thirties, a value-neutral justification for pacifism is impossible. Briefly stated, the reason is as follows: to claim that war is so destructive that there is a reasonable expectation that it will do more harm than good is merely a *pacificist*

---

[1] This word is used in this study in a broad (rather than strictly Benthamite) sense: to describe those who believe they have arrived at their pacifist position by weighing up the pros and cons of different courses of action in order to produce the 'best' result for everyone.

view; it does not obviate the need to consider the cause and likely consequences of each particular war on its merits. 'Utilitarian' pacifism is truly pacifist only if it goes further and states that the harm of any future war will *always* outweigh any conceivable benefit, and that, therefore, any war must be rejected without reference to its particular circumstances. For this to be the case its harm must tend to infinity, which is merely a way of re-stating in utilitarian language the assertion that war is the greatest evil.

But, although it is not the 'objective' pacifism it has been claimed to be, 'utilitarian' pacifism is nevertheless a new and distinct inspiration for pacifism. This is because it does not try to deduce the wrongness of war from higher ·religious or political principles but sees it to be self-evident in the harm inflicted on mankind—the suffering, destruction, and the denial of happiness war produces. Although the human values outraged by war include materialism and even hedonism as well as humanitarianism, in this study all absolute objections to war based on its consequences for human existence will be classified—using the term in a broader sense than is perhaps usual—as the humanitarian inspiration for pacifism. (The term 'utilitarian' will be retained, however, to denote that sub-category of humanitarian pacifism which erroneously believed its views to be objective.)

Humanitarian pacifism is thus no less a dogma than religious or political   pacifism. Although he usually ex-presses his faith in what purport to be empirically veri-fiable propositions, the humanitarian pacifist subconsciously redefines his key terms so that incompatibility with war is built into their meaning. For example, a non-pacifist might argue that a nation which beats off an invasion can be said to have preserved its liberty by war. But to a pacifist the resort to military measures will, by definition, be a denial of 'true' liberty so that the war will have failed to achieve its objective; to cite an example from the writings of a humanitarian pacifist active in the P.P.U.: 'The pacifist believes that because of the fundamental unity of man, the killing or maiming of any individual personality can only result in loss, never in gain for the whole species, *or for any section of it.* [1]

It is not only humanitarian pacifists, however, but those of all inspirations who, when attempting to express their negative attitude towards war in terms of more positive beliefs, merely rationalize their *a priori* rejection of all war. This explains the remarkable uniformity of the tenets to which religious, political, and humanitarian pacifists alike claim adherence: all reject war because it violates the dignity of the human personality or the unity of mankind, and all assert the impossibility of overcoming evil by evil methods. It follows from this that, although the pacifist movement has commonly organized itself in separate societies according to whether these tenets are seen as an expression of, for instance, Christian love, socialist brotherhood, or common sense and human decency, and although these societies have devoted much of their time to explaining to other Christians, socialists, or rationalists and humanists why their shared beliefs should lead to pacifist conclusions, the relevance of questions of inspiration to the practical dilemmas faced by pacifism can be exaggerated. Often more important in its historical development have been questions of orientation—in other words the pacifist's attitude towards the society in which he lives—which must now be considered.

Pacifism regards war as evil: therefore, though he must live in a political society, the pacifist cannot accept citizenly obligations to participate in or endorse war in any way. But how does this affect his wider role as a citizen? If the obligation not to endorse war-making activity is interpreted strictly, a pacifist must withdraw from all public activity within that society since this will be tainted by, for example, the allocation of social resources to defence. But if the pacifist withdraws in this way then he denies himself the chance of educating society in the direction of adopting either *pacificist* views on minimizing war or even, ideally, the complete pacifist position. In terms of his attitude to society, he has a choice of three orientations: the sectarian position of total withdrawal from society; the collaborative position of taking part

[1] Philip S. Mumford, *An Introduction to Pacifism* (P.P.U., 1937), p. 15 (italics added).

in political life to the extent of supporting *pacificist* campaigns; and the most optimistic position of all, which clearly presupposes exceptionally favourable circumstances, nonviolence (or non-violent resistance, as it was often described in the thirties to contrast it with non-resistance), which assumes that pacifism can be applied as an immediately effective policy in the world as it is.

In other words, pacifism is pulled in two opposed directions in its relationship with society: towards preserving its purity; or towards maximizing its political relevance. The relative strength of these pulls is determined by the society. If it is enlightened and has a strong *pacificist* tradition it will make political participation hard to resist; on the other hand the more repressive and hostile the society, the greater the pacifist's readiness to incur its displeasure and the more vital his pacifist witness.

This apparent paradox can best be understood if pacifism is seen as but one of the ways in which the individual conscience can conflict with the demands of political society. Though war is one of society's oldest and least defensible organized activities and one which brings out this conflict with unique clarity, it is not the only source of such conflict. The pacifist thus faces problems if he adopts what is, in effect, an attitude of selective anarchism. Why, it can be asked, does he not challenge the state over other social and political evils? If he accepts its authority and is integrated into society in every other respect can he not be accused of inconsistency and of letting down those with whom he has cultivated ties of common citizenship if he reserves the right to reject one, particularly onerous, social obligation? If on the other hand the pacifist is completely alienated from his society and able to condemn it over the full range of issues he will escape this accusation. Thus the more congenial the society and the more it offers him participation in practical efforts to prevent war, the harder the pacifist finds it to justify selective conscientious rejection of one citizenly duty. A major theme of this study will be that, whereas modern pacifism has often enjoyed a sympathetically anti-war environment, the most confident and impressive pacifism has resulted where pacifists have been driven, by disagreement with a society convinced of the inevitability of war, into a sectarian orientation.

To sum up: the typology used in this study excludes *pacificism* and quasi-pacifism, and classifies strict pacifism according to two separate criteria. As a result pacifism will at certain points be characterized as religious (e.g. Christian), political (e.g. socialist or anarchist), or humanitarian (including 'utilitarian') in order to make distinctions about its inspiration; and at other points as sectarian, collaborative, or non-violent, when its orientation is in question. The main types of both inspiration and orientation, briefly noted already, will now be reintroduced in their historical context.

3

BEFORE THE GREAT WAR

Before analysing pacifism in Britain in the era of the two world wars, it is necessary to outline briefly the pacifist tradition as it affected Britain before 1914. In this period the inspirations for pacifism were ill-defined: there was virtually nothing which could pass for a socialist or a humanitarian inspiration for pacifism (as distinct from *pacificism*); and, although most pacifists claimed to derive their belief from Christianity, on inspection many of these proved to be esoteric quasi-pacifists. The orientations of pacifism, as this chapter will also show, are largely determined by the state of political development of the society in which it finds itself. Pre-modern conditions encouraged sectarianism; but, as society became liberal and democratic and a *pacificist* movement developed, pacifists became collaborative—without, however, facing up to the question of how they could justify collaboration with non-pacifist measures. By the late nineteenth century sectarianism was showing vitality only in the still feudal circumstances of Tsarist Russia, where Tolstoy had begun to preach it. Since he did so partly in the belief that his non-resistance might prove politically efficacious, Tolstoy had sown the seeds of a new orientation (here called non-violence), which Gandhi was already exploring in the years before 1914. British pacifists knew surprisingly little about this, however: on the eve of the Great War their approach was still epitomized by the vague and shallow pacifism—Christian and collaborative—of an already senescent Peace Society.

To begin at the beginning: pacifism is, according to Peter Brock, nearly two thousand years old.[1] Its earliest and, throughout most of its history, its most vital inspiration has been Christianity. Members of the early Christian Church

[1] Brock, *Pacifism in Europe*, p. 3; see also Roland Bainton, *Christian Attitudes Toward War and Peace* (1961).

seem for the most part to have refused to fight in Roman armies, and Christian pacifists have always claimed that this attitude remains the most straightforward reading of Christian doctrine on war. But since AD 313, when the Emperor Constantine made Christianity the offical religion of the Roman Empire, pacifism has been abandoned by the Church in so far as the latter has agreed to support certain 'just' wars. The concept of the Just War was formulated in the fourth century by St Augustine, an African-born Roman citizen who was fully aware that the Roman military presence was necessary to protect the faith against barbarian incursions. As the doctrine was codified in the thirteenth century by St Thomas Aquinas, a Just War had to fulfil three conditions: (1) the war had to be fought with the permission of the sovereign; (2) there had to be a just cause for the war; and (3) the belligerents had to intend to advance good or avoid evil as the result of the war. To these conditions later medieval theologians added another, which became important as warfare grew more destructive: (4) the war had to be waged by proper means.[1] This has remained the orthodox Christian position ever since, although it has been held most explicitly and uniformly by the Roman Catholic church.

This post-Constantine compromise with war has been treated by pacifists—for example, by the distinguished ecclesiastical historian the Revd Cecil J. Cadoux (1883–1947)—as one of the many retreats the religion has made from its pristine purity:

In the life of the early Church, as in no other phase of history before or since, we see a moralising movement at work, visibly cleansing human society of its glaring transgressions, and bidding fair to establish the kingdom of God on earth . . . The acclimatisation of the Christian conscience, therefore, to the use of the sword is not to be considered as an accession of superior wisdom or as a necessary condition of the survival of the Church any more than is any other aspect of the general Christian surrender to the spirit of the world such as the love of wealth and luxury, intrigue and unbrotherly strife.[2]

Cadoux was writing in 1925, when, fear of war not being an issue, the main stimulus for Christian pacifism was that it

---

[1] F. L. Cross, *The Oxford Dictionary of the Christian Church* (1957). p. 1438.
[2] *The Early Christian Church and the World* (1925), pp. 612, 615.

seemed to offer a means of purifying the Churches after their worldly compromises in the Great War. A close friend, the Revd Charles Matthews, has noted how the inter-war period's leading pacifist, Canon H. R. L. ('Dick') Sheppard (1880–1937), who was converted to pacifism in 1927 at a moment of extreme disillusion with the Church of England and 'whose vision of the Church was always of the mystical, essential Church, was distressed by the contrast between this ultimate reality and the empirical Church. He dreamed of a Church here on earth which should manifest all the perfection of the mystical Church in its fullness.'[1]

Some non-pacifist scholars, however, have questioned whether the pacifism of the early Church can be taken as a paradigm of untainted Christianity.[2] They have argued that it was in reality based on a dislike of the pagan ritual—in particular, the idolatrous military oaths acknowledging the Emperor's divinity—which a Christian had to accept on joining the Roman army. By thus treating the basis of early Christian pacifism as analogous to the objection of twentieth-century Exclusive Brethren to being 'unequally yoked among unbelievers',[3] they have in effect interpreted it as what is here called esoteric quasi-pacifism. Quasi-pacifism has already been defined as a claim to exemption on grounds which do not amount to a universalizeable, principled, objection to all war. Sometimes, as in the case of objection to military oaths through fear of idolatory, it is not an objection to all war as such. An example of this in modern times is the 'interim ethic' of the Christadelphians and Jehovah's Witnesses, who do not really claim to be true and lasting pacifists since they look forward in the not-too-distant future to playing a militant role in the coming millennial crusade but refuse in the present sinful state of the world to submit to military authority. At other times the objection is undoubtedly to all war and killing, but on idiosyncratic grounds that are

---

[1] C. H. S. Matthews, *Dick Sheppard: Man of Peace* (1948), p. 51.

[2] e.g. Edward A. Ryan, 'The Rejection of Military Service by the Early Christians', *Theological Studies*, xiii (1), Mar. 1952, pp. 1–32. Some Christian pacifists accept this view: Geoffrey Nuttall, *Christian Pacifism in History* (Oxford, 1958), pp. 9–10.

[3] John Rae, *Conscience and Politics: The British Government and the Conscientious Objector to Military Service 1916–1919* (1970), p. 75.

regarded even by leading Christian pacifists as unable to with-
stand serious theological or philosophical scrutiny. One
example, the basis of the objection to war of the twelfth-
century Cathars, is an objection to shedding human (or even
animal) blood on the ground that it leads to ritual impurity;
another is the insistence of the Seventh Day Adventists that
their own literal reading of the Commandments in English
translation justifies a refusal of combatant (but not, apparently, of non-combatant) service.

Mainstream Christian pacifism, in contrast, derives its
objection to fighting not from selected biblical texts, nor
from the desire to avoid religious contamination, but from
the incompatibility of all war with its perception of Christ's
teaching as a whole. In its mature form, developed after
1914, it makes clear that its purpose is not to save the elect
from sin, nor even to save society from material disaster, but
to redeem mankind through the power of Christian love. The
extent to which the early Church was in this sense pacifist
rather than merely quasi-pacifist cannot be further discussed
here; but the historical importance of esoteric 'pacifism' to
the post-Constantine pacifist tradition must be emphasized.
In the fifteen hundred years from 313 to the foundation of
the first peace society and the gradual emergence, which
began not long afterwards, of tolerated pacifist minorities
within (especially the Protestant) Churches, the absolutist
attitude was kept alive only by the periodic emergence
of unorthodox Christian sects. In pre-Reformation times
these sects—such as the Cathars and Waldensians of the
twelfth century—were undoubtedly esoteric; only with the
foundation of the Mennonites in the mid-sixteenth and the
Quakers in the mid-seventeenth century did contributions of
lasting value to Christian pacifism *stricto sensu* begin to
be made.

But whatever the precise *inspiration* of pacifism during
the first seventeen centuries of its existence, esoteric or
truly Christian, it was undoubtedly sectarian in *orientation*.
In the case of the early Church this was largely a result of
persecution; and, after Constantine's conversion had rendered
sectarian withdrawal unnecessary for the Church as a whole,
pacifism was kept alive, as already noted, by the formation

from time to time of sects at odds with the political societies in which they found themselves, in the same way as the early Church had been in the Roman world. These sects seem to have traced little or no intellectual continuity with previous pacifist traditions; what they seem to have had most in common was a background of acute social tension.

In this sectarian orientation pacifism was characterized by pessimism. Whatever its inspiration for regarding war as the supreme evil, the implication of sectarian pacifism is that the evil cannot be ameliorated. War will never be abolished—unless by the complete moral regeneration of human society. Indeed, most pacifist sects were characterized by millennarian beliefs; where they differed from non-pacifist sects, of course, was in rejecting the alternative method for achieving the millennium: the violent crusade. For example, the Mennonites, founded in 1561 by Menno Simons, were a pacifist offshoot from the Anabaptists—who had themselves originally been predominantly pacifist before succumbing at Munster in the 1530s to the attempt to in-augurate God's earthly kingdom at once and by force. Pacifist sectarians believed they must wait patiently for the change in men's hearts, and tried in the meantime to dissociate themselves where possible from the evil of war and the society contaminated by it. However, while most felt their calling required them to witness to their values by submitting with quiet humility, some manifested a voluble and self-righteous defiance. The same was to be true of twentieth-century pacifists and was largely a matter of temperament: indeed the Chairman of the P.P.U. once went so far as to claim that the most significant observation that could be made about types of pacifist did not concern their beliefs, but was this 'fundamental psycho-logical division between the introvert and the extrovert'.[1]

It was inevitable that this sectarian orientation should have dominated pacifism until the nineteenth century, since it was possible to opt out of society to a meaningful extent, but impossible to do anything constructive about preserving peace as long as society remained undemocratic

---

[1] Alex Wood, in *PN*, 26 Apr. 1940.

and repressive. (The long tradition of proto-*pacificist* writing
and internationalist schemes merely peddled Utopian dreams.)
However, as societies became more modern they became
more complex and even the strictest of sectarian pacifists
could not avoid making continual compromises with the ever
more intrusive state by accepting the protection of the police
force and even by becoming dependent on others for food.
As Bertrand Russell observed in 1932: 'When I earn money
by pacifist activities, 8 per cent goes to building American
battleships and 30 per cent to building British battleships,
so that I do more harm than good.'[1]

Moreover, as societies became more modern they offered
for the first time the possibility of political change. In
Britain the new Benthamite faith in the power of public
opinion was expressed in the proliferation of pressure groups,
including the Society for the Promotion of Permanent and
Universal Peace, soon shortened to the Peace Society (or
International Peace Society). Founded in 1816, a year
after a similar foundation in the United States, it was Britain's
first peace society: pacifism thus ceased to be a faith confined to the static, self-contained sects and became instead a
proselytizing movement. Initially the Peace Society, which
had been established by Quakers, lacked any programme
beyond the conversion of individuals to Christian pacifism;
from the 1840s, however, it became permeated with the
newly popular ideas of *pacificism*.

The rise of *pacificism* in the early nineteenth century
was due to pessimism about the effects of war on civilized
values, combined with optimism that political progress had
made internationalism a realistic possibility for the first
time. The former was a result both of increased humanitarian
sensitivity to suffering of all kinds and of a growing awareness, in the troubled aftermath of the Napoleonic Wars,
that fighting also had unexpected social costs. The latter
was a product of the liberal conception of the world as a
community derived from a belief in free trade and from a
Nonconformist sense of morality. Britain's traditional lack

[1] Russell to Warder Norton, 29 Aug. 1932, in Barry Feinberg and Ronald
Kasritz, *Bertrand Russell's America: His Transatlantic Travels and Writings*,
i (1973), p. 124.

(as an island) of a large army and its deep-rooted aversion to conscription were thus reinforced by Cobden's influential critique of such military forces as it did possess as aristocratic vested interests. It was notable too that the labour movement did not develop any significant belief in a citizens' army.

The flowering of *pacificism* in Britain, and also in the United States, was an integral part of its liberal, protestant political culture. On the continent, in contrast, nationalism was more important and the peace movement much less vigorous: in Germany liberalism was too weak to nourish pacifism and, as in France, anti-militarism was to be increasingly dependent on socialist inspiration. Yet since the essence of *pacificism* is a belief that there is a middle position between pacifism and the doctrine 'si vis pacem, para bellum', it is clear that strategic factors are also relevant to its success or failure. For an expansionist nation such as Wilhelmine Germany, or for a defensively-minded nation such as inter-war France facing a more powerful neighbour, a middle position between submissiveness and Realpolitik was harder to locate than for powers like Britain and the United States, which lacked close-range threats to their national aspirations.

The possibility of political change and the emergence of a *pacificist* movement began to tempt pacifists out of their sectarian shells in order to participate in practical activity to prevent war. Leading the way—as already noted in the context of the foundation of the Peace Society—was the Religious Society of Friends, a pacifist sect which gradually diluted its sectarian outlook. Founded in the comparatively enlightened mid-seventeenth century, the Quakers had never been in conflict with society as acutely as had most earlier sects, and were favourably disposed to political participation for both social and doctrinal reasons. Socially, their upward mobility established them as a prosperous community of manufacturers, merchants, and professional men of considerable influence. Although some Friends were keen not to dilute their absolutism precisely because they had compromised on their original social radicalism, the majority came to be increasingly embarrassed by this sectarian survival. Doctrinally, too, they were well-equipped to co-operate with *pacificist* tendencies, since the Quaker objection to war was based not on any explicit law against bearing arms or taking life, but on an intuitive and subjective interpretation of the 'Inner Light'. The Inner Light could easily be identified with what non-Quaker Christians invoked, with equal subjectivity, as the 'Mind of Christ', or with what humanitarians, socialists, Theosophists, and non-Christian mystics understood as 'the spiritual unity of mankind'. Being so tolerant and undoctrinaire the Quakers found it so easy to co-operate with *pacificist* movements that many Friends feared that the distinctiveness of Quaker peace testimony was being forgotten. These fears were borne out in the case of the Peace Society which, from the 1840s onwards, was predominantly Nonconformist and *pacificist* rather than Quaker and pacifist.

The problems the Quakers were facing over how far they could endorse non-pacifist views in the interests of achieving political influence were inherent in what was, in effect, the new orientation they were pioneering. Already introduced here as collaborative pacifism (because it collaborated with *pacificist* activity), it proved to be undoubtedly the most popular orientation, in peacetime at least, during the century after about 1840, when *pacificism* took root in British political life. Its attraction was that it offered pacifists the chance to help prevent war; but it had two drawbacks. For one thing, it was hard to justify: how, in particular, could a pacifist explain both his own pacifism and his support of non-pacifist means of securing peace (such as the formation of an international police force in which he would personally be unable to serve)? This difficulty will be considered later, in the context of the 1930s when it was recognized for the first time.[1] More important for the present purposes is that the collaborative orientation blurred the difference between pacifism and *pacificism*.

It is a failure to keep these ideas separate which, it is here argued, vitiates the otherwise interesting attempt by David Martin to analyse pacifism wholly in terms of a distinction (derived from a synthesis of the sociological theories of

[1] See below, pp. 158–68.

Troeltsch, Weber, and H. Richard Niebuhr) between the 'sect' and the 'denomination'. The former category accords with what is here called the sectarian orientation and presents, therefore, no difficulties. The latter Martin defines as

a developed stage of the sect when perfectionist demands have been ameliorated, the adventist hope dimmed and compromise may be made with the world . . . In general the denomination may be distinguished from the sect because it is a reformist body which only rejects the wider society within the more embracing terms of an overall agreement.[1]

Into this category Martin places both the Quakers (here analysed as collaborative pacifists) and the Nonconformist Churches, which in the terminology of this study were mainly *pacificist*. As a description of the nineteenth-century peace movement this lumping together is understandable: because of their collaborative approach the Society of Friends worked closely with Nonconformist *pacificists*; and, indeed, a minority of the former became overtly *pacificist*, and a minority of the latter absolutely pacifist. But to categorize both as denominations is nevertheless, as Martin himself concedes, historically inaccurate, because whereas the Quakers had started as a sect and thereafter developed some of the characteristics of a denomination,[2] the Nonconformist Churches had taken denominational form right from the start, instead of having evolved out of a sect as his model implies. This had important consequences for the period 1914–45: because of its sectarian origins the Society of Friends remained, despite its *pacificist* minority, a resolutely pacifist body; whereas the Nonconformist Churches, despite their pacifist minority, endorsed the national cause in both world wars.

Martin's failure to distinguish between collaborative pacifism and *pacificism* illustrates the paradoxical position in which pacifism found itself once it ceased to be sectarian and became part of a wider (and tolerated) peace movement:

---

[1] Martin, *Pacifism*, p. 3.

[2] Elizabeth Isichei has argued that older sectarian characteristics co-existed with newer denominational elements over a long period: 'From Sect to Denomination among English Quakers', in Bryan Wilson (ed.), *Patterns of Sectarianism: Organization and Ideology in Social and Religious Movements* (1967), p. 161.

the more sympathetic society became to its formerly unique critique of war, the harder it was to make its own distinctive voice heard among the chorus of 'practical' schemes for war-prevention. To maintain the courage of its independent and unpopular absolutist convictions pacifism requires the stimulus of adversity. With Quakers feeling a declining sense of social alienation as the nineteenth century progressed, it was the newer Nonconformist tradition of conscientious conflict with the state—culminating in opposition to the Boer War and the Balfour Education Act—which, though not inspired by pacifism, did most to keep the sectarian spirit alive, thereby setting inspiring precedents for resistance to conscription when it was introduced in 1916. Walter Ayles (1879-1953), for example, later the Organizing Secretary of the No More War Movement, was to tell his military service tribunal that, in being an absolutist conscientious objector, he was merely suffering for his beliefs in the same way his Nonconformist forefathers had always done before him.[1]

It was significant too that, with the exception of the foundation in Victorian Britain of a few esoteric quasi-pacifist sects (such as the Christadelphians), the only interesting pre-1914 developments in absolute pacifist thinking occurred in repressive environments such as Tsarist Russia or South Africa. In Russia during the 1870s the novelist Leo Tolstoy (1828-1910), reacting in middle age against his dissolute early life as aristocrat and soldier, began to preach an extreme and ascetic doctrine of non-resistance to evil which repudiated all physical force and all compromise with society. His motive, however, was not the sectarian one of withdrawal for its own sake; he believed his non-resistance would somehow have the effect of discrediting and undermining the Tsarist state. He was thus an anarchist, believing himself to be working for political change, but doing so by means—in this case the uncompromising rejection of all force—which were essentially apolitical.

The hint that pacifism could have a political effect, rather than the content of his unorthodox Christian anarchism,

[1] Keith Robbins, *The Abolition of War: The 'Peace Movement' in Britain 1914-1919* (Cardiff, 1976), p. 195.

was to be Tolstoy's real legacy to modern pacifism. Although his thinking had aroused some interest before 1914 among British socialists, it made few thorough-going converts and by the inter-war period, when most pacifists were anxious above all to stress the realism of their strategy for averting war, it had come generally to be dismissed as an unnecessarily extreme position which risked tarring all pacifists with the brush of crankiness. The man who developed its practical possibilities—having in his intellectually formative years read and corresponded with Tolstoy—was Mohandas K. Gandhi (1869–1948). Working towards the more concrete and limited goal of civil rights for Indians in South Africa in the period after 1904 (and, later, that of Indian independence), Gandhi altered the emphasis of Tolstoy's anarchism from the apolitical to the political. Instead of seeing submission to evil primarily as a conscientious moral act, albeit with political implications, he saw it primarily as a calculated technique of political agitation, albeit also with moral implications. He thus abandoned Tolstoy's strict objection to physical force of any kind and planned organized mass exercises in civil disobedience.

Though (like Tolstoy) Gandhi had not formulated his views with international relations in mind, his ideas were, understandably, seized on by pacifists as the twentieth-century's most exciting initiative. This new hope—that pacifism might prove effective at once, instead of only after a slow evolution to a warless world—characterizes the third pacifist orientation used in this study: non-violence (or non-violent resistance). When pressed to justify this orientation, and to explain how pacifism would achieve immediate results in the international sphere, its advocates—of whom there were many in the early and middle thirties—had two lines of defence. The first was the assumption of moral deterrence: that a disarmed state could make any potential aggressor feel too guilty to launch an attack. The second—which Gandhi's campaign seemed to justify—was the technique of passive resistance: the assumption that an invading force could, even if moral deterrence had failed, still be overcome by civilian non-violence.

Both rested, however, on assumptions which were open to

question. The first, and to a lesser extent the second, represented an astonishing contrast with other pacifist orientations in their attitude to political society. Whereas sectarians regarded attempts to influence society as futile, and even the more sanguine collaborative pacifists limited their initial hopes to the efficacy of *pacificist* ideas only, non-violent resisters were so optimistic about the enlightened state of their own society (and its likely adversaries) that they expected non-violence to exert effective moral pressure. This was a perhaps not unrealistic expectation in the case of the relatively liberal British Empire against which Gandhi was directing his own nationalist efforts, or of the American south where the post-1945 peace movement has found non-violence to be a valuable technique for combating racialism. But in the sphere of international relations, particularly in the inter-war period, it was clearly Utopian. There was the practical difficulty, in an age which expected war to be carried on in the future almost exclusively by air bombardment, of setting up the face-to-face physical confrontation on which passive resistance relied for its psychological leverage. In addition, passive resistance was open to criticism on grounds of principle: to a strict Christian or Tolstoyan pacifist, it seemed to be itself a form of coercion rather than a true expression of love and reconciliation. Yet such was the optimism engendered by Gandhi's exploits in India in the early thirties that hopes for non-violent resistance were to reach a peak among pacifists of all inspirations even though the international situation was already deteriorating and prospects even for *pacificist* remedies had begun to fade.

Before 1914, however, Gandhi was little known in Britain and *pacificism* seemed to offer a real chance of preventing war. Despite the undermining in the late nineteenth and early twentieth centuries of the mid-Victorian assumptions about Britain's strategic interests and the harmony of international interests on which it had been based, internationalism had continued to gain in influence. Although confidence in the power of free trade had to some extent been supplanted by hopes for the development of international law and even a confederal system as the most favoured panacea for securing peace, Norman Angell's best-seller of 1910, *The Great*

Illusion, largely reaffirmed the Cobdenite thesis that there could be no rational motive for war. Admittedly, Angell had felt it necessary to reiterate this thesis because the increased economic and imperial competition faced by Britain from the later nineteenth century onwards had generated alternative socialist and radical critiques—the latter, and by far the more influential, developed mainly by J. A. Hobson and H. N. Brailsford—which both insisted that economic drives *could* produce war. But all three versions of *pacificism* agreed that a European war was far from inevitable and that if it nevertheless occurred then Britain could and should be kept out. Thus 4 August 1914 came as a stunning shock to the entire peace movement. Despite the partial precedent of the Boer War (and with the exception of a few individuals who had read Tolstoy, experienced compulsory military training abroad, or become alienated from the state on other issues) the pacifist movement—which still meant the now venerable and respectable Peace Society plus various Christian sects—had given little thought to what it would do if a major war came.

4

THE GREAT WAR

The Great War marks the beginning of the modern British pacifist movement. Two new fellowships were founded in 1914,
which formulated the Christian and socialist inspirations for
pacifism with unprecedented clarity, while the Peace Society
became moribund. The introduction of conscription in 1916
proved even more important: pacifism became a political issue
for the first time; and, although the number of conscientious
objectors (16,500) was small and the vast majority even of
these accepted alternative service, the small minority of
'absolutists' (who were prepared to go to gaol in protest against
any compulsory service) exerted a moral influence on the
whole nation. Yet the war bequeathed neither a strong
pacifist movement, nor a clear body of pacifist doctrine.
Indeed already in 1917, as *pacificist* hopes revived in response to the Russian revolutions and American backing for a
League of Nations, a number of absolutists—especially
socialist ones—began to retreat from strict pacifism without
making the fact fully clear. As this chapter will thus show,
the first four-fifths of the Great War did much to clarify and
dramatize the pacifist stand; but in the last fifth the confusion between pacifism and *pacificism* began to return.

(i) 1914: The New Fellowships

'Only two certainties seemed clear to them; firstly, that
Britain was bound in honour to help France; secondly, that
war was unchristian.' This was the conclusion reached by 'a
bewildered gathering' of Christians—including W. E. Orchard,
Henry Hodgkin, and Richard Roberts, whose contributions
to pacifism will shortly be noted—which was held privately
soon after the outbreak of war.[1] Collaborative pacifists such

[1] Vera Brittain, *The Rebel Passion: A Short History of Some Pioneer Peace
Makers* (1964), p. 33.

as these faced a stark choice: between following their *pacificist* allies into a new position of moral outrage against German aggression, or remaining pacifist and risking an unpopularity and isolation which pacifists had not experienced for at least a century—not even during the Boer War.

One who took the first option was J. A. Pease (1860–1943), the prominent Quaker who had to choose between remaining in the Cabinet (as President of the Board of Education) or in the Peace Society (of which he was Chairman). He settled for the former and resigned from the latter 'not because my views on peace principles have altered a tittle but because I might be regarded as being in a false position.'[1] Since, however, the Peace Society refused to condemn the declaration of war this precaution was probably unnecessary. Indeed, in spite of a short-lived attempt later in the war by the Revd Herbert Dunnico, a Congregationalist minister who became its Secretary in 1915, to give it a role as co-ordinator of the peace movement's campaign for peace negotiations,[2] the Peace Society never recovered its vitality. After the war Dunnico became a Labour M.P. (of anti-fascist, rather than pacifist views) while his society lapsed into a coma—in which state it even now enjoys a nominal existence, still in the hands of the Dunnico family.[3]

The failure of the Peace Society was underlined by the foundation in 1914 of two new fellowships—the No-Conscription Fellowship and the Fellowship of Reconciliation—both of which took the second option and reaffirmed the pacifist position (although in face of the prevailing

---

[1] Pease to J. B. Hodkin, 4 Aug. 1914, Gainford Papers. Stephen Koss is thus wrong to say that Pease did not resign from the Peace Society: *Nonconformity in Modern British Politics* (1975), p. 127.

[2] Robbins, *Abolition*, pp. 99–100. Much information for this chapter is derived from this useful book and from the thesis on which it is based.

[3] In common with other scholars, I have been unable to gain access to its records. In the inter-war period it still held annual meetings with politicians as guest speakers. Baldwin's decision to make his famous general election speech of 31 Oct. 1935 (urging a measure of rearmament but promising 'no great armaments') on one such occasion was a skilful (and so far unnoticed) device for highlighting his peaceful intentions. It is with this occasion in mind presumably that C. L. Mowat has misleadingly claimed: 'The Peace Society was strong and held large meetings addressed by men of eminence': *Britain Between the Wars 1918–1940* (1958), p. 422.

jingoism they stopped prudently short of calling publicly for a halt to the war).

The No-Conscription Fellowship (N.-C.F.) was founded in November 1914 by a young *Labour Leader* journalist, Fenner Brockway (1888-   ), initially at the prompting of his wife, Lilla, to mobilize men of military age against conscription.[1] The members of its National Committee were mostly young, middle-class I.L.P. socialists such as Clifford Allen (1889-1939), its Chairman, who, like Brockway, worked for the socialist press, and Morgan Jones (1885-1939) and J. H. ('Jimmy') Hudson (1881-1962), both schoolteachers. Only a few came from outside the ranks of socialist activists: the Revd Leyton Richards (1879-1948), for example, a Congregationalist who had already, unlike most British pacifists, found himself in conscientious disagreement with conscription in the form of the compulsory military training introduced in Australia in 1910, shortly before he came there to spend three years as minister of a Melbourne chapel[2]; and the philosopher Bertrand Russell, a Whiggish individualist who had espoused 'pacifism' during the Boer War but did not join the I.L.P. until 1915 and even then insisted that he was not a socialist.[3]   Though limiting itself to campaigning against conscription, the N.-C.F.'s basis was explicitly pacifist rather than merely voluntarist. Its statement of principles, adopted in 1915, required its members to 'refuse from conscientious motives to bear arms because they consider human life to be sacred.'[4] Its moment of ostensible failure, the introduction of conscription in 1916, was to prove its finest hour: from being a small propaganda body it became a substantial movement—though never as substantial as implied by its grossly exaggerated boast of 15,000 members in the summer of 1916—and the acknowledged voice of the whole conscientious objection movement. In particular, it proved an

---

[1] Fenner Brockway, *Inside the Left: Thirty Years of Platform, Press, Prison, and Parliament* (1942), pp. 45-6.

[2] Edith Ryley Richards, *Private View of a Public Man: The Life of Leyton Richards* (1950), pp. 44-9.

[3] Marvin Swartz, *The Union of Democratic Control in British Politics during the First World War* (Oxford, 1971), pp. 99-100; Bertrand Russell, *Autobiography*, i, 1872-1914 (1967), p. 146.

[4] Cited in Rae, *Conscience and Politics*, p. 91.

efficient information and welfare service for all objectors; although its unresolved internal division over whether its function was to ensure respect for the pacifist conscience or to combat conscription by any means, sincerely 'conscientious' or otherwise, had reduced it to a demoralized state by the last year of the war.[1]

The fact that socialists were first into the field with an active campaign against militarism and that they later provided leadership for the conscientious objectors marked the first challenge to Christianity's near-monopoly of pacifism. At the outbreak of the war the greatest disappointment for the peace movement—more disillusioning even than the patriotism of the Labour movement—had been the reaction of the Christian churches which, despite such encouraging pre-war signs of detachment from the political order as Nonconformist radicalism and Anglican Christian Socialism, had given the war their official blessing. For the long-term vitality of Christian pacifism, however, this proved a blessing in disguise. A theme of Christian pacifist history which has already been identified is how ecclesiastical condonation of war can crystallize a general dissatisfaction with the health of institutional religion into pacifist protest. This happened in the case of the Revd W. E. Orchard (1877–1955), who was in the process of taking up his ministry at King's Weigh House, a Congregational chapel in Mayfair, when the war broke out. Though he had been troubled about the morality of war since the Boer War and had been influenced by reading Tolstoy, the 'autobiography of religious development' which he wrote nearly two decades later recognized 1914 to have been a crucial intellectual watershed:

The war was, for me, simply the starting point from which Christianity had to be explored afresh, the problem which every consideration of Christianity compelled me to face. I used the war to show how far European nations had departed from the faith; for me it provided an indictment of vague and indefinite Christianity; to my mind it illuminated the Cross of Christ as nothing else had ever done.[2]

Before the war the pacifist minority within the Churches had

[1] Robbins, *Abolition*, pp. 90–2, 123–5, 207–10.
[2] W. E. Orchard, *From Faith to Faith: An Autobiography of Religious Development* (1933), pp. 120–1. Orchard was to become a Roman Catholic.

been small and unorganized and, because of its collaboration with *pacificism*, the distinctly Christian basis for its pacifism remained largely undefined. It was to remedy this deficiency, and to create a sense of community among isolated and bewildered individuals, that Orchard and 130 other anti-war Christians gathered at Trinity Hall, Cambridge on the last four days of 1914 for a conference on Christianity and war and agreed to form the Fellowship of Reconciliation (F.o.R.). In its early years the F.o.R. was predominantly, but not exclusively, Nonconformist and Quaker. Presiding over its Cambridge conference was Henry T. Hodgkin (1877–1933), a Quaker medical missionary who was to spend much of the inter-war period working in China. His sense of outrage at the outbreak of the Great War had been intensified by his experience as one of the delegates to the founding conference at Konstanz of the World Alliance for Promoting Friendship Through the Churches who had to scatter within hours of arriving because of the outbreak of war. Hodgkin's collaborator in organizing the Cambridge Conference, and the first Secretary of the F.o.R., was the Revd Richard Roberts (1874–1945), a Welsh-born Presbyterian who had been suddenly converted to pacifism on the first Sunday of the war when he realized that a number of regular German members of his congregation at Crouch Hill in North London were missing. In 1916 he was forced to leave his church on account of his pacifist views and he spent most of the rest of his life in the United States and Canada.[1]

Since both the original organizers of the F.o.R. were abroad for most of the inter-war years, it was the other members of the Fellowship who were to establish it as Britain's most thoughtful pacifist society and as the progenitor of an international movement whose American branch was to become that country's leading peace society. One of the most prolific writers on Christian pacifism in the inter-war period was the Revd Leyton Richards, whose opposition to the 1910 Australian Defence Act and membership (after his return to Britain to take over a church at Bowdon in Cheshire) of the N.-C.F.'s first National Committee,

---

[1] H. G. Wood, *Henry T. Hodgkin: A Memoir* (1957), pp. 148–64; Brittain, *Rebel Passion*, pp. 31–41, 77–80.

have already been mentioned. After conscription was introduced he felt obliged to resign from Bowdon and, having come to disagree with the N.-C.F.'s militant tendencies, he devoted himself to the F.o.R. as its General Secretary in 1917–18.[1] Other prominent early members of the F.o.R. were: the Revd Cecil J. Cadoux, later Professor of Church History at Mansfield College, Oxford, a Congregationalist who, after working for nine years in the Admiralty Office in Whitehall, was converted to pacifism around 1911 following 'a re-examination of the Synoptic Gospels, coupled with the perusal of a little book by Tolstoy'[2]; Dr Maude Royden, the pioneering woman preacher; George M. Ll. Davies, a Calvinistic Methodist and one of the most introspective of conscientious objectors; and George Lansbury, a rare representative both of the Labour movement and of Anglicanism.

Although by the end of the war the F.o.R. was claiming 8,000 members its public impact was, as in the case of its unobtrusive foundation conference, deliberately muted. It held some public meetings later in the war and was constantly urged by its activist minority to organize a campaign against the war, but on the whole its tone was quietist. This was not just from understandable diffidence about proselytizing pacifism in wartime: more than any other pacifist society it was content to reassure its members that they were not alone, rather than to mobilize them, and took the sectarian view that pacifism is essentially a matter for the individual conscience rather than for mass propaganda. This was inherent in its five-point 'Basis', adopted at the Cambridge conference, which was to gain increasing respect as a mature statement of Christian pacifism. Instead of basing itself on selective biblical texts or on an injunction against taking life, bearing arms, or other specific activities, it argued that 'Love, as revealed and interpreted in the life and death of Jesus Christ, involves more than we have yet seen, that it is the only power by which evil can be overcome, and the only sufficient basis of human society.' But, despite this confident assertion, it avoided making facile claims about the immediate

---

[1] E. R. Richards, *Private View*, pp. 59–71.
[2] C. J. Cadoux, *Christian Pacifism Re-Examined* (1940), p. 8.

efficacy of non-violence, insisting that those accepting this principle had to do so 'fully, both for themselves and in their relation to others, and to take the risks involved in doing so in a world which does not as yet accept it'. F.o.R. members were called 'to a life of service for the enthronement of Love in personal, social, commercial and national life'.[1]

It catered mainly, therefore, for clergy and intellectuals concerned to define a rigorous theological and spiritual basis for pacifism. That this problem was tackled represented an advance on pre-war thinking; but, as Orchard among others found, the F.o.R. was doctrinally too 'heterogeneous' for this to be an easy task, and even at the end of the war 'a really Christian pacifist philosophy was still in need of formulation'.[2] In part this was a result of inevitable clashes of personality: what leading members had most in common was confidence in their own spiritual intuition and the courage to stand by it even to the detriment of their careers. As Charles Raven, an Anglican who was to help the F.o.R. further to clarify and harmonize its interpretation of its Basis when he joined it in the thirties, emphasized nearly four decades later: 'In the First World War far more than today pacifism was apt to be the creed of uncompromising individualists, men or women inheriting the fine tradition of independence which its critics were apt to stigmatize as the "Nonconformist Conscience".'[3] For both doctrinal and personal reasons, therefore, the F.o.R. found 'reconciliation' embarrassingly hard to achieve in practice during its early years.

(ii) 1916: Conscription

Despite these early responses to the outbreak of war, a watershed for modern pacifism more decisive than 4 August 1914 proved to be 2 March 1916—the date conscription came into force. For exactly a hundred years after the first attempt to organize pacifism in 1816 British pacifists had suffered nothing worse than unpopularity for the sake of their cause

---

[1] The F.o.R.'s Basis is printed in Brittain, *Rebel Passion*, p. 35.

[2] Orchard, *From Faith*, p. 122.

[3] C. E. Raven, *Alex Wood: The Man and His Message* (F.o.R., 1952), p. 5.

but had as a corollary lacked opportunities to demonstrate the strength and extent of their conviction. It was widely assumed—for example, by the military service tribunals in the Great War—that pacifists merely desired personal exemption from fighting rather than complete dissociation from the war effort. It was conscription which, by bringing pacifists into sharp confrontation with the state, dramatized their views for the public mind and inspired all subsequent pacifist movements. Indeed the martyrdom of the absolutists has created a mythology which has coloured most accounts of pacifism in the Great War.[1]

The indisputable courage and integrity of the leading absolutists has focused attention on the shortcomings of the Military Service Acts: notably, the brutality of the army and prisons towards those whom the tribunals had failed to exempt. There has thus been understandable sympathy for the absolutists' view of themselves as fighting not just for pacifism but also for democratic liberties against the tyranny of the modern state. But it is rarely pointed out that from a comparative historical perspective the state was remarkably progressive in its legislative provisions: what went wrong with the conscientious exemption procedure—a radical provision for which the Vaccination Acts and recent defence Acts in the dominions were the only precedents—was that its two most liberal provisions proved unacceptable to the local worthies who had to implement them; and there is no evidence that they were in any way out of step with the public mind in this respect.

So deeply rooted was the *pacificist* tradition in Britain that even Conservative and military advocates of conscription had accepted the case for a conscience clause; but they had expected it to be confined, firstly, to exemption from military (or even, more strictly, from combatant) service only; and secondly, to objectors on religious grounds (or even to members of the historic peace churches) only. However,

---

[1] For the mythology see John W. Graham: *Conscription and Conscience: A History 1916–1919* (1922); W. J. Chamberlain, *Fighting for Peace*; and David Boulton, *Objection Overruled* (1967). For an excellent treatment to which the present attempt to provide a corrective is greatly indebted see John Rae, *Conscience and Politics.*

Asquith, prompted by his fellow Liberals whose defection from his coalition Government would destroy him as Prime Minister, introduced a broader clause allowing both unconditional and non-religious exemption—although, amidst the haste and confusion in which conscription for bachelors was introduced to supplement the existing scheme for voluntary attestation, a characteristically functional state of Asquithian ambiguity was allowed to persist as to what had actually been done. Since the exemption machinery was decentralized it was the particular interpretation favoured by the local tribunals which in practice determined the fate of the 16,500 who claimed conscientious objection.

Thus although on the first ambiguous point it was eventually made clear that the granting in appropriate circumstances of unconditional exemption (i.e. exemption from all, including civilian, service) was the Government's intention, only about 350 such exemptions were ever granted. Almost all went to Quakers:[1] largely because of the esteem in which the Society was held, and also its members' intelligence and knowledge of their rights. Aldous Huxley, for example, not yet a pacifist but an occasional spectator at the Oxford tribunal while an undergraduate, was considerably impressed by a Quaker's successful insistence on unconditional exemption, and no less unimpressed by 'half-baked, crude' political objectors.[2] Sometimes, however— as E. St. John Catchpool (1890-1971) admitted in his own case—Quaker social connections played a part.[3] Yet many demonstrably sincere Quakers failed to gain unconditional exemption, of whom the most famous was Stephen Hobhouse (1881-1961), who, rather than agree to serve in the Friends' Ambulance Unit as a condition of exemption, went to prison, where his treatment became a public scandal. It has rarely been remarked that the main criticism of the tribunals is thus not, as might have been expected, that they failed to grant the status of conscientious objector to those deserving it: more than 80 per cent of those who applied received exemptions of some sort; and, of the absolutists—a

[1] Ibid., p. 113.
[2] Grover Smith (ed.), *Letters of Aldous Huxley* (1969), pp. 91-4.
[3] E. St. John Catchpool, *Candles in the Darkness* (1966), p. 24.

category shortly to be analysed in detail—only 313 had been rejected as insincere by the tribunals compared with 985 who had been offered (and had rejected) the range of alternative options.[1] The failure of the tribunals had been to deny that the conscientious scruples of those whose sincerity they had accepted (such as Hobhouse) could extend to refusal of all—even civilian—compulsory service. But, as will be seen, the 'reformed' tribunals of the Second World War were themselves often to make this denial. The greater propensity of C.O.s in the Great War to defy them and go to gaol must thus be explained in terms of their greater self-confidence or stubbornness and not just of the greater harshness of the tribunals which pronounced upon their consciences.

The other main ambiguity was, however, to be resolved in the pacifist's favour in the Second World War: this was whether an objection to war on political grounds could be a 'conscientious objection'. The phrase had been adopted in preference to the 'conscientious beliefs' specified by the Australian Defence Act of 1910 partly because the Cabinet wished to accept non-religious objections, but this liberal intention was obscured by confusion between two types of political opposition to war. As already suggested, a political objection can be an objection to all wars or to certain wars only. The former type is impeccably pacifist; but its recognition as such by tribunals was prejudiced by their understandable reluctance to accept the latter type, which was indeed merely *pacificist*. When the Central Tribunal eventually ruled against recognizing *any* political objection, its published reasoning applied only to this latter type; and, although this ruling came too late to affect most of the decisions of the tribunals, they had already disallowed many political objections on these grounds. Admittedly, the effects of this confusion can be exaggerated: a significant number of political pacifists were exempted by tribunals (as were some political *pacificists*). Nevertheless the prudent objector—for example, the Catholic socialist Francis Meynell (1891–1975)—stressed

---

[1] Rae, *Conscience and Politics*, pp. 130–2, 167, 201–2. All statistics about Great War C.O.s cited in this book are based on the figures Rae gives here.

the religious aspect of his objection even it had also a strong political character.[1]

The result of the tribunals' erratic but generally cautious interpretation of the crucial ambiguities in the conscience clause has been to concentrate attention on the absolutists (and, more particularly, the politically-inspired absolutists). In one respect this is appropriate: their courage and intransigence constitute a major difference between the two world wars. But to set the record straight two facts must here be given due acknowledgement: nine C.O.s out of ten were not absolutists; and a substantial element was quasi-pacifist.

Sixty-four per cent of all objectors co-operated with the tribunal system: only 5,944 were resolved to resist it (of whom 1,234 had on conscientious grounds refused to apply for exemption in the first place, 2,425 had been rejected outright by their tribunal, 2,061 had found the type of exemption they were offered unacceptable, and an unclassifiable 224 fell into one of the latter two categories). These all experienced a painful confrontation with the civil or military authorities, often involving incarceration; but compromises were made on both sides and a majority eventually accepted improved offers of alternative service. Only 1,298 held out and thus qualify for the title 'absolutist'. Even assuming that every one of the 350 who had received unconditional exemptions would also have refused all compromise had they been less fortunate, the proportion of absolutists was no greater than one in ten. Most objectors were, in other words, 'alternativists'. That this was not always merely a result of human frailty in face of the ordeal to be endured as an absolutist can be shown by examining the attitude of the most respected group of C.O.s, the Quakers. The Society of Friends had come out in November 1914 with an unequivocal reaffirmation of its belief that all war was wrong (though it should be noted that, according to its own post-war survey, a third of its members nevertheless served in the armed forces;[2] and it is also known that a number of older Friends served on tribunals). Yet Quakers were not sectarian in their attitudes: their characteristic

---

[1] Francis Meynell, *My Lives* (1971), pp. 93–4, 253.
[2] Rae, *Conscience and Politics*, p. 73.

response to the war was epitomized by the formation of two relief units, which, though unofficial, did much to enhance the Society's reputation for compassionate efficiency. These were: the Friends' Ambulance Unit, which Philip Baker (afterwards Noel-Baker) had founded in 1914; and the 'Warvics', the Friends' War Victims Relief Committee, started in the same year and run for nine years with such whole-hearted dedication by Ruth Fry (1878–1962) that, after dealing with the post-war famines, she spent the rest of her life as a semi-invalid, issuing a succession of emotional pacifist pamphlets from her Thorpeness home. To a strict absolutist these units could be regarded as in practice helping the war to continue, and a number of members, particularly of the former (whose founder was a *pacificist*, not a pacifist) began to have doubts on this score. The introduction of conscription added what was in a number of cases a clinching voluntarist argument, since those who had formerly been volunteers now acquired the status of conscripts performing approved alternative duties: thus Corder Catchpool (1883–1953), a future P.P.U. treasurer, left the Ambulance Unit in order to seek, unconditional exemption and, not being granted it, went to prison.[1] Similarly Stephen Hobhouse, although offered service in the Unit as a condition of exemption, refused; and the Society's official attitude also became disapproving. But the fact that Quakers could not ignore evidence that the Ambulance Unit was benefiting the military authorities by patching up wounded soldiers and thereby expediting their return to active service, or that their liberal principles were offended by conscription, should not distract attention from the important difference between their preference for humanitarian activity and the belief held by the most famous absolutists that the main purpose of the C.O.'s stand was to be (in the words of a leading N.-C.F. member) 'a challenge not only to the military machine but to the capitalist order of society'.[2] It should thus be emphasized that the majority of Quakers accepted alternative service, that it was not unknown for those receiving

---

[1] W. R. Hughes, *Indomitable Friend: The Life of Corder Catchpool 1883–1952* (1957), pp. 32–7.

[2] C. H. Norman; cited in Robbins, *Abolition*, p. 125.

unconditional exemption (a rare privilege, it has been seen, even for Quakers) to volunteer for relief work, as did E. St. John Catchpool who joined the Warvics, and that the Ambulance Unit continued functioning. Its absolutist heroes were thus atypical of the Society. The best-known, the saintly Stephen Hobhouse,[1] was a recent convert of unusual intensity: a repressed and idealistic product of Eton and Balliol, he had renounced patriotism, capitalism and Anglicanism under the influence of a nervous breakdown and the works of Tolstoy, and, on joining the Society, felt unable to share what he regarded as the often too comfortable existence of his new co-religionaries and went to live in poverty in Hoxton. Like that of others, such as Barratt Brown, whose socialism was more militant and less mystical, his unwillingness to compromise owed much to his political beliefs. It was socialism (often allied with Nonconformity) rather than Quakerism which inspired the purest sectarianism; and it is thus significant that the body set up by the Society to deal with conscription was called the Friends' Service Committee.

The data which would permit an analytical breakdown of the 16,500 C.O.s does not, unfortunately, exist; but from the patchy records which survive the largest single group—constituting at least 10 per cent of the total—was the Christadelphian sect, which was less absolutist even than the Society of Friends: it was willing to help with munitions production, provided only that its members were not placed directly under military discipline. This classic example of esoteric quasi-pacifism illustrates another frequently-overlooked fact: that the common pre-war assumption that pacifism was largely the preserve of small Christian sects had a considerable degree of truth in it; as the journalist and poet Gilbert Thomas (1891-), an absolutist whose prison neighbour was a member of the Peculiar People, later emphasized: 'It was assumed that every pacifist . . . was a narrow-minded religionist, basing his creed upon the literal reading of Biblical texts . . . . And indeed, there *were* many conscientious

[1] See Stephen Hobhouse, *Forty Years and an Epilogue: An Autobiography (1881-1951)* (1951).

objectors of this type, as I soon discovered.'[1] Even in the Second World War, despite twenty more years of discussion of pacifist issues and improved general education, a high proportion of C.O.s were of surprisingly unsophisticated religious beliefs: pacifists were not unknown who, although basing their objections on biblical statements, were ignorant of other texts on the subject, or even of the fact that the Bible had not originally been composed in English.[2] Thus in view of the fact that so much has been made of the ignorance and stupidity of the tribunals during the Great War, it should in fairness be recognized that many of the objectors were themselves doctrinaire and unable to explain coherently their own, often esoteric, views.

Quasi-pacifism appeared, furthermore, in a new and rather different form as a result of conscription. Here described as elitist, it merits attention because, although its exponents were numerically insignificant, they were highly articulate and have acquired a certain prominence on account of their artistic reputations. 'Pacifists' of this type rarely existed in pure form, though one of the nearest to it was the letterer and carver Eric Gill (later to become a true pacifist) who privately admitted in 1916: 'Of course I shall try and get off —no conscientious objections—none whatever—but it would be such a rotten mess up for all my work, nationally unimportant tho it be, were I to be conscripted.'[3] Often, like the novelist David Garnett (1892–   ), who had done relief work with the Quakers, they had sincere *pacificist* feelings. But they can be regarded as elitist in so far as, like Garnett, they were not 'convinced that war was always wrong',[4] and in so far as they believed that their entitlement to be recognized as C.O.s depended on their higher personal obligation, as creative artists, to Beauty and Truth.

It must be admitted that a truly conscientious humanitarian

---

[1] Gilbert Thomas, *Autobiography 1891-1946* (1946), p. 128; see also pp. 122, 129, 143.

[2] See the account of his experiences as a member of the South-Western Tribunal 1940-4 by G. C. Field: *Pacifism and Conscientious Objection* (1945), esp. pp. 3-7.

[3] Gill to Geoffrey Keynes, 29 May 1916, in Walter Shewring (ed.), *Letters of Eric Gill* (1947), p. 79.

[4] David Garnett, *The Flowers of the Forest* (1955), pp. 58-93.

pacifism and mere quasi-pacifism based on one's own particular qualities and sensitivity to civilized values are easier to
distinguish in theory than in practice; but one of the characteristics which identified elitist objectors in the Great War was
their facetiousness. When, for example, the painter Duncan
Grant was asked by his tribunal whether he would push his
objection to war work as far as to refuse to make a pair
of boots, his response was that he 'was a gentleman and
objected to making boots'.[1] Similarly, although Lytton
Strachey's decision to go before a tribunal (when he was
medically unfit anyway) was itself a courageous gesture,
the episode is only remembered for his innuendo-laden
reply ('I should try and come between them') to the standard
question as to what he would do if a German tried to rape a
female relative of his; and in the same spirit a younger friend
of his, asked why he was not fighting for civilization like
most others of his age, could not resist replying: 'Madam, *I*
am the civilisation they are fighting for.'[2]

What enabled these 'Bloomsbury' quasi-pacifists, in particular, to stay so cheerful was the confidence that they
possessed the necessary connections and influence—J. M.
Keynes appeared for both Garnett and Grant, for example—
to impress the tribunals and to provide a congenial environment, such as existed, *par excellence*, at the Garsington home
of Philip and Ottoline Morrell, in which to carry out work
of national importance. Such privilege incurred suspicion
even among liberal opinion. Leonard Woolf, a devoted
internationalist though never a pacifist, remembered the
'quarrelsome and cantankerous' resident C.O.s as an 'unquiet
turgid sediment beneath the brilliant surface' of Garsington
weekends; while one of the mental obstacles which
Middleton Murry, also a visitor at this time, had to overcome in becoming a pacifist himself twenty years later was an

---

[1] Ibid, p. 122.
[2] Michael Holroyd, *Lytton Strachey: A Biography* (revd. Pelican edn., 1971),
pp. 628-9 (Mr Holroyd informs me that this, rather than the version given in
his original two-volume edition, is the one he now considers to be the authentic
version of Strachey's epigram); and *Lytton Strachey: A Critical Biography*, i
(1967), p. 416.

aversion to conscientious objectors based on those he had met there.[1]

However, before leaving the subject of elitist quasi-pacifism it should be noted how rare it seems to have been in its crudest form—'draft-dodging', as the Americans were later to call it (the absence of an English phrase being perhaps significant). Even making allowances for the fact that successful evasion will often leave no trace, there seem to have been remarkably few who, like the future Labour M.P. Fred Messer (1886–1971), managed to slip through the net by changing addresses frequently and who did so on pacifist grounds.[2] Adminstrative efficiency (and the vigilance of fellow citizens) may largely explain this; but it must also be recognized that in both world wars the majority of British pacifists desired to secure recognition of their rights from the state rather than simply shirk confrontation. Though few of them displayed the heroism of the absolutist, and though a significant element was quasi-pacifist, almost all had the courage of their convictions.

(iii) Socialist Pacifism and the Russian Example.

It does not derogate from the example of the Quakers to stress that it was the socialists who did most to dramatize the absolutist stand and to rescue it from the prevailing assumption that pacifism was merely the inbred eccentricity of the Nonconformist conscience or minor sects. They did so despite the fact that they probably comprised fewer than one in thirteen of all objectors: even the efficient and socialist-orientated N.-C.F. had details of only 1,191 political objectors —as compared with the 1,716 Christadelphians and 750 Quakers known to have received some form of exemption.[3]

The complexities of the socialist attitude to war require brief reiteration. In so far as the withering-away of war was one of the benefits they anticipated from the international

[1] Leonard Woolf, *Downhill All the Way: An autobiography of the years 1919–1939* (1968), p. 100; F. A. Lea, *The Life of John Middleton Murry* (1959), p. 196.

[2] Joyce Bellamy and John Saville (eds), *Dictionary of Labour Biography*, ii (1974), p. 261.

[3] Rae, *Conscience and Politics*, pp. 77, 82.

spread of socialism, all socialists were by definition *pacifists*. They accepted the morality of using military force for the defence of a socialist state and, more controversially, even for the overthrow of capitalism, but objected to the political ends for which capitalist governments fought wars. They interpreted the socialist's duty on the outbreak of an 'imperialist' war to be to give disciplined support to the mass 'war-resistance' which, ideally, the labour movement would organize. If this involved attempting to evade conscription, the purpose of so doing was not to salve the individual conscience but to subvert the state and stop the war.

A minority of socialists, on the other hand, regarded all war as contrary to socialist principles. Before examining this socialist pacifism, however, two factors must be noted which have contributed to a lasting confusion between these logically distinct positions. Firstly, war-resisters as well as socialist pacifists have been conscientious objectors in both world wars. Examples from the Great War were: Herbert Morrison, who seems to have based his objection very largely on the alliance with Tsarist Russia;[1] Robin Page Arnot and William Mellor, who based theirs on the Guild Socialist critique of the state;[2] and Douglas Goldring, who, having volunteered in 1914, became 'a whole-hog opponent of conscription on libertarian grounds' two years later.[3] Secondly, in the case of socialists the distinction between *pacificism* and collaborative pacifism was genuinely difficult to spot. In the case of non-socialists the former was based on a political analysis of the prospects of reforming international relations, while the latter was at that time usually based on a separate, and easily identifiable, religious affiliation—such as membership of the Society of Friends. But in the case of socialists both *pacificism* and pacifism were derived from the same, political, doctrine and were consequently much harder—even for their exponents—to tell apart.

The distinction lay, in effect, in differing conceptions of socialism. In contrast with the materialistic philosophy

[1] Herbert Morrison, *An Autobiography* (1960), pp. 61-2; Bernard Donoughue and G. W. Jones, *Herbert Morrison: Portrait of a Politician* (1973), pp. 40-1.

[2] J. M. Winter, *Socialism and the Challenge of War: Ideas and Politics in Britain 1912-1918* (1974), p. 124.

[3] Douglas Goldring, *Odd Man Out* (1935), p. 143.

of the war-resister, who saw the socialist cause in terms of a struggle for social and economic power, the socialist pacifist believed that a socialist brotherhood would necessitate change in individual moral values. It was at this more fundamental level that war was incompatible with socialist values. As a leading socialist absolutist, Clifford Allen, informed his Tribunal in March 1916: 'I am a Socialist, and so hold in all sincerity that the life and personality of every man is sacred, and that there is something of divinity in every human being, irrespective of the nation to which he belongs.[1] Like the N.-C.F.'s credo, this declaration defined a position which was undoubtedly both pacifist and political: it revealed that even when inspired by political values true pacifism springs from a 'moral' imperative rather than from 'political' expediency.

Indeed, once Allen and his fellow absolutists found themselves in prison they became more than ever convinced of the difference between pacifism, rooted in the individual's conscientious adherence to what he knew to be right, and the strategy of war-resistance which, however justified in political terms, was itself a form of coercion. By May 1917, after a year in gaol, Allen had come to realise that even by sewing mailbags he was releasing labour for the war-effort and decided to cease all co-operation with the prison authorities; yet he refused to urge others to do likewise as part of an organized campaign, since he believed that such a decision could arise only out of 'profound conviction'.[2] From this perspective an organized campaign against war could itself be regarded as riding roughshod over the individual conscience in the same way, albeit not to the same degree, as conscription.

Although Allen had thus defined an explicitly socialist pacifism which could scarcely be confused with *pacificism*, his clarification had almost no lasting effect, and throughout most of the inter-war period—and even after the Second World War—the exact nature of political pacifism was to

---

[1] Statement to Battersea Tribunal cited in Martin Gilbert (ed.) *Plough My Own Furrow: The Story of Lord Allen of Hurtwood as told through his writings and correspondence* (1965), p. 41.

[2] Allen to Lloyd George, 31 May 1917, cited ibid., p. 82.

remained surprisingly little discussed and little understood even within the labour movement. There were (in addition to the general confusion between socialist pacifism and *pacificism* just mentioned) two reasons for this, each of which must now be examined: the predominance of Christian socialism; and the distracting effect of the Russian revolution.

On close inspection most of those claiming to be socialist pacifists were Christian, rather than strictly political, in inspiration. Socialists like Allen, his absolutist colleague Brockway who had founded the N.-C.F., and Max Plowman, the poet and critic whose resignation of his commission in January 1918 on pacifist grounds will be discussed later in this chapter, were highly unusual in that their socialism was a complete surrogate for their former Christian beliefs; in other words, their socialism was their 'religion'. In contrast most socialists—as was to be expected within a socialist tradition such as the British in which liberal Christianity was the most significant 'ideological' impetus—retained a parallel religious inspiration; in other words, they were Christian socialists of one sort of another. This was true of the majority of Labour's pacifist M.P.s of the inter-war period. Some were Nonconformist minsters: the Revd Reginald Sorensen (1891-1971) was in charge of the Free Christian Church (inspired by the 'new theology' of the Revd R. J. Campbell but affiliated to the Unitarians) at Walthamstow from 1916 onwards and gained exemption from military service as a minister; and the Revd James Barr, reared, according to an I.L.P. colleague, 'in the traditions of the conventicles', was a prominent Glasgow preacher and temperance advocate: 'a brawny man, a farmer to all appearance, but garbed as a clergyman'.[1] Others saw their political careers as applications of deeper spiritual concerns: Dr Alfred Salter (1873-1945), who after childhood experience among both Wesleyans and Plymouth Brethren had become an agnostic, was reconverted by Dr Scott Lidgett and, soon after, became a Quaker without mitigating the full rigours of his Nonconformist conscience;[2] Cecil H. Wilson (1862-1945), also a

---

[1] Thomas Johnston, *Memories* (1952) p. 40.
[2] Fenner Brockway, *Bermondsey Story: The Life of Alfred Salter* (1947), Chs. 1-2.

temperance enthusiast, was a Congregationalist who joined the Society of Friends in 1934; and George Lansbury, a rationalist in his youth and a Theosophist in old age, was a rare example of an Anglican. None could be said to derive his pacifism from his socialism as much as to derive both from his Christianity.

Because of their experiences during the Great War, moreover, several leading 'socialist' absolutists became more committedly Christian-socialist in inspiration. Several joined the Society of Friends, including: J. H. Hudson, N.-C.F. National Committee member, temperance campaigner and, later, a Labour M.P.; Walter Ayles, an engineer and trade-union official from Bristol who became Labour M.P. for the North division of that city; and Will Chamberlain (1884–1945), a Birmingham journalist on various Labour papers who, in the early twenties at least, was still also a professed Tolstoyan.

The Society of Friends was, however, insufficiently radical on social and economic issues to attract the most remarkable Christian socialist pacifist of the inter-war period: Wilfred Wellock (1879–1972), an absolutist who became a Labour M.P. in 1927. Despite starting work in a Lancashire cotton mill at the age of ten, Wellock was driven by his puritan upbringing and remarkable self-discipline to improve and educate himself. As he did so, he became preoccupied with the need to restore the spiritual element in life which, from his experience in his Lancashire factory town, he believed had been steadily destroyed by industrialization. Because the Great War seemed to him to be the apotheosis of this corrupting industrialism, he seized on pacifism as the best means of rediscovering true values. 'Pacifism is simply applied Christianity', he wrote early in 1916.[1] Although eligible for exemption from conscription as an Independent Methodist lay preacher, Wellock opted to take his stand as an absolutist; and in March 1916 he launched from his home town a Christian revolutionary journal, the *New Crusader*, published by 'the Committee for the Promotion of Pacifism, Nelson'. After he went to prison, the paper was edited and

---

[1] *New Crusader*, 25 Mar. 1916, p.3.

financed by a Quaker novelist, Theodora Wilson Wilson (1865-1941), who had been converted to socialism during the Great War. It was to her that Wellock wrote a despairing letter from prison which illustrates how, by the end of the war, Christian-socialist pacifists believed they had inherited the authentic mantle of early Christianity:

What a country, what a world is ours! . . . Shameless selfishness, political and commercial corruption, self-indulgent looseness in manners—in a word, brazen materialism spreading on every hand fostered by national pride, by national and personal hypocrisy, aided, alas, by a soul sold Church—and all the fault of a Holy War! Whence did righteousness make claim to such a heritage? Can figs grow on thistles? And yet the Church is looking around aghast, and wondering why the people, after their intoxication of 'self-sacrifice', should show no disposition to pay tribute to formal religion and is attributing the remissness to every conceivable course rather than the true and, indeed, obvious one. In this, as in a thousand other directions, the obvious Christian truth must be proclaimed with clarion voice.[1]

The *Crusader* (as the *New Crusader* was known after 1919) was to be published throughout the twenties and played an important role, as will later be noted, in the setting up of the N.-C.F.'s successor organization, the No More War Movement, in 1921. It was thus one of the most significant developments of the Great War that, whereas pacifism had previously been almost exclusively Christian, a hybrid second strand, Christian-socialist in inspiration, became almost equally prominent. Because of its influence within the Labour movement it helped to ensure that the other, more sharply distinct, new strand—political pacifism strictly defined—lagged behind in third place and received little attention.

The second reason for the undeveloped state of political pacifist thought was that those who had done most to define it during the first year or so of conscription themselves *retreated* from it in the last year and a half of the war when an abrupt change in the political climate made them long to return to the mainstream of socialist activity. At the time of the introduction of conscription conscientious objection had seemed as constructive and revolutionary a stand as any then available for a socialist. Thus although Arthur Creech-

[1] Wellock to Wilson, 2 Feb. 1919, cited in *Crusader*, 28 Feb. 1919, p. 4.

Jones (1891–1964) had early in the war been worried that pacifism 'tended to encourage individualism and weaken collective action'[1] among socialists, he had nevertheless become a conscientious objector, albeit not an absolutist. But the sectarian position at which, as already noted, leading socialist objectors had arrived by the early summer of 1917, fully bore out his earlier prediction.

No sooner had absolutists become aware of the apolitical implications of strict pacifism than the political climate changed. The Russian revolutions of March and November 1917 and the growing war-weariness and industrial unrest in Britain suddenly raised expectations that the Labour movement might develop into a powerful anti-war force or even carry through a socialist revolution. In May 1917 Bertrand Russell, the N.-C.F.'s leading non-socialist activist, warned that body that, though 'a conscientious objector to the present war and to almost any imaginable war between civilised states', he had always reserved his position in respect of revolutions: 'Until lately, this was mere academic reservation, without relevance to the actual situation. Now, however, it has become a pressing practical consideration'.[2] He had already joined the I.L.P. and now decided to cease working for the increasingly demoralized N.-C.F.. It was ironic, therefore, that before he could give effect to this decision an injudicious sentence in an article he wrote for the N.-C.F.'s journal *Tribunal*, praising the Bolshevik peace offer and arguing that 'Labour holds the key', consigned him to gaol for sedition—just when he had lost all faith in the utility of imprisonment as a means of furthering the cause. Clifford Allen's diary entry for his 458th day of incarceration, 12 November 1917, showed that his priorities were changing in the same way:

The shaping of the future lies with the newly-organised Labour movement, which will without doubt have to contend with violent elements in its midst. If we on our part are so removed from the life and thought of the vigorous new movement around us as to refuse to distinguish the merits of wise aggressiveness from violence, when developing our

---

[1] Creech-Jones to Salter, undated letter (Feb. 1915), cited in Rae, *Conscience and Politics*, p. 84.

[2] Russell to members of the National Committee, 18 May 1917, cited in Ronald W. Clark, *The Life of Bertrand Russell* (1975), p. 332.

programme, then I fear lest whilst we may succeed in keeping ourselves unsullied from the world, we may find the world pays little heed to our formulas and shibboleths.[1]

The following month, contrary to his previous intentions, Allen accepted an offer of release from prison on grounds of ill-health (as did Stephen Hobhouse). By February 1918 he was recording in his diary that Brockway 'feels like me that Socialist movement has first claim on us', and that Morgan Jones—who was in August 1921 to become the first conscientious objector to be returned to Parliament—'seems to have no interest left in C.O. movement and is very much engrossed in personal chances of parliamentary candidature. How very sad it is to see how everyone has lost heart in the usefulness of C.O. stand.'[2]

For all his sadness Allen was to support the N.-C.F.'s decision to wind itself up in 1919 after the last of the C.O.s had been released and after the Government had clearly abandoned all thought of peacetime conscription. Three *ad hoc* committees were, in theory, to continue various aspects of the N.-C.F.'s work; but in practice socialist pacifism remained unorganized until the formation, in February 1921, of the No More War Movement. In his address to the N.-C.F.'s final convention at the end of November 1919, and in a notably more lukewarm preface to a book, published in 1922, commemorating the conscientious objectors of 1916-19,[3] Allen's message was that absolutist resistance was not an end in itself but the expression in special circumstances of socialist values which in peacetime should be expressed in other ways. Like many other political pacifists Allen saw his future in Labour politics, more particularly as part of the I.L.P.'s drive to radicialize the Labour Party. He ignored the activities of the peace movement until the early thirties when, standing out against the optimistic tide of pacifist thinking at the time, he powerfully reiterated the lesson he had learned as an absolutist: that pacifism was essentially apolitical and, therefore, irrelevant to the political task of war-prevention.

[1] Cited in Gilbert, *Plough*, p. 94.
[2] Diary entries for 21 and 27 Feb. 1918, cited ibid., pp. 108-9.
[3] See Graham, *Conscription and Conscience* (preface), which also reprinted Allen's speech to the N.-C.F. rally on pp. 332-8.

Thus in the period of the Russian revolutions and their aftermath, when the causes of pacifism and political socialism seemed to have diverged, a golden opportunity to establish once and for all the difference between these positions was missed because socialist pacifists lost confidence in their sectarian orientation and adopted the collaborative alternative of relying on the political initiatives of the Labour movement. Warnings that this might involve condoning revolutionary violence were astonishingly muted, except from such unrelenting scourges of laxity in any form as Alfred Salter[1] and Philip Snowden.[2] Russell, for example, was insisting in 1917 that pacifists were required by their principles to support 'a great change in our economic system' subject only to a particular obligation 'as pacifists . . . to do all in their power to secure that the changes should occur without the use of force and not in a spirit of violence or hate'.[3] In practice this frequently meant that, as he admitted nearly twenty years later, 'in meetings nominally opposed to all war, the threat of violent revolution was applauded to the echo'.[4] The explanation for what later seemed a puzzling inconsistency lay in the idealization of the Russian revolutions by those whose idealism had been pent up by years of war. In contrast with the detested Tsarist regime, Bolshevism seemed almost a spiritual liberation. A leading member of the *Crusader* group, the Revd Stanley James, told the 1919 National Peace Congress: 'A vital pacifism must ally itself with this creative force which has shown itself so strong in Russia',[5] and, according to Will Chamberlain, 'carried the majority of the delegates with him in his eloquent plea for sympathetic consideration behind the Bolshevik struggle for freedom'.[6] Similarly, Lansbury was claiming in March 1920, following a visit to Russia, that the Communist Third

[1] *Tribunal*, 24 July 1919, cited in Keith Robbins, 'The Abolition of War: A Study in the Organisation and Ideology of the Peace Movement 1914–1919' (D.Phil. thesis, Oxford, 1964), p. 431.

[2] Mary Agnes Hamilton, *Remembering My Good Friends* (1944), p. 112.

[3] 'The impact of the Russian revolution on the N.-C.F.', undated draft to branch secretaries, cited in Clark, *Russell*, p. 319.

[4] Bertrand Russell, 'Some Psychological difficulties of Pacifism in Wartime', in Julian Bell (ed.), *We Did Not Fight* (1935), p. 333.

[5] N.P.C. *Monthly Circular* No. 97, 21 July 1919, p. 193.

[6] *Crusader*, 4 July 1919, p. 4.

International did not advocate violence—a view with considerable support within the I.L.P.[1] The simple fact that the Bolsheviks had seized power during the worst of the military stalemate and had subsequently pursued a policy of revolutionary defeatism encouraged pacifists to regard Communism at first as primarily a stop-the-war movement. The question of whether a socialist might ever be called on to fight in defence of the embattled revolution did not arise as long as it appeared that the most useful protection that could be offered by the British Labour movement to the infant Soviet regime was resistance to wars of intervention; thus a recently released absolutist like Wilfred Wellock could in all conscience praise Lenin and devote himself to what he later called 'Hands off Russia' meetings even though 'as a pacifist I was sceptical of the success of any movement that depended on violence'.[2] It came widely to be accepted that Russia had been saved during 1920 by the dockers' celebrated refusal in May to load the *Jolly George* with munitions bound for Poland, and by the threat, three months later, of a general strike in the event of British support for Poland in its war against the Soviet Union. Both won lasting places in the mythology of the Labour movement—to the subsequent embarrassment of trade-union leaders such as Ernest Bevin, who had supported war-resistance in 1920 but came later to realize the burden reliance on such a strategy placed on the unions.[3] A more important consequence, in the present context, of this 'myth' of the general strike against war was that it obscured the distinction between pacifism and war-resistance which had seemed to be increasingly understood during 1916–17.

After an incisive start socialist pacifism had thus by the end of the war become a confused subject. Most socialists who were strict pacifists were in fact Christian in inspiration. And, of those who were genuinely political, a number had retreated from pacifism to the more orthodox policy of

[1] David Marquand, *Ramsay MacDonald* (1977), p. 260.

[2] Wilfred Wellock, *Off the Beaten Track: Adventures in the art of living* (Tanjore, 1961), pp. 100–2.

[3] Alan Bullock, *The Life and Times of Ernest Bevin*, i (1960), pp. 134–6; for his later criticisms of war-resistance see his interview with Lucy Cox, 'The Workers Would *Not* Resist War', *NW*, May 1931.

war-resistance in the excitement of the Russian revolutions. The resultant inability of most socialists to distinguish between the pacifist and *pacificist* interpretations of their creed was to persist for at least a further decade and a half.

(iv) The War's Legacy

It must be recognized that the Great War's legacy for absolute pacifism, though important, was much less decisive than its impact on *pacificism*. The war's unanticipated scale, horror, and dislocating effects, which dealt a lasting blow to both the glamour and the utility of warfare, were of only incidental interest to pacifists. In theory, in so far as they claimed that war was *always* wrong, the nature and consequences of one particular war were not relevant to their case; and, in practice, although during 1918 a detectable increase occurred in the numbers of soldiers facing military courts who professed to have developed conscientious objections, conversion to absolutism among those serving in the trenches was surprisingly uncommon.

In the few well-known cases of changes of heart among serving officers, such as those of two future Sponsors of the Peace Pledge Union, Siegfried Sassoon (1886–1967) and Max Plowman (1883–1940), conversion was, moreover, not attributed at the time to humanitarian objections acquired at the front and can in retrospect more easily be attributed to the unsettling experience of convalescence in Britain. Though Sassoon's 'pacifism' has become famous through both his own literary efforts and those of his friend Robert Graves, who saved him from court martial, his famous 'Soldier's Declaration' of July 1917 objected not to the war itself but to 'the political errors and insincerities for which the fighting men are being sacrificed'.[1] The discontent with the running of the war which the courageous (and even bloodthirsty) holder of the Military Cross began to express in his poetry in 1916 first developed while he was in England

[1] Cited in Robert Graves, *Goodbye to all that* (1929), pp. 320–1; for much information about Sassoon (though not the interpretation I have placed on it) I am grateful to Ted Bogacz, 'The Strange Protest of Siegfried Sassoon', paper read at the Institute of Historical Research, London, on 6 June 1978.

on leave between August 1916 and February 1917, during which time he was influenced by meeting a number of pacifists and by reading H. G. Wells's novel of stoical disenchantment, *Mr. Britling Sees It Through*. Returning to the front, he was wounded within two months; and it was when he found himself back in an English hospital, in April 1917, that he resolved, with the help of Bertrand Russell, Middleton Murry and Francis Meynell, to make his dramatic protest. After publishing his declaration he drew back, however, accepting psychiatric treatment from the pioneering neurasthenia specialist Professor W. H. R. Rivers, which Robert Graves arranged as the alternative to a court martial, and later returning to the front. As in 1936, when he agreed to be a Sponsor of the P.P.U. (though he never attended a single committee), Sassoon seems to have been not a pacifist but a *pacificist* with an unusually acute hatred of war compounded of a poet's sensibility towards the tragedy of war, a nostalgic aristocratic fear such as also motivated Lord Lansdowne's similar protest published in the *Daily Telegraph* on 29 November 1917 that the war was destroying the pre-1914 social fabric, and a lifelong political innocence which caused him to oversimplify the problem of securing peace by negotiation.

Although the circumstances of Max Plowman's protest were remarkably similar—like Sassoon he was a wounded poet who was briefly treated by Professor Rivers and who ultimately escaped military punishment—his objection to war was, in contrast, based on a profound and unshakeable pacifism. Even before the war Plowman had taken risks for his convictions, leaving his father's brick factory to eke out a precarious living as a writer. And, as a socialist, he had always had doubts about the war: he did not volunteer until December 1914, and then only for ambulance work. The first sign that his views on war were being clarified was his decision in July 1915 that there was no difference in principle between combatant and non-combatant service. At first he decided to fight and was commissioned into an infantry regiment, reaching the front in August 1916. In January 1917, however, he was concussed and invalided home, never to return to the trenches. It was during his sick leave that he gradually discovered he was a pacifist; and it was under the influence of Tagore's *Nationalism* that, in January 1918, after a year away from the front, he took the step of resigning his commission on the ground that his hatred of war 'has gradually deepened into the fixed conviction that organised warfare of any kind is always organised murder. So wholly do I believe in the doctrine of Incarnation (that God indeed lives in every human body) that I believe that killing men is always killing God'.[1] He was fortunate not only to escape with a simple dismissal from the army, but also, because of delays in the conscription procedure (to which he was now liable as a discharged volunteer), to avoid prison as an absolutist. He used his liberty to write an explanation of his position which was published in 1919 as *War and the Creative Impulse* and which defined the classic socialist pacifism which he unwaveringly asserted for the rest of his life. Although similar in most respects to the Christian socialism of, for example, Wilfred Wellock, it was clearly 'political' in that it was inspired not by any appeal to supernatural authority but by a mystical, almost anarchist, conception of socialism which Plowman had long admired in his literary hero, William Blake.

Revulsion against slaughter seems thus to have played surprisingly little part in Sassoon's and Plowman's objections to war, although it is, of course, possible that the danger of a court martial confusing humanitarianism with cowardice caused them to play it down. This risk was, of course, particularly acute for the rank and file, and it is noteworthy that one of the few ex-servicemen to attain prominence as a war-resister both during and after the Great War, C. J. ('Jim') Simmons (1893–1975), later a Labour M.P., did so only after being invalided out of the army with a leg amputated. This was self-evident refutation of any charge of cowardice: despite having taken part, as a serving soldier, in various of the anti-war socialist meetings of the summer and autumn of 1917, he was, as he later wrote, 'discharged from

---

[1] Plowman to the Adjutant, 52nd (Gr.) Bn. Durham Light Infantry, 14 Jan. 1918, in D. L. P(lowman). (ed.), *Bridge into the future: letters of Max Plowman* (1944), p. 92; for his reading of Tagore see his letter to Mrs Pethick Lawrence, 22 Dec. 1917, ibid., p. 87.

the Army with—incredibly—a "very good" character' (though he was to be imprisoned by the civil authorities in March 1918 for sedition); and as late as 1931, when he was campaigning to hold his parliamentary seat, his response to a heckler's shout of 'Conchie' was to pull up his trousers and to display his wooden leg. 'The crowd adequately silenced the interrupter.'[1]

Yet the removal of military discipline at the end of the war did not release any surge of pent-up pacifism. A few former soldiers changed their mind quite soon afterwards: for example, John Barclay, the future P.P.U. official (better known, perhaps, as Kingsley Martin's brother-in-law), was converted—on explicitly Christian grounds—to pacifism in 1920.[2] But, particularly in the twenties, the pacifist movement continued to depend for its leadership on those who had opposed the Great War from the start. While personal experience of the horror of war, or the loss of friends and relatives, undoubtedly played an important part in the growth of anti-war feeling in the inter-war years (although the writers who best captured the demoralizing effect of the war were those without direct personal experience of the fighting),[3] this cannot explain why some people became pacifists rather than merely *pacificists*. Indeed the war's ascertainable influence on the leading inter-war recruits to pacifism was surprisingly slight; and, where it can clearly be detected, for example in the cases of the Revd Dick Sheppard, Canon Charles Raven, Vera Brittain, and Sybil Morrison, it seems to have sown seeds which took many years to flourish. Although his few weeks as a chaplain on the Western front in 1914 precipitated an immediate breakdown and haunted him for the rest of his life, Sheppard did not become a pacifist until 1927, when his main inspiration seems to have been the need to find an issue which could revitalize the Church of England. The delayed progress towards pacifism

[1] Jim Simmons, *Soap-Box Evangelist* (Chichester, 1972), pp. 34, 36–8, 64. Simmons was a Primitive Methodist lay preacher.

[2] See his statement to a tribunal in the Second World War, printed in Denis Hayes, *Challenge of Conscience: The Story of the Conscientious Objectors of 1939–1949* (1949), pp. 28–9.

[3] Walter Allen, 'A Literary Aftermath', in George A. Panichas (ed.), *The Promise of Greatness: The War of 1914–1918* (1968), p. 504.

of Charles Raven (1885–1964) was identical to Sheppard's except for a three-year time-lag: his brief service as a chaplain was in 1917, during which he was gassed—yet he wrote from the front: 'Pacifists and C.O.s may talk of the sanctity of human brotherhood, we out here have discovered something of its reality';[1] his adoption of pacifism to an ecclesiastical purgative was in 1930. The tragic loss to Vera Brittain (1893–1970) of her fiancé, brother, and two close friends, all killed in battle, and her nursing experience as a V.A.D. in France, took her too only as far as *pacificism*; she did not embrace pacifism until 1936.[2] And although Sybil Morrison (1893–   ), a pillar of the Peace Pledge Union since the Second World War, now attributes her conversion to pacifism to revulsion at the sight of a Zeppelin catching fire over Harrow in 1917, its crew burning to death amid unseemly local rejoicings, she continued her job as an ambulance driver and took no part in pacifist activities of any kind until the later thirties.[3] Doubtless the memory of the trenches and of squandered lives was an ever-present unspoken factor; but as a stimulus to absolute pacifist recruitment it was certainly less conspicuous, and probably less important, than fear of the next war. Pacifism owed more to the bomber than to Passchendaele.

The most significant fact for pacifists about the Great War was thus not any revelation of an irreversible qualitative change in warfare but the imposition of conscription. Confrontation with the state provided the repressive conditions in which pacifism could rediscover its sectarian roots; and the resultant soul-searchings of the absolutists defined the implications of pacifism in modern society with an unprecedented rigour which still evinces respect today. Yet even this effect can be exaggerated, for its lesson was already being distorted before the war ended.

This was because of the remarkable revivial of *pacificism*, despite the war's continuous slaughter. The nineteenth-century peace movement had collapsed in 1914: no pre-war

[1] Cited in F. W. Dillistone, *Charles Raven: Naturalist, Historian, Theologian* (1975), p. 86; see also p. 211.

[2] Vera Brittain, *Testament of Youth: An Autobiographical Study of the Years 1900–1925* (1933); for her conversion to pacifism see below, pp. 210–11.

[3] Interview, 13 Oct. 1976.

organization, except the National Peace Council (N.P.C.), which aspired to be the co-ordinating body for the movement as a whole, played any significant role in the inter-war period. This was in contrast to the new societies formed in the war. As early as August 1914 radicalism organized itself into the Union of Democratic Control (U.D.C.); and internationalism revived with the wider recognition of the need for a League of Nations, leading at first to foundation of private study groups and, in May 1915, to the formation of a League of Nations Society. Combining radicalism and internationalism was a Women's International League (W.I.L.), founded by former suffragists, three of whom had managed, despite Governmental obstruction, to attend the International Women's Conference in the Hague in April 1915, out of which the W.I.L. grew. In the first half of the war all, despite considerable caution and moderation, were vilified as 'pacifist'; in 1917-18, however—during which period socialist *pacificism* revived, as already noted—their ideas (or, rather, those of the U.D.C. and League movement, since the W.I.L. was doctrinally too confused ever to become important) became respectable and influential. The U.D.C.'s demands influenced even the moderates of the Labour movement; and the League idea, reinforced early in 1918 by a second pressure group, the League of Free Nations Association (which wanted to use the wartime military alliance as the basis for an immediate, anti-German, League), won support in Government circles as a means of pleasing President Wilson and preparing for post-war economic co-operation against Germany. As *pacificism* thus recovered some of its former optimism, and as, except for a brief setback amid the jingoistic excesses following the Armistice, it continued to make progress throughout the twenties, the first three years of the Great War came to seem but a temporary setback in more than a century of growing *pacificist* optimism which was, as will be seen, to be checked only in the 1930s. The war enabled pacifism to establish inspiring (and sectarian) precedents; but until the final quarter of the inter-war period a majority of pacifists preferred to relapse into the same subordinate (and collaborative) position within the peace movement which had characterized their nineteenth-century predecessors.

5

AFTER THE GREAT WAR

The dozen years after the Great War were a paradoxical time for pacifism: many of its ideas were received with unprecedented sympathy; but as a distinctive position it was more than ever engulfed by the flood tide of *pacificism*. Fear of air power was widely voiced as a result of the wartime raids and, although for many years the public mind was too numb to discuss the trenches, by the later twenties their horrors were also being emotively recalled in a wave of novels, memoirs, and plays. The brand of *pacificist* thought which benefited from this anti-war feeling was internationalism, which became far more popular than its rivals, radicalism and socialism, as the superficial international calm of the twenties (particularly after the Locarno treaties of 1925) encouraged hopes that the League of Nations could secure disarmament and use its moral authority to ensure peace. After 1924 (in which year fifteen of its leading members left to join the first Labour Government), the U.D.C., whose attitude to European tensions was at bottom isolationist, lost the position it had enjoyed since the latter phase of the Great War as the most influential peace society to the League of Nations Union (L.N.U.), whose ideas gained ground even within a Labour Party normally sceptical of 'liberal' ideas. Founded late in 1918 by a merger of the two League societies, the L.N.U. acquired a membership unprecedented in the peace movement in terms of both quality and quantity. Offering as it did both arbitration and multilateral disarmament as ways to consolidate the post-Locarno euphoria into a permanent international peace, it was by the end of the twenties setting its sights on a gross membership target of a million.

Attracted by such positive proposals, far more pacifists joined the L.N.U. than joined the explicitly pacifist societies, which, apart from the Society of Friends, consisted of the F.o.R. for Christians and the newly-founded No More War

Movement for socialists (including Christian socialists). Although many promiscuously joined several or all of these, plus also the L.N.U.,[1] pacifist membership figures remained small and the most interesting ideas and activity emanated from an M.P.—Arthur Ponsonby—working on his own. The relatively poor showing of organized Christian and socialist pacifism, Ponsonby's almost solitary campaign for a new form of inspiration, and such impact as pacifism had made on public life by the end of the twenties are the subject of this chapter. Its dominant theme will be that the improving international outlook made the collaborative orientation the only appealing one; and that, as a result, the attention of pacifists was focused on the efficacy of *pacificism* rather than on the particularities of their own position.

(i) Christians.

The Society of Friends still consisted of birthright members for the most part, despite a number of wartime converts. (One discreditable motive which may have tempted officials of other peace societies to join[2] was improved access to Quaker money, on which most such societies relied to a certain extent.) Like its counterpart in the north of England, the Northern Friends' Peace Board (founded in 1913), the Friends' Peace Committee placed its considerable publishing and other resources enthusiastically at the disposal of all sections of the peace movement. Its annual reports to the Society's London Yearly Meeting were classic statements of the collaborative orientation. In 1927 it welcomed the 'greater readiness than formerly existed to admit the wrongfulness of war. Our work may therefore be more and more directed towards practical ways of abolishing it . . . '; and

[1] e.g. Lucy Cox, General Secretary of the N.M.W.M. 1924-32, interview, 23 Apr. 1975. This practice was defended by Sir Norman Angell, later a critic of pacifism, as late as the July 1933 National Peace Congress; see G. P. Gooch (ed.), *In Pursuit of Peace* (1933), pp. 43-4.

[2] According to Gerald Bailey (1903-72), Secretary of the N.P.C., 1930-48, interview, 18 Dec. 1970. Peace societies liked to have Quaker treasurers: the N.M.W.M. first approached Corder Catchpool (see Hughes, *Indomitable Friend*, p. 58), who later became P.P.U. treasurer following the death of Maurice Rowntree. The N.M.W.M. managed to secure the services of another Friend, Harold Morland.

two years later, when the *pacificist* tide was in full flood, it was insisting that Quakers 'should welcome every ally whatever uniform he wears' and 'unite with others who do not fully share our basic views, in working out their solution on political lines'. It even felt the need to add that it was 'none the less important that we should maintain our Quaker testimony based on Christ's teaching of the nature of man and his relation to God'.[1]   But, apart from thus appearing to treat the Society's distinctive pacifism as almost an afterthought, this collaborative approach presented few difficulties during the twenties. Not until the thirties did Quakers have to face up to the crucial issue which they had been fudging since the first mooting of the League idea in the Great War: their attitude to sanctions.

In the optimistic twenties—as at all times when there is neither war nor imminent prospect of it to concentrate the mind—it was the sectarian orientation, developed by the F.o.R., which proved more difficult to sustain. In the early stages of the Great War the F.o.R.'s very existence had served to reassure isolated individuals that others shared their interpretation of Christian duty; but once the difficult decision to carry on in peacetime was taken in 1919[2] there was continuous debate on how personal religious intuitions could be expressed in institutional form. The alternative organizational models between which it—like the P.P.U. a few years later—had to choose were specified with great clarity in January 1929 in the report of an internal inquiry into the purpose of the Fellowship:

We have asked ourselves: Is it that of a propagandist group, seeking along the ways of manifestoes and resolutions to get its message 'across' to the surrounding community? Or is it rather a kind of Order, a Fellowship of men and women, with a certain unmistakable attitude to life based upon a profound religious conviction? If this latter, then the aim would not be primarily that of securing a number of agreed conclusions on a number of intricate problems—it would be rather that of a living Fellowship, where organisation would count less, but the spirit would count more.[3]

Despite   protests   by   politically-minded   activists—such

---

[1] *London Yearly Meeting Proceedings*, 1927, p. 260; 1929, p. 293.

[2] Robbins, *Abolition*, p. 193.

[3] 'Report by Commission of Enquiry 1928/9', F.o.R. G.C., 21-2 Jan. 1929.

as Walter Ayles who in 1924, as its Chairman, urged the annual Council meeting to seize the opportunity of spreading anti-war views in the newly favourable climate of opinion—the latter view tended to prevail. As one member expressed it at that Council: 'The genius of the Fellowship was that it was not merely a propaganda body but something very like a religious order. We were called to commit ourselves to a certain way of life'.[1] And even in the later thirties a pacifist schooled in more militant societies could commit a solecism simply by inquiring at an F.o.R. ladies' tea-party 'whether they would help us in selling Peace News or on sandwich board parades or in giving out leaflets'. 'I shall never forget their faces', she reported later. ' . . . They looked dumb, obstinate and stupid . . . '[2] One who embodied the F.o.R.'s quietist approach at its most inspiring and courageous, however, was one its founder-members, George M. Ll. Davies (1880–1949). Of a saintliness comparable to that of Stephen Hobhouse—who himself soon abandoned the strains of public life after the Great War—Davies paid the price of idealistic sensitivity in recurrent bouts of intense depression and in an inability to stand the rough and tumble of politics. From a well-connected family (he was related to David Davies, the millionaire and future Baron Davies of Llandinam), he began as a banker (and even held a commission in the territorials) before succumbing to a nervous breakdown. A decision to devote himself to philanthropic social work did not prevent a second breakdown, in 1913; but on the outbreak of war the following year he realized that working for the F.o.R., and suffering imprisonment as an absolutist, enabled him to discover for the first time a worldly expression of his yearning for spiritual peace. Yet many aspects of the pacifist movement distressed him. In particular he found distasteful its personality clashes (even within the F.o.R.), and the crude militancy of some of the objectors he met in prison; and although in 1923 he became the only inter-war M.P. to be elected explicitly as a Christian Pacifist (albeit only for the tiny University of Wales constituency and with Labour backing against a split Liberal vote), he announced,

[1] F.o.R. Co., 8-9 Sept. 1924.
[2] Margery South to Ponsonby, 14 Apr. 1937, A.P.

characteristically, before taking his seat in Parliament that he did not 'feel free to enter into a sectarian obligation in which either hostility or antagonism to others is expected of one as a matter of party loyalty'.[1]   It was not surprising, therefore, that he abandoned politics after losing in the 1924 general election and subsequently confined his efforts to the F.o.R. (and, later, also the P.P.U., although it was significant that he did not become a Sponsor until after the Second World War had started), preaching always that pacifism could find true expression only through communion in one's personal life with the beauty of humanity and of all creation.

But such mistrust of organized activity came close to denying any role at all for the Fellowship as an organization, and in consequence it remained small and static: its General Committee noted in December 1929 that 'the rate of increase in the membership was very slow compared with the spread of pacifism'.[2] In the mid-twenties it had been claiming 7,500 members plus a thousand 'sympathizers', but a weeding-out of its dead files in 1928 reduced this to a core of about 3,300 members plus just over 300 'sympathizers'—at which level it was to remain until its threefold expansion in the last three years of peace. The one public sphere in which it had influence and collaborated with *pacificist* activity was, understandably, that of the Churches, where early signs of the Christian pacifist revival of the thirties—such as the founding within Congregationalism of a Christian Pacifist Crusade in 1926, and the reconstitution in 1929 of the Church of Scotland Peace Society (originally established in 1915 and disbanded five years later)—could already be detected. More significant for the cause of Christian pacifism, however, was the increased awareness within the Church of England that the memory of unseemly Christian enthusiasm for the Great War had urgently to be purged if the purity and prestige of organized religion were to be restored. At first concerned Anglicans had hoped that a radical stand on social and economic issues would inspire the Church; but the failure of

---

[1] *Friend*, 4 Jan. 1924, p. 7; see also George M. Ll. Davies, *Pilgrimage of Peace* (1950), which includes a biographical essay by Charles Raven.

[2] F.o.R. G.C., 10–11 Dec. 1929; the membership figures are taken from these Minutes.

the C.O.P.E.C. movement to produce a lasting change of attitude in the wake of its much-vaunted 'Conference on Politics, Economics and Citizenship' held at Birmingham in April 1924—which itself had made the *pacificist* declaration that 'all war is contrary to the spirit and teaching of Jesus Christ'—made them look for another issue. It was, of course, while going through a phase of acute disillusion with the Anglican church, which he got off his chest with the publication in 1927 of *The Impatience of a Parson*, that the former army chaplain, ex-Vicar of St. Martin-in-the-Fields and well-known radio parson, Dick Sheppard, first declared himself a convert to pacifism.[1]

Few others were then prepared to go as far as this, however, and Sheppard himself was not yet ready to devote himself exclusively to this issue and took no part in the F.o.R. As Canon Raven, who was himself converted to pacifism in 1930, later commented: 'Until 1928 it needed some courage to renounce war from a public platform, and with the exception of the Society of Friends no Christian Church had expressed any strong sense of its devotion. That autumn saw a definite change.' As Raven had noticed, the reaction against the Great War expressed itself in a sudden torrent of anti-war literature and propaganda, starting on the tenth anniversary of the armistice. This change of public mood seemed to evangelical Christians such as Raven who (jointly with Lucy Gardner, a founder member of the F.o.R.) had been the organizing secretary of C.O.P.E.C., to present the ideal follow-up issue: 'If a single issue was to be chosen, only the cause of peace was large enough and exciting enough to be a worthy expression of our studies.'[2]

In October 1929, therefore, a 'Christ and Peace' campaign was launched to awaken the Churches to the crucial need to condemn modern warfare. Although for the first time Church of England clergy took as active a part as their Nonconformist colleagues, this series of twenty-five meetings

---

[1] See Sheppard to Housman, 4 Feb. 1927, cited in L. Housman (ed.), *What Can We Believe? Letters Exchanged Between Dick Sheppard and L.H.* (1939), p. 298.

[2] C. E. Raven, *Is War Obsolete?: A Study of the Conflicting Claims of Religion and Citizenship* (1935), pp. 22–3, 35.

and conferences over seventeen months was far from satisfactory from the pacifist point of view. The campaign's lack
of clear organization and charismatic leadership, and its
failure to make clear the all-important distinction between
condemning war and preaching pacifism, both reflected the
weakness of the existing peace societies. Its one conspicuous
achievement was the declaration by the Anglican Church's
1930 Lambeth Conference: 'War as a method of settling
international disputes is incompatible with the teaching of
our Lord Jesus Christ'; but for all its radicalism as a statement from the Established Church this was no advance on
C.O.P.E.C.'s *pacificist* approach of six years before and
as a guide to Christian duty on the question of war-prevention
it was, in the words of a recent historian, 'an ambiguous
formula'.[1]

Though it must be interpreted as an aspect of the emotional *pacificism* of the late twenties, the 'Christ and Peace'
campaign served, nevertheless, as a stimulus to pacifism from
which the F.o.R., in particular, gained some new recruits.
Those involved in the campaign who were soon to cross the
Rubicon from *pacificism* to Christian pacifism included:
Raven, who joined the F.o.R. in June 1931;[2] the Revd
Herbert Gray (1868-1956) a senior Presbyterian pastor and a
former army chaplain, who joined the F.o.R. at the same time
as Raven and was the following year to be one of Sheppard's
partners in the abortive Peace Army; and also the Revd Henry
Carter (1874-1951), General Secretary of the Methodist
Social Welfare Department and a prominent temperance
worker, who was to announce his conversion early in 1933.[3]

Also active in the campaign were those such as Sheppard
and Leyton Richards who had already espoused pacifism.
Like many pacifists at that time Sheppard was still too
diffident and unsure of his views (as well as too ill) to press
the difference between pacifism and *pacificism*. Richards,

---

[1] E. R. Norman, *Church and Society in England 1770-1970: A Historical
Study* (Oxford, 1976), p. 298.

[2] F.o.R. G. C., 15-16 June 1931.

[3] E. C. Urwin, *Henry Carter, C.B.E.: A Memoir* (1955), pp. 79-81. He should
not be confused with the Revd Henry Child Carter (1875-1954) of Emmanuel
Church, Cambridge, an active Congregational pacifist: see R. Tudur Jones, *Congregationalism in England 1662-1962* (1962), p. 359.

however, was fully prepared to argue the merits of 'peace at any price' against internationalism and in January 1929 published *The Christian's Alternative to War: An Examination of Christian Pacifism*, one of the very few systematic attempts to explain Christian pacifism to a general audience before the mid-thirties. His book, which had run into a fourth edition within thirteen months, illustrates the limitations of even the best Christian pacifist thinking in the twenties.

The basis of Christian pacifism is, of course, straightforward and unchanging: the belief that, though condoned by the Christian Churches, war is contrary to the essential spirit and teaching of Christianity. The arguments used to justify this position have, however, undergone significant alteration. Before the Great War they were often derived from esoteric quasi-pacifist readings of Christian doctrine; while even those pacifists who did not belong to unorthodox sects seemed mainly to base their faith on selective scriptural tenets. From the foundation of the F.o.R. the most thoughtful Christian pacifists came to realize that there was no definitive biblical ruling on warfare, and that the pacifist case rested on a strict application to international relations of what all Christians acknowledged to be cardinal principles of their religion: love and redemption. Their case rested, therefore, on the validity of their interpretation of God's Will and Christ's Teaching, and all other considerations were, strictly, irrelevant.

But until the international events of the later thirties forced Christian pacifists to accept this view (or renounce their pacifism), they tended to hedge their bets by arguing that pacifism could also be justified on practical grounds. In the twenties, many seem to have assumed that *pacificism* would prevent war and did not discuss the possibility that Christian pacifism entailed a willingness to submit to invasion. The few who did so tended to make optimistic assumptions about the international situation. For example, when discussing the 'concrete case' of 1914, Richards admitted that pacifism involved a risk of 'martyrdom' but insisted that 'such martyrdom . . . would inevitably stir the conscience of mankind, and mark the beginning of the end

of war'. Moreover, when considering the morality of adopting
pacifism and thereby refusing to aid a third party such as
Belgium, he resorted to the utilitarian argument that, under
modern conditions, not coming to a nation's aid was 'always'
the best thing to do, 'for it is the merest make-believe to
suggest that war ever can or does defend those whose safety
we desire'.[1] Much of his space was devoted to an attempt to
show the irredeemable nastiness of war by stressing bayonet-
tings and syphilis in a manner characteristic of the memoir
writers of the period, and the main criticism the book received
was for its negativeness. Thus despite the greater support it
had gained within the Churches, and despite the continued
work of the F.o.R. and Society of Friends, the particular
message of Christian pacifism, as distinct from *pacificism*,
did not start to reach a wider audience until about 1934.

(ii) Socialists

The only outlet in the twenties for absolute pacifists who
were not of Christian inspiration was—although many of its
members were, in fact, devout Christians—the No More War
Movement (N.M.W.M.). Set up early in 1921, it was a direct
successor to the N.-C.F. which had been wound up less than
two years previously when conscription ended. By 1921 the
need for pacifists to avoid every distraction from the building
of socialism seemed less pressing; and former conscientious
objectors began to recover pride in their own distinctive wartime role and learn for the first time about their counterparts
abroad who might form the nucleus of an international
anti-militarist movement.

In addition some pacifists—particularly those of the
Christian-socialist *Crusader* group—had, despite their excitement at *pacificist* prospects during the last two years of the
war, been growing concerned at the extent to which violence
seemed to be gaining respectability on the left. Will Chamberlain, for example, was troubled not only by the provision for
sanctions in the proposed League of Nations Covenant but

---

[1] Leyton Richards, *The Christian's Alternative to War: An Examination of
Christian Pacifism* (1929), pp. 108-9.

also by post-war industrial militancy, and warned in February 1919 that

> it will be the duty of those who have resisted militarism during the war to do all we can to stem the tide of militarism in the Labour movement. The time may yet come when we shall have to face the bullets of our fellow workers in warning them that armed force is no remedy, whether in the hands of the capitalist or the worker.[1]

There was a reaction, too, against the blurring of pacifism and war-resistance; by October 1919 Gilbert Thomas felt the need to emphasize the distinction between them:

> The Conscientious Objector when he refused to handle a rifle did not dream that he might thereby compel the militarists to stay their operations. He did hope, it is true, that his example might challenge thought and win moral sympathy, but of coercing the public to enter upon peace negotiations he had not a thought.[2]

Similarly, Wilfred Wellock, a witness in Berlin to the successful defeat of the Kapp Putsch in March 1920 by working-class 'direct action', was careful to stress that he did 'not believe in preaching "direct action" as such but rather in appealing to the moral consciousness of the community . . . and making out a spiritual case for a new social order.'[3]

By May 1920 the *Crusader* group was growing frustrated at the inactivity of the *ad hoc* committees that were supposed to be carrying on some of the N.-C.F.'s work.[4] One was supposed to deal with military indoctrination in schools, another with the threat of conscription; but the most important was the Pacifist Union Committee, entrusted to lay the foundations of the British section of an international absolute pacifist organization.[5] By January 1921 the *Crusader* group was asking 'Where is the "C.O." movement? At the moment it is no longer mobilised—but a desire for mobilisation is in the minds of many.'[6] It was itself intending to launch a campaign in support of an 'Affirmation Against War' which it had drawn up, but an acute financial crisis forced it to set up this campaign on an independent footing.[7] On 15

---

[1] *Crusader*, 7 Feb. 1919, p. 3.
[2] Ibid., 17 Oct. 1919, p. 7.
[3] Ibid., 13 Aug. 1920, p. 6.
[4] Ibid., 14 May 1920, p. 3.
[5] Ibid., 5 Dec. 1919, p. 3; Boulton, *Objection Overruled*, p. 291.
[6] *Crusader*, 7 Jan. 1921, p. 6.
[7] Ibid., 28 Jan. 1921, p. 4.

February 1921, therefore, this Affirmation (which was, slightly expanded, to become the official pledge of the No More Movement) appeared in a letter published in the *Daily Herald* and in other papers over the signatures of Brockway, Chamberlain, Lansbury, and nine other pacifists—several of them (not surprisingly, in view of the need to attract financial support) Quakers. The letter informed those who felt able to endorse the Affirmation that a conference would 'shortly be called with the object of linking up with similar movements in other countries, and forming an international movement against war, pledged to work for complete disarmament in each and every country.'

At the Penn Club in London on 24 February 1921 eighteen pacifists attended such a conference, in the course of which the 'No More War International Movement' (as the N.M.W.M. was initially called) was formally established.[1] The next month the body that was intended to federate the various national movements was founded, under the name 'Paco', at an international anti-militarist congress at the Hague.[2] Despite optimism aroused in 1921-2 by 'Nie Wieder Krieg' (No More War) demonstrations in Germany, first held on the seventh anniversary of the outbreak of the Great War, the world anti-militarist movement proved no easier to organize than any other socialist international. In 1923 'Paco', changing its name to the War Resisters' International (W.R.I.), moved its headquarters from Holland to the private house of a small builder in Enfield. For the next twenty-five years it was run from his home by Runham Brown (1879–1949), a Congregationalist, socialist, and Great War absolutist, whose zest for organizing pacifism made him an indispensable, if not always popular, member of the N.M.W.M. and, later, of the P.P.U. The W.R.I.'s role during the period of his stewardship was far more comparable to a world-wide version of the old N.-C.F. than to the 'international movement against war' which pacifists had originally hoped for. Apart from organizing triennial international gatherings, it aimed to be an information service monitoring absolutist activity, most

[1] Chamberlain, *Fighting for Peace*, p. 118.
[2] Devi Prasad, *Fifty Years of War Resistance: What Now?* (W.R.I., 1972), p. 7.

of which, of course, took place in countries which retained conscription. The task of proselytizing 'war-resistance' was left entirely to its national sections; on the continent these sections were often decidedly more socialist than pacifist, but in Britain the task fell, until its official takeover by the P.P.U. in 1937, to the avowedly pacifist N.M.W.M..

That the N.M.W.M. was truly the successor organization to the N.-C.F. was illustrated by the fact that most of those who attended the Penn Club meeting on 24 February and went on to be the Movement's leading members were Great War absolutists and I.L.P. socialists. Its first Chairman was Chamberlain; the first editor of its journal, *No More War*, launched in February 1922, was Brockway; and its Organising Secretary after 1926 was Ayles. Right from the start it numbered some of the Great War's most remarkable absolutist personalities among its activists: Wellock, a vegetarian and believer in the simple life who rarely earned enough to enter the income-tax-paying bracket;[1] J. Allen Skinner (1890–1972), a Post Office clerk from Manchester who had contracted a serious tubercular condition in prison partly because, as a strict vegetarian, he had almost starved to death; and Harold Bing (1898–1975), believed to be the youngest absolutist of the Great War (and one of the most intelligent) who throughout his life was 'a keen vegetarian, against vaccinations, non-smoker and lover of the open air',[2] as well as a pacifist.

As befitted an organization set up by experienced absolutists of strong political views, the N.M.W.M. defined its socialist pacifism with great care. Its hundred-word membership pledge (which was abbreviated in 1926) contrasted with the P.P.U.'s memorably simple but imprecise declaration of a decade later. Beginning with the unequivocally pacifist statement that 'all war is wrong' and that the arming of any state in any way 'is treason to the spiritual unity and intelligence of mankind', it required the pacifist to 'declare it to be my intention never to take part in war, offensive or defensive, international or civil, whether by bearing arms, making or handling munitions, voluntarily subscribing to

---

[1] Wellock, *Beaten Track*, pp. 163, 165, 175.
[2] *Pacifist*, July 1975, p. 10.

war loans, or using my labour for the purpose of setting others free for war service.' This rigorous absolutist position had been set out in the *Crusader*'s 'Affirmation against War'; but at the second meeting of the N.M.W.M. held on 22 April 1921 a positive political obligation was added: 'to strive for the removal of all causes of war and to work for the establishment of a new social order based on cooperation for the common good'.[1]

The problem which was to dog the N.M.W.M. throughout its history was, in effect, whether the two halves of this pledge were compatible. To preserve the strict absolutism of the first part while making sufficient political impact to prevent war and establish the new social order prescribed in the second was, of course (although not understood in these terms), the central difficulty of pacifism in its collaborative orientation. The normal way out of this difficulty before the Great War had been for pacifists to play down their distinctive beliefs and campaign for *pacificist* measures; but the N.M.W.M., its absolutist rigour strengthened by suspicion of the newly-founded and disappointingly 'liberal' and 'imperialist' League of Nations, declared implacably that it did 'not believe that a vague sentiment against war is of much value, nor is it prepared to support any kind of half-measures or to compromise on the issue of war in any way whatsoever.'[2] The Movement's belief that it could collaborate with practical measures of war prevention without trimming assumed that socialist *pacificism* would make rapid and painless strides towards the eradication of militarism. This, in turn, presupposed the conversion of the Labour Party to a thoroughgoing policy of war-resistance, including total and unilateral disarmament.

At first there was some cause for cautious optimism, particularly in view of strong support for the pacifist conception of socialism within the I.L.P.. Wellock was attracted to this organisation at the start of the twenties explicitly because, as he later wrote, it 'inherited the spiritual idealism of the early Christian Socialists and the artist-poet-craftsmanship

---

[1] *Crusader*, 29 Apr. 1921, p. 11; at this point it had gathered 558 signatures for the Affirmation in its original form.

[2] *NMW*, 10 Mar. 1922.

school of William Morris'.[1] Also joining at this time was
Frank Dawtry, from 1927 onwards an active rank-and-file
member of the N.M.W.M. and, later, of the P.P.U., who
discovered it to be 'a body of almost spiritual character, and
it was not long before the very strong pacifist element in
that organization inspired me to throw what energies I had
into the cause of pacifism'.[2] Outside the I.L.P. there were
also encouraging signs: many Labour leaders had opposed
the Great War and continued to profess 'pacifist' opinions;[3]
at the Party's 1926 annual conference an unequivocal war-
resistance resolution, sponsored by Brockway and Arthur
Ponsonby, was carried by acclamation;[4] and on the ten
occasions between 1924 and 1931 when motions calling
for unilateral disarmament were pressed to a vote in the
Commons, 76 M.P.s recorded a total of 186 'ayes'.[5]

But the clear trend, once the Party had acquired experience in office, was to abandon such opposition-mindedness
and to accept the constructive *pacificist* opportunities
offered by a securely established League and, in particular,
by the long-awaited World Disarmament Conference. Mean-
while the I.L.P. lost influence as the Labour Party established
its direct-membership structure and, partly because of the
impetus given by the slump to a materialistic view of socialism, became less spiritual and more strident. The N.M.W.M.
was thus presented with a choice: either to accept the full
implications of its collaborative orientation, as had the
Quakers, and agree to support the very *pacificist* policies
it had previously criticized as half-measures; or to retreat
into a powerless sectarian purity. On this issue the Movement became increasingly divided in the late twenties.

The objection to collaboration with *pacifism* was not,
it should be noted, due to the usual difficulty of deciding

[1] Wellock, *Beaten Track*, p. 58.

[2] *PN*, 9 Feb. 1940, p. 2.

[3] Fifteen members of the 1924 Labour Government were members of the
U.D.C. which was commonly described as 'pacifist': e.g. by H. M. Swanwick,
Builders of Peace: Being Ten Years' History of the Union of Democratic Control
(1924), p. 180.

[4] *Report*, 26th Annual Conference, Margate 1926, pp. 253–7.

[5] Calculated from Hansard by the author. In 1929 Will Chamberlain claimed
that 116 members of the Commons had voted for total disarmament motions:
Fighting for Peace, p. 125.

how far to support coercive sanctions, since this issue was largely evaded until the thirties. Anyway, many socialist consciences were not, it seemed, greatly troubled by the issue of condoning a certain measure of force: there was, in particular, as a young recruit in the twenties, Leslie Paul, later remembered, 'a very rapid slurring of our pacifism' whenever the question of support for the Russian revolution arose.[1] Similarly John Lewis, later an organizer for the Left Book Club and a critic of pacifism, admitted in 1938 that although at this time he had been

a member of the Fellowship of Reconciliation and the No More War Movement it had never been possible for me to criticise the Russians for their defence policy. Very many pacifists shared this point of view. We were anti-imperialist pacifists at the time, and in the years immediately following the War this position was shared by all progressives and involved no difficulties.[2]

What socialists mainly disliked about *pacificism* was that its prevailing strand was too explicitly liberal in its political assumptions. They regarded the League, even at the peak of its international prestige, as merely a league of capitalist governments rather than of peoples, and repudiated Geneva's assumption that disarmament and peace were achievable on the basis of the capitalist status quo. The leadership of the N.M.W.M. was prepared, nevertheless, to accept the League and disarmament as steps in the right direction. In several cases at least this was a consequence of the success of many absolutists in starting careers in Labour politics and their understandable desire to remain in step with Party policy. The N.M.W.M.'s change of emphasis, which was accompanied by the streamlining of its pledge and by a membership drive, coincided with the appointment in 1926 of Ayles as Organising Secretary. Significantly, he was Labour's regular candidate in Bristol North, winning the seat in the 1923 and 1929 elections; likewise his loyal friend who had been the General Secretary since 1924, Lucy A. Cox (1894–   ), stood for Labour in the 1931 election (and five years later became the third wife of the Party's Secretary, James Middleton). Two

---

[1] Leslie Paul, *Angry Young Man* (1951), p. 124.
[2] John Lewis, *The Case Against Pacifism* ([1940)], p. 5. For this publication delay see below p. 293.

other prominent supporters of the leadership line also had Transport House connections: both Maurice Webb, its youth organizer in the thirties and, later, a Minister in Attlee's Government, and Will Chamberlain, whose views were in the process of traversing from impassioned Tolstoyan opposition to the League at the time the Covenant was first published to orthodox support for collective security in the mid-thirties,[1] worked in its press department.

In contrast, the vocal minority which rejected the leadership's policy as too great a compromise of both pacifist and socialist principles manifested an outlook that was becoming increasingly evident within the I.L.P. and which was to bring both organizations to disaster in the early thirties. The issue which first brought this opposition into the open in the late twenties was the reluctance of certain 'pacifist' Labour M.P.s to vote against the arms estimates (and also the Indian policy) of a Labour Government. A motion criticizing this reluctance was carried by the I.L.P's 1929 Conference[2], and the following year at the N.M.W.M.'s annual conference a similar attempt was made to rebuke some of its leading members—such as Lansbury, Wilson, and Barr—for placing Party before pacifism. Although narrowly defeated on this occasion the protests were to succeed in 1931.

More disturbing for the leadership than the resolution itself, however, was the evident confidence of those proposing it—led by Joseph Southall (1861-1944), an outspoken Quaker artist from Birmingham—in the right of the pure to root out sin: it was characteristic that Southall, asked to describe his work for the Society of Friends, answered: 'Telling the truth about the Peace question and sundry other matters that Friends would rather not know.'[3] Sectarians face, as had already been noted in the context of the medieval pacifist sects, a choice of how to express their dissent from the values of society. Most modern pacifists have seen their duty to be to withdraw or submit in a spirit of love and humility, and the minority which has adopted an attitude

[1] Compare his views in *Crusader*, 21 Feb. 1919, p. 3, with those in *Friend*, 24 Sept. 1937, p. 900.

[2] *War Resister*, No. 23 (Summer 1929), p. 21.

[3] *Friend*, 17 Nov. 1944, pp. 747-8. He was an I.L.P. activist who urged disaffiliation from the Labour Party.

of self-righteous defiance—most excusably, perhaps, under the stress of conscription—has caused them considerable embarrassment. Thus the saintly George M. Ll. Davies never fully recovered from the shock of meeting his first fellow conscientious objector in prison and hearing him immediately boast of his tribunal appearance: 'They asked me if I'd any objection to killing. I said I'd no objection to killing the likes of them and I shoved the table at them.'[1] As Russell shrewdly observed in an analysis of the psychology of Great War pacifists: 'In some men the habit of standing out against the herd had become so ingrained that they could not co-operate with anybody about anything.'[2] It was this same defiant minority-mindedness which surfaced from time to time within inter-war pacifism. It was, for instance, never very deep beneath the skin of two prominent Nonconformist Labour M.P.s and unswerving pacifists, J. H. Hudson and Alfred Salter. Hudson, who imported into his pacifism the sternness of his temperance campaigning, was described by Brockway as 'the most pugilistic of pacifists';[3] while Dr Salter was depicted by Lansbury's son-in-law, Raymond Postgate, as 'so intolerant that he seemed to ascribe any difference of opinion to moral turpitude'.[4] A suggestive distinction between pacifist attitudes was, moreover, offered by Postgate when he went on to note that, whereas his easy-going Anglican father-in-law was a teetotaller, the puritan Salter was (like Hudson) a prohibitionist. One did not have to be right at the opposite pole of sectarian psychology —Davies's introspective quietism, for example—to regard the 'prohibitionist' type of sectarian response exemplified by a section of the N.M.W.M. as out of harmony with true pacifism's respect for the individual conscience. Thus, although Southall could insist that all members should obey 'the organised conscience of the members as expressed at the Annual Conference',[5] many had become pacifists precisely

---

[1] *Rec.*, Feb. 1932, p. 34.

[2] Bell (ed.), *We Did Not Fight*, p. 333.

[3] Brockway, *Inside*, p. 68.

[4] Raymond Postgate, *The Life of George Lansbury* (1951), p. 310.

[5] *NW*, Jan. 1931. For an early expression of Southall's 'contempt' for the League see *Friend*, 25 Feb. 1921, p. 139.

because they were convinced that it was morally unjustifiable to attempt to 'organize' conscience.

Yet it was ironic that those, like Chamberlain, who now invoked the sovereignty of the individual conscience against such prohibitionism,[1] did so to support what it could not be denied were individual lapses from strict pacifism. This symbolized the N.M.W.M.'s underlying predicament after a decade of existence. It was organizationally too weak to stand on its absolutist dignity and go it alone: significantly, it had ceased publishing membership figures in 1927, when it claimed a total of only 3,000 and, although continuing to put *No More War*'s circulation at 15,000 copies, it was probably smaller even than the F.o.R. Its aspirations for the future—exemplified in its journal's change of name and format in 1930—were, therefore, increasingly focused on what had come to seem the most attainable *pacificist* goals even though they were not the socialist ones it had originally hoped to achieve. Thus the last edition of *No More War*, before it was reborn under the less explicitly pacifist title *New World*, pointed out that, after years in which it 'steadily advocated uncompromising pacifism', it had now to recognize 'the passing of an epoch', in that war was now 'entirely discredited':

The moment has come when we must add to our work for war resistance and disarmament that constructive work of international reorganisation which alone will make possible the birth of the New World of our dreams—a world delivered from the terrible menace of war. THE NEW WORLD . . . will be a paper which, alongside of this uncompromising pacifism, will attempt to make practical contributions to the solution of the difficulties which beset the world reconstruction to which we are pledged.[2]

Although it had in no sense diluted its own pacifism it was clearly now prepared—to the fury of the Movement's sectarian element—to adopt an overtly collaborative orientation towards those same 'half-measures' it had been careful to condemn in its opening numbers.

---

[1] *NW*, Dec. 1930.
[2] *NMW*, Apr. 1930.

(iii) Humanitarians: Ponsonby and the 'Utilitarian' approach

It was a sign of the failure of all the pacifist societies to make any real impact on the public mind in the decade following the worst war in history that the most enterprising attempt to promote absolute pacifism as a distinct alternative to *pacificist* half-measures was a personal initiative outside the framework of organized pacifism. This was the campaign launched in 1925 by the courtier's son and former diplomat turned Radical politician, Arthur Ponsonby (1871–1946), whose switch of allegiance from Liberal to Labour immediately after the war[1] had been followed by what was, in effect a conversion from *pacificism* to pacifism. In 1925 he published a statement of his beliefs, *Now is the Time*, and launched his ambitious Peace Letter—a petition committing its signatories to 'refuse to support or render war service to any Government which resorts to arms'.[2] After two years he was able, in a deputation to Stanley Baldwin in December 1927, to present 128,770 signatures—a total impressively near the P.P.U.'s peak membership of 136,000. The reason for Ponsonby's sudden emergence as the leading British pacifist of the later twenties and early thirties was his belief that he had discovered a new type of pacifism which was both common-sensical in outlook and irrefutable in inspiration. Throughout what proved a long pacifist career he was concerned to stress that he had no eccentric objection to physical force used by individuals in self-defence or for the protection of the weak;[3] indeed, when assaulted in the course of addressing U.D.C. meetings during the Great War, he had been known to punch his assailant in the face.[4] The basis of his pacifism was his 'discovery'—perhaps influenced by the growing awareness of the extent of the economic dislocation caused by the Great War—that war could be objected to, not just on

[1] For his previous career see Swartz, *Union of Democratic Control*, pp. 14–17, 103–4, 212–13, 216.

[2] *The Times*, 9 Dec. 1927. Some of the petition forms survive in the Baldwin Papers.

[3] See Lord Ponsonby *et al.*, *What Shall I Do About War?* (undated pamphlet of speeches delivered in the autumn of 1933), p. 10.

[4] According to Bernard Shaw, *What I Really Wrote About the War* (1931 edn.), p. 208.

religious, moral, humane or political grounds, but on the grounds of 'its failure to achieve a single desirable object, whatever the gigantic cost may be'.[1]

Ponsonby appeared to believe that this amounted to a new and 'objective' inspiration for pacifism—one which, unlike all previous inspirations, did not depend on prior religious or political assumptions. He seemed to assume, moreover, that on any simple utilitarian calculation the unhappiness and destruction caused by war would invariably be seen to outweigh its benefits: hence, pacifism was proved to be always the best policy. This 'utilitarian' pacifism is, it must be recognized, worthy of attention as the first attempt to adapt pacifist inspirations to take account of both the increased suffering and destruction, and the dislocating side-effects, produced by modern war, which made any net benefit from fighting undeniably harder to justify. But it was not the value-neutral justification for pacifism its adherents hoped it to be. For reasons already discussed, 'utilitarian' pacifism proved to be a form of what is here classified as the humanitarian inspiration for pacifism.

Humanitarian pacifism was, in fact, to prove the major pacifist innovation of the inter-war period, though it was not to come into its own until the thirties when the imminence of aerial holocausts focused attention on the pain and suffering to be expected in the next war. During the twenties attempts to calculate the relative costs of settling a dispute by war or adopting a peaceful settlement at any price were characterized less by preoccupation with the high price of the former than by complacency about the assumed low cost of the latter. Thus one reason for Ponsonby's marked failure to develop his 'utilitarian' critique more systematically than he did was his conviction—to quote his Peace Letter—'that all disputes between nations are capable of settlement either by diplomatic negotiations or by some form of international arbitration'. In reply to Baldwin's polite rebuttal of this Letter, he asserted even more explicitly: 'We are of the opinion that unprovoked aggression is a war myth.'[2] To this belief in the harmony of international relations was added

[1] Arthur Ponsonby, *Now Is The Time: An Appeal for Peace* (1925), p. 102.
[2] *The Times*, 21 Dec. 1927.

a second reason for optimism: his conviction—which can
be traced back to his U.D.C. days—that democratic opinion
was essentially peaceful unless inflamed by propaganda.
Ponsonby's intention, therefore, was simply 'to develop
the instinct which will make a man when he hears rumours
of war say *No* without knowing the facts, which indeed he
can never know however much he may try'.[1] It was thus a
logical development from his Peace Letter campaign to
expose the manipulation of public idealism, by means of
invented atrocity-stories, which had prevented the public
taking a rational decision as to the merits of British participation in the Great War; this he attempted to do in his book
Falsehood in Wartime which, appearing in 1928, marked an
important stage in the public's reaction against the Great War.

When scrutinized, Ponsonby's pacifism of the middle
and later twenties thus amounted to a tactical threat of
civil disobedience designed to jolt the Government into the
realization that a *pacificist* remedy, which the public mind
also favoured, was within its grasp. He had virtually admitted
this at a Cambridge Union debate on 8 March 1927—which
anticipated the result, though not the public impact, of the
Oxford Union's 'King and Country' debate of six years
later—when he had argued that all disputes could be settled
by diplomatic negotiation: 'The acceptance of pacifism
would therefore lead to a wider use of that method of
deciding disputes'.[2] Equally revealing in this respect was his
reluctance to recommend total disarmament and, when in
1929 he again became a junior minister, to oppose a Labour
Government's arms estimates. His defence of this decision to
the Secretary of the Sheffield I.L.P. contrasts sharply with
the hostility to all gradualist half-measures which, as will
shortly be seen, he was to manifest in the early thirties; his
case was that

---

[1] Ponsonby, *Now*, p. 20.

[2] *Granta*, 11 Mar. 1927, p. 245. Apart from its timing, a factor explaining this
debate's lack of impact was the clumsiness of the successful motion's wording:
'That lasting peace can only be secured by the people of England adopting an uncompromising attitude of pacificism.' The best speech against Ponsonby was by a
recent ex-president, Patrick Devlin, who argued that 'uncompromising Pacifism
refused to recognise that one war in ten might be both just and necessary.'

so long as the Labour Government shows a disposition to reduce armaments, to pursue a policy of peace and to avoid all wars, so long in fact
as I think they are the best Government for advancing towards my ideal
I am not . . . going to vote against the Government because they won't
go the whole way and abolish the war services at once.[1]

Even in the hands of its most confident exponent, therefore,
pacifism in the twenties was parasitic upon *pacificism*.

(iv) The Pacifist Impact

By the end of the twenties pacifism had achieved a certain
recognition in British public life, although it was not yet
treated as the matter for serious intellectual attention it was
to be by the mid-thirties, and its implications were far from
fully understood even by pacifists.

'Extreme pacificism' (or 'extreme pacifism') was regarded
by its critics as synonymous with dissent from prevailing
attitudes on many questions of value and life-style. There
was considerable truth in this view; Frank Parkin's discovery
about support for unilateral nuclear disarmament in the
sixties applies also to pacifism in the twenties: it was 'a
capsule statement of a distinctive moral and political outlook'.[2] Whereas for centuries this outlook had been that of
Christian sects of more or less esoteric attitudes towards the
world, after the Great War it had broadened into recogniz-
ably the same 'capsule' of lower-middle class idealism which
George Orwell later disparaged so effectively in *The Road to
Wigan Pier*. Orwell's cruel caricature of the I.L.P. socialist
of the thirties was perhaps more accurate as a satirical portrait of a rank-and-file pacifist of the twenties: 'typically, a
prim little man with a white-collar job, usually a secret
teetotaller and often with vegetarian leanings, with a history
of Nonconformity behind him, and, above all, with a social
position he has no intention of forfeiting'.[3]

To apply this intolerant observation is, of course, simplis-
tic and unfair to the pacifist movement in the twenties; yet,
unless the small advertisements in its journals were misdirected,

---

[1] Ponsonby to Rawson, Aug. 1929, A.P.
[2] Parkin, *Middle Class Radicalism*, p. 3.
[3] Penguin edn., 1962, p. 152.

it was indeed characterized by many of the left-wing idio-
syncracies which, in Orwell's famous list, ranged from
fruit-juice drinking to feminism.[1] (There was one major
exception, however: nudism. In contrast with the thirties
when the movement acquired a more libertarian strand, in
the twenties pacifism meant Nonconformist puritanism.)
The minority attitude most strongly represented was
vegetarianism, for which, in Leslie Paul's words, 'pacifism
had an extraordinary affinity'[2] and for which, as has already
been noted, Allen Skinner of the N.M.W.M. had nearly died
as an absolutist rather than modify his diet. The unwillingness to take life explains this connection; less logical but
almost as strong was pacifism's affinity for strict temperance,
epitomized by Hudson and Salter, and for feminism, on
which almost all women pacifists had cut their teeth and
towards which most male pacifists—most notably Lansbury—
had a record of consistent sympathy. Other causes attracting
equally committed, but less widespread, support included:
Esperanto and other artificial international languages; the
Woodcraft Folk, a left-wing, William Morris-inspired alternative to the 'militaristic' Boy Scouts; and the handicraft and
self-sufficiency movement of which Wellock, who wove
his own clothes, was the most enthusiastic exponent.[3]
Although the particular strength in Britain of the Nonconformist tradition helped many of these ideas to take deeper
roots, they were a feature of European pacifist movements
too. As an 'official' account of the W.R.I.'s progress in the
twenties recently pointed out: 'Various movements—esperan-
tist, vegetarian, war resistance—were growing and coming
together. At the annual conference of the Association of
Vegetarians in Kozanlik, Bulgaria, in 1927, nearly all the
participants were war resisters as well as vegetarians.'[4]

Transposing Orwell's comments on socialism in the thirties
it can be admitted that, in the twenties, 'to . . . an ordinary
man, a crank meant a pacifist and a pacifist meant a crank'.[5]

---

[1] Ibid.
[2] Paul, *Angry Young Man*, p. 117.
[3] Wellock, *Beaten Track*, p. 163.
[4] Prasad, *Fifty Years*, p. 11.
[5] Orwell, *Wigan Pier*, p. 153.

In informing Laurence Housman of his conversion to pacifism in February 1927 even Sheppard, normally the most
tolerant of men, went out of his way to emphasize his
reservations about the character of the *majority* of the Great
War's conscientious objectors and his strong distaste for 'the
fanatics and freaks who rush into every progressive cause,
getting badly in the way of its triumph'.[1] By the late twenties
pacifism had gained relatively little support which could
escape this stigma. Its Bloomsbury and Garsington sympathizers remained detached. In the Churches, apart from
certain intellectuals in the F.o.R., and the unique case of
the Society of Friends, it had little prominent or 'respectable'
support and was, in particular, only just beginning to win
support from charismatic and socially influential Anglicans
such as Sheppard and Raven. Parliamentary support had,
however, reached a peak: no fewer than thirty supporters
among the Labour ranks were claimed by the N.M.W.M.
alone after the 1929 election,[2] compared with only twenty-
one 'peace' M.P.s identified by the National Peace Council
at the equivalent moment six years later—of whom, moreover, only a third were pacifists.[3] Yet the trade union leaders
were already unhappy about a policy of war-resistance; and
many Labour M.P.s were soon to make the discovery which
the Party's most influential 'pacifists', MacDonald and
Snowden, had already made: that their pacifism had, all
along, really been an isolationist form of *pacificism*. While
it was clear that the institutional power of the Churches and
of the Labour movement had been successfully mobilized in
support of the League and of the disarmament campaign
which began in earnest in 1927, the strict pacifist position—
in so far as the distinction was understood—could call on few
advocates of any public prominence. Almost the only writers
committed to pacifism were the minor poet and critic Max
Plowman and the Quaker playwright Laurence Housman,
neither of whom were then devoting much of their energies
to peace work. With leading opponents of the Great War
such as Russell and Allen having lost interest, and Sheppard

[1] Sheppard to Housman, 4 Feb. 1927, in Housman (ed.), *What . . .?*, p. 88.
[2] *NMW*, June–July 1929.
[3] *P*, Dec. 1935, p. 145.

not yet wholeheartedly committed to the cause, its best known figures at the end of the twenties were Ponsonby (created Baron Ponsonby of Shulbrede in 1930) and Lansbury.

In the thirties, in contrast, it would be able to call upon the services of many more writers, artists, clergy, and leaders of youth opinion. Pacifism was thus one of the beneficiaries of the radicalization of previously apolitical British intellectuals which occurred as a result of the slump and, more particularly, of the 1931 political crisis and which was given further impetus by Hitler's accession to power. With the prospect of war beginning to loom, many of these new recruits were inspired by the feeling that modern war had changed qualitatively and, even when resorted to in self-defence, could no longer be justified in terms of its net contribution to human happiness. In the twenties, however, this 'utilitarian' or (more correctly) humanitarian pacifism had received surprisingly little attention. In part this was because the existing pacifist societies remained wedded to either Christian or socialist principles. But it was mainly because a utilitarian approach to the international situation in the twenties led an overwhelming majority of war-haters to a *pacificist* (rather than a pacifist) conclusion.

6

'EXTREME' PACIFISM 1931-2

The basis of *pacificist* optimism at the start of the thirties was the belief that disarmament was achievable and that the League, though empowered to ask for military sanctions, would in practice be able to police international agreements by bringing the disapproval of world public opinion to bear on a defaulting nation—'moral sanctions', as this was often called. The first doubts were raised by the League's inability to deal with the Japanese invasion of Manchuria in September 1931; but though accepted with hindsight as a watershed of the inter-war period, at the time the crisis had little real effect on *pacificism*. The World Disarmament Conference had at long last been arranged for February 1932 and the discredited belief in the power of moral sanctions was simply superseded by the assumption (which the Abyssinia crisis was to prove no better founded) that in a similar crisis the threat of economic sanctions would enable the League to impose its will.

Since the Manchuria crisis thus made only a small dent in *pacificist* optimism, it was not surprising that it had only a slight effect on pacifism. Most pacifists maintained their collaborative orientation: they felt enthusiastic about disarmament and able to support the League since, apart from a strident campaign for an international police force by the abrasive millionaire and ex-Liberal M.P., David Davies (created Baron Davies of Llandinam in 1932), and his specially-founded New Commonwealth Society, military sanctions were almost never discussed. There were, nevertheless, two categories of pacifist for which 1931-2 was a time not for concentrating on pacifism's common ground with the rest of anti-war opinion but for pioneering a positive and distinctively pacifist contribution to policies. One will be considered in the next chapter: the socialist pacifists who struggled to relate their views to what the 1931 political crisis had led them to believe was an incipient revolutionary situation in Britain. The other will be considered here: the heterogeneous collection of 'extreme' pacifists—Gandhi (or, more accurately, his British disciples), Ponsonby, Einstein, the Peace Army, and popular intellectuals such as Nichols, Joad, and Storm Jameson—who were either enthusiasts for the as yet largely unexplored orientation of non-violence or spokesmen for the still surprisingly neglected humanitarian inspiration for pacifism, or both.

(i) Non-violence

The increased interest at this time in non-violence—the belief that pacifism could immediately and successfully be applied to politics—was a result of the increased optimism about international affairs inherited from the late twenties, reinforced by two new factors which fortuitously coincided: the inspiring reports of Gandhi's campaign in India; and the increased sense of urgency inculcated by events in Manchuria.

It was in the early thirties that Gandhi emerged as the most influential external influence on the British peace movement. Although (as the next chapter will show) his anti-imperialism had won him enthusiastic support among socialist pacifists since the early twenties, he did not become a household name until his 1930 campaign against the salt tax; and his claim that his doctrine of 'Satyagraha' ('holding firmly to the truth')[1] was both the basis for an effective political technique and also a process of self-realization that was ethically valuable in its own right was not systematically considered by Christian pacifists until his twelve-week visit to London for the Round Table Conference in the autumn of 1931.

Although most would have liked to believe, with Wellock, that 'India has forged a new weapon of freedom, developed and proved a new technique of revolt which ere long will supersede in every part of the world the old technique of

[1] H. J. N. Horsburgh, *Non-Violence and Aggression: A Study of Gandhi's Moral Equivalent of War* (1968), p. 35.

violence',[1] and flocked to meet Gandhi at a meeting in
Friends' House, many were as disappointed as was the F.o.R.
that Gandhi 'had not seemed to respond to the idea of uniting
with the peace movement in an effort towards constructive
reconciliation'.[2] Another report of the meeting concluded
that, whereas 'Mr Gandhi seeks to redress wrong-doing, Jesus
sought to redeem the wrong-doer', and went on to reduce
the points at issue to two questions: 'Is willingness to suffer
itself morally efficacious? or does it depend upon the intention behind it?'[3] George M. Ll. Davies of the F.o.R. questioned Gandhi personally on this point and, as a long-standing
critic of every attempt to justify pacifism as a political
method, expressed dissatisfaction with Gandhi's answer because (in the words of Dr Johnson's aphorism, which he was
fond of quoting) 'a man who is honest because it is policy
is a rogue'.[4] Likewise the *Friend*, reporting another meeting
with Gandhi, was saddened to discover that 'he did not
believe that all who passively resist must have spiritual
backing'.[5]

Yet despite such doubts it was clear that Christian pacifists were generally encouraged by Gandhi to explore the
possibility that pacifism might itself have the power to make
a decisive contribution to world peace. Bertram Pickard,
for example, a Quaker who had as early as 1930 expressed
his misgivings that Gandhi's methods were coercive,[6] changed
his tune soon after meeting him in November 1931, and
began to argue that

the force of true pacifism is not in the negative absence of violence, but
rather in the positive presence of conquering love, or soul-force, as Mr
Gandhi calls it. Quakerism at its very best has exemplified this type of
pacifism . . . Mr Gandhi and his friends are making the stupendous
venture of trying to apply it in the field of politics. The difficulties
and dangers are obvious, but the successes are of great significance
for a world riven by the spirit of violence and hate. The problem still
remains for Quaker pacifists—how to put this positive method of

[1] *NW*, Apr. 1931.
[2] F.o.R., E.C. 18 Nov. 1931.
[3] Quoted in Leyton Richards, *Christian Pacifism After Two World Wars*
(1948), p. 37.
[4] *Rec.*, Jan. 1933, pp. 5-6.
[5] *Friend*, 18 Dec. 1931, pp. 1150.
[6] F.P.C., 5 June 1930.

conquering love into effect in political situations like the present conflict in Manchuria?[1]

Gandhi had arrived in London on 12 September 1931, just six days before the start of Japanese aggression in Manchuria. Although, as already stressed, the check this crisis administered to the collaborative orientation was very slight, a minority of pacifists seemed to have responded to it in positive but paradoxical fashion. Perceiving that a gradualist policy was running into difficulties, they assumed that what was needed was not less but more optimism and faith in human nature.

The most articulate exponent of an all-out policy as an act of faith was Lord Ponsonby, whose outlook had recently become significantly bolder. His reaction to the Manchurian situation was to insist that non-violence would have worked:

Had China been unarmed, had no Chinese been able to fire a single shot, Japan had she attacked China would have been a *self-confessed aggressor before all the world*, including her own people. Knowing therefore that she could not bamboozle her own people by any possible pretence that an armed attack on a completely unarmed people was not aggression, she would never have attempted to take such action.[2]

And, in a book on disarmament published around this time, he made it clear that his remarkable confidence in the liberal scruples of a potential aggressor was not confined to Japan:

Say for instance that Denmark were completely disarmed. It is conceivably possible that any nation having a sharp dispute with the Danish Government would proceed to drop bombs on Copenhagen? Low as my opinion of international morality may be I do not for a moment believe such a thing possible. I am convinced that Disarmament really constitutes the only absolute security.[3]

The basis of Ponsonby's pacifism had always been his optimistic view both of the harmony of international interests and of the peaceableness of democratic public opinion; as the former became less self-evident he came to place increasing emphasis on the latter. Unprovoked aggression, he now explained, could only occur if

[1] *Friend*, 28 Nov. 1931, p. 1052.
[2] *NW*, Mar. 1932.
[3] Lord Ponsonby, *Disarmament: A Discussion* (1932), p. 31. The author's views are placed in the mouth of 'The Layman' who takes part in a number of Socratic dialogues with 'The Officer', 'The Advocate'.

the Government of the nation in question can persuade its people that it has a high motive, a defensive motive, a noble purpose. How could it do that when by making war on a disarmed nation it would be proclaiming to the world that it was a blatant aggressor, a self-confessed indisputable agressor? No Government, however immoral you may think them, could do it.[1]

It was, it is worth noting, this same critique which was to cause him, four years later, to explain the League's failure to apply military sanctions against Italy in 1935-6 in terms of a recognition by its leading member governments that they could not whip up public support for a war on so remote an issue.[2]

The Manchuria crisis had, of course, been an unwelcome distraction from the peace movement's main priority, its disarmament campaign, and it was on this subject that Ponsonby's increased boldness since the twenties was even more conspicuous. In 1925 he had written that he

would neither vote for, nor advocate, the abolition of the standing army and the scrapping of the navy. Public opinion is not ready for such a step. No greater error could be made than to present them with the ultimate and concluding stage of our policy when up to now we have failed to convince them and draw them through the preliminary stages.[3]

In contrast with this definitive statement of the collaborative orientation his 1932 book on disarmament was a dogmatic statement of non-violence. It was highly critical of the cautious approach of the Disarmament Conference: 'A more senseless and dangerous policy than reduction of armaments by international agreement cannot be imagined. It is asking for trouble . . . I am fully convinced that in this matter of disarmament there is no half-way house'.[4] Whereas it was not uncommon for some socialists to argue that the Disarmament Conference was futile because capitalism could never abandon armaments, Ponsonby's criticism was more unusual: he appeared to be suggesting that, even if successful in its

[1] Ibid.
[2] Royal Institute of International Affairs, *The Future of the League of Nations* (1936), p. 164.
[3] Ponsonby, *Now*, p. 173.
[4] Ponsonby, *Disarmament*, pp. 26-7.

own terms, it would increase the risk of war. It was not surprising, therefore, that his attack on the whole approach
being adopted at Geneva in a debate in the House of Lords
on 10 May 1932[1] provoked dissent from most leading
Quakers, who believed that any step in the right direction
should be welcomed.[2] Unabashed, Ponsonby three weeks
later extended his personal campaign against the Conference
by stage-managing a critical tour of inspection of Geneva
with Albert Einstein as his star.

Einstein (1879-1955) was a guarantee that the stunt
would secure the necessary limelight: the physicist enjoyed
an astonishing world popularity which was somehow corre-
lated positively with the abstruseness of his research. On
international questions, however, his views were simple to the
point of innocence, though bafflement could still arise
because of his propensity to endorse internationalism,
socialist anti-militarism, and pacifism all at the same time.[3]
However, his widely-reported statement to the New History
Society of New York in December 1930 that war would be
impossible if as little as two per cent of the population
declared themselves conscientious objectors, seemed to show
that he had settled down as a pacifist and advocate of non-
violence. Although in Britain the vogue for 'two per cent'
badges never caught on as it did briefly across the Atlantic
(perhaps, it has been suggested, because it was mistaken
for a drive to reduce the proof content of alcoholic be-
verages),[4] Einstein had been taken up by the N.M.W.M. as a
hero second only to Gandhi, and Ponsonby found him an
ideal ally in his personal campaign. After visiting a session
in the Disarmament Conference in which Japanese and
Russian delegates were both applying resourceful sophistry
to the question whether the mobility of an aircraft-carrier
increased its offensive or defensive character, he forthrightly

[1] 84 H. L. Deb, cols. 361-3.

[2] Harrison Barrow to Ponsonby, 20 May 1932, A.P.

[3] See Martin Ceadel, 'Pacifism in Britain 1931-1939' (D. Phil. Thesis, Oxford
1976), pp. 58-60.

[4] This explanation is offered in Hughes, *Indomitable Friend*, p. 77. For an
enthusiastic response see Ruth Fry's letter in the *Spectator*, 7 Nov. 1931, p. 590;
for a sceptical one see Russell to Runham Brown, 21 Mar. 1931, in Russell,
Autobiography, ii (1968).

condemned it at a press conference arranged by Ponsonby and called for a complete end to the manufacture of munitions.[1]

Although few pacifists were prepared to endorse Ponsonby's and Einstein's condemnations of Geneva, some were to take their optimism about non-violence even further. Indeed what was perhaps the most sanguine pacifist initiative of the entire twentieth century occurred in February 1932: the attempt by a trio of leading Christian pacifists to form a Peace Army of unarmed passive resisters to intercede between the combats in the world's military confrontations, starting with the one in Manchuria.

The prime mover of this scheme was one of the inter-war period's best-known woman pacifists, Dr Maude Royden (1876-1956), a former suffragist who, after joining both the F.o.R. and the W.I.L. during the Great War, had devoted herself to the cause of peace. The Oxford-educated daughter of a wealthy Liverpool shipowner (and the sister of the Chairman of the Cunard Steamship Company), she had fallen under the influence, while in her early twenties, of the unorthodox Anglican preacher, the Revd Hudson Shaw. She began work as his lay curate and fell in love with him, living for forty years with Shaw and his wife in platonic triangular intimacy, until in 1944 Mrs Shaw died and Dr Royden became his wife for the few remaining weeks of his life.[2]

Encouraged by Shaw, she became assistant preacher at the City Temple in 1917, and in 1921 acquired her own church, the Guildhouse (in Eccleston Square, Pimlico), where she preached until her retirement in 1936. Her religious views were a non-denominational form of Christian socialism and their combination of religious and political concerns was reflected, not altogether harmoniously, in her pacifism. Her Christian impulses drew her to the strict pacifism of the F.o.R.; but her equally strong commitment to political relevance made her receptive to any non-military means of preventing war, even if sectarians might consider it a departure

[1] Ronald W. Clark, *Einstein: The Life and Times* (1973), pp. 353-5.
[2] Maude Royden, *A Threefold Cord* (1947), pp. 9, 16, 24-8, 114-15; see also *Time and Tide*, 1 Sept. 1922, pp. 832-3, and her obituary in *The Times*, 31 July 1956.

from rigorous pacifism. Thus only a few weeks after her Peace Army proposal had been making headlines, she was informing David Davies that she was in full agreement with his book *The Problem of the Twentieth Century*—which forthrightly argued the case for all, including military, sanctions as the only guarantee for peace and security.[1] She had, however, as she later acknowledged when she withdrew her support from Davies's New Commonwealth Society, failed to realize that an international police force would have to be armed 'with the most terrible of all modern weapons'.[2] When Davies remonstrated with her, she disarmingly confessed her difficulty: 'I quite see that your reasoning is sound, but then I have really abandoned the attempt to be rigidly logical in my pacifism'.[3] For the next five years she sought to stave off the choice between pacifism and *pacificism* (as did many members of the W.I.L.) by professing to believe that economic sanctions could prevent war. At the time of Munich, as will be seen, she opted for strict pacifism; after the outbreak of war, however, she came to see this as a mistake. Her 'much-criticised wartime vacillations' were later attributed by Vera Brittain, herself a thoroughgoing Christian pacifist, to an incomplete understanding of Christianity and an excessively political preoccupation with short-term success: only half-jokingly, she traced Dr Royden's problems back to 'the chance that as an Oxford student she read Modern History and not Theology (a school closed to Oxford women until 1935)'.[4]

Maude Royden's Peace Army proposal had first been mooted in one of her regular sermons at the Guildhouse, shortly after the start of the Japanese occupation of Manchuria:

I would like now to enrol people who would be ready if war should break out to put their bodies unarmed between the contending forces, in whatever way it be found possible—and there are ways you do not think of now in which it would be possible.[5]

---

[1] Royden to Davies, 23 Apr. 1932, D.D.
[2] Royden to Davies, 27 Oct. 1933, D.D.
[3] Royden to Davies, 2 Nov. 1933, D.D.
[4] Brittain, *Rebel Passion*, p. 75.
[5] Quoted in *NW*, Nov. 1931.

The idea received little publicity until the last week of February 1932 when, in response to the renewed Japanese aggression in Shanghai, she went into a weekend retreat with Herbert Gray and Dick Sheppard, to consider what they could do in a situation in which the League had failed. They decided to recruit a contingent of unarmed volunteers to be sent to Shanghai, under Sheppard's leadership, to form a human barrier between the Japanese and Chinese and thereby end the fighting. This decision was ventilated in the national press on 26 February, eliciting 800 replies[1] and a question in the House of Commons which caught the Foreign Secretary unprepared. A week later, however, Sir John Simon was able to reply that 'since there are good grounds for hoping that active hostilities are now at an end, the conditions which inspired the gallant and humanitarian offer of Miss Royden and her co-signatories will not again arise.'[2]

None of the volunteers saw action (and there seems to be no basis for the story that they actually set out for Tilbury).[3] When the League of Nations was asked to transport them into the fighting area the Secretary-General, Sir Eric Drummond, replied that he was unable to consider any scheme that did not originate from the government of a Member State. Moreover, a lull in the fighting and a patched-up peace removed the situation for which the Peace Army had been tailored. In addition, Sheppard, whom Gray acknowledged to be the 'real leader',[4] had a relapse on 2 March of the recurrent asthmatic illness which had led him to resign as Dean of Canterbury the previous year. When he recovered briefly, however, he made a surprising attempt to interest Lloyd George in the leadership of the Peace Army—an attempt which demonstrated how far Sheppard saw the peace question in terms of mobilizing men of good will behind an

[1] *Peace Review*, Apr. 1932; R. Ellis Roberts, *H. R. L. Sheppard: Life and Letters* (1942), pp. 216-17.

[2] For the original question on 16 Mar. 1932 see 263 H.C. Deb. col. 258; for Simon's answer on 23 Mar. see col. 1013.

[3] For this story see William Purcell, *Portrait of Soper: A Biography of the Reverend Lord Soper of Kingsway* (1972), p. 124; and Carolyn Scott, *Dick Sheppard: A Biography* (1977), p. 191. The contemporary evidence makes quite clear that the plan never got this far.

[4] *Rec.*, Apr. 1932, pp. 74-5; see also Sybil Morrison, *I Renounce War: The Story of the Peace Pledge Union* (1962), p. 7.

inspiring leader, rather than in terms of defining a specific pacifist policy which could be applied to the international situation. When he met Lloyd George at Churt on 23 October 1932, his discovery that the ex-Prime Minister, though charming, was 'more intellectual than I had expected'[1] and unable to co-operate, reveals more about Sheppard's outlook than about Lloyd George's.

Though the Army's brief moment of celebrity was soon over, its volunteers were, in theory at least, kept on standby by one of their number, Mrs Joyce Pollard, and a Peace Army Council was formed consisting of the original trio plus two new recruits. Although it undertook such tasks as distributing leaflets at the Hendon Air Pageant in the summer in 1933,[2] and offered its services to the Danish Government early in 1933,[3] the organization became dormant; and, after an unsuccessful bid by Vera Brittain to revitalize it early in 1934,[4] it was disbanded in June of that year. In 1935, however, by which time the Christian pacifist movement was beginning to gather momentum, Mrs Pollard sought to revive it and wrote—unsuccessfully again—to the League's Secretary-General.[5] Although the reconstituted Peace Army did see active service it was only on a minute scale which negated its original strategy: in 1937 and 1938 two members spent time in Palestine to carry out work of reconciliation. The gesture ended in tragedy when one, Hugh Bingham, was shot and fatally wounded.[6]

The Peace Army's original strategy had been the equivalent at the collective level of Lytton Strachey's recipe for dealing with a German soldier raping his sister—trying to come between them[7]—and, although it merely sought to put to the test some frequently expressed pacifist assumptions about the power of non-violence, it was received even by pacifists

[1] Roberts, *Sheppard*, p. 220. There appears to be no reference to this in the Lloyd George Papers.
[2] *Rec.*, Aug. 1932, p. 157.
[3] Royden to Gilbert Murray, 17 Jan. 1933, G.M.
[4] W.I.L. Exec., 9 Jan. 1934.
[5] *P*, Apr. 1935, p. 12; *Friend*, 22 Nov. 1935, p. 1084.
[6] *Friend*, 4 Feb. 1938, p. 98, 1 July, p. 584; *Christian Pacifist*, June 1939, pp. 163–4, Aug., p. 200.
[7] See above, p. 45.

with some hilarity. *Reconciliation* described it as 'impracticable and slightly theatrical',[1] and even Laurence Housman tactfully told his close friend Sheppard that he doubted its feasibility.[2] The Friends' Peace Committee also considered it impractical, even if useful as a protest,[3] and the *Friend* acknowledged that 'already it has been mocked as sentimental folly'.[4] The Peace Army was vulnerable to the objection, more commonly levelled at defence staffs, that it was a preparation for the last war rather than a future war. Writing in 1938, Maude Royden attempted to turn the charge against her critics by stressing the peculiar nature of the battle at Shanghai in February 1932:

It was an unparalleled opportunity, for the fighting there was not guerilla warfare, nor in the air, nor along a vast front of trenches; it was across a street. Few of our critics realised this. The flood of correspondence which followed like a spate on the appearance of our letter in the press showed that most of the writers were hypnotised by the ideas of modern warfare that had been generated by the conduct of the last war.[5]

However, at the time in late 1931 when she had first made the proposal, the fighting was in Manchuria and of a more conventional kind. Moreover, other Peace Army leaders made uninhibited claims for the wider applicability of its methods: this was particularly true of the two new recruits to its Council, the Revd Donald Soper and Brigadier-General Crozier, and of the author of a book on its strategy, Henry Brinton.

It is appropriate that Soper should have begun his career as pacifist leader in the Peace Army since he has proved himself over five decades to be Christian pacifism's most unshakeable political optimist. Born in 1903 and thus too young for service in the Great War, Soper had inherited from his devout Wesleyan parents a faith in the conquering power of Christian truth which remained intact even after exposure to the intellectual scepticism of Cambridge, or to the dispiriting social conditions to be tackled by the

[1] *Rec.*, Jan. 1934, p. 6.
[2] Housman to Sheppard, 28 Feb. 1932, in Housman (ed.), *What . . . ?*, pp. 172–3.
[3] F.P.C., 3 Mar. 1932.   [4] *Friend*, Mar. 1932, p. 188.
[5] Maude Royden, 'Dick Sheppard: The Peace Maker', in William Paxton *et al.*, *Dick Sheppard: An Apostle of Brotherhood* (1938), p. 77.

South London Mission where he went as a newly-ordained Methodist minister in the year of the General Strike. The effect of the latter was simply to encourage him to attach to his Christianity radical—even Marxist—social views.[1] When the Far Eastern crisis began, however, he started to place increasing emphasis on the international aspect of his radicalism, adopting a pacifist stance of equal simplicity and conviction. Despite the deterioration of the international situation he continued to assert not only 'that pacifism contains a spiritual force strong enough to repel any invader', but even that 'pacifism can be applied as a solution to most of the world problems of the day'.[2] As later as November 1937 he was predicting that Europe was on the verge of a pacifist landslide, and the failure of his prophecies did nothing to alter his belief that pacifism was not only morally right but also politically realistic.[3]

Soper's confidence was shared by his colleague on the Peace Army Council, Brigadier-General Frank P. Crozier, although they had very little else in common. Crozier (1879–1937) was the most colourful and unlikely pacifist of the inter-war period. A former mercenary soldier, rejected by the regular army on medical grounds, he had served in Africa and Canada as well as in the Ulster Volunteer Force before the Great War gave him the chance of more orthodox soldiering. He won rapid promotion, and after the war continued to hunger for active service, working as an officer in the newly-formed Lithuanian army and then as commandant of the Black and Tans. In February 1921, however, his career was finally ended by his resignation, amid a blaze of headlines and questions in the House, on the grounds that the punishments he had ordered for men in his charge who had looted a grocery store near Trim had been countermanded by higher authority. In view of his pre-war Ulster connection, it is likely that he had, in reality, been moved to resign less by the revulsion at barbarous military methods to which he later tended to attribute his action than by a

[1] Douglas Thompson, *Donald Soper: A Biography* (1971), pp. 24–5, 38–9.
[2] *P*, July 1933; *Friend*, 30 Mar. 1934, p. 284.
[3] Purcell, *Portrait of Soper*, pp. 79, 134–6.

rigid concern for strict soldierly discipline.[1] Even after he
had taken his dispute with the army to the point of campaigning for the peace movement his new colleagues wanted,
in the words of Viscount Cecil of the L.N.U. (to which
Crozier had in 1929 applied for work), 'to know a little more
about his quarrel with Government over the Black and Tans'.
'I think', Cecil commented, 'there must be another side to
it.'[2] When Crozier died suddenly in August 1937, *The Times*
refused to print brief tributes sent in by Sheppard and
Ponsonby,[3] and upset his widow[4] by publishing an un-
generous obituary which baldly stated: 'General Crozier,
making no allowance for "political expediency", proved
difficult in a series of trying situations and resigned over a
question of discipline'.[5]

Unemployed and short of money, Crozier undertook what
speaking engagements he could for the L.N.U., and when the
boom in war books began late in 1928, turned his hand
to writing his war memoirs with a combination of 'energy
and lack of subtlety' which *The Times* obituary believed
to be his major characteristics. Published in 1930, *A Brass
Hat in No Man's Land* made great play with the (by then)
well-worn themes of cowardice and sexual licence in order
to prove his contention that 'war is a dirtier game than is
generally known'.[6] This metaphor was apt, for Crozier
seemed, indeed, to regard war as a game, albeit not for the
squeamish. His views on how to prevent war, never very
clearly articulated, seem to have been conventionally internationalist at this time. Early in February 1932, shortly
before the announcement of the Peace Army, he had been
professing to David Davies his unqualified enthusiasm for an
international police force,[7] although a desire to be taken on
to Davies's sizeable private payroll may explain this.

---

[1] Charles Townshend has concluded that Crozier's account of his resignation
'should be treated with some caution': *The British Campaign in Ireland 1919-21*
(Oxford, 1975), p. 165 n.
[2] Cecil to Murray, 13 Feb. 1929, G.M.
[3] Sheppard to Kingsley Martin, 4 Sept. 1937, Martin Papers.
[4] *PN*, 25 Sept. 1937.
[5] *The Times*, 1 Sept. 1937.
[6] p. 80.
[7] Crozier to Davies, 7 Feb. 1932, New Commonwealth files, D.D.

It was thus as an unemployed muchraker of militarism in search of a surrogate for military adventure, rather than as a convinced pacifist, that Crozier joined the Peace Army. Through it, however, he fell under Sheppard's spell—he was to act as a key organizer in his subsequent pacifist campaigns —and became an enthusiastic advocate of non-violence. The governments of the world, he was telling the *Manchester Guardian* by the end of February, had no answer to the Peace Army strategy: 'What would they do, supposing Dick Sheppard and I were to walk with 10,000 unarmed people along No Man's Land, or if we were to send over from forty to a hundred civil aeroplanes between the opposing armies? If our people were shot public opinion would be shocked.'[1]

Already thinking along similar lines was a pacifist member of the L.N.U. staff, Henry Brinton (1901-77), who had in 1931 started on a book which anticipated the Royden-Gray-Sheppard proposals. It was not published, however, until the late spring in 1932, when it appeared under the title *The Peace Army* and with a foreword jointly contributed by Maude Royden, Gray, Crozier, Raven and Richards. In it Brinton argued, with supreme optimism, that an attack on an unarmed group of volunteers 'would be such a ghastly weight on the conscience of any nation that it seems incredible that all the innate feelings of decency of the people would not rise in revolt and lead to such a reaction against was that it would vanish for ever'.[2] In places, however, he sounded less confident. Unlike Crozier, he admitted that the Peace Army could not cope with air warfare; and, although the book's preface had stated the Peace Army's main merits to be that it was a 'positive proposal for action', he backtracked on this point, claiming it was

not so much intended to be a detailed plan which could be immediately put into operation, as an indication of a possible line of approach to the great question facing the world today. It is also intended to show that, if the principles of Christianity were boldy applied, they need not consist merely of holding aloof from the events in the material life of mankind, but could be shaped to play a leading part in the destiny of mankind.[3]

[1] *M.G.*, 27 Feb. 1932.
[2] Henry Brinton, *The Peace Army* (1932), p. 74.
[3] Ibid., p. 77.

As in the case of other believers in non-violence, Brinton's belief that pacifists were obliged to seek a practical way of preventing war was stronger than his confidence that any watertight method had yet been found. Their burning desire to adopt this orientation meant that pacifists failed to scrutinize its central assumption: that an enemy would be answerable to a liberal and humane public conscience. The Manchuria crisis had already disproved it, but British pacifists were ignorant of Japan's warrior culture and remote from its area of expansion; in addition, as Russell later noted in explanation of his own excessive faith in non-violence at this time, they had been conditioned by Gandhi's campaign to believe that all adversaries would be similar to the rulers of the British Empire and were thus wholly unprepared for one like Hitler.[1] As late as November 1932 Ponsonby was enthusiastic even in private about the 'immense stir' which unilateral disarmament by Britain would cause: 'The effect on other countries would be electrical and I am quite convinced that other nations would immediately follow';[2] while the following month Ruth Fry could still dismiss a call for the strengthening of sanctions with an observation that 'the real sanction required as a growth of world conscience, not of world force'.[3] However, once the advent of Hitler began to make it clear that no response would be made to a disarmament gesture, and that the world's conscience was not growing but becoming hardened, less was heard of non-violence. It was not to recover the popularity of 1931-2 until 1936 when disarmament and collective security had both been seen to fail and, for all its evident risks, it was almost the only policy of war prevention as yet untried.

(ii) Humanitarianism

Non-violence appealed to pacifists of all inspirations; but its greatest impact was on humanitarian pacifism, which it helped to become markedly more popular during 1931-2. This was understandable: most of those here classified as of

[1] Russell, *Autobiography*, ii, p. 192.
[2] Ponsonby to Hardie, 10 Nov. 1932, F.H.
[3] Fry to G. N. Barnes, 20 Dec. 1932, New Commonwealth files, D.D.

humanitarian inspiration believed themselves, as already noted, to be concerned simply with the consequences of human actions. They were drawn to pacifism only when they could regard it as an effective way of minimizing suffering. In the twenties the prospects for *pacificism* looked so good that a calculation of consequences was rarely felt to justify the extra risks involved in pacifism. After 1931, however, a number of pacifists—Crozier for one—were ready to take the plunge. The new factors encouraging them to do so were: the first hint, dropped by the Manchuria crisis, that *pacificism* might fail or prove unexpectedly risky; and an increased sensitivity to the suffering any war would involve—induced not only by the flood of books about the Great War which had appeared in 1928-30, but more especially by the horrific visions of a future air gas war depicted in the pro-Disarmament Conference propaganda of 1931-2.

The type of humanitarian pacifism put forward in the early thirties was different, moreover, from that advanced by its rare exponents—notably Ponsonby—in the previous decade. It is one of the themes of this book that pacifists of this inspiration were slow to discover the difficulties of specifying precisely which values of human existence whose violation by all war made the resort to arms invariably counter-productive. Ponsonby had seemed to be adopting Normal Angell's critique, in *The Great Illusion*, of the irrationality of war; but whereas the latter had merely derived *pacificism* from it, Ponsonby felt it necessitated pacifism—thereby implying that it was the mainly economic and material dislocation caused by war which could never be outweighed even by considerations such as political liberty.

In contrast, the humanitarian pacifism of 1931-2 did not seem so materialistic; but, resting as it did largely on revulsion against pain and physical suffering, it could be criticized instead for espousing a narrowly hedonistic scale of human values. In addition, because it was based on strong emotions it tended to be unstable; and, as the decade progressed, the pacifism of the best-known converts of 1931-2—notably the writers Beverley Nichols, Cyril Joad, and Storm Jameson—tended to undergo confusing fluctuations.

The most prominent of these at the time was Beverley

Nichols (1900-   ), who after a glittering Oxford career un-
interrupted by war service (for which he was just too young)
had achieved instant fame as a fashionable littérateur. His
output in the twenties, written in an affected style now considered characteristic of that decade, consisted of novels and
books on gardening. In 1934, irritated by a suggestion that
the pacifism for which he became suddenly famous in the
early thirties was merely 'a passing mood',[1] Nichols was to
claim that his peace campaign had begun as early as 1928
when he debated with G. K. Chesterton at the Cambridge
Union the motion 'That this House is for peace at any price'
and published a book in which 'the entire emotional framework' of his thirties pacifism was 'foreshadowed in several
pages'.[2] But although he had indeed condemned war on both
these occasions,[3] and done so from an emotional perspective
similar to that which was to become his hallmark in the
thirties, his claim to have been consistent was misleading in
two respects. Firstly, his views in the twenties were *pacificist*
and made no reference to the individual's need to refuse to
fight. (Indeed, apart from the occasional reference to the
need to sacrifice 'the Imperial idea', no mention at all was
made of how actually to prevent war.) Secondly, his emotionalism was markedly less extreme than it was to become
in the thirties.

It was not until the start of the new decade that Nichols
stopped 'drinking cocktails and talking nonsense while the
clouds were gathering over Europe',[4] and progressed from a
vague *pacificism* to an explicit pacifism of formidable intensity. The first signs of this new commitment were revealed
by his play *Avalanche*, first performed in July 1931. In retrospect it can be seen to mark the start of a trend for popular
anti-war writers to turn from the last war to the next and
from *pacificism* to pacifism; being thus somewhat ahead of
its time, it was a flop. The play was set in a snowbound

---

[1] *Spectator*, 13 July 1934, p. 59.

[2] Ibid., 27 July 1934, p. 133. Nichols wrongly dated his Cambridge Union
appearance as 1927.

[3] *Granta*, 8 June 1928, p. 517; Beverley Nichols, *The Star-Spangled Banner*
(1928).

[4] Beverley Nichols, *All I Could Never Be: Some Recollections* (1949),
pp. 197-8.

Swiss chalet where a group of holidaymakers, hoaxed into
believing that a world war had broken out, discussed their
attitude to war. A young writer called Nigel, who turned
out to be the hoaxer, declared that he would stay in Switzerland and continue writing plays. For this he was roundly
condemned by his companions; but his reply to those urging
him to return to Britain to fight was—with the stage direction
'almost screaming'—memorably vehement:

How dare you ask me to go where bodies—human bodies—are being
blown to pieces—where men are running round with their entrails
hanging on the ground—where they are staggering through the mud
with their eyes blown out—where their lungs are swelling and bursting
with gas. It's blood, blood . . .[1]

'I lived the part of Nigel—I approved of everything he said
and did',[2] Nichols later made clear; and in 1932 he eschewed
the device of the fictional mouthpiece and openly proclaimed
his new pacifism. The forum he chose was an unusual one:
the September issue of *Good Housekeeping*, although his
article was soon reprinted in pamphlet form. Under the title
'In the Next War I Shall Be A Conscientious Objector' it
explained that six months previously he and four friends
had met in a Berlin hotel and signed the following pledge:

We, the undersigned, do solemnly swear that in no circumstances
whatever will we engage in any form of warfare, should our respective
countries become involved in hostilities. Moreover, to prove the integrity of our purpose, we hereby pledge ourselves to offer our lives,
as a gesture of peace, to submit, without protest, to death at the hands
of our respective governments, within forty-eight hours of the declaration of war, by being shot through the heart, by a chosen tribunal
of our countrymen.

But, Nichols went on to point out, the appalling horrors of
an air war 'of desperate haste and quick extinction' would
make a mockery of future attempts to summon conscientious
objectors before tribunals. Despite the graphic description
he offered ('the whole of the city . . . destroyed . . . the
streets . . . an inferno of fire and gas and smoke . . . hideous
with the groans of the dying') the prospect was, to Nichols,
'not devoid of a certain grim humour'.[3] Indeed part of the

---

[1] Beverley Nichols, *Failures: Three Plays* (1933), p. 178.
[2] Ibid., p. 17.
[3] *Good Housekeeping*, Sept. 1932, pp. 16, 103.

appeal of such writing (including the spate of 'next war' novels which also began to appear on a larger scale than ever from 1931 onwards[1]) was that its seriousness was leavened by a whimsical exhuberance which was acceptable while the next war seemed still a distant nightmare. Despite expressing irritation with a critic of *Avalanche* who had accused him of not being serious,[2] the recommendation Nichols made in his article stressed the more trivial aspects of war's causation. 'Women could stop war in the nursery,' he argued. 'I should like to manufacture a brand of toy soldiers that would help them do it. They wouldn't be pretty soldiers. They'd be so hideous and so horrifying that they would give any children nightmares for weeks.'[3]

A couple of months after the article was published Nichols appeared on the platform of a disarmament demonstration organized by the L.N.U. at the Albert Hall on 15 November 1932, and stole the show with his ringing declaration that he was for peace at any price.[4] However, he missed the chance, three months later, of playing a leading role in what proved to be a far bigger pacifist sensation, when he had to turn down an invitation to propose the Oxford Union's 'King and Country' resolution.[5] This was because he was visiting Geneva as part of the research for *Cry Havoc!* which, published in July 1933, proved to be the decade's most successful 'pacifist' book. As will later be seen,[6] however, the act of setting down his views forced him to abandon his former faith in the efficacy of non-violent resistance; and, looking back after the Second World War, he was to admit that his pacifism had been 'entirely emotional, and . . . due to a very acute awareness of physical pain . . . It was

[1] See Martin Ceadel, 'Popular Fiction and the Next War, 1918-1939, ' in Frank Gloversmith (ed.), *Class, Culture and Social Change: a New View of the 1930s* (Brighton, 1980).

[2] Nichols, *Failures*, p. 23.

[3] *Good Housekeeping*, Sept. 1932, p. 106; see also 'A Child's Guide to Peace' in Beverley Nichols, *For Adults Only* (1932), pp. 215-22.

[4] For the impact of this speech see *Friend*, 18 Nov. 1932, p. 1007; Cecil to Noel Baker, 16 Nov. 1932 (copy), Add. MSS 51107, R.C.; *Spectator*, 10 Aug. 1934, p. 194.

[5] Unpublished memorandum by Frank Hardie, F.H.

[6] See below, pp. 139-41.

a cloudy and unstable foundation for any philosophy.'[1]

Taking his place at the 'King and Country' debate (after several other refusals) was Cyril Joad (1891-1953) who, as a result, attained prominence as an exponent of pacifism based on an identical belief (expressed in an autobiography in 1932) 'that of all the evil things in the world, physical pain is by far the worst'.[2] If Nichols's sensitivity to the mutilation of young men in war can in part be attributed to his homosexuality, Joad's similarly acute aversion to suffering can be linked to the (heterosexual) hedonism and love of sensual pleasure for which he was notorious.[3] Highly gifted, but restless and opportunistic, he was a puckish and lightweight amalgam of Bertrand Russell (who believed Joad plagiarized his ideas) and H. G. Wells, tending to the former's iconoclastic optimism rather than to the latter's Olympian seriousness. After twenty years professing to be a revolutionary I.L.P. socialist, Joad—like many others—changed his views after the 1931 crisis. After a flirtation with Mosley's New Party, Joad in 1932 set up the Federation of Progressive Societies and Individuals (F.P.S.I.) as an attempt—with the master's blessing[4]—to implement the Wellsian vision of an enlightened élite of intellectuals uniting to plan rational solutions for the problems of the world.

The F.P.S.I. began with strong pacifist overtones: it declared its long-term aim to be a world government but, according to its Manifesto: 'As first steps this involves (i) progressive disarmament by example on the part of this country, and (ii) war resistance on the part of individuals in the event of an outbreak of hostilities'.[5] For Joad, therefore, its significance was as a bridge from his former revolutionary socialism to the 'utilitarian' pacifism for which he was best known in the thirties. Although he always saw himself as a philosophical rationalist his thinking, particularly

---

[1] Nichols, *All*, pp. 211-12.

[2] C. E. M. Joad, *Under the Fifth Rib* (1932), p. 90.

[3] See the evidence cited in Martin Ceadel, 'The "King and Country" Debate, 1933: Student Politics, Pacifism and the Dictators', *Historical Journal*, 22, 2 (1979) p. 401.

[4] Norman and Jeanne MacKenzie, *The Time Traveller* (1973), p. 375.

[5] C. E. M. Joad (ed.), *Manifesto: Being the book of the Federation of Progressive Societies and Individuals* (1934), p. 23.

on pacifism, was highly emotional: hence its popular appeal.
Characteristic of his method was his evocation, in a N.M.W.M.
pamphlet published in 1932, of the horror of the Great War:

Men were burned and tortured; they were impaled, blinded, disem-
bowelled, blown to fragments; they hung shrieking for days and nights
on barbed wire with their insides protruding, praying for a chance
bullet to put an end to their agony; their faces were blown away and
they continued to live . . . [1]

Not only were these sentiments and tone strongly reminiscent of Nichols's but they were also to be modified in a
similar direction and at exactly the same time (in 1933) when
Joad also ceased exclusively to consider his emotional feelings about war and began to appreciate the limitations of
non-violence as a means of preventing it.

A further example of an emotional pacifism which was
first declared in 1932 and modified the following year was
that of the novelist Margaret Storm Jameson (1897–   ). Her
sense of outrage at the Great War in which so many of her
contemporaries ('class 1914 people'),[2] including her brother,
had been killed suddenly erupted into overt pacifism while
writing memoirs of her early life—'an otherwise polite book
that had every chance of pleasing by its polite simplicity',[3]
as she later described it. Brooding upon the depressing consequences of the war, she felt an acute sense of guilt at having
supported it, and turned her book into an outspoken anti-war
polemic:

In 1932 what lying gaping mouth will say that it was worthwhile to kill
my brother in his nineteenth year? You may say that the world's
account is balanced by the item that we have still with us a number
of elderly patriots, army contractors, women who obscenely presented
white feathers. You will forgive me, if as courteously as is possible in
the circumstances, I say that a field latrine is more useful to humanity
than these leavings.

By the end she had gone so far as to declare herself a pacifist:

If this country . . . is got into another Great War I shall take every
means in my power to keep my son out of it. I shall tell him that it
is nastier and more shameful to volunteer for gas-bombing than to run
from it or to volunteer in the other desperate army of protestants. I

[1] C. E. M. Joad, *What Fighting Means* (N.M.W.M., 1932), p. 15.
[2] Storm Jameson, *No Time Like The Present* (1933), p. 112; see also p. 94.
[3] Storm Jameson, *Journey from the North: Autobiography*, i (1969), p. 285.

shall tell him also that war is not worth its cost, nor is victory worth the cost.[1]

Yet soon after the book appeared in 1933 she had started to realize that non-violence might not be the best means of preventing war in practice and, like that of Nichols and Joad, her pacifism never recovered its former confidence.

The years 1931–2 thus represented the pinnacle of pacifist political optimism during the inter-war period. Not only were most pacifists still as hopeful as ever about the fruits of collaborating with the League and disarmament movements, but also an 'extreme' minority had emerged, characterized by a belief in non-violence and, in many cases, by so exaggerated a picture of war's horrors that it seemed impossible ever again to justify it. In such a heady atmosphere it was not surprising that the sectarian orientation, represented by the F.o.R., had reached its nadir: at the end of 1932 Cadoux was admitting that, even to many of its former stalwarts, 'the Fellowship has virtually ceased to be worth maintaining'.[2] Yet within a short time Hitler's accession to power on 30 January 1933 had marked a turning-point: thereafter the pendulum of pacifist opinion began to swing back—albeit slowly and unevenly—to the F.o.R.'s view that the rightness or wrongness of pacifism did not depend on whether or not it prevented war. Before crossing this watershed, however, it is necessary to turn to the other context in which the distinctiveness of pacifism and the possible direct application of non-violence to current problems were being discussed during 1931–2: the debate among socialist pacifists about their response to what they hoped might develop into a revolutionary political situation.

[1] Jameson, *No Time*, pp. 39–40, 237–8.
[2] 'Should the Fellowship survive?', *Rec.*, Jan. 1933, p. 1.

7

PACIFISM AND REVOLUTION, 1931-2

Confusion between the demands of socialism and pacifism (or, more strictly, between the political conception of socialism favoured by a majority of the socialist movement and the moral one advocated by its pacifist minority) was rife in the early twentieth-century peace movement—in spite of the opportunity to resolve it presented by the Russian revolution. Socialists now admit this, having come to believe that the overdue bifurcation took place in the thirties in response to external aggression starting with the Japanese in 1931 and concluding with Franco's rebellion of 1936. In one respect, however, this orthodoxy is misleading. In 1931-2 left-wing opinion, responding to the formation of the National Government in the economic crisis of August 1931, was wholly preoccupied with the domestic situation; and the first real awareness that there was an internal contradiction with socialist pacifism was occasioned by the question of the pacifist role in what was believed to be an incipient revolutionary crisis. What demoralized the N.M.W.M. was thus not any militarist or fascist threat but the realization that, unless it could show that non-violence was the most effective strategy for toppling capitalism, pacifism would be an embarrassing hindrance to the socialist cause in Britain.

In the worst of the economic depression, in 1931-2, the N.M.W.M. experienced perhaps the most unpleasant internal row in the history of the British peace movement. Not only did the ideological disagreement inherited from the late twenties grow more acute but it was exacerbated by allegations about the behaviour of the two Secretaries: so far did relations thereafter deteriorate that, when a fire broke out at the home of a member in possession of sensitive documents relating to the dispute, suspicions were privately entertained that it had been started deliberately[1] —an ironic state of affairs for a pacifist society.

[1] Private information.

The worsening of relations between the Movement's pro-Labour Party, pro-League leadership and its pro-I.L.P., sectarian left wing was one of the symptoms of the way the August 1931 financial crisis radicalized political attitudes. Despite the fact that Labour's return to opposition had made the question less urgent, the N.M.W.M.'s 1931 conference, held in November at Cheltenham, finally passed Joseph Southall's resolution that M.P.s who voted for war-credits should resign from the movement.[1] This increase in radical support alarmed supporters of the leadership such as Maurice Webb who in forthright language condemned the minority-minded attitudes manifested at Cheltenham:

Suggestions that it was our purpose to create a big mass movement were very frigidly received, and apparently held to be unorthodox. Such empty generalisations, however, as 'we want quality and not quantity' aroused comparative enthusiasm. . . . From the immaculate heights of our unassailable righteousness we threatened with expulsion such valiant pacifists as George Lansbury, Cecil Wilson, and James Barr, if they dared in future to yield to their conscientious belief that it is better to retain a Government with a progressive peace-making policy than to leave the field to a party of reactionary swash-buckling imperialists, even if the temporary price of a vote for war credits must be paid.[2]

He further gave vent to his feelings in a piece of astringent doggerel, entitled 'The Pacifist Saga' or 'How the N.M.W.M. Saved its Soul':

Ten little pacifists; a thin but brave red line;
One joked at an N.C. meeting—then there were nine;

Nine eager pacifists; trying to conquer hate;
One whistled a military march—then there were eight;

Eight righteous pacifists; praying hard for heaven;
One praised a government—then there were seven;

Seven careful pacifists; with others would not mix;
One dared to doubt their sense—then there were six;

Six pompous pacifists; thought brotherhood must revive;
One pleaded for tolerance—then there were five;

Five fearless pacifists; defying the cannon's roar;
One revealed views of his own—then there were four;

[1] *The Times*, 30 Nov. 1931.
[2] *NW*, Feb. 1932.

Three puzzled pacifists; wondered why they never grew;
One told them the reason—then there were two;

Two lonely pacifists; their movement almost gone;
One shook a Colonel's hand—then there was one;

One perfect pacifist; purity personified;
Thought this was a wicked world—and laid him down and died.[1]

With similar forthrightness Walter Ayles, who continued to defend the League as 'the biggest thing which has ever happened in history',[2] condemned the W.R.I.'s triennial conference held at Lyons in 1931 (which had failed to elect his colleague Lucy Cox to its executive): 'Ask them to report on work in their country and they will tell you for half-an-hour about the evils of capitalism and militarist imperialism, but hardly a word of how they are organising to bring disarmament and peace.'[3]

During 1932, however, the leadership's rearguard action against the left suddenly crumbled when both Secretaries resigned following an inquiry into the Movement's financial state.[4] The slump had reduced the flow of benefactions on which all peace societies—even the huge L.N.U.—relied, and in February 1932 the National Committee set up a financial commission to effect immediate economies. Its task proved unexpectedly protracted; and, moreover, by April the two Secretaries were refusing to co-operate with the commission. Although as early as 1926, when Ayles had joined his friend Miss Cox as a second full-time Secretary, the generosity of their salaries had been criticized,[5] the issue did not now simply concern their remuneration. Ayles's successor was later candidly to describe his predecessor's resignation as an 'enforced dismissal' following 'some uneasiness on the part of certain influential pacifists regarding the financial administration';[6] no convincing explanation for the departure of the Secretaries was ever offered to the Movement; and, for

[1] Ibid. The verse about four pacifists was not printed.
[2] NW, Sept. 1931.
[3] NW, Oct. 1931.
[4] N.M.W.M., N.C. 9 Apr. 1932; for a fuller account of the crisis see Ceadel, thesis, pp. 88-9.
[5] Report, N.M.W.M. Annual Conference, Birmingham 2-3 Oct. 1926, p. 38.
[6] Reginald Reynolds, My Life and Crimes (1956), pp. 94, 96.

the most confidential portions of the key National Committee
meetings in June 1932 at which the 'Labour Party' group
of Webb, Chamberlain, and Creech-Jones unsuccessfully
attempted to refer back the financial commission's report,
minute-taking was suspended.[1] The exact issue at stake thus
cannot be established; but it seems that the outgoing Secretaries were believed to have put their own personal and
political ambitions before the urgent needs of the N.M.W.M.
In particular, Ayles, a man of considerable personality who
had just lost his parliamentary salary following his 1931
election defeat, was suspected of cultivating good relations
for his own purposes with some important donors on whose
money the Movement depended.[2]

His former colleagues were upset but not surprised when,
on resigning from the N.M.W.M. he refused to co-operate
with an audit, attempted to have the Post Office redirect
office mail to his private address,[3] and also immediately
announced that he was to become Secretary of a new peace
organization for which he had been able privately to arrange
finance. This was the British Commonwealth Peace Federation (aim: 'To unite the Empire for World Peace and
Progress'), a nebulous body the function of which—apart
from providing Ayles with a salary—was never clear. Lucy
Cox eventually took a job at Transport House and, like
Ayles, was to be elected a Labour M.P. in 1945.

The departure of Ayles and Cox removed the obstacles
to the drift to the left. During the interregnum the Movement was run by Ben Parkin (1906-69), a young schoolteacher
of Marxist views who, shortly after leaving Oxford, had
visited the Soviet Union (and was after 1945 to become a
left-wing Labour M.P.), and Muriel Nichol, daughter of the
I.L.P. M.P. Richard Wallhead, with Runham Brown of the

---

[1] N.M.W.M. N.C. 11-12 and 25 June 1932.

[2] This is the explanation for criticisms of Ayles by his colleagues now offered
by Lucy Cox: interview with Mrs Middleton (née Cox), 23 Apr. 1975. For further
evidence of Ayles's 'powerful, attractive personality' which many admired but
which 'aroused considerable antagonism' in others, some of whom found him
'objectionable', see Joyce M. Bellamy and John Saville (eds.), *Dictionary of
Labour Biography*, v, (1979), p. 12.

[3] For the mutual recriminations surrounding the departure of the Secretaries
see N.M.W.M. N.C. 10 July; Control Committee 20 July, 20 Aug.; Letter from
N.C. to Branch Secretaries 5 July, 1932.

W.R.I. in charge of the finances. And when, in September 1932, they appointed a new General Secretary, they reacted against the dangers of careerism by choosing a candidate whose excessive zeal and militancy was itself to prove controversial.

The successful candidate—chosen on the casting vote of office secretary Mabel Eyles[1]—was Reginald Reynolds (1905-58), a Quaker (and family friend of Laurence Housman) and a lapsed member of the N.M.W.M., who in 1929 had travelled out to meet Gandhi and had attained minor celebrity by being entrusted with Gandhi's letter to Lord Irwin announcing the 1930 civil disobedience campaign. His I.L.P. views and identification with Gandhi were welcomed by the N.M.W.M., as were his idealism and asceticism: it was characteristic that, though initially offered a lower salary than either of his predecessors (both of whose jobs he was combining) he insisted on cutting it by a further 50 per cent, saving money by sleeping in the office. But the price the Movement had to pay for such dedication was intolerance. Shortly after writing the reference which helped Reynolds get the job, Housman had pointed out to Sheppard that Gandhi was almost the only person of whom Reynolds was not severely critical, and observed: 'That poor lamb does give himself a bad time of it, by his bitter judgements on people who disagree with him.'[2] And Reynolds himself, who was destined in 1935 to meet and in 1938 to marry his match in controversial socialist pacifism, the novelist Ethel Mannin, later acknowledged that he was in his day 'probably the most choleric pacifist in the British Isles, a man who believed in loving his enemies but quarrelled with an alarming number of his friends.'[3]

The appointment of the abrasive Reynolds was one factor encouraging the N.M.W.M. wholeheartedly to pursue the revolutionary line it was already adopting; two other factors require brief mention. The first was the decision in July 1932 of the I.L.P., to which many N.M.W.M. members also belonged, to disaffiliate from the Labour Party—a bold gesture

[1] N.M.W.M., N.C. 10-11 Sept. 1932; Reynolds *My Life*, pp. 94-5.
[2] Housman to Sheppard, 1 Sept. 1932, in Housman (ed.), *What . . ?*, p. 180.
[3] Reynolds, *My Life*, p. 100.

which consigned the I.L.P. to the political wilderness. The second, which requires more comment, was the holding in Amsterdam on 27–9 August 1932 of a World Anti-War Congress, nominally at the behest of two French anti-militarist writers, Henri Barbusse and Romain Rolland, but actually as a result of the behind-the-scenes efforts of Willi Münzenberg, the pioneer of the Communist front organization. Although Rolland, like Einstein, failed to attend (allegedly for reasons of ill-health), and although the Soviet delegation, which was to have included Maxim Gorki, was kept out by the Dutch authorities, the Congress was a considerable *coup de théâtre* for Münzenberg and attracted 2,196 delegates. Among them were Parkin and Reynolds (who met each other in Amsterdam for the first time, the way being thus smoothed for the latter's appointment to the N.M.W.M. Secretaryship) and three representatives of the Peace Army: Sheppard, Brinton and Mrs Pollard.[1] These British pacifists were given food for thought by having to sit through vehement attacks on the German Social Democrats and warnings of the need to protect the Soviet Union against the Japanese threat—preoccupations which betrayed the Congress's Communist domination. More particularly, they were left in no doubt as to Communist contempt for what the official Manifesto discussed under the rubric 'Futile Pacifism'; as Parkin noted in his report on the Congress: 'Lord, how the word "pacifism" stinks in the nostrils of most delegates! A pacifist is a man who believes in the *status quo* and the League of Nations, a man whose grandfather knocked you down and who now urges you not to stand up.'[2]

Such hostility, combined with crude attempts to win them over to sympathy for Soviet foreign policy, offended most non-N.M.W.M. pacifists. Thus when a British Anti-War Movement (also calling itself variously a Council or Committee and here abbreviated to B.A.-W.M.) was launched in England in the immediate aftermath of the Amsterdam Congress it failed to attract the degree of fellow-travelling support for

[1] See the report *Report and Manifesto of the World Anti-War Congress at Amsterdam* (1932), pp. 13–15. For Sheppard's attendance see Housman (ed.), *What . . . ?*, pp. 178–9; for Reynolds's see *My Life*, pp. 94–5.
[2] *NW*, Oct. 1932.

which it had hoped.[1] It was a sign, therefore, of the particular susceptibility of the N.M.W.M's new leadership to
criticisms that pacifism showed a 'bourgeois' inability to
grasp the revolutionary nettle that it, in contrast, initially
agreed to affiliate to the B.A.-W.M. (a decision which was
altered, however, to simple co-operation after a month of
experiencing the drawbacks of direct membership of a
Communist-controlled organisation). Similarly, when its
National Committee discussed the Amsterdam Congress's
criticisms of 'Futile Pacifism', it concluded (with only
Wellock dissenting) 'that this described the work of the
Movement.'[2]

The first public indication that the Movement's outlook
was changing in this direction had come in an article in *New
World* for July 1932 under the portentous title 'A New
Situation Calls: The Future Policy of the N.M.W.M.: New
Conditions Demand New Measures'. The new situation
was, the article made clear, that produced by both the
domestic political crisis and the deadlock at Geneva, as a
result of which 'a large body of people are now for the first
time being driven to accept the view that far-reaching social
changes are inevitable, and are ready to explore new lines
of approach to the solution of the problem of disarmament.'
But what if the collapse of capitalism proved violent? 'Civil
war . . . must be avoided for obvious reasons. But that does
not mean that we should meekly accept whatever reaction
may bring upon us.'

This decision to work actively for revolution on the
grounds that it was both desirable and inevitable was greeted
with enthusiasm within the N.M.W.M. in the following
months, despite the fact it logically committed pacifists to
approving whatever violence was necessary to defeat the
forces of reaction. The Movement's hope was to avoid
violence altogether by itself assuming a leading role in the
revolutionary struggle; as Harold Bing argued, in the course
of a National Committee discussion of the problem, 'the
greater the number of convinced pacifists on the provisional
administration the more likely the new state of affairs

---

[1] Ceadel, thesis, pp. 107-13.
[2] N.M.W.M. N.C. 10-11 Sept., 17 Oct. 1932.

would be established without bloodshed.'[1] It aspired, in particular, to persuade the socialist movement to carry out the revolution by the same non-violent means which Gandhi was using in India.

The N.M.W.M's enthusiasm for Gandhi was no sudden whim. As early as 1921, for example, Brockway (himself born in India) had, under his inspiration and with the assistance of his supporter, V. J. Patel, compiled a list of historical examples of the successful political application of non-violence.[2] The following year Wellock had described Gandhi as 'the greatest and most Christ-like figure in contemporary history. We cannot think of him and of his wonderful endeavours and heroic achievements without thinking about Christ.'[3] And in 1931 Reynolds, who had served Gandhi in India, offered what was for him the equivalent tribute when he called him 'a greater revolutionary than Lenin'.[4] So strong and durable did such admiration for Gandhi prove that by 1935 it was felt necessary to ask: 'Why . . . this constant talk about India in the organ of the No More War Movement?' By way of answer it was admitted that 'several of those in the Movement happen to be friends and admirers of Mahatma Gandhi' and that 'some of us have an Indian bee buzzing in our bonnets'; but it was nevertheless insisted that the attention given to Gandhi was justified because he had 'tried to discover a means of destroying power without the weapons of power. He has tried to set soul force against brute force.'[5]

But, though Gandhi had indeed tried valiantly, he had not succeeded in abolishing violence and the net effect of his campaign had been to increase the amount both of violence and repression. New World's July 1932 policy statement had warned against this: after calling for 'a new technique . . . a policy of non-violent resistance which must be worked out beforehand', it had pointed out that in so far as such a technique was 'imperfect and inadequate it will but invite the adoption of violent means on the part of those who have no faith in the policy of non-violence.' The recognition that non-

[1] Ibid., 10–11 Sept.
[2] Non-Co-Operation in Other Lands (Madras, 1921).
[3] Wilfred Wellock, India's Awakening (1922), p. 67.
[4] Reginald A. Reynolds, India, Gandhi and World Peace (n.d. [1931]), p.6.
[5] NMW, Mar. 1935.

violence was fallible should, logically, have brought pacifists face to face with the dilemma of the revolutionary pacifist position: could a pacifist argue that socialist ends justified violent means? Few were prepared to give a direct answer, although the comments of several National Committee members implied that they thought he could. Ben Parkin, for example, though professing to believe non-violence would work, was prepared to admit that 'if there were no alternative to an armed struggle we should be on the side of the oppressed'; he also criticized 'the notion that to admit the inevitability of the class struggle or to take part in it, is somehow a betrayal of our principles.'[1] Similarly Brockway argued that 'we have passed into a revolutionary period' and suggested that a pacifist would be doing no violence to his conscience if he worked for the revolution 'to be carried through successfully with the minimum of violence which the conditions of the struggle and the psychology of the population allow'. This was a far cry from his absolutism in 1916; and it was significant that, having resigned the chairmanship of the N.M.W.M. in 1928, he now also resigned that of the W.R.I., and made explicit the extent to which hatred of capitalism had usurped the central position in this thinking formerly occupied by hatred of war:

Capitalism incarnates the principles of War; it has the results of War. It is not so dramatic, its horrors are not so obvious—but every day that passes it is starving men, women and children in the midst of plenty; it is crushing the mind and imprisoning the spirit of millions; it is beating down the workers and peasants of the world to hunger conditions in order to maintain the profits and power of the possessing class. That is War—War as damnable and unnecessary as military conflict.[2]

So many of the N.M.W.M's most forceful members thought the same way that by the autumn of 1932 the voice of absolute pacifism could scarcely make itself heard within the N.M.W.M. above such revolutionist rhetoric. One member complained: 'The November issue of the *New World* was simply a statement of the I.L.P. revolutionary policy . . . '; while another insisted: 'The man who is a socialist first and a pacifist second should say so and stop masquerading.'[3]

[1] N.M.W.M., N.C., 10–11 Sept. 1932.
[2] *NW*, Feb. 1933.
[3] *NW*, Jan. 1933.

Not only were few prepared to do so, as already suggested, but the Movement's leading strict pacifists were reluctant to press the issue. One of the few to assert 'I am a pacifist first and a socialist second' was Cyril Joad, whose iconoclastic temperament (and the fact he had already offended the left by supporting Mosley's New Party) equipped him to make clear, in an N.M.W.M. pamphlet published in the summer of 1932, that 'although I can see there are good arguments in favour of a revolution . . . I should nevertheless do my best to prevent a revolutionary situation from arising.'[1] Although Joad's worries were privately shared by at least three members of the National Committee—Bing, Wellock, and Runham Brown: the three who were to become Sponsors of the P.P.U.—they were more cautious in expressing them. The most outspoken was Bing, who warned in a *New World* article: 'In our new-found righteousness we must avoid any kind of heresy hunting. There is a tendency among some of our members to assume that a consistent pacifist must necessarily be a socialist. I dissent . . .' But, for fear of being though bourgeois, he was careful to insist that pacifism had, nevertheless, to be 'applied': 'Certainly no one can logically be a member of the No More War Movement who does not adopt a revolutionary attitude towards the present society.' His strategy for defending his strictly non-violent approach was thus to insist that it was truly radical ('my social conceptions are so much more revolutionary than those of most socialists') and offered more chance of winning mass support than did 'falling into the sort of class-war jargon which will alienate many pacifists who should be working with us.'[2]

The debate was, of course, between two conceptions of socialism and the strategies that went with them. Bing's conception was avowedly spiritual. 'Our influence is not so much as a propaganda body as an organic growth', he told the National Committee. '. . . We cannot reform the world without reforming ourselves.'[3] But this had lost further

[1] Joad, *What Fighting Means*, p. 20; see also his *Pacifism and the Class War* (N.P.C. pamphlet No. 6, 1933).

[2] *NW*, Feb. 1933.

[3] N.M.W.M. N.C. 10–11 Sept. 1932.

ground since the 1931 political crisis and was given very short shrift indeed in the Committee's policy statement which was duly endorsed by the 1932 annual conference at Sheffield in November. Stressing that revolutionary changes could occur 'at any moment', this dismissed the policy of 'cravenly accepting oppression for ourselves or tolerating injustices for others, whilst calling upon our fellows not to use wrong methods.' Instead it deliberately defined pacifism in such a way as to exclude those who had the best claim to use the word. 'The purpose of the Pacifist Movement' it claimed,

is not to keep 'peace' by such means but to work for human progress and the righting of wrongs . . . The practical implications of this position must not be evaded in order to retain a paralysing unity between ourselves and those 'pacifists' who wish to preserve the fruits of violence and oppression without themselves fighting for it. We recognise no common interest between such an attitude and pacifism as we understand it.[1]

It was not surprising that, when the Sheffield Conference met to consider the report, even *New World* had to admit: 'A few of the delegates were alarmed at what was described as the departure from the historic mission of the movement.'[2] The N.M.W.M.'s leaders did nothing, however, to assuage that alarm. Their attitude was typified by Parkin's assertion in the February 1933 issue of *New World*: 'There is a good deal of dead wood to cut away before the old type of pacifist breaks out of his thicket of isolation and self-sufficiency to join the fight for the new society.'

Parkin's metaphor was ironic in view of the N.M.W.M.'s real organizational position at that time. Far from needing pruning, it had long been in need of all the supporters it could muster: in February 1932 the National Committee had been informed that of little over four thousand nominal members only 346 had cast votes in the election for that committee.[3] More important in the short term, however, it needed money, the slump and its revolutionary policy having cut off its supply of benefactions. The resulting financial

---

[1] 'Recommendations on Policy by the National Committee of the No More War Movement (For consideration at the Annual Conference at Sheffield, Nov. 1932)'.

[2] *NW*, Dec. 1932.

[3] N.M.W.M., N.C. 13 Feb. 1932.

deficit forced it, in February 1933, to reduce its paid staff to three—Reynolds, Miss Eyles and a clerical assistant—and, three months later, entirely to halt publication of *New World*, which had managed only spasmodic publication during the previous year. Announcing the journal's demise Wellock made clear how far the demoralization of the N.M.W.M. had gone: 'Far too much time has been devoted to what might be called "pathological" work, that is to the painful task of trying to keep lukewarm branches alive. This task is felt to be a waste of time and money . . . ' Instead, the Movement had decided to establish, from its own members and through co-option, 'Groups of Action' which would study social and world issues of practical relevance to pacifists.[1]

The N.M.W.M. had thus suspended most of its propaganda activities and abandoned all pretence of being a mass movement. Since it did so in the early months of the Third Reich an uninformed observer might be forgiven for surmising that this occurred because Hitler had discredited pacifism. However, as the next chapter will show, the advent of Hitler initially *stimulated* pacifism in Britain; and, as this one has shown, the N.M.W.M.'s difficulties preceded the Third Reich and arose largely from the decision to put revolutionism before pacifism on the assumption—still voiced as late as December 1932 by Maynard Bennett, a Quaker member of the N.M.W.M. National Committee, when attempting to sell the new policy to his fellow Friends—that a revolution 'is perhaps nearer to us than another world war'.[2] Hitler's securing of the Chancellorship late the following month falsified this prediction; in consequence pacifism, which in 1932 had seemed of doubtful relevance to immediate problems, suddenly appeared more salient than revolutionism.

An illustration of this change is provided by the response of two of the period's most unorthodox socialists: the literary critics (and best friends) Middleton Murry and Max Plowman. Murry, editor of the *Adelphi*, was probably the most sensitive barometer of the changing currents of inter-war

[1] *NW*, May 1933. A quarterly news-sheet *Points for Pacifists* was still issued.
[2] *Friend*, 2 Dec. 1932, p. 1074.

opinion: his sudden enthusiasm for war-resistance (though
not as yet for pacifism) even anticipated Hitler's coming to
office by a fortnight. In the second half of 1931, like many
other previously apolitical intellectuals, he had been converted to Marxism, pouring out his new convictions in *The
Necessity of Communism*, written in a fortnight and published early in 1932. He also joined the I.L.P., welcoming
its disaffiliation from the Labour Party in July 1932, and
even hailing Brockway as 'an English Stalin'.[1] At this time
he was openly contemptuous of pacifists (whom he had disliked since his visits to Garsington in the Great War) and
considered their sole utility would be to serve as ambulance
workers of the revolution. Nor did he have any time for
the argument that non-violent methods acceptable to pacifists could ensure a humane revolution; on the contrary, he
argued, what was required to keep bloodshed to a minimum
was to make it 'short and sharp' by a 'firm determination in
the revolutionary party to betake itself to force, if necessary'.[2] But in the new year he suddenly came to believe
that war-resistance, rather than revolution, was the most
effective and popular way of undermining capitalism. With
the precision of one well used to charting his own changes of
intellectual tack he recorded his arrival, at precisely 10.15
p.m. on 18 January 1933, at the conclusion: 'The main long-
view policy in Revolutionary Socialism in the proximate
future is to organise resistance against war.'[3]

Murry's change of heart was welcomed by Max Plowman,
even though it took him a further three and a half years to
persuade Murry to make the next step—from *pacificism* to
pacifism; in addition Plowman himself became suddenly
excited about the prospects for socialist pacifism. An un-
wavering pacifist since his resignation from the army in
January 1918, he had a strongly 'moral' conception of
socialism which had helped to keep him aloof from the
N.M.W.M. and also caused him to be greatly upset by Murry's
sudden lapse into materialism in 1931. While assuring his
friend that he was 'in complete agreement . . . about the

---

[1] Lea, *Murry*, pp. 193, 196.
[2] *NW*, Nov. 1932.
[3] Cited in Lea, *Murry*, p. 200.

necessity for, and the inevitability of, a social revolution',
Plowman constantly complained of being unable to 'feel the
religious sentiment in your Communism'.[1] When Murry
suddenly decided that war-resistance was more constructive
than planning for a seizure of power, Plowman welcomed
his decision warmly as a step in the right direction. 'Rightly
handled,' he enthused to Murry, 'war-resistance would grow
into the religious idea that would resuscitate the West, just
as Gandhi's idea will bring the East to life . . . '[2] Murry's
conversion was, however, not the only factor to cheer Plowman, who thought he detected a new climate of opinion.
'Unless I am very much mistaken,' he predicted late in
February 1933, 'the pacifist issue is going to be the deter-
mining one after all . . . I mean it will be the birth-place of
the true positives—the real determinant of values . . . '; and
a few days later he was asserting with even greater certainty:
'I know now that the pacifist issue is *primary*.'[3] In one sense
he was right: in 1933 pacifism was to become a major issue
for the first time (except during a war), even though the
organization which saw itself as Britain's leading pacifist
society was in no position to avail itself of this opportunity.

[1] Plowman to Murry, 9 Jan., 15 Mar. 1932, M.P.
[2] Plowman to Murry, 9 May 1933, M.P.
[3] Plowman to West, 26 Feb., to Marr, 5 Mar. 1933, in D.L.P(lowman), (ed.),
Bridge, pp. 459-60.

8

THE IMPACT OF HITLER, 1933

Hitler's elevation on 30 January 1933 was the critical international event of the inter-war period. In retrospect it has
therefore been seen as an intellectual watershed—like the
Manchuria crisis, only more so—marking the point at which
many who had clung to their belief that the Great War had
abolished war came reluctantly to accept the need to fight,
in a last resort, for international justice against fascist aggression. This view is, of course, broadly correct: growing
awareness of the nature of Hitler's regime, particularly after
it walked out from Geneva on 14 October 1933, did force
the peace movement and the public mind to give serious
attention not merely to condemning war but to the more
practical question of preventing it. Before 1933 the *pacificist* consensus in support of the League and the Disarmament
Conference had prevented the various strands latent within
the peace movement from fully appreciating their differences
of approach. However, once the most dangerous power in
Europe had withdrawn from the League, and disarmament
had been seen to fail, the movement was forced to choose
between pacifism, war-resistance, internationalism, and
other, logically distinct, peace policies which previously it
had tended to blur together as an undifferentiated 'pacifism'.
Faced with this choice some formerly vague 'pacifists'
accepted the rigorous implications of strict pacifism for the
first time; but many more came to realize they were not
pacifists at all.

Yet this process of clarification was, in practice, neither so
swift nor so straightforward as has often been suggested.
Indeed a common response to the deterioration of the international situation in which many detected disturbing echoes
of 1914 was simply an emotional 'never again!'. And, although many who succumbed to this pacifist reflex soon
came to discover its limitations as a practical means of

making sure another world war did not happen, acceptance
of the need to resort to sanctions as a deterrent was delayed
both by an upsurge of isolationist feeling and by a reluctance
to face up to the logical distinction between pacifism and
internationalism. Thus the old *pacificist* consensus did frag-
ment in 1933; but it did so in a complex fashion—as historians
struggling to make sense of, for example, the 'King and
Country' debate or East Fulham by-election have discovered.
Although by the end of the year the dust had largely settled
and the key division within the peace movement, that
between *pacificists* and pacifists, had started to become
apparent, there was still some way to go—as the considerable
but still incomplete clarification of the usage of the word
'pacifism' illustrated.

(i) Never Again!

The appointment of Hitler as German Chancellor at the end of
January 1933; the renewal of Japanese aggression in China in
February; the rapidly worsening economic situation in the
United States preceding Roosevelt's inauguration in March; the
continuing disarmament difficulties at Geneva which a belated
British initiative, also in March, failed to resolve; and the short-
lived British trade embargo against Russia following the arrest
in Moscow of the Metropolitan Vickers engineers in April: all
combined to produce in the opening months of 1933 the first
sustained concern about European war since the end of
the Russo-Polish conflict in 1920. Comparisons between
1933 and 1914 were frequently made and, although they were
almost as frequently dismissed, war talk was a distinctive
feature of serious public discussion throughout 1933. When
accepting delivery, in March 1933, of the manuscript of *Testament of Youth*, soon to be hailed as one of the classic memoirs
by a member of the 'War Generation'[1] of 1914-18, Vera
Brittain's publisher, Victor Gollancz, commented to her: 'I
hope there won't be a war before your book comes out'.[2]

[1] The book began and ended with the poems 'The War Generation: Ave' and
'The War Generation: Vale'.
[2] Vera Brittain, *Testament of Experience: An Autobiographical Story of the
Years 1925-1950* (1957), p. 86.

That month a *New Statesman* article entitled 'Remember 1914' compared the Anti-War Congress then being organized at Bermondsey by the B.A.-W.M. with the socialist anti-war rally in Trafalgar Square on the Sunday before Britain entered the Great War: 'In 1914 war was imminent and everyone knew what the war would be and broadly how the European Powers would be grouped. Today everyone fears war, but no one is sure which war, or when it will come.'[1]   Many feared it would be with Germany again; but Kingsley Martin warned the delegates at Bermondsey: 'I believe you should be on your watch for the war against Russia, which we must not have'.[2]

Such war talk was too hypothetical to have any adverse effect on pacifist morale in Britain. There was no immediate recantation comparable to that of Einstein, who, in a letter to the King of Belgium published in *La Patrie Humaine* on 18 August 1933, admitted that 'in the present circumstances, I, if I were a Belgian, should not refuse military service, but accept it with my whole conscience, knowing that I was contributing towards the salvation of European civilisation'.[3] Soon afterwards he transferred his allegiance within the British peace movement from the N.M.W.M. to the New Commonwealth Society. This change of heart—which, embarrassingly, coincided with the publication of an anthology of his pacifist writings[4]—reflected the speed with which, as a Jew domiciled in Germany, the unprecedented evil of Nazism and the need to resist it was brought home to him (literally—his house was attacked by stormtroopers, although he was abroad at the time). To the British peace movement, however, Hitler at first seemed merely one symptom (albeit the most dangerous) of a world-wide militarist revival which risked plunging the world into war unless the peace-loving powers exercised a restraining influence. The 'never again!' mood was thus isolationist rather than deterrent.

Isolationism is conducive to pacifism: this was evidenced

---

[1] *NS*, 11 Mar. 1933, pp. 283–4.
[2] *War* No. 4 (15 Mar. 1933) p. 6. For further evidence of fear of war see Ceadel, thesis, pp. 115–17.
[3] Reprinted in *P*, Oct. 1933.
[4] Rosika Schwimmer and Alfred Lief (eds.), *The Fight Against War* (1933).

by the increased enthusiasm shown in February and March (as already noted) by the longstanding but formerly inactive pacifist, Max Plowman; and, even more so, by new conversions directly attributable to the world events of those months. The most famous example was the leading Methodist temperance reformer, Henry Carter, who early in 1933 attended two conferences on the Christian attitude to international affairs: one in mid-February, at which he was still a *pacificist*, as he had been during the Christ and Peace campaign of 1929-31; and one in mid-March, by which time he had embraced pacifism.[1]   Between these two conferences, as he explained in the *Methodist Recorder* on 23 March 1933, 'stupendous events have brought mankind face to face with the fact of war in the Far East, and the possibility of future war in Europe. The world situation looks startlingly like July 1914.' The Great War, he went on to argue, had failed to end war and had itself generated social and economic troubles; but another war would be even more horrific. Explicitly on these grounds Carter announced his conversion to pacifism: 'This requires me to say that in the unhappy event of a future war I should reason, preach, and write against it, and should use any lawful means to dissuade others from recourse to fighting.' By November 1933, moreover, his initiative had helped to set up a Methodist Peace Fellowship—an early symptom, like Leyton Richards's revival in May of the (Congregational) Christian Pacifist Crusade, of the growth of organized pacifism within the clergy which was to provide a launching pad for the 'new pacifism' of 1934-5—and throughout his life Carter remained a leader of Christian pacifism.

However, not all pacifism fostered in this favourable isolationist climate proved as durable as Carter's. His belief had survived because it was deeply rooted in Christianity and, despite what he had written in his *Methodist Recorder* article, was attributable to the international crisis of early 1933 only in the sense that it was that which pushed him over the edge after he had long been wavering on the brink. In contrast, where pacifism was simply an emotional response

<hr>

[1] Urwin, *Carter*, pp. 79-81.

to a deteriorating international situation—as was often the case in 1933, in 1936, and at the time of the Munich Conference—it tended to be inspired only by an unstable humanitarianism, and often lasted no longer than the 'never again!' mood which engendered it. In many cases its exponents confused total *opposition* to militarism and the horrors of war with the adoption of the total *opposite* position to militarism and war—namely, refusal to fight. When they realized that the real problem was not to express hostility to war but to prevent it, they mostly retreated to some form of *pacificism*.

The most celebrated illustration of this reflex and its recoil is the controversy provoked at this time by the 'King and Country' debate at the Oxford Union.[1] At one of its weekly debates, on 9 February 1933, the Oxford Union Society passed by 275 votes to 153 the motion 'That this House will in no circumstances fight for its King and Country'. After a few days this unselfconscious undergraduate Thursday evening's relaxation was built up by the press into an international news story. In the United States the pledge to take no part in war came thereafter to be known as the Oxford pledge;[2] and it has even (erroneously) been alleged that the debate helped to convince Hitler, who had come to power only ten days before, of Britain's unwillingness to honour her European commitments.

It is, of course, easy to point out the limitations of the debate as an indicator of public opinion: for one thing, the outcome was largely a tribute to the oratorical skills of the visiting proposer of the motion, Cyril Joad; for another, the Union Society's aim was to produce entertainment, not to express undergraduate opinion even in the way modern student unions are constitutionally supposed to do. Moreover, the press controversy occurred largely as the result of a letter published in the *Daily Telegraph* on the Saturday following the debate (11 February 1933) under the

---

[1] For a full account of the debate, its aftermath, and its mythology, see Ceadel, 'The "King and Country" Debate', *Historical Journal*, 22, 2 (1979), pp. 397–422.

[2] See e.g. John K. Nelson, *The Peace Prophets: American Pacifist Thought 1919–41* (Chapel Hill, 1967), p. 37; Charles Chatfield, *For Peace and Justice: Pacifism in America 1914–41* (Knoxville, 1971), p. 260.

name 'Sixty-Four', which was in fact written by the paper's leader writer, J. B. Firth. Firth, a devoted Oxonian (he had as early as 1908 published an anthology of poetry about Oxford) expressed the dismay of older generations of Oxford men at this manifestation of 'Red tendencies' at Oxford, and urged that they expunge the shameful motion. This suggestion was taken up by Randolph Churchill, who, along with other former Union members, put down a motion to this effect on 2 March 1933. Largely because the issue had by then developed into the right of 'old Oxford' to interfere with the current members' running of the Union, Churchill's expunging motion was massively defeated by 750 votes to 138 at the excitable and much publicized second debate. Undoubtedly, therefore, what the 'King and Country' controversy revealed most clearly was Oxford's newsworthiness and the public's sensitivity about taking the monarch's name in vain, rather than any widespread interest in pacifism.

Nevertheless—and this constitutes its importance for the present study—the controversy had the effect of forcing people to think out their views on war prevention more carefully than they would otherwise have done. In addition, the debate itself offered a number of clues as to the state of public thinking on this subject early in 1933. One major clue was an unprecedented willingness to endorse explicitly pacifist, rather than vaguely anti-war, sentiments. Despite frequent assertions to the contrary,[1] the proposers of the 'King and Country' motion did *not* advocate fighting for international or socialist justice: they attacked war of any kind. Admittedly, this would probably not have been the case if Angell, Russell, or John Strachey—who, along with Nichols, had been asked to speak before Joad was approached—had been able to accept the invitation to propose the motion. In the event, however, it was Joad who agreed to come and who made the debate-winning speech; his emergence in 1932 as an outspoken pacifist has already been noted, and it is clear that at the Union he explicitly argued the case for Gandhi-style non-violent resistance in face of an invasion of unarmed Britain.

[1] Most recently by Howard, *War and the Liberal Conscience*, p. 91.

The reason why the pacifist content of the Oxford Union resolution has so frequently been denied is that many of its supporters, having succumbed unthinkingly to the pacifist reflex, soon came to realize that it was not the best way of preventing war. It was thus not surprising that they should retrospectively seek to explain away their, now regretted, support for the resolution by seizing on its obligingly (but unintentionally) ambivalent wording and claim that all along they had mentally reserved the right to fight for internationalism or socialism and had only opposed jingoism of the 'King and Country' variety. They were encouraged in this rationalization by those who had not attended the debate and who explained the motion in the same way. One of the first to do this was Jonathan Griffin, a journalist active in peace circles throughout the thirties, who wrote in a *New Statesman* letter published a fortnight after the debate:

When I read of the motion . . . I found myself underlining the words 'for its King and Country'; for I realised simultaneously two things: first, that there can be no question for me any more of fighting in a national war; secondly, that if a war arose because the Covenant of the League of Nations required the use of the ultimate, military sanctions against an aggressor country, I would have to fight.[1]

Within a short time it had become an orthodoxy of progressive opinion that the motion had been passed by a coalition of pacifists, internationalists, and war-resisters. Thus, writing in a symposium, published in 1934, on *Young Oxford and War*, Michael Foot, then still a Liberal and recent ex-President of the Union, listed these three positions and claimed: 'The students who voted for the King and Country motion at Oxford comprised persons holding all these different points of view. They were united in their refusal to respond to the sentimental appeal made in the name of King and Country.'[2]

But although the supporters of the Oxford resolution had, by the time Foot was writing, indeed divided into these distinct camps, at the time of the debate they had *not* constituted a self-conscious coalition of separate viewpoints uniting under the banner of a skilfully-worded slogan. Early

[1] *NS*, 25 Feb. 1933, p. 219.
[2] Michael Foot *et al.*, *Young Oxford and War* (1934), pp. 31-2.

in 1933 the logical differences between pacifism, internationalism, and war-resistance were no better understood than
they had formerly been (as Foot's own propensity to confuse
pacifism and internationalism showed).[1] All that had
happened was that the previous *pacificist* consensus had been
radicalized, albeit temporarily and unthinkingly, into a
pacifist consensus. The underlying reason for this was the unprecedented international uncertainty which undermined
pacificist optimism and produced the 'never again!' reflex.
But two contributory factors played an important part in
intensifying this feeling: the use of the phrase 'King and
Country', and the gulf between the generations in their
attitudes to the Great War.

The phrase 'King and Country' powerfully and instan-
taneously evoked the recruiting posters, patriotic propaganda,
and war hysteria of 1914. Indeed its emotional connotations
had been spelled out only three days before the debate in a
private letter to Sheppard from his pacifist friend Housman.
Describing a recent peace meeting at which he had addressed
an enthusiastic and youthful audience Housman had specu-
lated: 'I wonder would they hold out if war came? I doubt
it. "Call of King and Country" would then once more
atrophy conscience and abolish common sense.'[2] It was
because it evoked the jingoism of 1914 that the motion
appealed to those who might not otherwise have supported a
pacifist motion. It touched, moreover, on a second emotional
chord: the growing sense of identity among the post-war
generation. Having assimilated the anti-war literature of the
twenties in their formative years, many students in the early
thirties had developed a cynical view of conventional defence
policy, and indeed of the Great War itself. They also felt that,
since they would be the ones to fight a future war, they had
a right to speak out.

---

[1] In his contribution to *Young Oxford and War* Foot (whose 'genuine pacifism
and conscientious objection to the use of arms' had been emphasized by *Isis*,
18 Oct. 1933, p. 7) began with a confident assertion (pp. 45–50) of the morality
and efficacy of non-violence; but he shifted to the argument that the 'most
extreme pacifist . . . would be justified in supporting a collective force; for the
reason that the force, the purpose of which is to provide a backing of law, does
not contain the elements objected to by the pacifist' (pp. 58–9).

[2] Housman to Sheppard, 6 Feb. 1933, in Housman (ed.), *What . . . ?*, p. 203.

Only the more sympathetic commentators on the controversy realized that this was what largely accounted for the
wide appeal of an extreme pacifist resolution, since Fleet
Street mostly preferred to attribute the result variously to
Communism, degeneracy, or disrespect for the monarchy.
The *Manchester Guardian* was one of the few papers to
insist, as it did on 13 February, that the 'obvious meaning
of this resolution' was youth's deep disgust 'at the national
hypocrisy which can fling over the timidities and follies
of politicians, over base greeds and commercial jealousies
and jobbery, the cloak of an emotional symbol they do not
deserve'. The most forceful expression of this view came
however, from the humorist A. A. Milne (1882–1956) who
began a career as a prominent pacifist by coming to the
defence of the Oxford debate in a *News Chronicle* article on
23 February: 'There is no infamy for which the words "King
and Country" do not provide adequate cover. "My Country,
right or wrong!" How tragically easy war becomes waged in
these mists of sentimentality.' Another supporter of the
Union, Ponsonby, found the same argument very effective
in his own propaganda; on 22 April 1933 he informed the
President of the Union at the time of the debate:

I have used it at several meetings with great success. Even at the Manchester Luncheon Club a fortnight ago to an audience of heavy business
men I worked it in and was told afterwards that many had not understood the significance of the resolution before—the determination of
the young generation not to be carried away by the so-called patriotic
wash which was poured out in 1914. [1]

Essentially, therefore, the 'King and Country' motion,
like other manifestations of the emotional pacifist reflex
of early 1933, was a backward-looking protest at what had
happened in August 1914. It seemed to assume that British
involvement in an unnecessary war could be engineered
without warning by an unscrupulous Government prepared
to resort to the psychological trickery of jingoism, and concentrated on what the individual's duty would be if such a
crisis recurred. When, almost immediately, the motion's
supporters were forced by Hitler's consolidation of power

---

[1] Ponsonby to Hardie, 22 Apr. 1933, F.H.

in Germany and further Japanese aggression in China to look to the future, they began to realize the limitations of pacifism as a means of preventing crises arising in the first place. Within a short time most had settled for being *pacificists*: of these a minority at first declared themselves socialist war-resisters, but before the end of 1933 most of these had joined the majority in espousing internationalism.

(ii) The Drift to Pacificism

A particularly clear-cut example of how involvement in the debate stimulated first a dramatic commitment to pacifism then, almost immediately, an awareness of its practical limitations was the young Christ Church post-graduate who had organized it, Frank Hardie, President of the Union in Hilary Term, 1933. Hardie, whose Oxford career had already included a First in Modern History and the Chairmanship of the Labour Club, was one of the most promising of a highly-talented generation of young Oxford socialists. Having helped at his school to found a branch of the L.N.U. he had been a supporter of the League when he first came up to Oxford in 1929. In a Union debate in May 1931 he had spoken in support of the motion 'That Pacifism is the only true form of Patriotism' (which was carried by 79 votes to 47), declaring explicitly that he 'was opposed to conscientious objection unless it was organised on an international scale'. This episode illustrates not only the prevalence at that time of pacifism's original, vaguer, meaning,[1] but also the lack of public attention normally paid to Union debates—even when pacifist resolutions were adopted—unless (for example, through the use of the phrase 'King and Country') they fortuitously touched a raw nerve. After the Manchuria crisis he became disillusioned with the League and, under the stimulus of the 'King and Country' controversy, came to declare himself an absolute pacifist. Writing a week after

---

[1] Another proposer of the May 1931 motion 'divided pacifism into two sorts; compulsory arbitration and peace at any price' and supported only the former. The *Isis* reporter emphasized the confusion over definitions: 'Pacifists said they were patriots, patriots said they were pacifists, and patriotic pacifists probably said they were pacific patriots . . . '. *Isis*, 3 June 1931, p. 11.

the debate in the *New Statesman*, he insisted 'that the best method of ending war was of individual resistance to any future war'.[1]

But no sooner had he adopted this position than he had to defend it against criticisms the cogency of which he was too perceptive to ignore. On 22 March 1933 the Professor of International Relations at Oxford, A. E. Zimmern, who was one of those who believed the debate had 'helped to intensify the reign of terrorism in Germany', wrote Hardie a long letter criticising his motion for obscuring the issue it purported to discuss

because it blurs over the vital distinction between Individual Resistance ('Quakerism', Ponsonby's propaganda etc) and Resistance in the name of a law superior to that of the individual State (loyalty to Covenant, Kellogg Pact etc). This distinction is absolutely vital and it is a great dis-service to pander to the mental confusion in which most people are on the subject.[2]

A week later, replying to correspondence in the *New Statesman*, Hardie admitted the limitations of the motion for the first time: 'It has served to give dramatic expression to the extreme pacifism of my generation; it does not serve to define precisely the method by which peace is to be preserved'.[3] By the time he came to sum up the whole controversy in the *Manchester Guardian* on 29 May 1933, he had begun to stress that the motion could indeed be interpreted in different ways by Quakers, Marxists, and League supporters. Adapting the words of Nurse Cavell, he argued: ' "Pacifism is not enough." To be in favour of peace as opposed to war is only a first and small step. The next step is to think out clearly what are the means to peace.'

The means to peace of which Hardie became an enthusiastic advocate in the summer of 1933 was war-resistance, which he defined as 'not merely the resistance of individual pacifists basing their action on humanitarian or religious motives, but the mass resistance of the working classes basing their action on economic motives . . .'.[4] This brand of *pacificism*

[1] *NS*, 18 Feb. 1933, pp. 181-2.
[2] Zimmern to Hardie, 22 Mar. (see also 16 Mar.) 1933, F.H.
[3] *NS*, 1 Apr. 1933, p. 412.
[4] *NS*, 4 Nov. 1933, p. 547; see also his contribution to Foot *et al., Young Oxford*, p. 181.

reached a level of support in the summer and early autumn of 1933 which surpassed its previous upsurges of popularity in 1920 and 1926.[1] Its success, which culminated in the adoption by acclamation of a war-resistance motion at the Labour Party's annual conference at Hastings in the first week of October, was a symptom of public fear of war which was more widespread and politically salient than at any other time in the inter-war period, except for the Munich period itself.

This was due to the mounting difficulties at the Disarmament Conference, on which so many hopes had for so long been focused. It had been an orthodoxy since the Great War that armaments themselves caused war; therefore it was feared that a failure at Geneva would initiate an arms race which could result only in war. When on 14 October 1933 Germany walked out of Geneva altogether—a withdrawal astutely timed by Hitler to follow an admonitory speech by the British Foreign Secretary—European affairs were believed to be balanced on a knife-edge. Even those to whom Nazism was ideologically anathema were unwilling to upset the unstable equilibrium by offering any criticism of Germany: the N.M.W.M.'s annual conference, which was in session at the time, resolved 'that public opinion must be educated to understand the nature of the protest that Germany had made';[2] while Sheppard and Maude Royden immediately proposed an Albert Hall meeting to express Britain's goodwill towards Germany.[3] Blame for the crisis belonging properly to Germany had to be laid elsewhere: for example, at the doors of the arms traders who were more vilified at this time than at any other in their already twenty-year long career as bogeymen of the peace movement;[4] and at the doors of the British Government. A sign of the public willingness to accept these scapegoats was the loss on 25 October of the safe Conservative seat at East Fulham, the most spectacular of a series of by-elections in which the

[1] War-resistance is treated more fully in Ceadel, thesis, pp. 144–93.
[2] *P*, Nov. 1933.
[3] L.N.U. Executive, 19 Oct., 2 Nov. 1933.
[4] See e.g. Fenner Brockway, *The Bloody Traffic* (1933) and the article by Philip Noel Baker in *Recovery*, 10 Nov. 1933, cited in John Wheeler-Bennett, *The Disarmament Deadlock* (1934), p. 12.

Labour Party supplemented its stock-in-trade of social and economic complaint by playing the 'peace' card.[1] This mainly consisted of what Baldwin angrily condemned as 'the calculated and mischievous lie' to the effect that 'the Conservative Party does not believe in Peace and Disarmament'.[2] It was these tactics, to which Labour was again at times to resort following the start of air rearmament in the summer of 1934, which convinced Baldwin that he could not beat *pacificism* and had, instead, to capture it. (This he did very astutely in the November 1935 general election, timed so that he could exploit League rhetoric to sugar the pill of rearmament.)

Blaming the government did not, however, solve the problem of formulating a constructive alternative policy. What the autumn by-elections of 1933 revealed was a considerable amount of confusion and wavering between three conflicting options: pacifism, war-resistance, and internationalism. Of these pacifism was undoubtedly the least popular, but far from negligible, nevertheless. At many of the 1933–4 by-elections, for example—though not at East Fulham—Labour adopted pacifists as candidates, including two future P.P.U. Sponsors: James Barr at Kilmarnock and Alex Wood (1879–1950), a local physics don and F.o.R. member, at Cambridge. Moreover, the Hastings Conference was informed by J. R. Bellerby, a former Professor of Economics at Liverpool and a Labour candidate, of a private poll he had carried out, which indicated an unexpected degree of public pacifism. Bellerby (1896–1977), who had won a Military Cross and lost an arm in the Great War, was an active and extreme *pacificist*, but not himself a pacifist; yet his referendum, based on 17,000 answers in selected areas of the country, found that no less than 57 per cent supported, and only 43 per cent

---

[1] Some historians have denied that foreign affairs played a significant role at East Fulham. For a discussion of the controversy, which concludes that (although it is naïve to look for a single-issue explanation and although pacifism in the strict sense can be ruled out) the disarmament issue added to the prevailing suspicion of the National Government and was the reason given by the local Liberals for supporting Labour, see Martin Ceadel, 'Interpreting East Fulham', in C. Cook and J. Ramsden (eds.), *By-Elections in British Politics* (1973), pp. 118–39.

[2] *The Times*, 28 Oct. 1933.

opposed, unilateral disarmament by Britain in 1933.[1] This poll, was of course, obviously unreliable and considerably exaggerated support for pacifism: even Bellerby admitted privately that its results needed 'to be viewed with some reserve. They do not seem to me to justify unilateral disarmament by a Government'.[2] Nevertheless it did reflect the undoubted fact that pacifism was stronger at the end of the year in which Hitler reached power than at the beginning.

However, most of those opposing a return to a conventional balance of power policy and an arms race were not pacifists, and the main debate was between two fundamentally different *pacificist* strategies: either accepting the inevitability of Franco-German conflict and pursuing a policy of isolationism, as recommended by both the war-resisters of the left and the press lords on the right; or standing by the commitment to preserve peace and security in Europe, as advocated by both internationalists and 'orthodox' official opinion. In the heat of the disarmament crisis isolationism won the argument within the left, and the process of accepting the need to deter Hitler was thus delayed. Admittedly, the set-back did not prove a long one: soon the negativeness and fatalism of war-resistance caused a return to internationalism, as the evolution of Frank Hardie's thinking again illustrates. Since early summer he had been stressing the economic nature of war's causation, expressing scepticism about the League, and had even helped draft the war-resistance motion passed at Hastings.[3] Before the end of October, however, he was taking the lead in an attempt, under the auspices of the National Peace Council, to formulate a peace package that would entice Germany back to the conference table; and, after a period of ambiguously supporting both Geneva and war resistance, he soon developed into an orthodox internationalist and supporter of collective security.

[1] *Report*, 33rd Annual Conference, Hastings 1933, pp. 192–3; see also *NS*, 21 Oct. 1933, p. 475. Although Bellerby had late in 1932 formed an 'Association for the Peace Ballot of Great Britain' to undertake this poll, it had no connection with the famous 'Peace Ballot' of 1934–5 instigated by the L.N.U.

[2] Bellerby to Hardie, 22 Nov. 1933, F. H. For his constructive proposals for disarmament and pooled security see his pamphlet *World Order Without Arms* (1933).

[3] Interview with Frank Hardie.

Most of the pacifists who retreated towards *pacificism* when they developed doubts about the efficacy of pacifism as a means of preventing war had, however, progressed straight to internationalism. Yet, although they had thus become aware of the important difference of principle between pacifism and internationalism (and had avoided confusing the issue by a flirtation with war-resistance), they failed to make the distinction as crystal-clear as they might have done. They did so for a variety of reasons ranging from sheer confusion to a reluctance to admit personal inconsistency: as can be seen in the case of three pacifists converted to emotional humanitarian pacifism in 1931–2, Joad, Nichols, and Storm Jameson, and also of two of the peace movement's elder statesmen, Allen and Angell.

In his speech to the Oxford Union, Joad had declared his faith in world government as an ultimate ideal, but had urged unilateral disarmament and non-violence as the best short-term policy. When the press furore started, he defended his position with characteristic insouciance, musing rhetorically in the *Daily Herald* of 20 February 1933: 'We have promised to renounce war in the future. Why, then this hullabaloo because young men take our promise seriously by promising in their turn to refuse to fight?' After the defeat of the expunging attempt on 2 March he wrote in similar vein: 'I and those who voted with me happen to take the view that the best way to ensure peace is to refuse in any circumstances to make war';[1] and in his contribution to *Peace* for April 1933 he reaffirmed his position at greater length:

The biggest step for peace which could be taken in 1933 would be the inauguration of an intensive campaign to induce the maximum number of young people to announce their refusal to fight in any war between nations. The response to the direct individual appeal not to fight is at the moment overwhelming. Say simply: if you want to stop wars, refuse to fight in them and you will be staggered at the response.

However, during April 1933, Joad began for the first time to acknowledge the practical limitations of pacifism. Previously most of his intellectual efforts had been devoted

[1] C. E. M. Joad, *The Oxford Resolution* (1933), p. 5 (reprinted from the *Sunday Referee*, 5 Mar. 1933).

simply to emphasizing the horror of war. Probably the most
effective part of his 'King and Country' speech had been
where he had made great play with the fact that he had
attended a similar debate shortly before the Great War
and that only a few months later his best friend 'had hung
on barbed wire with his entrails hanging out for twenty-
four hours, screaming to be put out of his agony'.[1] Similarly,
one of his newspaper articles had been largely spent on the
stock argument that the next war would be even more
horrifying:

The next war will not see young men fighting young men; it will see
men poisoning women with bacteria, choking men with gas; it will
see children retching out their insides in the convulsion produced by
the inhalation of mustard and chlorine . . . A thousand aeroplanes
would bomb London to pieces in a few hours and plague and famine
would complete the work done by bacteria and explosives.[2]

Concentrating as it did on building up hatred of war, Joad's
pacifism was, as his critics pointed out, 'open to the charge
normally levelled against the War Office—that is always being
prepared for the last war'.[3] As another critic of Joad and his
followers, J. L. Garvin, put it: 'They seem to think of conscientious objection en masse. In the air age the notion is
hopelessly antiquated.'[4]

Such criticism forced Joad to modify his position. In
Peace for May 1933 he admitted that conscientious objectors
had been numerically insignificant in the Great War and that
even if as many as 25 per cent of all those who had endorsed
the Oxford resolution in all the student Unions at which it
had been debated actually refused to fight, it would do no
more than embarrass the Government since 'until more than
50 per cent of the young men in all European countries are
of the same mind, this method alone cannot be trusted to
prevent war. For my part I think it useless to urge it alone.
The ways of preventing war are as numerous as the causes
which produce it.'

The way Joad favoured was internationalism: he advocated

[1] Oxford Mail, 10 Feb. 1933.
[2] Joad, The Oxford Resolution, p. 7.
[3] Gerald Gould, 'The Pacifist's Dilemma', NS, 28 Oct. 1933, p. 506.
[4] Observer, 26 Feb. 1933.

an international army, and during the Abyssinia crisis was prepared to endorse the application of sanctions by the League. But, instead of abandoning pacifism, he insisted that he himself would be conscientiously unable to serve even in an international force (and in the later thirties, when the internationalist cause seemed dead, he returned to a position of outright pacifism which he sustained until his total recantation in 1940). In the terminology of this study this can be explained as simply a change of orientation from non-violence to collaboration; but to contemporaries it was confusing and even Joad found it hard to justify.[1]

Nichols was prepared much sooner to admit his views were changing, but found himself a prisoner of his 1932 reputation as the most extreme of pacifists. As late as December of that year he was still insisting to Lord Davies that, while accepting international government as an ideal, the immediate need was 'to bring home to the authorities the fact that there really is a far greater body of strong pacifist opinion than they imagine'.[2] He was conscious, however, that his pacifism rested merely on revulsion at war and suspicion of the Government, and it was to explore its more positive implications that he set out, early in 1933, to write *Cry Havoc!* It was because he was in Geneva pursuing research for this book that he had rejected the invitation to speak at the 'King and Country' debate. This visit was described in the book, along with his experiences of visiting an arms factory, testing a gas mask, and holding discussions on war prevention with such contrasting thinkers as Robert Mennell, Francis Yeats-Brown, G. D. H. Cole and Sir Arthur Salter. While working on *Cry Havoc!* he made a resolution, recorded in *Peace* for April 1933, 'that I would make one pacifist a day . . . cannot every citizen do the same? . . . But it is a full time job.' When the book appeared in July 1933—predicting another world war within a year[3]—it became probably the best-selling anti-war tract of the thirties. The author's technique both for generating emotional heat and for reflecting the bafflement of the man in the street at the range of conflicting views

[1] See below, p. 160.
[2] Nichols to Davies, 8 Dec. 1932, New Commonwealth files, D.D.
[3] Beverley Nichols, *Cry Havoc!* (1933), p. 237.

that had suddenly emerged on what caused war was shrewdly dissected by the *Spectator*:

He often uses the language of hysteria; almost every sentence is in implied italics, and might be appropriately ended by a mark of exclamation. This is not so much a book as a scream . . . All this is, no doubt, entirely deliberate. Moreover, if more than two sentences of the book are linked by a logical chain of thought Mr. Nichols apologises profusely.[1]

Canon Raven exercised a fellow pacifist's privilege of being even blunter. 'To read even so sincere and passionate a *cri du cœur* as Mr. Beverley Nichols's *Cry Havoc!*', he argued the following year, 'is to be constantly reminded of the neurosis from which he is manifestly suffering.'[2]

But the process of writing the book had already led Nichols to realize that his emotional pacifism had been ill-thought-out. Two-thirds of the way through, he acknowledged: 'I began this book by swearing that I wouldn't fight. That oath was broken. I now seem to have committed myself to serving in an international army.'[3] By the end of the book he had not only confirmed this interim conclusion but had indicated that his change of view was only partly because he had discovered the merits of internationalism in the course of his Genevan trip; it owed as much to his realization that to expect pacifism to be positively effective, as he had formerly done, was to adopt the non-violent orientation. In the open letter to a supporter of the 'King and Country' resolution with which *Cry Havoc!* ended, Nichols wrote:

If you have read this book, you will realise that, though in theory I am for peace at any price, I am not absolutely certain that the theory will work . . . What I am getting at is this . . . the policy you tell me most of you really voted for, in that Oxford resolution, was the policy of passive resistance.[4]

And, asked to endorse this policy as the most practical way of dealing with a growing risk of aggression, Nichols found himself unable to do so.

It was symptomatic of the intellectual confusion prevailing

---

[1] *Spectator*, 4 Aug. 1933, p. 165.
[2] Raven, *Obsolete?*, p. 40.
[3] Nichols, *Cry Havoc!*, p. 165.
[4] Ibid., p. 242.

in 1933 that, though the book thus explicitly preferred internationalism to pacifism, it was almost universally regarded
as an extreme pacifist statement: even its publisher em-
blazoned 'Never, in any circumstances, to fight for King and
Country' across its dust-jacket.[1] In consequence, it contributed less than it should have done to the clarification of
public thinking, the need for which can be judged from even
Storm Jameson's inability to decide where she stood once
her erstwhile pacifist certainties had deserted her. As she
later recalled:

For some years after 1933 I lived in equivocal amity with pacifists
and combative supporters of the League of Nations, adjusting my
feelings, in good and bad faith, to the person I happened to be with.
I swayed between the two like a tightrope walker. My only immovable
conviction was my loathing of war.[2]

She further hedged her bets by simultaneously endorsing
the war-resistance policies of the B.A.-W.M. through one
of its offshoots, the Writers' Anti-War Council.

This growing awareness that, whatever should be set in its
place, pacifism was not the best instrument for containing
aggression was also driven home by the leading speakers
at the National Peace Congress held at Oxford on 7–10 July
1933—although here again their reluctance actually to abandon their claim to be pacifists spoiled the clarity of their
message. The Congress was the first since 1930 of what had
formerly been annual events organized by the National Peace
Council, and was to be the most important of the inter-war
period; as the *New Statesman* commented: 'It was not surprising to find the National Peace Congress better attended
than any of its predecessors. It is fear of war that makes
people interested in peace, and it is only in the last year that
people have become afraid.'[3] Its highlight was the return to
active efforts to influence the peace movement of two of its
veteran peace campaigners, both of whom had recently been
honoured and both of whom had recently undergone considerable changes of outlook: Clifford Allen, since 1932 Lord
Allen of Hurtwood; and Sir Norman Angell, knighted in 1931.

[1] Nichols, *All*, p. 221.
[2] Jameson, *Journey*, i, p. 326.
[3] *NS*, 15 July 1933, p. 63.

In a carefully prepared but impassioned speech aimed at pacifist opinion, Allen expressed the fears about European security which, in stark contrast to both his Great War pacifism and his subsequent detachment from European affairs, had been preoccupying him since late the previous year:

The world is crying out for security, law and order. This need must be satisfied now and not postponed until we have had time to change the whole outlook of mankind. Its satisfaction involves not only disarmament, but the setting up of a machinery of government equipped with at least some of the judicial and police powers that we have conferred on our national governments. The Peace Movement, however, hesitates to agree to this because of a doctrine called Pacifism.

He then confronted the Congress with the conclusion at which he had first arrived (although he did not mention this fact) sixteen years before when, as an absolutist conscientious objector, he became aware of the political futility of his position:

I submit to you that Pacifism is not and never can be a political method so long as it is chiefly concerned with abstaining from the use of force . . . You can, of course, *define* Pacifism by a reference to force, but you cannot thereby save the world from the use of force . . . You must cease taking part in practical affairs and go instead into the wilderness as an educator of opinion or as a religious evangelist . . . Either therefore insist upon believing in Pacifism as something measured by the use of force and go out of politics, or define Pacifism as something emphasising the power of reason and stay in politics.[1]

Allen's recommendation that the pacifists of 1933 should accept the minimum of internationally-controlled force necessary to provide the security essential for international peace was strongly supported by Angell. In marked contrast both to the isolationism he had espoused during his U.D.C. days, and to the war-resistance views to which he had paid occasional lip-service during an unhappy excursion into I.L.P. politics in the twenties, Angell endorsed Allen's new involvement in the European situation. The only difference was that, instead of stressing the guiding principles of reason, Angell preferred to justify his change of approach by his doctrine of the lesser evil. Though he professed to accept, like Allen, that the arguments for non-resistance were 'logically and intellectually, the strongest case of all', they were also

---

[1] Gooch (ed.), *In Pursuit*, pp. 16, 18–19.

'the least likely to be accepted by any great nation; or to enter the realm of practical politics.' In practice, therefore, he argued: 'The choice is between an armed anarchy and an armed society. Both are evil. But I suggest that the armed society is less evil; that a good society, though armed, is on the way to becoming an unarmed one . . . '.[1]

Speaking with one voice, two of the peace movement's leading veterans had thus produced classic statements of the distinction between pacifism and *pacificism*; but each had somewhat pulled his punches by refusing to abandon his claim still to be a pacifist in his private beliefs. In Allen's case, as a former absolutist, this at least had the logic of personal consistency in his favour; his change of emphasis could be analysed as a simple change from a sectarian to a collaborative orientation. But Angell's claim to be a pacifist ('I am a non-resister and would be prepared to vote for uni-lateral disarmament irrespective of what other men do', as he expressed it in *Peace* for May 1933) was more puzzling because it did not tally with his past record, which had been consistently *pacificist*; indeed, his autobiography was to make no mention of his ever having been a pacifist. There seem to be two explanations for Angell's apparent mis-representation of his true position. The first was that his venture into left-wing politics (which, despite becoming a Labour M.P. in 1929, he admitted to have been a mistake)[2] taught him the tactic of exaggerating his own radicialism when trying to moderate the ideological enthusiasms of his political associates. The second was that until the mid-thirties the key to his real views was still the unadulterated Cobdenite *pacificism* he had preached in *The Great Illusion*, so that he really believed that the difference between pacifism and support for sanctions in a last resort would, in practice, be almost negligible. Asked in 1933 to frame a definition of pacifism he acknowledged that the 'tendency to divide organised effort to secure peace into two categories of "paci-fist" and "internationalist" seems to be a growing one'; but he professed to doubt 'whether there is . . . in truth any

[1] Ibid., pp. 30, 42.
[2] Sir Norman Angell, *After All* (1951), p. 227.

fundamental conflict of principle at all'.[1] Similarly, at the Oxford congress he insisted that it was perfectly consistent for a member of the L.N.U. to be also a member of the N.M.W.M. or of a Christian pacifist society.[2] This attitude contrasted with the outspoken criticisms of pacifism for which he became known after 1936 when, like all who remained loyal to the League, he found himself advocating what was, in effect, a conventional defence policy of rearmament and alliance. His position in 1933 showed that the gulf between pacifism and *pacificism* had become appreciable but was not yet seen to be unbridgeable.

(iii) Semantics

With both these concepts in circulation, and only partially differentiated, the confusion surrounding the meaning of the word 'pacifism' throughout 1933 was considerable, although by the end of the year a measure of clarification had been achieved. Its new, more precise, meaning was far more commonly used than previously: appropriately *The Times* introduced 'pacifism' for the first time as a separate entry in its Index in the volume covering the third quarter of that year. But the older, vaguer, meaning still remained in use: when the word made its first appearance in the full *Oxford English Dictionary*, in the Supplement published in 1933, it was still defined in this *pacificist* sense. The two meanings were, moreover, in clear rivalry. Thus Vyvyan Adams, the leading Conservative campaigner for disarmament in the Commons, was troubled by a letter from Frank Hardie which described him, in passing, as a pacifist. Adams felt moved to reply on 12 June 1933:

I am . . . sorry that you say I am a 'pacifist'. Labels are terribly dangerous things. For example, a vast number of people quite erroneously identify the word pacifist and conscientious objector. If pacifist means a friend of peace and an enemy of war, I am one. But if it means a conscientious objector, I am not a pacifist.[3]

Adams preferred the wider sense of the word, but was

[1] Cited in Louis R. Bisceglia, 'Norman Angell and the "Pacifist" Muddle; *Bulletin of Institute of Historical Research*, May 1972, p. 109.

[2] Gooch (ed.), *In Pursuit*, pp. 43-4.

[3] Adams to Hardie, 12 June 1933, F.H.

becoming aware of the need to recognize that two quite different meanings existed; on 8 August 1933 he drafted a letter to *The Times* intended to make this point:

The hideous word 'Pacifist' is often the delight of the *ex parte* controversialist. It begins with an expectorative mute and contains two hisses . . . It commonly has two interpretations. It is frequently identified with 'Conscientious Objector' . . . The second connotation is 'one who regards war as the greatest calamity which can overtake mankind'.[1]

Whereas Adams, a *pacificist*, disliked the narrowing of the word's meaning, pacifists were critical of what they regarded as its continuing dilution. The Revd A. D. Belden argued in *Peace* for August 1933:

One of the ways in which the Devil defeats the idealist is by stealing his vocabulary. Take the word 'Pacifist'. Originally used to designate the Quaker non-combatant and the Tolstoyan non-resister, it is today insolently stolen by American admirals and British generals to describe themselves as they plead for adequate resources of guns and planes and poison gas 'purely for national defence'.

Etymologically, Belden was wrong: the word had not been originally used exclusively for non-resisters. Yet he was right in so far as the word was often inappropriately arrogated by statesmen who, in the emotional climate of the early thirties, were afraid of being branded as militarists. Churchill satirized this trend when in July 1934 he described MacDonald and Baldwin as 'these world famed pacifist Ministers—I use the term in order to put myself in harmony with modern modes of thought and because it is the greatest compliment that can be paid'.[2] But, as the decade wore on, the use of pacifism in this wider sense became less acceptable. By the autumn of 1934, when the meaning of the word was aired for the first time in the L.N.U.'s journal *Headway*, a senior and long-serving staff-member, discovering to his surprise what the *Oxford English Dictionary* definition was, could confidently assert: 'The definition of a "pacifist" is one who is desirous of peace at practically any price; one who is probably a conscientious objector, and who disapproves of military service.'[3]

---

[1] Draft letter dated 8 Aug. 1933, Adams Papers.
[2] 292 H.C. Deb. col. 2373 (30 July 1934).
[3] Col. H. F. T. Fisher, *Headway*, Nov. 1934.

Well before the end of the decade the *O.E.D.* definition was regarded as deliberately obfuscating. Thus, when in February 1938 Wickham Steed claimed during a radio discussion to be a pacifist because he was working to eradicate war, he merely provoked immediate incredulity ('I beg your pardon. But *you* a pacifist?'[1]) from his interlocutor, Ponsonby; and, reporting on the National Peace Congress at Bristol a few months later, Kingsley Martin, whose own usage on the point had formerly not been very precise, noted critically: 'Many advocates of collective security still like to be called "Pacifists". The word confuses the issue.'[2]

The point after which this old usage could be considered wilfully archaic was 1936, when an important clarification of public thinking took place; but 1933 marked the first general awareness that it had outlived its usefulness. As Frank Hardie was observing in the columns of the *New Statesman*:

In the sense of preferring peace to war, we are all pacifists now. But that kind of pacifism is not enough. There would be less confusion if the word 'pacifist' were always to be taken to mean one who, on account of certain principles, philosophical or religious, will, in no circumstances whatever, take part in war.[3]

During 1933 there had been considerable progress towards accepting this view and understanding the distinction between pacifism and *pacificism*; but the next two years were to show that much remained to be clarified.

[1] *Listener*, 16 Feb. 1938, p. 341.
[2] *NS*, 4 June 1938, p. 946.
[3] *NS*, 18 Nov. 1933, p. 630, replying to 11 Nov., p. 580; he made the same point in Foot *et al, Young Oxford*, pp. 169-70.

9

PACIFIST INTERNATIONALISM, 1934-5

After the upsurge of pacifism and war-resistance during 1933 had subsided, the peace movement began at last to polarize over the central but long-evaded question of whether or not a threat of force, such as sanctions applied through the League, was essential to preserve peace. Only a small, albeit articulate and dedicated, minority opted for pacifism, while the majority accepted the need for some form of deterrent. In consequence internationalism came into its own in 1934 and reached a peak of popularity the following year: during this time the Labour Party committed itself to what by the spring of 1935 was generally known as collective security; and the Peace Ballot seemed to show considerable public support for the idea.

But, although a considerable clarification of peace thinking did thus take place in 1934-5, it was less thoroughgoing than sometimes suggested. Collective security was commonly assumed to be achievable without the risk of military entanglement. Thus although some pacifists—notably Sheppard, who appealed in the national press on 16 October 1934 for support for his absolutist 'peace pledge'—were starting to recognize the conflict between pacifism and *pacificism*, most were so reluctant to make a clean break that the P.P.U. was not set up until nineteen months after Sheppard's letter. The practical steps taken during 1934-5 towards the launching of an independent pacifist movement will be reserved until the following chapter. What will here be analysed is pacifist thinking during a period in which, despite increased recognition of the distinctiveness of pacifist ideas, a majority of pacifists were engaged in a rearguard action to prevent pacifism and internationalism finally parting company. The critique they put forward, best described as pacifist internationalism, was characterized by two beliefs. The first, most widely voiced in 1934, was that the main priority for pacifists was to expose conventional patriotism (including what was interpreted as its most extreme manifestation, fascism) because it culturally conditioned nations to go to war unnecessarily—a conditioning described by its most popular critic as the 'War Convention'. The second, which tended to replace it, was that, if aggression nevertheless occurred, pacifists were justified in supporting certain coercive *pacificist* measures even though as individuals they were conscientiously debarred from assisting directly: in other words they were starting, in face of the growing support for sanctions, to become self-conscious about the collaborative orientation. This was particularly true of certain Christian intellectuals, whose attempts to justify their collaboration were part of a wider attempt to refine the Christian pacifist position, which revealed with unprecedented clarity the extent to which that position depended on liberal assumptions both in theology and politics.

(i) The War Convention

In 1933 many pacifists had discovered that they had been indulging their hatred of war when they should have been analysing its cause. Attempting to remedy this a majority of former pacifists diagnosed the cause to be nationalist pressures: Nichols, for example, had asserted in *Cry Havoc!* that 'the generic name for all these poisonous germs which cause war is . . . patriotism.'[1] This view swept through the peace movement (except for the minority loyal to the alternative view that capitalism caused war). 'The first cause of war is religion . . . this religion of patriotism', wrote George Catlin, one of the contributors to a book of essays, edited anonymously by Storm Jameson and published in 1934, which propounded this theme with remarkable uniformity;[2] while Leyton Richards was among many others also arguing that 'the real enemy of world peace' was the 'amalgam of

---

[1] Nichols, *Cry Havoc!*, p. 209.
[2] G. E. G. Catlin, 'The Roots of War', in Storm Jameson (ed.), *The Challenge to Death* (1934), pp. 21, 39. The other contributors included Vera Brittain, Vernon Bartlett, J. B. Priestley, Rebecca West, Winifred Holtby, Mary Agnes Hamilton, Julian Huxley, Ivor Brown, and Philip Noel Baker.

tribal instincts and traditions and historic memories and sentimental attachments and unthinking loyalties' called nationalism.[1]

By far the most famous statement of this cultural critique of the causation of war was by a writer formerly known only for his humorous writings, A. A. Milne. As already mentioned, Milne had first been moved to tackle this subject by the 'King and Country' controversy of February 1933; and five months later he began to develop his ideas in book form. This process took him nearly a year and it was not until September 1934 that *Peace With Honour* appeared. When it did it soon began to repeat the success of *Cry Havoc!*, thanks both to Milne's technique as a professional writer—it was, according to one reviewer, 'brilliantly written in so straightforward a way that Pooh, though a bear of very little brain, could not err therein'[2]—and to his experience as a propagandist in the War Office during the Great War.[3] Its argument was summed up in the sub-title, 'An Inquiry into the War Convention', and in the syllogism: 'When a nation talks of its honour it means its prestige. National prestige is a reputation for the will to war. A nation's honour, then, is measured by a nation's willingness to use force to maintain its reputation as a user of force.'[4] The 'War Convention' was thus a system of values which ensured that governments could declare wars impulsively, secure in the knowledge that their peoples were brainwashed into uncritical support.

This critique attributed considerable potency to even the trivial trappings of jingoism. Although this was an almost constant feature of the peace movement's thinking—even in March 1939 a pacifist could argue: 'The greatest thing we can do for peace is to establish nursery schools for all children aged two to seven'[5]—it seemed particularly marked around 1934. In that year, for instance, Francis Meynell insisted that the immediate task was 'the "debunking" of

[1] Leyton Richards, *The Christian's Contribution to Peace: A Constructive Approach to International Relationships* (1935), pp. 29, 48.

[2] *Rec.*, Nov. 1934, p. 305.

[3] A. A. Milne, *Autobiography* (1939), p. 266.

[4] A. A. Milne, *Peace With Honour: An Inquiry into the War Convention* (1934), pp. 27-8.

[5] *PN*, 17 Mar. 1939.

patriotism', to which end he dwelt on the insidious effects of the 'martial music, the medals, the religious blessing of banners, the uniforms to catch the eye of the child as well as that of the nurse, the picture of the soldier always as a saviour' and other forms of militarist conditioning.[1]

Whether this was a justified or an exaggerated view, however, two opposed deductions could be made from it, depending on whether foreign or domestic nationalism was believed to be the real threat. The first was that, in view of the ease with which an enemy could mobilize its population, an international army was needed to act as a deterrent. The second was that, in view of the strength at home of this patriotic reflex, an immediate refusal to fight in any circumstances was essential. Many were unable to choose (or perceive the difference) between these two deductions—including Storm Jameson, who later admitted that her essay in *Challenge to Death* 'could have been written either by a devout supporter of the League or an out-and-out pacifist'[2]—and the effect of the 'War Convention' critique was thus to obscure the difference between internationalism and pacifism. However, some (including Nichols and Catlin) clearly opted for the former; while others (including Richards, Meynell, and the influential Milne) took the more controversial latter option.

'To renounce aggression is not enough', Milne asserted unequivocally. 'We must also renounce defence.'[3] Implicitly he was putting forward a 'utilitarian' argument for pacifism on the grounds that, since there were never any real issues on which to go to war, there was no gain that could result from fighting rather than from seeking a peaceful settlement free of the suffering and dislocation involved in fighting. Ponsonby had been arguing this explicitly for at least nine years and when, following the appearance of *Peace With Honour*, he sent Milne an example of his work, the latter felt 'ashamed that I had not read it before, and proud that, starting to

---

[1] Francis Meynell, 'What Shall I Do In The Next War?', in Joad (ed.) *Manifesto*, p. 137.

[2] Jameson, *Journey*, i, p. 328.

[3] Milne, *Peace With Honour*, p. 130; in the *News Chronicle*, 23 Feb. 1933, he had argued: 'It is impossible to ensure peace so long as a distinction is drawn between aggressive and defensive war.'

think out war all over again, I have used exactly your arguments, and reached so finally your conclusions.'[1] Unlike Ponsonby, however, Milne had not fully thought out his position. Despite his occasional recognition that the success of pacifism in preventing war depended on similar developments in other countries—as, for example, when he claimed that the best way to prevent war being regarded as 'practical politics' would be to place all the leading statesmen of Europe under a sentence of execution to be carried out if their nation became involved in hostilities[2]—he appeared to believe (since he made no claims for non-violence) that the main threat to peace came from Britain. Indeed his positive recommendations were based explicitly on the assumption 'that Germany is as amenable to reason as Italy (or any other nation), and that, with certain limitations imposed on her by the Versailles Treaty, she is as anxious as any other nation for the securing of peace.'[3]

Faced with Italian acquisitiveness towards Abyssinia Milne was forced to modify his position, conceding that outside Europe aggression might still occur and accepting the case for sanctions against Italy.[4] In 1940 he finally abandoned his pacifism altogether and urged wholehearted support for the war effort; yet even so he insisted that *Peace With Honour* had outlined the correct policy for the time it was written.[5] In retrospect the circumstances of 1934 which caused him to propound and subsequently to defend so extreme a view require some comment. In addition to continued political mistrust of the National Government and reluctance to criticize Germany, two factors explain the willingness of Milne and others to see the main danger to peace as British militarism: continued jitteriness about the danger of an arms race as a result of Germany's walk-out from Geneva in October 1933; and a misunderstanding of the threat posed by fascism.

While any hope still remained that the Disarmament Conference could be revived, the peace movement was

[1] Milne to Ponsonby, 29 Dec. 1934, A.P.
[2] Milne, *Peace*, pp. 81–4.
[3] Ibid., p. 144.
[4] See the preface dated 23 Sept. 1935 to *Peace With Honour* (5th edn., 1935).
[5] A. A. Milne, *War With Honour* (1940), pp. 11–13.

outraged by any attempt to return to a conventional defence policy, which it assumed to be motivated by reactionary patriotism. For example, the Tory loser at East Fulham had, as Baldwin later complained in the speech which made the by-election notorious, been 'mobbed' merely because he had 'made a most guarded reference to the question of defence.'[1] That Baldwin's complaint was in large part justified can be judged from the emotive maiden speech in the Commons by the Labour victor, John Wilmot, in which he claimed, in all apparent sincerity, that no distinction could be drawn between the Government's policy and that of Lord Rothermere's *Daily Mail*, which, campaigning for a massive increase in the air force, could legitimately be termed patriotic (and even militarist) but which Wilmot described tendentiously as 'the principal organ, which represents—so nearly, as a rule—the opinions of the government.'[2] In such an atmosphere (which contrasts with that obtaining four or so years later when public discussion of pacifism was conducted in a more dispassionate fashion), to express doubts about disarmament was to risk having one's motives impugned—as was discovered, for example, by two Oxford dons. The historian Llewellyn Woodward later indignantly remembered that 'once in those years after 1933 I was told point-blank that I was "against the cause of righteousness"' for opposing disarmament;[3] while the economist R. F. Harrod, when even as late as the 1935 general election campaign he told the Labour candidate on whose platform he had been speaking that he could no longer believe that Hitler and Mussolini would disarm even if Britain showed the way, was greeted with the cry: 'Oh, Roy . . . have you lost all your idealism?'[4] This rhetorical hegemony was, moreover, self-reinforcing: those prepared to call for rearmament tended to be more extreme in their views and more combative in temperament than most who had private doubts about the peace movement's basic assumptions. Thus the one systematic attempt

[1] 317 H.C. Deb. col. 1144 (12 Nov. 1936).
[2] 283 H.C. Deb. col. 983 (29 Nov. 1933).
[3] E. L. Woodward, *Short Journey* (1942), p. 239.
[4] R. F. Harrod, *The Prof: A Personal Memoir of Lord Cherwell* (1959), p. 168.

to refute Nichols's *Cry Havoc!* came from an outspoken admirer of both Mosley and Mussolini, Francis Yeats-Brown. Although his book *Dogs of War!*, which appeared in July 1934, made a case against pacifism which Raven respected and which Nichols himself later admitted to be 'unanswerable',[1] it went on—as befitted the author of an earlier article on this theme in the *Spectator* provocatively entitled 'Why I Believe in War'[2]—to add controversial further arguments based on an overtly fascist preference for 'the dangerous world of the creative will'.[3] This merely reinforced pacifist suspicions that only fascists could reject their views.

It also encouraged pacifists to see fascism as a confirmation of the 'War Convention' thesis rather than a challenge to it: in other words, to see it as itself an extreme manifestation of traditional patriotism, rather than as a distinctive political phenomenon for which an acute and deep-seated national frustration with the international status quo was a necessary (albeit not a sufficient) condition. This meant that during 1933-4 fascism was often regarded as a domestic (rather than a military) danger;[4] and its growth in Britain, which was exaggerated by the peace movement, thus helped rather than hindered pacifism. It was perhaps significant that three of the P.P.U.'s most active future sponsors, Huxley, Vera Brittain, and Storm Jameson, attended Mosley's notorious Olympia meeting of 7 July 1934[5]—as did Sheppard himself, whose outrage with what he witnessed was a major factor in his decision to launch his peace pledge three months later. Many pacifists seem to have believed that their own idealism was a particularly effective means of neutralizing fascism; as the Revd Lewis Maclachlan, a leader of the Methodist Peace Fellowship, put it in April 1934: 'Fascism is a moral disease, dreadfully infections . . . The Christian pacifist will oppose the menace of Fascism by the power of ideas, in which

---

[1] Raven, *Obsolete?*, pp. 39-40; Nichols, *All*, p. 221.

[2] *Spectator*, 30 Dec. 1932, pp. 911-12. For the evolution of Yeats-Brown's views see Ceadel, thesis, pp. 213-4.

[3] F. Yeats-Brown, *Dogs of War!* (1934), pp. 90, 96, 123; see also John Evelyn Wrench, *Francis Yeats-Brown 1886-1944* (1948), pp. 171-2.

[4] See Ceadel, thesis, pp. 212, 215-16.

[5] Brittain, *Testament of Experience*, p. 109.

indeed we have too little faith.'[1] Similarly and also in 1934 Delisle Burns, one of the L.N.U. Executive's leading exponents of the view that sanctions were unnecessary, criticized what he called the 'defence complex' and insisted:

The final attack upon war is not to be made among the politicians and the officials, or by the signing of Treaties, or even by the establishment of new institutions, but by the spiritual and intellectual enlightenment of the Nobodies who have fought all wars and will always have to fight whatever wars may occur.[2]

(ii) Collaborating with sanctions.

Although pacifists never ceased to denounce British jingoism and were even more inclined than were progressives generally to detect creeping fascism in the Government's every air-raid precaution or rearmament scheme, they came to realize— by the end of the international lull which had lasted from the collapse of the Disarmament Conference until Hitler's announcement of a powerful air force in March 1935 and the first signs of Mussolini's preparations for war against Abyssinia over the following months—that Britain was unlikely itself to start the next war. Pacifists had thus to consider fascism and aggressive nationalism as an external danger outside the range of their cultural counter-bombardment.

In 1931–2 a vocal minority had proposed to defeat external threats by non-violence; but after the embarrassing ingenuousness of the Peace Army (and after the accession of Hitler), there had been fewer confident affirmatives to the question with which the General Secretary of the F.o.R. had, in March 1933, bluntly confronted his General Committee: 'Could the Christian, or the pacifist, or anyone else prove that evil could be conquered by good and that the good would work?'[3] As Raven pointed out in 1934: 'It has been left to Mahatma Gandhi . . . to raise doubts about whether the weak things of this world are not even today stronger

[1] Rec., Apr. 1934, pp. 90, 92.

[2] C. Delisle Burns, War—and a changing civilisation (1934), pp. 130–1. Despite the strong resemblance between his views in 1934 and Milne's, Burns was later to make clear that he was not a strict pacifist: see his Civilisation: The Next Step (1938), p. 225.

[3] F.o.R., G.C. 20–1 Mar. 1933. The General Secretary was Percy Bartlett.

than the strong.'[1] Most pacifists adopted, in effect, the same evasive stance as the W.I.L. (which, though *pacificist*, had an influential pacifist minority): urged in July 1935 by two Peace Army veterans, Maude Royden and Crozier, to endorse their plea to the Abyssinians to practice non-violent resistance in the event of any invasion, its Executive resolved 'to send a letter to Dr Royden saying that the Committee was in agreement that peaceful passive resistance was the right answer to threats of aggression but it did not feel it suitable to urge such action on the Abyssinian Government at the present time.'[2] Only with the well-timed publication, shortly before Italy's attack on Abyssinia, of the English edition of Richard B. Gregg's highly influential book *The Power of Non-Violence*, and the endorsement of its arguments by Huxley, Heard, and others shortly to come together within the P.P.U., did non-violence enjoy a new burst of popularity.

The approach still favoured by most pacifists was collaboration with the League movement, which (with the exception of a minority led by Lord Davies and his New Commonwealth Society which wanted an international police force) assumed that economic sanctions would provide an adequate means of coercing an aggressor. The difficulties inherent in both these policies began, however, to trouble pacifists for the first time during 1934-5.

The efficacy of economic pressure had been one of the revelations of the Great War; as a Quaker pacifist enthused in January 1919: 'The power of the economic boycott is simply incalculable.'[3] Yet, as a number of pacifists soon learned for themselves on visits to Germany in the aftermath of the Allied blockade,[4] this power was not automatically humane simply for eschewing actual violence. Did the end— the preservation of peace without resort to military weaponry —justify the means? Few pacifists had ever considered the

---

[1] Raven, *Obsolete?*, p. 161.

[2] W.I.L. Executive, 30 July 1935.

[3] *Friend*, 24 Jan. 1919, pp. 53-4.

[4] See Wellock, *Beaten Track*, p. 45; Victoria de Bunsen, *Charles Roden Buxton: A Memoir* (1948), p. 151; Leah Manning, *A Life for Education* (1971), p. 69; Hughes, *Indomitable Friend*, p. 81; Vera Brittain, *Testament of Friendship: the story of Winifred Holtby* (1940), pp. 147-8.

question. When, therefore, the Manchuria crisis broke some—for example, Wellock—called for 'steady pacifist pressure upon Japan', involving the withdrawal of 'all loans, credits and munitions',[1] but the N.M.W.M.'s National Committee could not agree whether a refusal to unload Japanese ships in the world's ports was compatible with pacifism.[2] Only when the Peace Ballot confronted the whole nation with a blunt inquiry about, amongst other issues, economic sanctions, did the pacifist movement define its attitude systematically.[3] Meeting in August 1934, shortly after the Ballot had first been announced, the Friends' Peace Committee gave a qualified answer: 'Yes, to the extent of refusing all war material and financial aid . . . but not including starvation methods.'[4] This probably reflected the normal pacifist view up to then; but once actual polling began in November 1934 doubts began to be felt whether any economic sanction existed which was mild enough to be acceptable yet also tough enough to be effective. Summing up the debate among pacifists in January 1935 Gerald Bailey, Secretary of the N.P.C., noted considerable opposition to *all* economic sanctions;[5] indicative of the trend in pacifist thinking was Salter's change of heart on this issue in March 1935, when he began to urge a 'no' vote.[6] The final results of the Ballot, declared in June 1935, showed far greater support for economic than for military sanctions among the public at large; but, among the tiny minority who insisted on their ill-publicized right to put 'I take the Christian pacifist position' as their answer, only one in five seem to have found economic measures any more acceptable than military ones.[7] The pacifist conscience had become more exigent; yet it was not until after the

---

[1] *NW*, Mar. 1932; *Manchester Guardian*, 22 Feb. 1932.

[2] N.M.W.M., N.C. 13 Feb. 1932.

[3] See e.g. the discussion in *Manchester Guardian*, Oct.–Nov. 1934, prompted by the Ballot.

[4] F.P.C., 2 Aug. 1934.

[5] *Friend*, 4 Jan. 1935, p. 18.

[6] Brockway, *Bermondsey Story*, pp. 188–9.

[7] Of the 11,640,066 who voted in the Ballot, only 14,169 availed themselves of this option in respect of the question on economic sanctions, and 17,536 in respect of that on military sanctions. Thus of this minute minority only about one in five distinguished between the two types of pressure.

risks involved in economic sanctions sank in during 1936 that it became uncompromising. Thus by May 1937, Carter, who exactly two years previously had been willing to support financial sanctions and a boycott on war materials (though not stronger measures), was refusing to contemplate even the mildest of economic pressure because of its 'coercive significance'.[1]

The same partial progress towards clarification could be detected also in attitudes to the international police force. This proposal had always been inherently ambiguous: if the force was to be set up only *after* (or at the same time as) general disarmament was achieved, then it would in many respects be comparable to a domestic police force; yet, if the force was to be set up in a still armed world in order to provide security as a precondition for disarmament, it would have to be equipped to defeat the most powerful opposition. The initial enthusiasm for the New Commonwealth Society shown by Maude Royden, Sheppard, and others, indicates that pacifists tended to interpret the force only in the former sense; however, once the last hopes for a revival of the Disarmament Conference had died in the spring of 1934, they became increasingly aware that its leading enthusiasts had in mind a very different, 'militarist', conception. This new awareness was propagated by pamphlets with self-explanatory titles such as *Frankenstein and his Monster* and *New Wars For Old*, written in 1934 for the W.I.L. by Mrs Helena Swanwick, a veteran radical campaigner against all types of sanctions whose isolationism (like that, during the Great War, of her former U.D.C. colleague Ramsay MacDonald) was so extreme and emotional as at times to be indistinguishable, even to herself, from pacifism.[2] Yet, although pacifists had in general become aware of the ambivalence of the police force idea, a minority continued to find it confusing and seductive. For example, the N.M.W.M.'s National Committee was told in March 1934 that one of the

[1] Compare his letter, *Manchester Guardian*, 11 May 1935, with his letter to Murray, 3 May 1937, G.M.

[2] Mrs Swanwick opposed unilateral disarmament and was sceptical about non-violence (see *NMW*, Oct. 1923, and H. M. Swanwick, *I Have Been Young* (1935), p. 371). Yet at times she talked as if her opposition to sanctions was a matter of moral principle (see her references to the need for 'a strong ethical faith': *I Have Been Young*, p. 261; see also her *Collective Insecurity* (1937), p. 265).

Movement's leading speakers had been 'completely hazed' at a public meeting by a question about it,[1] even though the N.M.W.M. was officially critical; similarly, when a year later the Southampton Branch of the L.N.U. debated the New Commonwealth's version of the scheme, the 'considerable Pacifist support for the idea' could still be put forward as one of its advantages.[2]

But not all support for the international police force was based on confusion: some of it arose from the deliberate adoption of the collaborative orientation. One of the signs of a reinvigoration of pacifist thinking in 1934 was the realization, particularly among Christians, that, while an international force was in no sense a pacifist measure and pacifists could not themselves serve in it, it was none the less preferable in political terms to armed anarchy. For example, when in January 1934 the Friends' Peace Committee discussed the force, it refused to endorse it but acknowledged that it might be a step towards world peace.[3] Similarly, after a number of prominent members of the N.M.W.M. and the Society of Friends had, in *Peace* for March 1934, outlined their objections to 'any attempt to turn the League of Nations into an armed power', eighteen leading Quakers, including Charles Roden Buxton and Bertram Pickard, issued a reply arguing that it was wrong to place obstacles in the way of political leaders and movements struggling 'against the dangerous conception of the absolute sovereignty of the single state'.[4] The issue had been discussed during February and March in a series of articles in the *Friend* and, drawing the threads together, Pickard recognized that a pacifist who shared his views was dividing life into two spheres and applying separate standards in each:

On the one hand, he must attempt to apply, within the relatively narrow orbit of his personal activity, the pacifist principle or method (i.e. the overcoming of the evil will by the good will). On the other hand, having accepted political responsibilities, he must cooperate in forming and executing political judgements which of necessity take

[1] N.M.W.M., N.C., 24 Mar. 1934.
[2] L.N.U. Southampton branch, E.C., 21 May 1935.
[3] F.P.C., 4 Jan. 1934.
[4] *Rec.*, May 1934, pp. 139–40.

the form of compromises between opinions and attitudes of which his is only one.[1]

The same distinction was developed more systematically by Leyton Richards in his book *The Christian's Contribution to Peace*, which, completed in November 1934 and published the following January, was intended 'to show how personal pacifism is related to world peace in a political sense.' In it Richards emphasized for the first time 'the difference between Christian pacifism and the desire for international peace', and the fact that to achieve the latter

it may be necessary to accept half a loaf rather than no bread at all; for in this matter the Christian must work with others who do not share his personal faith, and he must therefore be willing to go with them as far as they will go with him.[2]

This was a marked change of emphasis from his former unwillingness to make any compromises; as late as January 1932 he had informed David Davies that, while he readily admitted that his proposals 'may be the next step along which an imperfect world will go', he himself was not prepared to 'urge that "next step" when I think I know a better one'.[3] By 1934, however, he had modified this view to the extent of recognizing that 'an International Police Force equipped for military operations . . . would be a striking and significant step towards the realisation of a Christian world order.'[4]

Raven was in broad agreement. His own, more recent, conversion to pacifism had occurred at the high tide of *pacificist* optimism in 1930, and it was to this, rather than to pacifism itself, that he looked for a practical way of preventing war in the shorter term. In *Reconciliation* in January 1934 he had shocked other pacifists by his assertion that 'mere abstention will not suffice to make war impossible.'[5] Although confident that a strong pacifist movement could have a beneficial political impact, he questioned the value of premature

[1] *Friend*, 30 Mar. 1934, p. 270.

[2] Richards, *Christian's Contribution*, pp. 7, 9.

[3] Richards to Davies, 2 Jan. 1932, D.D.

[4] Richards, *Christian's Contribution*, p. 142. For this change of view also compare the revised (1935) edition of his *Christian's Alternative to War*, p. 30, with the original (1929) edition, p. 36.

[5] *Rec.*, Jan. 1934, pp. 4-5.

disarmament, particularly in situations such as the North-
Western frontier of India.[1] He thus supported the L.N.U.,[2]
and insisted: 'While refusing to submit our own consciences
to the dictates of political common sense or to make the
Church an appendage of the League of Nations, it ought
surely to be possible for Christians to acquiesce in the inter-
nationalisation of armed force while advocating and developing
another way of reconciliation.'[3]

In the period between the collapse of the Disarmament
Conference and the Abyssinia crisis, pacifists thus came self-
consciously and articulately to profess the collaborative
orientation which most pacifists had unthinkingly adopted
for nearly a century. Admitting to different standards of
behaviour in the personal and political spheres was, however,
easier than *justifying* the difference—as an early attempt by
Joad was to show. Having recently come to support internationalism while still proclaiming himself a pacifist, he was
driven by attacks on pacifism in the *New Statesman* in
November 1933 to defend his position. In doing so he asked
himself 'by what logic . . . does the pacifist, conceding the
occasional legitimacy of force in theory, himself refuse to
fight in practice?' His answer proceeded by analogy with the
average citizen's reluctance to be a policeman, to slaughter
sheep, or to take on other uncongenial or onerous jobs
which were nevertheless necessary for social existence: 'The
whole of civilised society is indeed based on the assumption
that we may legitimately employ or appoint other people to
carry out for us functions which we would not or could not
carry out for ourselves.'[4] This argument, however, confused
objections to socially necessary jobs because they were of a
vocational, specialized, or low-status kind, with objections
based on conscientious grounds. What Joad was putting forward was, in effect, elitist quasi-pacifism: he seemed to be
claiming exemption from fighting for a cause he knew to be
right on the grounds that his refined sensibility would find
the experience more distressing than would an ordinary

[1] Raven, *Obsolete?*, pp. 153–4.
[2] Dillistone, *Raven*, p. 219.
[3] Raven, *Obsolete?*, pp. 182–3.
[4] *NS*, 25 Nov. 1933, p. 653.

citizen. Even less satisfactory, however, was the attempt made by a contributor to *Reconciliation* in May 1934 to solve this problem by combining complacency about mild sanctions with overt dishonesty:

I am quite sure that we have to make up our minds about this in a very realistic way and have jotted down one or two things that have occurred to me lately . . . I suggest—tentatively, I admit—that pacifists should urge their Government to pledge the country up to the hilt in support of the League idea. The fact that 'up to the hilt' means to the Government and to all non-pacifists 'military measures' and does not mean that to us, does not matter from a practical point of view, for firstly, war to us is so insane and immoral that no pledge could be looked upon as binding us to it, and secondly, in actual practice there would be so many previous steps—all of them much more effective than war—in the support of the League before the question of war became a live issue, that it is quite literally inconceivable in real politics that the League should think of declaring war upon an enemy state.[1]

When, also in 1934 and after ten years during which there had (as Raven admitted) 'been very little effort to think out the issue',[2] the leaders of Christian pacifist thought began to give it their attention, they too found it fraught with pitfalls. For example, Leyton Richards seemed concerned mainly to convince his readers—and, as a recent convert to supporting sanctions as a second best, perhaps also himself—that these could be mild enough not to outrage the pacifist conscience. He thus argued that, since 'a graduated scale of pressure' could be applied, it was 'by no means certain . . . that the military power of an International Police Force would ever be called into action'; indeed, the authority of such a force would 'lie not so much in the armed sanctions at its disposal as in the public opinion by which it was directed and upheld', and even if armed sanctions proved unavoidable, the evacuation of civilian populations would ensure that only property, rather than life, would suffer.[3]

But this was to make a case for *pacificism* only: it failed to explain why, in view of the benign nature of sanctions as he had depicted them, he nevertheless insisted that a pacifist 'cannot himself enlist in an International Police Force'.

---

[1] R. E. Fenn, 'The Pacifist and the League of Nations', *Rec.*, 1934, pp. 118-19.

[2] Raven, *Obsolete?*, p. 24.

[3] Richards, *Christian's Contribution*, pp. 137-8, 143.

Richards recognized, however, that he was applying a double standard and defended it by arguing that a pacifist 'accepts Courts of Law, for instance, even though they may resort on occasion to capital punishment'.[1] But this analogy raised its own difficulties. If his argument was that, albeit reluctantly, he accepted the legitimacy of capital punishment, then he was implying that the taking of life by an international force was legitimate in the same way. As earlier discussed,[2] however, any analogy with the domestic judicial system was relevant only for a full world state; what Richards and other pacifists failed to consider until the Abyssinia crisis was upon them was how near to this ideal an international organization had to be for its judicial and punitive processes to be acceptable. Since pacifists advocated an international force as a practical measure it was relevant to ask whether they were prepared to accept the right of the existing League, based as it was largely on the British and French conception of what a just international order was, to punish Germany or Italy for challenging it.

If on the other hand Richards was asserting that he did not personally accept the legitimacy of capital punishment, yet was not prepared to withdraw his co-operation from the whole of the judicial system simply because of this, then he was defending the right of the conscientious objector to make compromises in practice over relative inessentials. But even if this principle is accepted, it has drawbacks if used as a justification for supporting a new international police force. For one thing, to accept existing blemishes is not the same as to create new ones. For another, to refuse to let a minor blemish such as capital punishment blind one to the overall merits of a legal system like the British which rests very largely on consent backed up by humane punishments is very different from supporting an international judicial system in which the 'blemish'—its power to take life—was clearly (for all Richards's optimism about sanctions) completely indispensable to the system's successful functioning and would remain so for the foreseeable future.

Richards's formal attempts to justify the collaborative

[1] Ibid., p. 142.
[2] See above, pp. 11-12.

orientation were thus, like those of the few other pacifists who had attempted this, not wholly successful. All showed an enthusiasm for *pacificism* which made it all the harder to explain why they themselves could not personally take part. But whereas socialist and humanitarian pacifists seemed to have no explanation to offer, Christian pacifists were beginning to develop one. In the case of Richards it was only implicit in his writing; but it was made explicit during 1934 by Canon Raven whose first attempt systematically to expound his pacifism was also the first Christian pacifist work to make clear the extent to which all Christian pacifists, consciously or unconsciously, took a liberal view of theology not acceptable to all Christians.

(iii) Christian Liberalism

Pacifist Christians (the vast majority of whom were, of course, Protestants)[1] viewed Creation optimistically: they saw man not as irredeemably sinful but as capable of growing in Grace, and the world as capable of responding to Love. This was true even of the sectarian pacifists of the F.o.R., although these did not expect the growth of Christian understanding to be anything but slow and painful and were very sceptical about the likelihood of immediate progress in the political sphere. The majority of Christian pacifists, however—particularly after the growing signs of public anti-war feeling in the late twenties—held an evangelical faith that an important moral awakening could be generated by the Churches within society as it stood and that this could have a significant political effect. By 1929, for example, Richards could assert that if the Churches refused in a 'thoroughgoing and absolute fashion' to endorse war, governments would 'speedily discover other and better ways of dealing with international disputes than by the customary threat of armed force';[2] while Raven later confessed to having entertained

---

[1] Of the pacifists mentioned in this book only W. E. Orchard (who does not seem to have remained a pacifist after becoming a Catholic), Francis Meynell (who abandoned pacifism in 1935) and Eric Gill were Roman Catholics. The last two were both of radical views (Meynell a Communist and Gill in effect an anarchist) and can be classified as political as much as Christian pacifists.

[2] Richards, *Christian's Alternative*, pp. 143-4.

an 'apocalyptic hope' in the twenties that evangelism could produce signs even of a 'Second Coming'.[1]

This optimism reflected a liberal interpretation of both theology and politics. In theological terms it was an immanentist (rather than a transcendental) view: it presupposed God's presence everywhere within the 'secular' world and refused (in Raven's words) 'to regard the natural order as only the scene or theatre in which the divine drama of redemption is played out', insisting instead 'that the Universe derives its value from the manifestation of deity within it'.[2] This view was implicit in all Christian pacifist writing: for example, in Richards's assertion that the 'authority of Christ' rested 'on the fundamental spiritual likeness between His nature and ours . . . and it is for this reason that our God-given human nature agrees with and responds to the God-like in Him.'[3] Richards seemed unaware that there was any other theological approach (attributing non-pacifism in the Churches merely to worldly compromise): like those of most Christian pacifists his inter-war apologetics always focused on the political prospects for war prevention—joining in the emotional attacks on war in 1929, supporting internationalism in 1935, and endorsing appeasement in 1938[4]— rather than on the theological basis of pacifism.Only when the Second World War forced him to abandon his *pacificist* hopes did he define his personal position: significantly, he then espoused the extreme liberalism of Quaker theology, came to acknowledge that much Christian pacifist writing had been 'dated'[5] by Hitlerism (because it rested on transiently political and not timelessly theological arguments), and set out belatedly to remedy this deficiency by explaining clearly his reasons for deriving pacifism from Christianity. Raven, however—as befitted a theologian who had been elected Dean of Emmanuel College, Cambridge, at the age of twenty-four and who had returned to the University in 1932 as Regius Professor of Divinity—was one of the few

---

[1] Charles Raven, *The Theological Basis of Christian Pacifism* (1952), p. 3.

[2] Raven, *Obsolete?*, p. 155.

[3] Richards, *Christian's Alternative*, p. 58.

[4] See Richards, *Christian's Aternative, Christian's Contribution,* and *The Crisis and World Peace* (S.C.M., 1938), respectively.

[5] Richards, *Christian Pacifism After Two World Wars*, p. ix.

to have done so already in the early thirties, and in the full knowledge that the pacifist view of Christianity was controversial and coming under attack from transcendentalists (who regarded the secular and the sacred as entirely separate and who exalted God as superior to and independent of the universe). Inspired mainly by the eminent Swiss theologian Karl Barth, transcendentalism was increasingly to confront the British pacifist movement in the second half of the thirties, following the translation of Barth's writings and, more important, their popularization by the American social theorist and lapsed pacifist, Reinhold Niebuhr, who came increasingly to dismiss his former colleagues in the American F.o.R. as 'soft Utopians'.[1] Barth and Niebuhr implied that to expect progress in the secular world was to show insufficient humility towards God's mystery. Thus when, as will later be seen,[2] Christian pacifists were forced to focus on the doctrinal justification for their beliefs, they found themselves swimming against the tide of theological fashion.

The expectation that pacifism could inspire a moral crusade rested on a distinctively liberal view of politics too. That Richards was steeped in this tradition was dramatically symbolized by the fact that his mother had died of excitement when the success of her beloved Liberal Party in sweeping Manchester in the 1906 general election proved too much for a weak heart.[3] Raven, a keen amateur naturalist, saw political and spiritual progress in explicitly evolutionary terms: he belonged to the minority current within social-darwinist thought which interpreted the doctrine of survival of the fittest as an argument, not for armed preparedness, but for pacifism since it was clear 'that in the course of human evolution the struggle for existence has become increasingly an effort to achieve moral and spiritual values';[4] pacifism was thus a necessary adaptation to ensure human survival in an era of total war, as well as a step nearer the Christian religious ideal. Their political assumptions became very clear when they addressed themselves to the socialist

---

[1] Cited in Raven, *Theological Basis*, p. 15.
[2] See below, pp. 207-9.
[3] E. R. Richards, *Private Life*, p. 2.
[4] Raven, *Obsolete?*, p. 52.

challenge that pacifists were isolating war by arbitrarily limiting their conscientous objections to a single evil. In 1929 Richards had retorted that

it is not irrational to isolate the problem of war from those other problems and practical difficulties which call for the exercise of coercive force in human relationships. The history of moral achievement suggests that organised evil is eliminated from the common life of man by a succession of attacks in detail rather than a mass attack all along the line.[1]

The historically proven strategy for progress was, he thus insisted, to pick an issue which could become the thin end of a reforming wedge, as had the abolition of slavery which had marked the beginning of a series of humanitarian reforms in the nineteenth century. War was obviously the equivalent issue for the twentieth century; as Raven, also citing the slavery precedent, put it in 1934: it was 'in the campaign against war' that the first blow against 'the evils of competitive capitalism' could be struck.[2]

But even if this liberal domino theory of reform was correct, and the abolition of war was a seminal issue capable of setting off a chain of further social breakthroughs, the analogy with the liberal reforms of the nineteenth century was misleading. For one thing, it was far harder to opt unilaterally out of war than out of the slave trade. For another, the fact that the chain of nineteenth-century progress had failed to eliminate war might have been taken as an indication that it was a more intractable problem than they had supposed. In the event, however, the outbreak of the Great War tended to be treated by pacifists as simply a freak revival of a ritual which had been believed to be already obsolete. For example, four decades after the event Raven was still reminding audiences of his sense of shock when 'in 1914 the unbelievable happened and the world, which to my generation had plainly reached a stage where war was an anachronism and armies a picturesque pageantry, plunged suddenly to destruction'.[3] Yet instead of concluding that he and his contemporaries had been mistaken he reaffirmed (in

[1] Richards, *Christian's Alternative*, p. 58.
[2] Raven, *Obsolete?*, p. 52.
[3] Raven, *Theological Basis*, p. 1.

his 1934 Halley Lectures, significantly entitled *Is War Obsolete?*) an unshaken belief that moral and spiritual progress occurs in history 'step by step as accepted standards are challenged and primitive instincts sublimated, and that in this matter of war we have now reached a point at which it has become a terrible anachronism.'[1]

This Christian liberalism, based on both political and theological assumptions, explains why Raven, Richards, and other Christian pacifists felt able to adopt the collaborative orientation. Their belief in political progress enabled them to accept the *pacificist* argument that measures such as an international police force would be a practical first step in the right direction. But, though they could support it politically, they could not serve in such a force personally because their pacifism was (in Richards's words) 'a matter of personal conviction which admits of no compromise; those who see the will of God in Christ's reaction to evil can "do no other" than try to be faithful to that revelation, whatever the cost to themselves or to any worldly interest.'[2] But, in thus. claiming that personal revelation exempted them from considerations of political logic, they were aware they seemed merely to be elitist quasi-pacifists—as Raven put it, their attitude seemed to be: '80 per cent of you are unchristian, and of course may fight: I am a Christian and I won't.'[3]

To this they had, in effect, two answers. The first was to stress the limitations of revelation. 'Absolute truth is and must remain beyond us . . .', Raven insisted. 'Hence it by no means follows that a judgement valid for me is necessarily valid for another . . . To assume that God's will for me, even if I am confident of its intention, is universally binding, is an act of arrogance.'[4] In this light the pacifist's refusal to fight in international army appeared a question of humility rather than of inconsistency or elitism. Their second answer was to imply that, instead of being wholly parasitic upon *pacificist* attempts to prevent war, they had their own

---

[1] Raven, *Obsolete?*, p. 52.
[2] Richards, *Christian's Contribution*, p. 8.
[3] *Rec.*, Mar. 1934, p. 66.
[4] Raven, *Obsolete?*, p. 86.

practical policy and that, even if a majority rejected it in favour of gradualism, they could still play a constructive complementary role. They were, it must be admitted, vague about how, say, a declaration in favour of pacifism by the Churches in Britain would prevent war: there was little talk about non-violence (as already noted) or appeasement (which did not become fashionable until the second half of 1935 at the earliest). But they sincerely saw themselves as helping to inspire the attack on war by serving as the vanguard of the peace movement in the march of progress to the warless world all believed to be attainable.

Thus during 1934–5 pacifists had begun to see the limitations of explaining war purely as a conditioned jingoist reflex; and most accepted the desirability of collaborating with collective security—some, including Joad, Milne, and Pickard, being prepared to endorse sanctions even during the Abyssinia crisis.[1] A number of pacifists had started to become conscious of the difficulties of this collaborative orientation, though only a few—notably certain leading Christian pacifists— were able to offer a coherent justification for supporting *pacificism* while remaining pacifist; and they did so on the basis of liberal assumptions about theology (which were coming increasingly under attack from their fellow Christians) and about political and international conditions (which were becoming less realistic). Only after 1936, when faith in *pacificist* progress was undermined as it came to be feared that internationalism was a retrograde step which increased the risk of war, could the clarification of pacifist thinking proceed.

[1] See, respectively, *NS*, 9 Nov. 1935, pp. 665–6; Milne, *Peace* (preface to 5th edn.); *Friend*, 18 Oct. 1935, p. 972.

10

THE NEW PACIFIST MOVEMENT, 1934-5

Pacifism's progress during 1934-5 towards setting itself up as an independent movement was, like its progress towards clarifying its ideas, significant yet incomplete. The ailing N.M.W.M. was goaded by the rise of collective security into a revival of activity, but this proved to be a final fling. Of greater long-term significance was the emergence of a pacifist movement within the Churches and the commitment to almost full-time campaigning of the one man, Sheppard, who possessed the charisma to attract not just Christians but also the increasing numbers inspired by humanitarian concern at the prospect of war. Even so, this 'New Pacifism' (as it was often called) was not to achieve its full expression until 1936.

(i) 'Old' Pacifism: the N.M.W.M.

The N.M.W.M.'s decline, which had forced it early in 1933 to abandon the attempt to keep going either its journal or its 'lukewarm' branches, continued into 1934. In March an emergency meeting was told by Allen Skinner that local branch activity in general had become ineffective and that it would be better 'to make the basis of our Movement the organised individual activities of our members on the "Fabian" principle'.[1] This confession of institutional failure reflected the extent to which it had fallen between the two stools of pacifism and revolutionism. Of the strict believers in the former who objected to the latter many had left; yet this had not produced greater doctrinal cohesion since a number of them, seemingly impervious to the new line, remained. The National Committee's policy 'had made little impression on the Movement', Muriel Nichol complained to

[1] N.M.W.M. Federation Secretaries' Conference, 25 Mar. 1934.

the emergency meeting. 'There were still too many points of view in the Movement and we were trying to reconcile them. That was the cause of our ineffectiveness. A pacifism that is to have any edge presupposes the acceptance of socialism.'[1]

By 1934, however, it was hard to make a socialist case for pacifism. With the Labour Party committing itself to internationalism and with the B.A.-W.M. also changing its attitude towards the League (which the Soviet Union joined in September 1934), pacifists found themselves more isolated than ever before from the mainstream of socialist thought. The only strand within the European tradition which remained both socialist and non-violent was the minority one of anarchism. It was not surprising, therefore, that there was increased interest at this time—particularly during and after the W.R.I.'s triennial conference held at Welwyn in 1934—in the ideas of the Dutch anarchist Barthelemy de Ligt.[2] De Ligt appealed to the N.M.W.M. because, unlike 'bourgeois' pacifists, he emphasized 'the importance of not suppressing the impulses to struggle, to conquer, to sacrifice and to rise higher than the self—impulses so typically human—but of sublimating them.'[3] Yet it was significant that his greatest support was to come from P.P.U. mystics such as Aldous Huxley, who contributed the introduction to the English edition of his magnum opus, or R. H. Ward, who later described him as 'a Gandhi of the west'.[4] Those in the N.M.W.M. who most enthusiastically endorsed Mrs Nichol's call for a socialist policy were losing interest in non-violence. Reynolds, for example, could write: 'The oppression of the subject classes and races is worse than war . . . What does death matter to those who have never been suffered to live . . . ? To support the Great Powers and to call it peace is to sell justice to the highest bidder.'[5] Later he was to admit that he and many of his colleagues 'had ceased to be pacifists without

---

[1] Ibid.

[2] De Ligt's *Plan of Campaign Against All War and All Preparation for War*, discussed at Welwyn, was published as a P.P.U. pamphlet in 1939.

[3] Bart. de Ligt, *The Conquest of Violence: An Essay on War and Revolution* (English edn, 1937), pp. 207.

[4] R. H. Ward, *Names and Natures* (1968), p. 150.

[5] *NMW*, Jan. 1935.

clearly recognising the fact';[1] they remained loyal to the Movement, but many rank-and-file members were seduced away by the overt Marxist rhetoric of the B.A.-W.M. The once-thriving Manchester branch (the National Committee was told in September 1934) found

> themselves more or less absorbed, as far as their active membership is concerned, by the activities of the Anti-War Council, which incidentally they were instrumental in forming some eighteen months ago . . . But this has not been the only drain from the branch; there has also been a considerable secession from the Right, arising out of certain fears of a too close collaboration with the B.A.W.M. and also in view of the new economic emphasis of our Movement. For example the Friends have slackened in their support . . . For these several reasons the paper membership has rapidly dropped and barely two dozen out of 200 are now paying their subscriptions regularly . . .[2]

It was not surprising, therefore, that by December Runham Brown was reiterating that the branch system had failed;[3] or that, to save money, Reynolds resigned as General Secretary becoming instead Honorary Joint Secretary on a part-time basis (with an outside job to make up his pay and with an enthusiastic Christian revolutionary, Robert Entwhistle, replacing him without salary).[4]

It was not all retrenchment, however: at the same time the National Committee decided to concentrate the Movement's remaining resources on reviving a national journal, taking as its basis the local newsheet *No More War*, which the enterprising Birmingham Council had launched. This decision was well-timed: the Movement recovered its voice—and seemed, in consequence, to enjoy a brief revival—in January 1935 when growing public discussion of collective security (passionately condemned by Reynolds) and the Peace Ballot (sarcastically parodied by Southall as a questionnaire on temperance organized by the liquor trade)[5] gave it scope for what it enjoyed most: destructive criticism. It was not surprising that some readers of *No More War* 'were greatly disturbed to find in the first number three of the eight pages devoted to thinly-veiled insults by Joseph Southall

---

[1] Reynolds, *My Life*, p. 139.
[2] Memorandum, N.M.W.M., N.C. 8 Sept. 1934.
[3] N.M.W.M., N.C. 1 Dec. 1934.
[4] N.M.W.M., N.C. 9 Feb. 1935.
[5] *NMW*, Jan. 1935.

and Reginald Reynolds against the League of Nations Union, an organisation of which we in common with other members of the N.M.W.M. are members',[1] for the journal seemed to have adopted the deliberately sectarian aim of eliminating all such double membership. Southall thus reaffirmed his determination 'to resist to the last and expose to the uttermost the demon of militarism in all his crafty disguises';[2] and, as the Abyssinia crisis approached, the N.M.W.M.'s leaders became more outspoken in their conviction that 'the supreme triumph of the militarists' was, in Wellock's words, their 'conversion of the Collective Peace System into a Collective War System'.[3] *No More War* even became willing to accept that 'the militarist politician is anxious for peace'[4] in order to impugn the motives of advocates of collective security. By the end of 1935 support for the League had become such an emotive issue that, when a Bradford member informed her local branch she had been invited to join the L.N.U., 'it nearly caused a civil war—feelings ran so high about it!'[5]

However, the Movement was not protesting merely about sanctions. It was contemptuous even of the 1935 National Peace Congress, organized by the N.P.C. which took a neutral line on this question, and yet was aggrieved when its own speakers were not given sufficient chances to be heard—a complaint which drew from an N.P.C. supporter the retort: 'I cannot be surprised that, with the narrow-minded prejudice against peace makers who differ from themselves that so many of the leaders of the "No More War Movement" display, they are not selected to speak from the platform of the Congress.'[6] It was no less critical of the new Christian pacifist movement which, it believed, preached the 'bourgeois' pacifism on which the N.M.W.M. had turned its back in 1932. As Robert Entwhistle explained:

It is their cardinal weakness that, in the main, they are still in the stage of pacifist thought of the Conscientious Objector. Their main concern is the vindication of the Christian conscience by non-participation in

[1] *NMW*, Feb. 1935.
[2] *NMW*, Oct. 1935.
[3] *NMW*, Nov. 1935.
[4] *NMW*, Oct. 1935.
[5] South to Ponsonby, 6 Jan. 1936, A.P.
[6] *NMW*, July 1935.

war. This is the line of Christian pacifist leaders like Canon Raven and Dr. Maude Royden. It is utterly inadequate to the circumstances of today. Or where they react against so-called 'negative pacifism' they tend to conceive the creation of a new social order, either by the re-creation of individual souls or as a peaceful and orderly development of capitalism into something better, both points of view entirely ignoring the stern realities of the class struggle and the Fascist danger.[1]

Yet such carping on the deficiencies of others came strangely from a society whose membership not only remained small but included—as its leaders were shocked to discover from a correspondence in *No More War* for July and August 1935—those who believed that its pledge did not imply support for unilateral disarmament. Moreover, when the National Committee met on 2 November 1935 to draft a statement of policy on the Abyssinia crisis, it failed to agree[2] —an indication of the extent to which its ostensible recovery of vitality in 1935 had been based on a negative hostility to collective security. It was thus a fair comment on the state of the Movement that, whereas in the 1929 edition of *The Christian's Alternative to War*, Leyton Richards had written of the great impact the N.M.W.M. was then making all reference to it had disappeared from the revised edition of 1935.[3]

(ii) 'New' Pacifism: the Sheppard Peace Movement.

The true yardstick of the N.M.W.M.'s failure was Sheppard's success during 1934-5 in demonstrating that an unequivocal pacifist position could attract a mass following. He enjoyed two assets which the N.M.W.M. lacked: the support of a growing Christian pacifist movement; and a charismatic personality which attracted the unsophisticated hater of war alarmed by the Abyssinia crisis.

Pacifism had been gaining influential adherents among ministers of all denominations since the later twenties, and in 1933 an increase in tempo had occurred. In May Leyton Richards had revived the Christian Pacifist Crusade, originally set up in 1926, on the basis of his own Congregational church

[1] Ibid.
[2] N.M.W.M., N.C. 2 Nov. 1935.
[3] Compare the 1929 edition, p. 138, with 1935, p. 108.

at Carrs Lane, Birmingham; and on 3 November Henry Carter's Methodist Peace Fellowship was formally launched at simultaneous services during which 500 ministers accepted its Covenant.[1] (Carter became chairman, and the other leading officials were Soper and the Revd Leslie Keeble.) By the following month the Revd Gwilym Davies of the L.N.U.'s Welsh National Council was expressing concern at the

decided drift towards out and out pacifism in the big religious denominations of Wales. The Welsh Baptist denomination, for instance, has become, by resolution, 100% pacifist; the other denomination [sic] are going the same way . . . In their present mood there is some danger of a real landslide in the Welsh religious denominations away from the League of National Union . . .[2]

During the autumn an attempt had been made to co-ordinate these burgeoning denominational movements by setting up a Council of Christian Pacifist Groups (C.C.P.G.), of which the founder members were the Methodist and Congregational groups, the revived Unitarian fellowship, plus the Society of Friends and the F.o.R.[3] In 1934 these were joined by: the Presbyterian Pacifist Group, whose leading figure was the Revd Lewis Maclachlan; the Baptist Pacifist Fellowship, organized by the Revd W. H. Haden; and the Church of England Peace Fellowship, which was largely the result of an initiative by Canon Stuart Morris.

Morris (1890–1967) was destined to be Britain's most important pacifist organizer during the quarter-century after Sheppard's death. A Cambridge graduate, he served as a Chaplain to the Royal Flying Corps in the Great War and afterwards became a parish priest in Birmingham. There he met the one pacifist bishop of the time, E. W. Barnes (1874–1953), who made him a Canon of Birmingham Cathedral and appointed him his secretary. He first became prominent as a pacifist in 1934, arguing a case for Christian pacifism similar to Raven's, and urging the formation of a pacifist group affiliated to the L.N.U.[4] He seems also to have had discussions with Sheppard on the possibilities of organizing

---

[1] Rec., Aug. 1933 p. 148; Dec. 1933, p. 234.
[2] Davies to N.B. Foot, 29 Dec. 1933, D.D.
[3] Peace Year Book 1935, p. 103; F.o.R., G.C. 11–12 Dec. 1933.
[4] F.o.R. Co., 31 July–7 Aug. 1934; Rec., Sept. 1934, p. 250–1; Nov. 1934, p. 307–8.

an independent pacifist movement—an idea which Sheppard was starting seriously to contemplate in 1934.

It was Sheppard, the man for whom the cliché 'magnetic personality' might have been invented, whose charisma gave Christian pacifism mass appeal. Brought up on the fringe of the royal circle—his father, whom he described as 'something of a courtier',[1] was a Minor Canon who sang in the Royal Chapel at Windsor—Sheppard was educated at Marlborough and at Cambridge, where he was a rather 'hearty' undergraduate, and at one stage even contemplated following his elder brother into the professional army. He decided instead to do a period of social work in the East End, and then took another short-term job as a lay secretary to Cosmo Gordon Lang, the future Archbishop of Canterbury, who was then Bishop of Stepney. It was as a result of this experience that he decided to become ordained. After a brief but harrowing spell as chaplain in the first weeks of the Great War, he took over in November 1914 as Vicar of St. Martin-in-the-Fields. It was immediately clear that, in his mid-thirties, he had discovered his vocation in life. For the twelve years of his incumbency, his congregations were packed to overflowing, thanks to his personality and his willingness to experiment—his most successful experiment being to allow the B.B.C. in 1924 to broadcast a church service for the first time, thereby ensuring himself national fame as the radio parson. After his resignation from St. Martin's in 1926 he was made a Companion of Honour, and in 1929 became Dean of Canterbury, an office he held until 1931. Thus for all his outspoken and unconventional criticisms of the Church of England he was highly successful in worldly terms. He officiated as a family friend at Sir Oswald Mosley's first marriage and at his first wife's funeral, voted Tory in 1931, and died a wealthy man—to the embarrassment of his followers.

Yet he was saved from complacent orthodoxy by the tragic side of his life. Despite his extraordinary charm he was (at least according to the Freudian and, it has been suggested, distorted portrait painted by his major biographer, R. Ellis

---

[1] Cited in Roberts, *Sheppard*, pp. 219-20.

Roberts)[1] deeply unsure of himself and found fulfilment only by devoting himself to others with a compulsive energy that invariably ended in physical collapse because he suffered painfully from asthma. It was acute asthma which had necessitated his premature resignations from both St. Martin's and Canterbury, and which also prevented the development of the Peace Army into a significant pacifist movement. In November 1932, moreover, he had collapsed while attempting to address a disarmament meeting. Only late in 1933, when he acquired a breathing machine, did he secure partial relief for the first time.

This improvement in his health enabled him to decide how best to develop his careers as a pacifist and a clergyman, both of which had been in virtual abeyance for the previous six or seven years. While he took this decision he returned temporarily in 1934 to St. Martin's where his successor, Pat McCormick, was on sabbatical until the autumn. Declining a generous invitation from McCormick to remain at St. Martin's (with McCormick as his deputy), and also an offer from Maude Royden to join her at the Guildhouse, he finally agreed on 27 September to become a Canon of St. Paul's. For a parson who had vaunted his 'impatience' with the stuffiness of established religion, this long-pondered and soon regretted decision was a surprising one. It is tempting, therefore, to see his simultaneous decision to renew his pacifist stand as in some way a compensation for accepting a conventional preferment. Earlier in the year he had seemed no more certain of his views than he had been in 1932 when he had endorsed both the Peace Army and the New Commonwealth Society, and made his approach to Lloyd George. When, as late as April 1934, Lord Davies had asked him to reaffirm his support for the New Commonwealth, Sheppard's reply had been sufficiently non-committal for Davies, who

[1] In *H. R. L. Sheppard: Life and Letters* (1942), Roberts interprets Sheppard's personality as a struggle between the introverted, insecure young 'Lawrie' (as Roberts labels this tragic side of Sheppard's life) and the extrovert, confident adult 'Dick'. (For the debt to Freud, see p. 27.) Roberts knew Sheppard only late in life and his emphasis on Sheppard's unhappiness has been criticized by an older friend, Charles H. S. Matthews: *Dick Sheppard*, p. 15. Carolyn Scott's *Dick Sheppard* is impressionistic, but draws on useful reminiscences by Sheppard's daughters.

professed to 'sympathise with your reluctance to commit yourself in any way till you have been able to clarify your mind in regard to the issues involved', not to give up hope.[1] But, responding to the progress of pacifism in the Churches, to the Olympia meeting, to the encouragement of Canon Morris, and to the exhortations of his Peace Army colleague Crozier, Sheppard clarified his mind in favour of the uncompromising pacifism he had first professed in 1927. This time he proclaimed his decision in what proved to be a seminal letter to the press published on 16 October 1934.

He gave as his reasons for writing this letter, which ran to over five hundred words, the urgency of the international situation, the increasing tendency to violence exemplified by the Fascist and Communist movements, and his belief that the average man was seeking an alternative policy because he was 'now convinced that war of every kind or for any cause, is not only a denial of Christianity, but a crime against humanity, which is no longer to be permitted by civilised people.' To test this belief he called on all men—he believed that the peace movement already derived considerable support from women—to send him a postcard indicating that they would be ready to attend a meeting to vote in favour of the 'uncompromising' resolution: 'We renounce war and never again, directly or indirectly, will we support or sanction another.' He disclaimed all intention of founding any new organization or of calling pacifists together 'to abuse those who conscientiously are not able to agree with them', and recognized that many potential recruits were put off by the methods of existing peace societies.[2]

Although the letter was dated 15 October it must have been written before 29 September when Sheppard left on a cruise to gain strength for his new post at St. Paul's in mid-November. He had thus given as his address Crozier's house at Walton-on-Thames and it was there that 2,500 cards arrived within two days, 99 per cent of them endorsing his pledge.[3] On 19 October even *The Times* (which had not

[1] Davies to Sheppard, 11 Apr. 1934 (copy), D.D.
[2] See e.g. *News Chronicle, Daily Herald, Manchester Guardian*, 16 Oct. 1934; the letter is reprinted in Sybil Morrison, *I Renounce War*, pp. 99-100.
[3] *Daily Herald*, 18 Oct. 1934.

carried his letter) was quoting Sheppard's secretary's assertion that his 'peace appeal was sweeping the country'.
Although, on his return in November, Sheppard was clearly
delighted by this response, he used it as a reason for procras-
tination. 'I believe that we shall be able to obtain half a
million signatures,' he predicted—wrongly, since the total
received was only 50,000—and declared that he was 'determined not to act until we know our full strength'.[1] Thus
although he made the occasional pacifist speech—for example
on 9 November at a gathering organized by the C.C.P.G.
where, sharing the platform with Raven, Richards, Barnes
and Carter, he attracted a capacity audience of 2,700 with a
further thousand at an overflow meeting[2]—and started to
work out his pacifist views by writing a book, *We Say 'No'*,
which was completed by July 1935 (with all proceeds going
to his peace work), he did no more to follow up his original
letter until his Albert Hall rally nine months later.

Apart from spasmodic ill-health and the demands of his
new position, the reason for this delay was that he sincerely
had no desire to start a new organization. The sole purpose
of his letter had indeed been 'to attempt to discover how
strong the will to peace has grown'. It is possible that in
this he was deliberately attempting to pre-empt the Peace
Ballot's attempt to mobilize support for sanctions, and
indeed he was accused by *Peace* for November 1934 of
dividing the peace movement and repudiating the approach
for which the Ballot, 'the most ambitious enterprise in its
history', stood. But, as the Peace Ballot's results came in
from late November, and with the peace movement uniting
in support of it and in condemnation of the Government
and its rearmament proposals, Sheppard seemed reluctant to
press his criticisms of collective security. With his characteristic generosity towards those disagreeing with him he paid
fulsome tribute to all Ballot workers[3] and concentrated on
issues upon which the peace movement was united. For
example, in a letter to the *Manchester Guardian* of 11 May

---

[1] *Friend*, 30 Nov. 1934, p. 1114.
[2] *Peace Year Book 1935*, pp. 104–5; F.o.R. G.C. 10–11 Dec. 1934.
[3] *Ballot Worker*, No. 6 (25 Apr. 1935), p. 3.

1935 he protested at the Government's A.R.P. proposals and announced his categorical refusal to co-operate.

This letter included, however, the remarkable admission for a pacifist that 'like everyone else, I should do my best to be of assistance in the unthinkable event of another European war, but the idea of now getting ready, especially in view of the fact that gas masks, as I am told, cannot be of service to children, fills me with unspeakable repugnance.' What Sheppard meant by 'assistance' in wartime, and whether he was implying that pacifism was a 'bluff' which could be abandoned if it failed to prevent war, was unclear. Indeed, the cloudiness of his thinking was evident in *We Say 'No'*, which he was writing at this time. It began with an account of the death in 1914 of a soldier he had known whose wife was then about to give birth and whose child would, in 1935, be of military age, and proceeded to argue that all armaments and alliances, including collective security, would merely lead to another futile war. His characteristic combination of unconcern for intellectual and theological difficulties and acute sensitivity to the human difficulties of applying ideals in practice meant that in several cases he deviated from his own proclaimed absolutes.[1] Typical of his approach was his belief that pacifists should undertake ambulance work, which he refused to condemn as merely helping the military machine to patch up troops and return them to the front:

When I think of this question, however, I do not see it in terms of logic, but of wounded men who lie, perhaps for hours, with no one to bring them aid, or dress their wounds, or give them the drink of water or the cigarette for which they crave.[2]

Although Sheppard liked to exaggerate his own confusion and perplexity, the Abyssinia crisis troubled him as much as the hypothetical issues he had considered in his book. On 10 July 1935 he confessed to Laurence Housman: 'Abyssinia and Italy simply beats me. I don't know what we pacifists

---

[1] His biographer pointed out that he claimed the Commandment 'Thou shalt not kill' to be absolute but never questioned capital punishment and also implied that to defend a frontier arms might be sometimes justified: Roberts, *Sheppard*, p. 335.

[2] H. R. L. Sheppard, *We Say 'No': The Plain Man's Guide to Pacifism* (1935), p. 144.

ought to be at.'[1] Nevertheless the crisis stimulated him to hold the meeting of signatories of his original pledge which he had promised nine months before. On 14 July 1935, a sweltering Sunday, they flocked to a highly successful Albert Hall rally, at which the speakers apart from Sheppard were Edmund Blunden, Siegfried Sassoon (who read his poetry instead of making a speech), Crozier, and—the only woman present—Maude Royden. Sheppard was delighted by it, informing Ponsonby: 'Our Albert Hall meeting was, I think the most impressive show I was ever at, not because of the speakers but because of the astonishingly young and keen audience of over 7,000.'[2] After the meeting what Housman jokingly called Sheppard's 'beastly blooming organisation'[3] —the Sheppard Peace Movement, as it was first known— was launched. In thus going against his original intention not to found a new society, Sheppard seems to have been swept along by the momentum of the crisis (and perhaps, too, by that of Crozier); in December 1935 he was to write: 'It seems the tide or the gale of God is with us—blowing almost too strongly (too strongly to last).'[4]

Three factors contributed to this pacifist wind, of which the first stirrings could be detected as the Abyssinia crisis began to loom in the summer of 1935, and which reached gale force from 1936 onwards. These were: doubts about the moral validity and efficacy of the League; a sudden interest on the part of a few leading intellectuals in justifying pacifism on humanitarian grounds; and popular enthusiasm for economic appeasement as a peaceful way of avoiding war.

As already noted, when collaborative pacifists had talked of the internationalization of armed force as a step in the right direction, they had rarely specified how 'international' a body had to be before ceasing to be a conventional military alliance. Indeed, apart from the stock left-wing denunciation of the League as an alliance of dominant capitalist governments

---

[1] Housman (ed.), *What . . . ?*, p. 240.

[2] Sheppard to Ponsonby, 24 July 1935, A.P. The best account of the meeting is by Hannen Swaffer (who was called up from the press table to say a few words), *Daily Herald*, 15 July 1935; but even *The Times* mentioned it, albeit a day late: 16 July.

[3] Housman to Sheppard, 30 July 1935, in Housman (ed.), *What . . . ?*, p. 241.

[4] Sheppard to Housman, 10 Dec. 1935, in ibid., p. 244.

with a selfish interest in preserving the status quo, there was remarkably little discussion in any section of the peace movement (with the obvious exception of the New Commonwealth Society) of the quality of internationalism. When, for instance, the L.N.U. was considering the international police force and its Conservative members objected—on the grounds that it altered the basis of the League from a limited confederal structure nearer to a world state—few internationalists seemed to understand what the issue was.[1]

Only in the late summer of 1935 did the credentials of the League as an international authority begin to be challenged. One challenger was Nichols, who had in 1933 declared his support for internationalism, but who at an early stage in the Abyssinia crisis began 'to suspect that an ultimate solution does not rest in the League as it stands. It is not a League at all, but an Anglo-French alliance. When I wrote *Cry Havoc!* the prospects were different. Germany was there, and Japan was there.'[2] The fact that, in reality, Japan had announced its departure from the League before *Cry Havoc!* was completed and that Nichols had not used any of the book's later editions to modify his views in the light of the German withdrawal suggested that the issue had not previously occurred to him. Now that it had, however, he abandoned internationalism and, under the influence also of the Oxford Group Movement, declared his support—briefly, it transpired—for Sheppard.[3]

Another who was moving back towards pacifism under the impact of the crisis was Bertrand Russell. Although over the seven decades in which he was to pronounce upon international questions the detailed policies he recommended varied sharply from pacifism to a pre-emptive nuclear strike, each was an attempt to apply the same utilitarian principles to different situations. As he put it in 1935, in an article explaining his opposition to the Great War: 'The view which I took, and still take, was that, while some wars have been

---

[1] See L.N.U. Executive, 1 Nov. 1934; *Report*, L.N.U. General Council, Dec. 1934, pp. 51–75. Almost the only internationalist consistently to question the League's legitimacy (other than on anti-capitalist or anti-French grounds) was C. Delisle Burns.

[2] Cited in Alan Campbell Johnson, *Peace Offering* (1936), p. 131.

[3] See Sheppard to Martin, 2 Oct, 1935, Martin Papers.

justified (for instance the American Civil War), the Great War was not justified, because it was about nothing impersonal and raised no moral issues.'[1] He had therefore given qualified support to socialist war-resistance (which, as already noted, he had discovered to be more effective than individual non-resistance) as the best available means of ending it; and, although after the war he devoted little time to the question, he became increasingly interested in the idea of an international government which could prevent future aggression by nipping it in the bud. The possibility of military sanctions against Italy, however, made him realize that the League was incapable of achieving this. As he informed Kingsley Martin on 7 August 1935:

I am against a League war in present circumstances, because the anti-League powers are strong. The analogy is not King v. Barons, but the Wars of the Roses. If the League were strong enough, I should favour sanctions, because either the threat would suffice or the war would be short and small. The whole question is quantitative.[2]

The question this raised in his mind was whether any armed force could be justified in quantitative terms; and, further influenced by the events of 1936, Russell was to decide it could not and to pledge his support to Sheppard.

The position which Russell was to define in 1936—and which he was later to admit was a 'creed' rather than the strict utilitarian analysis he believed himself at the time to be putting forward—was, in the terminology of this study, humanitarian pacifism. Previous attempts to justify this inspiration had oversimplified it: the 'utilitarian' approach of Ponsonby and Milne had been based on too rosy a view of the nature of international tensions; while the 'humane' emphasis on the sufferings of war to be found in the pacifist writings of Nichols, Joad, and Storm Jameson ignored the miseries of subjugation to an invading tyranny. Taken together, moreover, they had all tended to ignore the spiritual dimension of human happiness, implying that a loss of hedonistic or materialistic satisfactions was all that pacifists needed to prove. The threat of war over Abyssinia and the

---

[1] Bell (ed.), *We Did Not Fight*, p. 334.
[2] Martin Papers; it is printed in Kingsley Martin, *Editor: A Second Volume of Autobiography 1931–45* (1968), p. 194.

personal ministrations of Sheppard, attracted to the pacifist movement, however, two thinkers who were to elevate humanitarian pacifism by adapting it to a more integrated view of human values: Aldous Huxley, and his friend and fellow polymath, Gerald Heard.

Huxley (1894-1963) had taken no stand of principle against the Great War in which, nearly blind from an infection contracted at Eton, he was exempt from service: after an eight-month stay at Garsington, which followed an Oxford career in which he had shown the distinction expected of a member of his illustrious family, he worked briefly for the Air Board, before becoming a schoolmaster. Privately, however, he admitted to his brother Julian while still an undergraduate that 'now, if I could (having seen all the results), I think I'd be a conscientious objector, or nearly so. But I shudder to think what England will be like afterwards—barely habitable.'[1] This feeling that the war had irrevocably corrupted the liberal civilisation in which he had been raised found its first expression in the novels satirizing the post-war waste land which made his reputation. Not until after the world slump had begun, and he had visited both Italy and Germany, did he begin to channel his whimsical astringency into overt political comment. *Brave New World*, the turning point in this respect, was completed in August 1931; while the following year he was moved sufficiently by the Disarmament Conference to contribute journalistic commentaries to *Time and Tide*. In May 1932, for example, he attacked the strategy of 'qualitative disarmament', which had been adopted at Geneva, since it was believed to hold out the best hope of sparing the civilian population in any future war:

What is needed is to make it unequivocally clear to civilians of every age and sex that the next war is meant for them; that there will be no soldiers to suffer vicariously for them; and that all the bleeding and choking, all the groaning and dying will have to be done personally, even by the most respectable bankers and archdeacons and Dames of the British Empire, even by heads of government departments and Cabinet ministers. [2]

[1] Aldous to Julian Huxley, 31 Mar. 1916, in Smith (ed.), *Letters*, p. 97.
[2] *Time and Tide*, 7 May 1932, p. 514.

Underlying Huxley's apparent cynicism about modern civilization was, however, a real yearning to discover alternative and more profound values. The first attempt to express these in his writing was in *Eyeless in Gaza*, the most ambitious of his novels which, though begun late in 1932, was not completed until late in 1935. The delays in its composition reflected Huxley's difficulties in formulating his views—difficulties which often took physical form as incapacitating bouts of insomnia. The breakthrough in both the book and his health occurred in the last quarter of 1935 when he both committed himself to pacifism and overcame his aversion to speaking in public, appearing with Sheppard at the Albert Hall in November 1935 and lecturing at Friends' House on 3 December in a lunch-hour series on 'The New Pacifism'.

The link Huxley recognised between the curing of his insomnia and his emergence as a pacifist campaigner is dramatized in *Eyeless in Gaza* through the figure of Miller, the pacifist doctor who collaborates with Purchas, the parson with a 'muscular-jocular Christian manner',[1] who has founded his own pacifist society. Purchas is clearly based on Sheppard; while Miller, in part suggested by Heard, was mainly a fusion of two unorthodox medical theorists: F. M. Alexander and Dr J. E. R. McDonagh. F. Matthias Alexander (1869-1955) had been a semi-professional orator who had developed acute hoarseness which no doctor could explain, but which he, after laborious self-examination, discovered to be the result of involuntary and uncontrollable muscular reflexes. The only solution was to improve his 'Use of the Self'—to quote the title of his best known book— which involved a fundamental psychological reorientation. Alexander became a full-time therapist, dealing with stutterers and other sufferers from nervous ailments, and tried in his writings to elevate his technique (which was endorsed by Lord Lytton, among others) into a medical philosophy based on the indivisible unity of the human organism.[2] He also introduced Huxley to Dr J. E. R. McDonagh, F.R.C.S.,

---

[1] *Eyeless in Gaza* (1936), Penguin edn., p. 14.
[2] F. Matthias Alexander, *The Use of the Self: Its Conscious Direction in Relation to Diagnosis, Functioning and the Control of Reaction* (n.d. [1931]).

an energetic campaigner on behalf of his own dietary theory that most illness was caused by poisoning of the bowels.[1]

Huxley, whose willingness to suspend his critical faculties in relation to unorthodox medical theories was later rewarded by the success of the 'Bates Method' in improving his eyesight, was attracted to such theories largely because, by linking physical and mental ailments, they accorded with his quest to reduce 'irrational multiplicity to comprehensible unity'. At the physical level this unity meant sleep; at the spiritual level, repose; and at the intellectual level, true coherency and consistency. By the winter of 1935 Huxley had come to discover all three levels of unity in the conception of peace—by meditating on which the pacifist hero of *Eyeless in Gaza*, Anthony Beavis, achieves spiritual fulfilment in the last pages of the book:

In peace there is unity. Unity with other lives. Unity with all being, beneath the countless identical but separate patterns, beneath the attractions and repulsions, lies peace. The same peace as underlies the frenzy of the mind. Dark peace, immeasurably deep. Peace from pride and hatred and anger, peace from cravings and aversions, peace from all the separating frenzies. Peace through liberation, for peace is achieved freedom. Freedom and at the same time truth. The truth of unity actually experienced.[2]

Thus, for Beavis as for his creator, pacifism, being the mystical perception of truth, was excellent therapy both for the individual and for mankind; as he told his lunch-hour audience at Friends' House: 'if enough people set out to experience spiritual reality . . . then there will be peace; for peace . . . is a by-product of a certain way of life.' He also pointed out that any judgement of either the morality or the efficacy of pacifism

must be prefaced by a more general discussion of the relation of means to ends. Two questions at once propound themselves, one concerned with ethics, the other concerned with observable facts. Do good ends justify bad means? That is the first question. And the second is this: Can bad or even merely unsuitable means ever in fact lead to a realisation of the good ends desired by their users?

To both these quesions Huxley offered an emphatic negative and affirmed instead a positive conviction that pacifism

[1] Sybille Bedford, *Aldous Huxley: A Biography*, i (1975), p. 313.
[2] Penguin edn., p. 319.

'prescribes the appropriate means for attaining the ends desired by all';[1] but to clarify his mind and demonstrate his case he set out on perhaps the most rigorous justification for humanitarian pacifism ever attempted, *Ends and Means*, which eventually appeared in 1937, by which time he had withdrawn to the United States.

Accompanying Huxley in his progression to pacifism in 1935, and in his emigration to America in April 1937, was Gerald Heard (1889-1972), whom he had known since 1929. A journalist who specialized in scientific popularization, he had a formidable reputation as an intellectual—'said to be the cleverest person in the world', Evelyn Waugh noted in 1930, having encountered him over the dinner table and found him 'well-informed about theology and spiritualism' though 'personally unattractive'[2]—and had been working since the late twenties on an abstruse trilogy written to find out 'why it is that men manage to live socially'.[3] In the thirties he came to believe that the defect in the social mechanism which had divided mankind into anarchic sovereign states would soon precipitate a war in which those states would further disintegrate into anarchic city-states. The extremity of Heard's pessimism about the future of the world in the autumn of 1933 amused Huxley, who wrote to his brother on the day of the German departure from Geneva that Heard was 'more pessimistic than ever, advising us all to clear out to some safe spot in South America or the Pacific Islands before it is too late. He enjoys his glooms: but the fact does not necessarily mean that the glooms are unfounded. The German spectacle is really too frightening.'[4] Two years later, however, Heard became hopeful that the positive social values which his researches had indicated to be the key to harmonious social existence could be fostered through pacifism. Late that year he completed his trilogy with the publication of *The Source of Civilisation*, which defined

[1] Aldous Huxley, 'Pacifism and Philosophy', in G. K. Hibbert (ed.), *The New Pacifism* (1936), pp. 25, 29.

[2] Michael Davie (ed.), *The Diaries of Evelyn Waugh* (1976), p. 321.

[3] Gerald Heard, *The Source of Civilisation* (1935), p. 11. The first two parts of the trilogy were *The Ascent of Humanity* (1929) and *The Social Substance of Religion* (1931).

[4] Aldous to Julian Huxley, 14 Oct. 1933, in Smith (ed.), *Letters*, 374-5.

his central preoccupation in terms that had clear relevance
to pacifism:

Our dilemma is that we want peace and justice but seem only to be able
to attain these values by acts which destroy them. Values without sanctions are only dreams, but in attempting to make the dream come true
we may destroy it and reality also . . . Nevertheless a force which is
both real and yet non-violent does exist, a power which can meet both
the requirements of our case.[1]

Like Huxley, Heard believed that bad means were unable to
produce good ends but that an intense contemplation of
reality led to a realization that non-violence was the means
on which all good ends depended: like Huxley, too, he
appeared on pacifist platforms, lectured at Friends' House,
and gave his support to the Sheppard Peace Movement.

Although the prestige of pacifism was considerably en-
hanced by Huxley's and Heard's uncompromising refinement
of its humanitarian inspiration, its growing popularity in the
last five months of 1935 owed far more to the discovery of
economic appeasement as a practical policy for pacifists to
recommend. Formerly, when pacifists had been asked what a
pacifist government would have done about, for example,
the Japanese invasion of Manchuria, they had either boldly
asserted the efficacy of non-violence or pinned their faith in
economic sanctions. Only the occasional pacifist responded
as the Revd Lewis Machlachlan did when Japan renewed its
aggression in 1933: by arguing that the proper question to
ask was not what pacifists would do in this crisis, but 'what
would the Christian Pacifist have done before the situation
was aggravated by militarist action and the rousing of
national passion?'[2] The reason for this seems to have been
that, beyond curbing the jingoistic tendencies in his own
country, the pacifist had no practical policy to recommend
which could prevent aggravation in the international sphere.
Although,for example, Bishop Barnes was informing the
C.C.P.G.'s rally in November 1934 'that it would be well
worth while to forego all the fancied gains of the Treaty of
Versailles that thereby we might gain Germany's good

---

[1] p. 47.
[2] *Rec.*, May 1933, p. 93.

will',[1] pacifist enthusiasm for appeasement was not, except in the immediate aftermath of Germany's departure from Geneva, conspicuous.

But as a result of Mussolini's propaganda about his need for the economic resources provided by colonies, the peace movement discovered the economic grievances of what suddenly became known as the 'Have Not' nations. Almost overnight, economic appeasement, like support for the League before sanctions were an issue, became the panacea with the broadest range of support in the peace movement. Internationalists were compelled to pay lip-service to it even though they feared it lent a moral credibility to aggression and sapped the political will to enforce collective security; Christian pacifists could give it an unqualified welcome: to work for the fairer sharing of the world's raw materials seemed to be the practical expression of their ideals of love reconciliation, and atonement. While established pacifists were reassured by the prospect of achieving political relevance without compromising their objection to force, others became pacifists as a result of appreciating the political case for appeasement. For example, the Revd Leslie Weatherhead, the Methodist preacher who was to achieve fame at the City Temple, seems to have started to move from *pacificism* to pacifism—a conversion influenced by a personal heart-to-heart with Sheppard—in August 1935 when he came to realize that Britain, a sated imperial power denying Italy her share of the spoils, was 'a successful but unbranded burglar, now converted'. This led him to argue:

Are we not hypocrites in branding Italy, unless to all our prayers, we add deeds? . . . Let us cease talking about sanctions, armed or economic . . . Britain should ask Italy what territory now British would help in her legitimate and obvious desire for extension and then make her a definite offer of such territory.[2]

The pioneer and leader of Christian appeasement was George Lansbury who, for the first time in his long pacifist

[1] *Rec.*, Dec. 1934, pp. 317-8.

[2] Cited in Kingsley Weatherhead, *Leslie Weatherhead: A Personal Portrait* (1975), p. 83. Since this book wrongly dates the start of the Italo-Ethipian war as 24 Aug., it is possible that this quotation is also given an earlier date than it should be.

career, threw himself wholeheartedly into a campaign on this issue. Never a systematic thinker—'No brains to speak of ... certainly no capacity for solving intellectual problems', as a hostile witness, Beatrice Webb, had put it[1]—his subtle blend of simple emotionalism and political shrewdness had enabled him to sustain a serene pacifism while loyally supporting Labour policy. This became far harder when the 1931 electoral débâcle left him, as the Party's sole surviving elder statesman, to shoulder the burden of the leadership at precisely the moment when the aggression of the militarist powers was starting. Up to the summer of 1935,[2] however, he was able to salve his pacifist conscience by hoping that economic sanctions would, in practice, suffice, and by regarding himself as morally dissociated from Labour's adoption of collective security in 1934 because he had been in hospital at the time the Party had repudiated war-resistance.[3] He was also touched by the expressions of support he received whenever he explained his dilemma. But it is not clear how long he would have felt able to remain leader even if Ernest Bevin had not cut impatiently through the Party's protestations of loyalty at the Brighton Conference on 1 October 1935 and told him to make up his mind whether or not he could accept its policy. In retrospect, though initially bitter at the circumstances of his resignation,[4] he came to accept that he had compromised his pacifism and that it was wrong for a pacifist to accept political responsibility of that kind.[5]

The sign that Lansbury, who in his mid-seventies was starting to show signs of physical infirmity, had decided to make his pacifism his priority even before Brighton was his influential letter to *The Times* on 19 August 1935, which he described as his 'Plea for a Truce of God'. Protesting at 'the terrible acceptance of future war as something we must prepare for as unavoidable', Lansbury called for a world

[1] Cited in Robert Skidelsky, *Oswald Mosley* (1975), p. 181.
[2] Anthony Eden told Viscount Cecil that Lansbury had been 'most satisfactory' on the Abyssinian question: 'Note on Conversation with Mr. Eden, Foreign Office, 21 Aug. 1935', Add. MSS 51083, R.C.
[3] See *Report*, 35th Annual Conference, Brighton 1935, p. 180.
[4] See 'A Page of History by G. L., Oct. 1936', Lansbury Papers.
[5] George Lansbury, *My Quest For Peace* (1938), pp. 12-13.

conference to be held in the Holy Land[1] —sending copies of his letter to the Pope and other religious leaders—to secure a juster distribution of the world's plenty:

> No one will say there is not enough room, enough raw materials, enough markets for us all . . . In this day of ours, through the providence and mercy of God, science and invention enable us to say there is power to give the highest and noblest life for the children of men, no matter whether they are born brown, black, yellow or white.

The letter provoked immediate enthusiasm from his fellow pacifists. Sheppard wrote in the following day's issue: 'Of course Mr. Lansbury is right. It is the only way, and we know it. I can promise the support of well over 50,000 men, probably 250,000 by Christmas, for some such scheme as Mr. Lansbury proposes.'[2]   Since Sheppard's lack of expertise on political, and more especially economic, matters was seen as a handicap by some socialist pacifists, his alliance with Lansbury strengthened his Movement's appeal; on 13 September 1935 both men united for a meeting at Central Hall, Westminster, attended by a packed house of 4,000 with a further 1,500 having to be turned away.[3] By the end of the year the call for a world conference to inaugurate a new international order, which was a theme voiced at three well-attended Armistice Day rallies held by pacifists in London in November 1935 (in addition to a notably less successful effort by the N.M.W.M.), was being endorsed also by Barnes, Carter, Raven, Richards, Soper, and other leading Christian pacifists.[4]

It was a sign of strict pacifism's unprecedented influence that it was no longer treated with the same tolerance as before in the two institutions where it had grown accustomed to the status of an accepted minority: in the Labour Party, where Lansbury's enforced retirement from the leadership in October 1935 followed Ponsonby's resignation from the leadership in the Lords on the same issue; and in the Church of England, where, in the same month the Archbishop of

---

[1] Ibid., p. 20.

[2] *The Times*, 20 Aug. 1935.

[3] F.o.R., G.C. 23-4Sept. 1935; other speakers included Henry Carter, Gerald Heard, and Lady Parmoor.

[4] Letter dated 18 Dec., *Rec.*, Jan. 1936, p. 27.

York, William Temple, described pacifism as a heresy,[1] provoking an angry reaction from Raven, who later concluded nevertheless that all such criticisms proved valuable in stimulating a deeper examination of pacifist principles.[2] Pacifists were granted the right of reply to a radio broadcast by Temple and, despite protests from Lansbury who felt he should have been invited,[3] Morris delivered it on 9 January 1936.

The Abyssinian affair enabled pacifism to discover a distinct and confident voice because its circumstances were so clear-cut: collective security meant war; pacifism meant peace. Pacifists were thus able to ignore the possibility that collective security might have a defensive value for Britain. Characteristic of their propaganda even in 1935 was an article by Ruth Fry, in which she related a fairy-tale about the miraculous election in Britain of a pacifist Government, and asked her readers to consider what their reactions would be if it came true: 'You, I believe, would wake up your children and tell them that, thank God, they were now safe, for the terrfying fear of war was gone forever.'[4] They had yet to face up to the question of *why* pacifism was preferable to *pacificism*. Was it because it was, as Miss Fry seemed to believe, more effective as a practical policy? At the Labour Party's 1935 Conference, Salter had taken this line:

Pacifists are told they are not practical people. I want humbly to submit to you that we are the true realists, and we are the only practical people. The world has tried again and again every other method except that method laid down in the Sermon on the Mount.[5]

Or did the espousal of pacifism constitute a recognition that no practical policy of war-prevention existed and that anyway pacifism was not just 'a stop-the-war trick' (as *Reconciliation* expressed it in August 1935) but 'a spiritual way of life'?[6]

[1] In a York Diocesan Leaflet. Temple admitted later: 'I should perhaps have qualified my expression by saying "heretical in tendency", for I do not know of any formal condemnation by the Church of pacifism as such.' *The Times*, 29 Oct. 1935.

[2] See e.g. *The Times*, 31 Oct. 1935; *Rec.*, Dec. 1935, pp. 320-2.

[3] Reith to Lansbury, 22 Nov. 1935, 6 Jan. 1936; Lansbury to Reith, 8 Jan. 1936 (copy), Lansbury Papers.

[4] *Rec.*, Aug. 1935, p. 201.

[5] *Report*, p. 167.

[6] pp. 145-7.

This was one of the major difficulties facing the P.P.U. when it was finally founded in May 1936 as part of that year's important and overdue upheaval within the peace movement.

11

THE 1936 CRISIS AND PACIFIST INSPIRATION

The threefold international crisis of 1936—the final subjugation of Abyssinia, the remilitarization of the Rhineland, the
civil war in Spain—was a major watershed in a way the crises
over Manchuria and Hitler's accession to power had not
been. The illusion of non-military sanctions collapsed, and
for the first time public discussion faced up to Britain's
strategic vulnerability. The peace movement finally and
dramatically polarized. The L.N.U. remained courageously
committed to collective security even though it was now
clear that it would involve a policy of rearmament and
alliances indistinguishable from conventional defence
measures. Although some former pacifists were jolted by this
realization into accepting the need to arm against fascism,
the L.N.U. suffered a heavy net loss of members, since most
pacificists believed that only 'peaceful change'—the phrase
adopted to describe what was, in effect, a policy of isolationism and economic appeasement—offered any chance of
avoiding an arms race ominously reminiscent of that before
1914. Some, however, went as far as espousing pacifism,
while those who were already professed pacifists finally
severed all links with internationalism.

The effect of 1936 on pacifism was thus sharply to intensify a two-way traffic, towards and away from it, which had
been flowing on a small scale since the crises of 1931 and
1933. Defections were straightforward: those moving away
from pacifism did so because they had come to doubt its
practicality as a policy for preventing war and securing justice. Conversions, however, were of two contradictory
kinds. Some were attracted towards pacifism because it was
the last untried practical policy. But, as hopes of preventing a
second world war by any method receded, the only converts
—and, indeed, the only pacifists retaining their beliefs—were

those who had ceased to expect immediate results from any policy. The position in the pacifist movement in the aftermath of the 1936 crisis was thus complex: some had already concluded that pacifism was essentially apolitical; others were in the first flush of enthusiasm that pacifism could be practical politics.

The way to simplify this complexity is to examine the impact of 1936 on the three pacifist *inspirations* separately, since each responded differently at first—although by 1938-9 they were all agreed that pacifism was a faith and not a policy. Socialists were the first to be forced into this realization by the facts of fascist belligerency: only a tiny minority remained pacifist during the Spanish Civil War, although those who survived that test tended to be unshakeable thereafter. A proportion of Christians also abandoned their former assumption of the immediate triumph of love over evil in response to these same events, though their reaction was less sudden, and offset by continued recruitment from those accepting that pacifism was politically irrelevant. It was humanitarian (or, as many probably still saw themselves, 'utilitarian') pacifists who were the last to accept that pacifism was moral rather than practical: they accounted, therefore, for much of both the recruitment to pacifism during its period of rapid growth in 1936-7 and the defections thereafter.

(i) Socialists

Summing up the recent upheaval in pacifist opinion in a letter to Lord Ponsonby on 27 August 1936, Mrs Helena Swanwick noted shrewdly: 'Most of the more politically minded pacifists have gone sanctionist, while the religious ones don't care about the plea of impracticability.'[1] Reformulated in the terminology of this study, what the events of 1935-6 had achieved was the destruction of the long-standing compatibility between pacifism and the needs of the socialist movement. War-resistance, a political rule of thumb based on the assumption that the cause of socialism was so unlikely to

[1] A.P.

be advanced by fighting (to which, however, no objection in principle was raised) that it would always be prudent to plan for a general strike, was largely discredited during 1936. Even before the Abyssinia crisis the Communists (though not the I.L.P. and the Socialist League) had abandoned war-resistance and insisted that sanctions were in the best interests of socialism; but it was the Spanish Civil War which proved to be so incontrovertibly a people's war that the vast majority of war resisters could not avoid modifying their whole attitude to British defence and foreign policies. Most came to accept that, although it was embarrassing for socialists that their anti-fascism forced them into partnership with a British ruling class which had (they believed) its own selfish, imperialist, reasons for quarrelling with its counterpart in Germany, a war against Germany would also be a people's war. Only a rump, mostly to be found in the I.L.P., was prepared to fight in Spain but felt that to prepare for a general war against Nazism would be merely to favour, in the words of George Orwell who took this view, 'British Fascism (prospective) as against German Fascism'.[1]

With the majority of socialists advocating a 'peace front' against fascism, the only political forces with which pacifists shared a common anti-war approach were right-wing isolationists and pro-Germans. This was illustrated by the changed strategy from 1936 onwards of Beverley Nichols. Having only recently moved back towards pacifism in the autumn of 1935, on the rebound from internationalism and under the influence of Buchmanism, Nichols at once began to fall under Mosley's spell. Unusually, however, he did not renounce his pacifism until 1938: up to then he combined his support for the P.P.U. and the Oxford Group Movement with a growing interest in two groups he considered to be making the most practical contribution to peace: the British Union of Fascists and the Anglo-German Fellowship.[2] It was an ingenious and logical application of the collaborative orientation to the

[1] Orwell to Gorer, 15 Sept. 1937, in Sonia Orwell and Ian Angus (eds.), *The Collected Essays, Journalism and Letters of George Orwell*, i (Penguin edn., 1970), p. 313.
[2] Beverley Nichols, *The Fool Hath Said* (1936), pp. 238–75 (esp. p. 263); *News of England: A Country Without A Hero* (1938), Chs. 20–1 (esp. pp. 303–6.); *Men Do Not Weep* (1941), pp. 14–33.

circumstances of the later thirties, but it offended most
pacifists: the N.M.W.M., considering the possibility of in-
viting Nichols to join their advisory panel in March 1936,
decided he was 'definitely not pacifist';[1] while ten months
later Crozier of the P.P.U. felt that he had gone 'out of his
way to let us down, having signed the pledge and his card
still being on the file.'[2]

Without the reassurance that they were also advancing
the interests of political socialism, socialist pacifists faced
a major crisis from which only a few emerged unscathed.
As already noted, the 'socialist' inspiration had two strands:
Christian socialism, which was strictly a religious inspiration;
and political pacifism proper. As Mrs Swanwick's generaliza-
tion suggested, it was the former—exemplified by such figures
as Salter, Hudson, Barr, Wilson, and Alex Wood—which survived the test; albeit not without difficulty, particularly
over Spain. Even Lansbury, who had been confirmed in his
pacifist convictions by Mussolini, confessed to a son-in-law
that if he had been a Spaniard he would have found it hard
not to fight Franco;[3] but his faith endured nevertheless.
When, as will shortly be noted, the N.M.W.M. faced its final
crisis over this issue, the Christian socialists such as Wellock
and Runham Brown were prominent among those remaining
pacifist and joining the P.P.U.

For those pacifists for whom religious belief was a strong,
but not quite preponderant, ingredient in their socialism,
acceptance of the political case for combating fascism by
force could co-exist, schizophrenically, with an almost
equally strong emotional regard for non-resistance. Kingsley
Martin, for example, the son of a Congregationalist minister
and himself a veteran of the Friends' Ambulance Unit, in
which he had served as a conscientious objector in the Great
War, had been converted to sanctions by Abyssinia and was a
passionate supporter of the Spanish Government's fight
against Franco. Yet he 'saw no intellectual difficulty', he informed *New Statesman* readers in August 1936, 'in at once
working for the victory of the Spanish people and in being

[1] N.M.W.M., N.C., 28 Mar. 1936.
[2] Crozier to Ponsonby, 7 Jan. 1937, A.P.
[3] Ernest Thurtle, *Time's Winged Chariot* (1945), p. 121.

glad of the growing pacifist movement in England.'[1] As late as 1938 he was offering his services as editorial adviser on *Peace News*, the journal of the P.P.U. with which he kept in touch, partly through his sister's husband, John Barclay, a full-time P.P.U. official. A similarly schizophrenic approach was maintained by his friend Victor Gollancz who, re-reading fifteen years later a call for an anti-fascist alliance which he had written after reluctantly abandoning his pacifism, was struck by the fact that 'there is more real conviction in my plea for sympathy with pacifists than in the insistence on collective security that follows it.'[2] In both cases their religious sensibilities drew them back towards a position they rejected on political grounds.

It was socialist pacifism *stricto sensu* which, as soon as the Abyssinian and Spanish issues finally demonstrated its full implications, proved most vulnerable. As already emphasized in this study, the conception of socialism from which pacifist beliefs could be derived was a moral or spiritual one which could neither be promoted nor exterminated by resort to violence. Yet, in practice, few socialist pacifists were prepared to be indifferent to the material interests of the socialist movement, and the onset of fascist aggression showed to many that they had been *pacificists* not pacifists.

During the 1935 Brighton Conference, at which Labour committed itself to military sanctions if needed in the imminent confrontation with Mussolini over Abyssinia, Morgan Jones, the Labour M.P. and (though not active in the peace movement since his release from prison) a former absolutist, turned in to dismay to his neighbour and said: 'I have never before voted for arms in my life but what am I to do?'[3] At the same Conference Dorothy Woodman, a former secretary of the W.I.L. before hatred of Nazism had led her to turn the U.D.C. from an anti-war into an anti-fascist society, publicly announced her conversion to sanctions;[4] while other 'political pacifists' who were quietly renouncing this label at this time included Francis Meynell and three

[1] *NS*, 22 Aug. 1936, p. 245.

[2] Victor Gollancz, *More For Timothy* (1953), p. 381; see also his *Reminiscences of Affection* (1968), pp. 82–3.

[3] Cited in George Catlin, *For God's Sake, Go* (1972), p. 243.

[4] *Report*, p. 171.

M.P.s, Leah Manning, F. W. Pethick-Lawrence, and Ernest Thurtle.[1]

Spain proved an even more damaging blow to socialist 'pacifism' than Abyssinia. Striving to keep the W.R.I. pacifist, Runham Brown predicted stoically to Ponsonby on 27 September 1936:

In these days of crisis may will depart from us but we shall be proved right and ultimately we shall win. Our job is to keep our Movement steady. We now have to face a more difficult position raised by the Spanish War. Some like Fenner Brockway will leave us, but we shall go on.[2]

Spain did, indeed, complete Brockway's gradual process of realization, which had begun with the Russian revolution and was later considerably furthered by the political and economic crisis of 1931, that the absolute socialist pacifism which had led him to found the N.-C.F. in 1914 was, in reality, an extreme socialist *pacificism*. He explained this painful discovery in a chapter of his autobiography written in August 1939:

I had long put on one side the purist pacifist view that one should have nothing to do with a social revolution if any violence were involved ... Nevertheless, the conviction remained in my mind that any revolution would fail to establish freedom and fraternity *in proportion to its use of violence*, that the use of violence inevitably brought in its train domination, repression, cruelty.

Visiting Catalonia in 1936, and being immensely impressed by the anarchists he met there, however, he came to be in

no doubt that the society resulting from an anarchist victory would have far greater liberty and equality than the society resulting from a fascist victory. *Thus I came to see that it is not the amount of violence used which determines good or evil results, but the ideas, the sense of human values, and above all the social forces behind its use.* With this realisation, although my nature revolted against the killing of human beings just as did the nature of those Catalonian peasants, the fundamental basis of my old philosophy disappeared.[3]

Spain also hammered the final nail into the coffin of that chronic but stubborn invalid, the N.M.W.M., which, having

[1] See, respectively, Meynell, *My Lives*, p. 250; Manning, *Life for Education*, p. 142; Lord Pethick-Lawrence, *Fate Has Been Kind* (n.d. [1943]), pp. 185–6; Thurtle, *Chariot*, pp. 132–4.

[2] A.P.

[3] Brockway, *Inside the Left*, pp. 339–40 (italics in original).

survived the Abyssinian crisis, albeit with growing signs of division, wound itself up within a mere seven months of Franco's rebellion. Although as early as June 1936 it had been having talks about its relationship with the incomparably more popular P.P.U., its decision to accept a merger was a direct result of the Spanish Civil War. An influential group of activists began a campaign to exempt civil wars from the Movement's pledge; when the October 1936 annual conference postponed a decision on the issue, the staff sent a collective letter of resignation in protest. But, despite considerable sympathy for the Spanish Government, a majority felt that a pacifist society could not endorse a conflict prosecuted with all the bitterness and modern weaponry of an international war; so the leader of the staff revolt, Reginald Reynolds, found himself in the unaccustomed position of pleading for a compromise and for toleration of a minority viewpoint.[1] His sympathy for the anarchist cause in Spain drove him finally to admit, in the course of a decisive confrontation between the staff and the Committee members, that 'he did not understand what pacifism is: it did not exist for him . . .'[2]

Since it was clear that the secession of Reynolds and his supporters would destroy the N.M.W.M., the National Committee, which for all its doubts had not wavered from its pacifism, debated the issue at considerable length and even considered the possibility of redrafting the Movement's declaration. It finally accepted that the individual branches of the N.M.W.M. should be presented, at a special delegate conference, with a straight choice between continuing its independent existence with its socialist priorities more clearly acknowledged or putting its pacifism indisputably before its socialism and merging with the P.P.U. So that its members could make a rational choice the National Committee made a final effort to clarify the terms on which an understanding could be reached with the P.P.U. Talks had been taking place intermittently for at least six months, but had failed to make progress owing to a fundamental contradiction in the N.M.W.M.'s attitude to the P.P.U. It strongly disliked what it regarded as the P.P.U.'s 'bourgeois'

---

[1] See e.g. his article 'On compromise', *NMW*, Oct. 1936.
[2] N.M.W.M., N.C., 21 Oct. 1936.

desire to avoid responsibility for the world's military, political, and economic conflicts. In contrast, as Allen Skinner had insisted in the summer of 1936: 'The primary purpose of the No More War Movement is not to provide a spiritual refuge for pacifist dissenters . . . The purpose of the No More War Movement is to seek to stop war and on its fitness for that purpose it . . . must be judged.'[1] But the logic of this argument forced it to recognize that the P.P.U.'s greater popularity made it far more likely to stop war than was the N.M.W.M. As Frank Dawtry, a leader of the anti-P.P.U. faction, later admitted, Sheppard's baby was 'a much larger child than its parent has ever been' and offered prospects 'for the greater advancement of the ideas to which the No More War Movement has subscribed for nearly twenty years.'[2]

The National Committee agreed, therefore, provisionally to accept the concessions offered by Canon Morris (who was representing the P.P.U. during one of Sheppard's bouts of illness) to Allen Skinner in December 1936.[3] Apart from allowing the N.M.W.M. to nominate two Sponsors, the major concession was the P.P.U.'s promise to introduce a formal democratic structure at some unspecified time in place of Sheppard's and his fellow Sponsors' benevolent despotism. These concessions helped the merger with the P.P.U. to carry the day by a substantial majority—although the powerful Birmingham branch refused to accept the decision and continued its independent existence—at the Special Conference held at Friends' House on 6 February 1937, after a debate which had been notable for the complete lack of enthusiasm for the P.P.U. in its present form.[4] It was with the intention of gingering it up that the formal merger was carried through in February 1937, with Wellock and Bing (joining Runham Brown, who had already transferred his allegiance to Sheppard) chosen as P.P.U. Sponsors.

What the voluntary but reluctant liquidation of the N.M.W.M. revealed was that, in contrast to the increased vitality of religious and humanitarian pacifism, political

[1] *War Resister*, No. 40 (Summer 1936), p. 3.
[2] *NMW*, Mar–Apr. 1937.
[3] Morris to Skinner, 15 Dec. 1936: N.M.W.M., N.C., 19 Dec. 1936.
[4] N.M.W.M. Conference, 6 Feb. 1937; *NMW*, Mar–Apr. 1937.

pacifism was too weak after being forcibly parted from its *pacificist* allies to survive on its own. But political pacifists such as Bing who had come through this test had demonstrated that their convictions were no less impervious to political adversity than those of religious pacifists. Indeed there were a few political pacifists—Max Plowman, for one—whose commitment to pacifism seemed stimulated by the Spanish war, and also some new recruits to the cause, such as Middleton Murry. Almost invariably, however, their socialist vision was spiritual and, involving as it did a repudiation of the mainstream of political socialism, it can be likened to non-violent anarchism.

Unusually for a socialist of twenty-five years standing and a pacifist who had risked a court martial in the Great War, Plowman had taken no part in pacifist activities until inspired by the non-socialist Sheppard to do so. Despite Spain, he threw himself full-time into the work of the P.P.U., and restated his pacifism in a collection of essays published in the autumn of 1936 with the revealing title *The Faith Called Pacifism*. It was appropriate, too, that Kingsley Martin, who considered that the effect of this book 'must have been to stop many doubters from being pacifists' since they were asked to adhere to 'so revolutionary and difficult a religion',[1] was later to describe the atheistic Plowman as 'a religious pacifist if ever there was one'.[2]

Plowman's greatest pacifist satisfaction at this time came when in October 1936 he finally succeeded in converting his close friend and fellow critic Middleton Murry to pacifism. After abandoning the extreme Marxism which had nearly put an end to their friendship during 1931–2, and espousing war-resistance in January 1933, Murry had gradually, like a majority of socialists, come to pin more faith in the League, particularly after leaving the I.L.P. in 1934. His main interest, however, was in developing the *Adelphi* summer schools into a permanent socialist community, for which purpose he bought, in November 1935, a house near Colchester which became the Adelphi Centre. Plowman, however, was doubtful

---

[1] *NS*, 14 June 1941, p. 599.
[2] Martin, *Editor* (Penguin edn.), p. 211.

about the basis of his desire for communal living. 'Is it the
spontaneous expression of a deep, germinal, religious faith
. . .?' he inquired. 'Or is it a gesture of fatigue . . . made
without a more specific purpose than amiability and goodwill to nice people . . .?'[1]

This question was a shrewd one: Murry's enthusasm for
community life was largely explained by his corresponding
lack of enthusiasm for his disastrous third marriage. His
second wife, Violet Le Maistre, had died in 1931 of consumption—like Katherine Mansfield nine years before—and
Murry thereupon married Violet's former maid Betty, a
robust and formidable woman who, as one acquaintance
observed, was unlikely to die of consumption,[2] but whose
violent temper verged on insanity. His conversion to pacifism
involved, therefore, a very personal commitment to non-
violence since it went hand in hand with a decision to return
to Betty (who was seeking custody of their daughter) and
thereby endure her aggressive rages which often left him
conspicuously bruised.[3] This decision followed a brief but
intense love-affair with the American wife of his doctor
which left both parties so distraught that Max Plowman,
whose skill and appetite for soothing the distressed was probably his most remarkable talent, found it hard to calm both
of them down.[4] The affair had occurred in August 1936 at
the *Adelphi* summer school at which Murry, despite the
pacifist propaganda he was forced to absorb with his food
from Rayner Heppenstall, then a young writer who was
acting as cook at the Adelphi Centre, was implacably anti-
pacifist. On the 20th of that month he had recorded in his
diary that Spain convinced him 'as I have never been convinced before, and could never have been convinced otherwise,
that one must fight . . .'.[5] But having decided not to fight
his wife, and having spent a holiday on the Norfolk broads
with Plowman, he resolved not to fight fascism either and

[1] Plowman to Murry, 16 Sept. 1935, M.P.

[2] Rayner Heppenstall, *Four Absentees* (1960), p. 68.

[3] When Sybil Morrison first met him she thought he had a disfiguring birth-
mark, which turned out to be a bruise: interview, 13 Oct. 1976.

[4] Helen Young to Dorothy Plowman, 14 Oct. 1936, M.P.; and Colin Middleton Murry, *One Hand Clapping: A Memoir of Childhood* (1975), pp. 115-18.

[5] Cited by Lea, *Murry*, p. 232.

signed the peace pledge on 14 October 1936. 'To have
walked that mile along with you', Plowman informed him the
following day, 'is worth a whole life.'[1]

Murry's conversion to pacifism was as shocking to his
other friends as his simultaneous return to Betty (and involved him equally in personal hardship since the wealthy
socialist Sir Richard Rees withdrew his important financial
backing for the *Adelphi* in protest). Yet Murry was anxious
to justify his pacifism in explicitly socialist terms. *The Necessity of Pacifism*, which he published in the summer of 1937,
stressed the total lack of appeal to 'the average plain-man of
this country' of materialistic socialism. He also advanced his
new conviction 'that this capitalist society will not be transformed by anything other than a movement of human
brotherhood,' and that since 'there is nothing in a capitalist
world more revolutionary than international peace', pacifism
would save Britain from war.[2]

But especially in the book's Epilogue—which probably
reflected his meeting Sheppard for the first time in March
1937 and his discovery that he was unexpectedly impressive—
this political emphasis was overlaid by an explicitly Christian
message. Thus not only did he make the point: 'The teaching
of our Lord was far more revolutionary than materialistic
socialism', but he concluded the book on an intensely spiritual note: 'The new Community, the new Communion, the
new Church: these are to my imagination, inseparable and
one.'[3] This new emphasis came as a shock to Plowman—
who, after half a decade of carefully nurturing Murry's
religious sense, now found himself seeking to curb it—particularly when Murry toyed with the idea of becoming
ordained. Mrs Swanwick's observation, cited earlier, that it
was 'religious' pacifists who tended to retain their faith while
the 'more politically minded' ones reneged can thus be confirmed as generally accurate: provided that it is granted that
political pacifists were also, as the case of Murry's unpre-
meditated transition from socialist to Christian pacifism so
neatly illustrated, in a sense 'religious'.

[1] Plowman to Murry, 15 Oct. 1936, M.P.
[2] pp. 26, 40, 54.
[3] pp. 121, 124.

(ii) Christians

Although escaping the virtual destruction suffered by socialist pacifism, and well placed to benefit from the longer-term trend towards recognition of the moral or spiritual nature of pacifism, the Christian inspiration was also shaken by the events of 1935-6. As Cecil Cadoux, whose own views were undergoing significant modification in the later thirties, remembered: 'It was during the monstrous attack on Abyssinia that a veteran Christian remarked to me that there were a good many people who thought they were pacifists but who now find they are not.'[1] Raven agreed: 'Pacifist opinion was unquestionably shaken' by the Abyssinia crisis, in which 'pacifists found themselves forced into an apparent alliance with Lord Beaverbrook in advocating isolation' or were 'thrilled by the tale of John Cornford's heroic death' in the Spanish Civil War; and many, 'among them some who had been leaders of the movement', had changed their minds. Yet, he pointed out, 'especially among the Churches' pacifism continued 'to gather strength'.[2]

The relative resilience of Christian pacifism demonstrated the extent to which it had already clarified its ideas during 1934-5; for, as Raven emphasized, 'only those who had serious grounds for their faith and had learnt to see the issue plainly and take long views were likely to stand firm.'[3] Although most Christian pacifists had taken an optimistic view of the international situation which was shattered in 1936, their leaders had begun to emphasize that the justification of their faith, as a matter of personal revelation, was separate from the politics of war prevention. Furthermore, being predominantly middle-class and in many cases content with the existing social order, Christian pacifists tended to be less strongly anti-fascist than socialist pacifists, and more inclined, therefore, to see the suffering of the Spanish people in their civil war as confirming pacifist predictions about the nature of war, rather than to see the political issues involved as upsetting all previous assumptions. Christian pacifism was thus

---

[1] Cadoux, *Christian Pacifism Re-Examined*, p. 5.
[2] Charles Raven, *War and the Christian* (1938), p. 45.
[3] Ibid.

able to recruit disillusioned internationalists over Abyssinia
without immediately losing them over Spain.

For both new recruits and established supporters, however, the implications of Christian pacifism became a little
clearer as a result of these events. This change must not be
exaggerated: Christian pacifists never fully emancipated
themselves—largely because of the lack of subtlety of their
opponents, it must be acknowledged—from reliance on
certain stereotyped arguments. One such argument concerned the merits of the same handful of biblical texts
mentioning force or killing: Raven noted wearily in 1938
that every relevant allusion had been 'scrutinized, discussed,
interpreted and employed as an authority a hundred times
during the past twenty years'.[1] But in trying to break away
from inconclusive text-swapping, pacifists often resorted to
what became another stock debating point: that (again in
Raven's words) 'it is utterly inconceivable that Christ could
be the pilot of a bombing aeroplane'[2]—an argument which,
however, owed as much to anachronism as to genuine insight
into the Mind of Christ since it was no less impossible, as a
shrewd critic of pacifism pointed out in 1939, to 'imagine
Christ driving a car along the Kingston By-Pass, or taking a
ticket to a Walt Disney film'.[3] Leading Christian pacifists
were aware of the limitations of such polemic and came in
1934–5, as already noted, to lay more stress on the positive
aspects of their beliefs. Yet when they did so they spent a
lot of time discussing the pacifist's attitude to internationalism
as if they regarded it as the best long-term policy for war
prevention, saying less about either the political efficacy of
pacifism itself, or its theological basis. By discrediting internationalism and exposing pacifism to allegations of heresy,
the Abyssinia crisis demonstrated that, as Professor G. H. C.
Macgregor pointed out in the first study to take account of
the crisis, Christian pacifists had formerly been 'too apt to
assume without a sufficient proof that Jesus' ethic is incon-
testably "pacifist" and that, even if so proved, he intended

---

[1] Ibid., p. 93.
[2] Rose Macaulay *et al.*, *Let Us Honour Peace* (1937), p. 45.
[3] Kenneth Ingram, *The Defeat of War: Can Pacifism Achieve It?* (1939),
p. 53.

that pacifist ethic to be applied to the wider sphere of social and national politics.'[1]

As Professor of Divinity and Biblical Criticism at Glasgow, President of the Church of Scotland Peace Society, and a member also of the F.o.R., Garth Macgregor (1892–1963) was well equipped to remedy this deficiency, and his book, *The New Testament Basis of Pacifism*, completed in September and published in December 1936, has come to be accepted as perhaps the most valuable study of Christian pacifism to emerge from the inter-war period. Its difference of emphasis from previous writings can be judged from his insistence that 'nothing is more important than that we should ask, "What *is* the teaching of Jesus?" before we confuse the issue by going on to ask, "Is it practicable for us today to follow that teaching?" '[2] The answers he gave to both these questions, which will be considered in turn, added up to a justification for Christian pacifism which was undoubtedly more rigorous intellectually, but also less reassuring politically, than any that had previously been offered to the British pacifist movement.

Rather than emphasizing literalistic formulae (although he included an exhaustive analysis of the relevant texts) or dwelling on the horror of modern warfare, Macgregor concentrated on defining 'the positive imperative of the Christian ethic'. This he summarized as the three 'basic principles' of Christ's teaching and example: firstly, 'love towards one's neighbour'; secondly, the 'belief in a Father God who loves all men impartially and sees an infinite value in every human soul'; and, thirdly, the principle that all Christ's teaching 'must be interpreted in the light of his own way of life, and above all of the Cross.'[3] Any attempt to apply these principles, he argued, involved practising pacifism: not merely in its negative aspect of refusal to fight, but in its more important positive aspect of love and sacrifice.

Yet it must be observed that any attempt to distil so complex a blend of differing historical, cultural, doctrinal influences and traditions as Christianity into a pure essence,

[1] G. H. C. Macgregor, *The New Testament Basis of Pacifism* (1936), p. 7.
[2] Ibid. (preface).
[3] Ibid., p. 10.

about which all its adherents could agree, was bound to fail, since fundamental disagreements existed over first principles which could not be resolved. Pacifists were, as already noted, immanentists, believing (as the fifth article of the Basis of the F.o.R. had put it): 'That since God manifests Himself in the world through men and women, we offer ourselves to Him for His redemptive purpose, to be used by Him in whatever way He may reveal to us'; or, as in the case of Leslie Weatherhead, emphasizing 'the humanity of Jesus rather than the divinity'.[1] Until the thirties this approach was in the ascendant; Richards, for example, enthused in the late twenties that 'modern scholarship' had 'rescued Jesus and set Him once more in the midst of the world He came to save.'[2] Yet during the new decade the theological tide turned in favour of transcendentalism, and it was the need to consider all accusations such as 'slurring over the sterner side of the Divine nature', or tending to exalt 'love at the expense of righteousness',[3] which stimulated Macgregor to produce so impressively thorough and durable a study. The turning of this tide was due to the gloomy theology of Karl Barth and its trenchant application to pacifism by Reinhold Niebuhr.

Barth (1886–1968) was a Swiss-born theologian of socialist views who had been educated at Marburg and had been deeply shocked when in 1914 his former university teachers had endorsed the German Government's actions. Like Raven, he had recognized that the catastrophe of the Great War was incompatible with his previous belief in spiritual and political progress; but whereas Raven's response was to assert that it would be possible to set progress in motion once more by attacking what was clearly the most important obstacle, war, Barth's was, in contrast, to abandon all hope of human reason and reform. Re-examining the theological roots of his faith during the war years, in a major commentary on Paul's Epistle to the Romans which he published in 1919, he decided that Christian socialists like himself had been guilty of overlooking the word of God in their enthusiasm for improving society: 'Everything had always been settled without

---

[1] Weatherhead, *Leslie Weatherhead*, p. 57.
[2] Richards, *Christian's Alternative*, p. 32.
[3] Macgregor, *New Testament*, p. 69.

God. God was always thought to be good enough to put the crowning touch to what men began on their own accord. The fear of the Lord did not stand objectively at the beginning of our wisdom . . .'[1] It was the revised edition of this work, published three years later, which established his reputation by advancing the uncompromising argument that 'the theme of the Bible—contrary to the critical and orthodox exegesis which we inherited—certainly could not be man's religion and religious morality, nor his own secret divinity. The Godness of God—that was the bedrock we came up against.'[2] This belief in the mystery of God led to a greater emphasis on the sinfulness of man which was reinforced, perhaps, by the circumstances of his own life: in 1929, to the consternation of his friends and the distress of his wife, he embarked on a *ménage à trois* by bringing an attractive young woman, thirteen years his junior, into his home; and, having taken up a professorship in Bonn in 1930, he felt obliged to return to Switzerland in 1935 after being suspended for his opposition to the Nazis' German Christian Movement.

Since Barth's writings were not translated into English until 1933, and he did not visit the country until March 1937, his impact on English-speaking pacifist circles was slight until the later thirties, and even then owed much to the popularization of his views by the influential American Protestant pastor and theologian, Reinhold Niebuhr. For many years Niebuhr had been a leading figure in the most respected of American peace societies, the F.o.R., which, in view of the severity of the depression, America's immunity from air attack and her policy of isolationism, had devoted itself increasingly to the social—rather than international— aspects of pacifism. Like the British N.M.W.M. the year before, the F.o.R. had split itself in 1933 on the issue of the pacifist role in the class struggle; as a result, under the influence of both Marxism and a strong sense of man's original sin, Niebuhr rejected his former liberal pacifist belief that man was capable of living harmoniously in society

---

[1] Cited in Eberhard Busch, *Karl Barth: His Life From Letters And Autobiographical Texts* (translated by John Bowden) (1976), p. 99. This account of Barth's career is mainly derived from this study.

[2] Cited ibid., p. 119.

without conflict and left the F.o.R. Within four years he had
ceased to be a pacifist even in international matters and soon
came to support American entry into the Second World
War.[1] The extent to which his writings drove Christian
pacifists on to the defensive was later acknowledged somewhat
bitterly by Professor Macgregor in a second justification of
pacifism devoted exclusively to challenging Niebuhr's arguments: 'To the non-pacifist majority in the churches his
writings have come as a veritable godsend, and no one has
been so successful in salving the conscience of the non-
pacifists, and even in weening the pacifist from the pure milk
of his faith.'[2]

The Barth–Niebuhr assault made Christian pacifism a less
easy position to sustain intellectually than it had been in or
just after the Great War. Then, although the social and institutional pressures to support the war were greater, the liberal
approach to theology had been taken for granted by its supporters as the purest form of Christianity and the Churches'
reluctance to embrace it was attributed to worldliness. It was,
therefore, a shock for Christian pacifists to be accused in the
later thirties of being themselves insufficiently Christian and
to be branded as humanists or utopians.

For intellectuals, who, like Raven or Macgregor, were conscious and convinced immanentists, this was no more than an
irritation. The real impact was on two types of person. One
was the devout Christian layman who was anxious to base his
personal behaviour on his faith and who was discouraged
from pacifism by the argument that it ignored the question
of righteousness and over-simplified the problem of evil. The
other was the passionate hater of war who, if driven to es-
pouse pacifism, was less likely than previously to express
this in purely Christian terms, and was more inclined to use
humanitarian arguments. In particular, the P.P.U., though led
mainly by Christians, catered most explicitly for humanitarian
pacifism—a fact about which its Christian members became
increasingly unhappy. A debate in the correspondence

---

[1] Nelson, *Peace Prophets*, p. 94; Lawrence S. Wittner, *Rebels Against War: The American Peace Movement 1941–60* (1969), pp. 15–16.

[2] G. H. C. Macgregor, *The Relevance of the Impossible: A Reply to Reinhold Niebuhr* (F.o.R, 1941), p. 11.

columns of *Peace News* in July and August 1938 on the
difference between 'religious' and 'humanitarian' pacifism[1]
testified to a feeling that the P.P.U. was not a wholly satisfactory focal point for Christian pacifists. So too did the
continued growth of explicitly Christian pacifist societies:
the Anglican Pacifist Fellowship, founded in the summer of
1937, had attracted over 1,500 members by September 1939;
the Methodist Peace Fellowship had grown to 3,500 by that
time; and the F.o.R.—as will shortly be noted—was also growing with unprecedented rapidity.

The decline in the prestige and influence of the Christian
Churches over the inter-war period, and the increased emphasis on the horror and suffering to be expected in a bombing
war, help to explain why Christianity bulked less large in
relative terms within the mainstream of the pacifist movement than twenty years previously. Another reason was that,
particularly after 1936, it was less reassuring in its answer to
the second of the questions posed by Macgregor: that concerning the practicality or otherwise of pacifism. It was
humanitarian pacifists who, in the optimistic early years of
the P.P.U., made the most uninhibited claims for its policy
of non-violence. More characteristic of Christian pacifists
was Macgregor's insistence that 'it is no part of our purpose
to argue that the way of Jesus Christ . . . offers the world an
easy way out of its difficulties. If it did, it would not be the
way of the Cross.'[2] Although even he could not resist claiming that if the 'Church as such' were to become pacifist 'the
whole world situation would be radically changed' (an assertion which had to be modified to 'might well be' in the book's
1953 edition, which also dropped many of his optimistic
earlier statements about appeasement),[3] the expectations
held by Christian pacifists in the later thirties about the conquering power of love over evil were less facile than, for
example, those of the Peace Army half a decade previously.

This is illustrated by the conversion to pacifism in 1936 of
Vera Brittain, who was aware that 'to follow Dick meant
treading the Way of the Cross in modern guise. He pointed

---

[1] *PN*, 23 and 30 July, 6 and 13 Aug. 1938.
[2] Macgregor, *New Testament*, p. 135.
[3] Compare ibid., p. 143 and 1953 edn., p. 105.

to a path which might end, not in crucifixion or a den of lions, but at internment, the concentration camp, and the shooting squad.[1] An internationalist since the Great War, she did not waver from her belief in the League until she found herself the only advocate of collective security on the platform of a large open-air peace meeting held at Dorchester on 20 June 1936 in front of 15,000 people. Her subsequent account of what she came to see as 'the turning point of my life' suggests that she had not yet lost faith in the League as a political expedient and that she was impressed by the meeting mainly on account of the strong religious faith of her fellow-speakers, Lansbury, Soper, and—above all—Sheppard. Though Sheppard had immediately detected her interest in pacifism and invited her to become a Sponsor of the P.P.U., she prevaricated, and even continued to appear on L.N.U. platforms to test her beliefs. She discovered that she was increasingly in sympathy with the political case against the League as a 'mere French-dominated instrument for continuing the unjust *status quo*', which was put forward by P.P.U. hecklers; but her discussions with her husband, and her visit to Germany in 1936, had left her in no doubt that in the short term the L.N.U. had the more practical policy. Her decision—which she never regretted—to accept Sponsorship of the P.P.U. soon after Christmas 1936[2] sprang explicitly from her Christianity, which was of an extreme liberal kind. As she later expressed it:

I was . . . not even sure that I believed in God; but the effect of Jesus upon human history was a fact of experience. As a man He had died on the Cross believing that, whatever the immediate results of a course determined by conviction and ending in apparent total defeat, His Father would reveal in time's long perspective that an action performed in accordance with the Divine Will would produce the results that He desired for His world.[3]

This change of emphasis away from short-term political success was, understandably, welcomed by George M. Ll. Davies, who told the F.o.R. in December 1936 that

the passage of time had brought to the pacifist movement a deeper discernment. A phase of self-righteousness had passed and we were more humble: a wave of reaction had left us stripped and bare of outward success and disillusioned in politics. There remained a

[1] Brittain, *Testament of Experience*, p. 170.
[2] Ibid., pp. 164-70.
[3] Ibid., p. 172.

possibility of forming little 'islands of peace'—and perhaps that was the way rather than expecting high things in high places. He stressed the value of direct action by the individual.[1]

Among Christian pacifists the sectarian orientation thus became more attractive, as the trebling of the membership of the F.o.R. between the Abyssinia crisis and the outbreak of the Second World War illustrates. From the late twenties till the end of 1934 its total had stagnated at about 3,300; in 1935 it grew by 11 per cent and in 1936 by almost another 20 per cent. More remarkable, however, was the fact that its rate of increase grew more rapid thereafter: in 1937 it went up by 37 per cent and in the period from the beginning of January 1938 until the outbreak of war its growth rate averaged 32 per cent per year, reaching 9,813 members on the outbreak of war. Nor did it stop there: it grew throughout the war and by 1945 the figure stood at over 13,000.[2] A comparison with the membership pattern of the much larger P.P.U.—which grew rapidly in 1936, reached a plateau stage by early 1937 and, though climbing again from the summer of 1938 onwards, did so at less than 8 per cent per year—is revealing. It suggests that Christian pacifism, shown after 1936 to be a religious impulse which involved the risk of martyrdom, failed to attract its share of 'practical' pacifists whose conversion was a direct response to the crises of 1936, but proved a durable and satisfying inspiration for those still prepared to be pacifists when the prospects of preventing war had faded. As Soper, reflecting after five years of the Second World War, was to put it:

The utilitarian argument for non-violence breaks down under the overwhelming pressure of brute fact . . . I would not disguise the fact that many of the arguments we used to proclaim, the senselessness, the cruelty, the wastefulness, the indecisiveness of modern war have for me lost most of their coerciveness in this nightmare of corporate evil. I am alone sustained by the Christian faith which assures me that what is morally right carries with it the ultimate resources of the universe . . .[3]

(iii) Humanitarians

A majority of the enthusiastic pacifist recruits to pacifism during 1936, who enabled the P.P.U. to achieve a membership

---

[1] F.o.R., G.C. 14–15 Dec. 1936.
[2] Membership figures are from the General Committee minutes.
[3] *PN*, 15 Dec. 1944.

unmatched before or since in the history of British pacifist
societies, were those who saw their pacifism as (in Sheppard's
words) 'a logical deduction, a philosophical necessity, an intellectual reality based on a study of the science of sociology,
anthropology, politics, history, economics'[1] and who are here
classified as of humanitarian inspiration. Most of them,
having become aware of the risks inherent in collective
security, hoped that pacifism would be a safer and more
effective means of preserving peace. The precise ways they
expected to do this will be discussed later;[2] but all such
practical pacifism rested ultimately on the same belief:
that international disputes involved no vital interest and that
no nation could be foolish or indecent enough to resort to
the incalculable and uncontrollable horror of modern war
when offered a 'reasonable' solution. The sudden increase
during 1936 in support for the position which Ponsonby had
been advocating for over a decade (and Milne, with some
doubts, since 1934) was due to the reminders of the costs of
a full-scale war delivered by the limited but inhumane fighting in Spain and Abyssinia. For a time the *alternative* lesson
of these wars and of the narrow escape over the Rhineland—
that conflicts of interest too important to be negotiable were
appearing in Europe—could be overlooked.

The first of the former League supporters to respond to
the events of 1936 by espousing pacifism were, predictably,
those whose commitment to collective security had previously been qualified by strong pacifist inclinations. For example,
Storm Jameson, already noted as a classic pacifist internationalist, found herself, as the result of a discussion with
left-wing journalist friends on the very day of the remilitarization of the Rhineland, asking herself the question: 'If
I believe that concentration camps, the torture of Jews
and political opponents are less vile than war, I must say so
plainly, not pretend that the price is something less.'[3] Although she later admitted that she was never, in her heart of
hearts, able to convince herself that the answer was really
yes, she publicly opted for absolute pacifism, attending the

---

[1] Rose Macaulay *et al.*, *Let Us Honour Peace*, p. 7.
[2] See below, pp.248–65, 274–82.
[3] Jameson, *Journey*, i, pp. 341–2.

founding meeting of the P.P.U. on 22 May 1936 and becoming one of its earliest Sponsors.

Convinced sanctionists were slower to change their minds although the abandonment of sanctions against Italy was for many a time to take stock of their beliefs. As late as the early spring of 1936, Captain Philip Mumford had published a book, *Humanity, Air Power and War*, strongly arguing the case for an international police force. A former professional soldier, who had fought with the cavalry for much of the Great War before joining the Royal Flying Corps and who later served with the Royal Air Force in Iraq from 1927 until his retirement in 1932, Mumford had become interested in the League movement as an extension of his interest in the international control of air power and had been critical of pacifists who disliked the idea. In October 1934 he had argued in the L.N.U.'s journal *Headway*

that the accusation that we who press for an international air force are introducing the idea of the use of armed force to implement League policy can hardly stand. It is the pacifists and not ourselves who wish to alter a principle—that of eliminating the use of armed force.

Sometime in the summer of 1936 he started, however, to work for the P.P.U., becoming a Sponsor and member of the Executive Committee. This abrupt change of heart seems to have been a response to the failure of collective security; but another possibility cannot be ruled out. This is that his affair with the P.P.U.'s first organizing secretary, the attractive Margery Rayne—which, since he was already married, resulted in her resignation in February 1937—was the cause, rather than a consequence, of his arrival in the P.P.U. office.[1] In any case, by the end of the year he was devotedly nursing Sheppard, whose health had broken down under the strain of the P.P.U.'s opening burst of activity, on a recuperative visit to the south of France;[2] the following year he committed his new allegiance to print in *An Introduction to Pacifism*, a confident, if not always coherent, popularization of the ideas of the P.P.U.'s more abstruse humanitarian theorists.

The conversion of another former internationalist, Rose

---

[1] Interviews.
[2] Roberts, *Sheppard*, p. 294.

Macaulay (1881–1958), whose support for sanctions against Italy had been enthusiastic, took place shortly after Mumford's, and seems to have been a result both of the Spanish war and Sheppard's persuasiveness. Like that of her fellow novelist Storm Jameson, her conversion was accompanied by lingering doubts. As early as October 1936 she admitted to Gilbert Murray, whom she had just heard argue the case for collective security, that 'all the time you spoke I was agreeing . . . I am haunted by your saying that you thought the advocates of complete pacifism were doing harm; it is a fearful thought, that I often have';[1] and in March 1938 she resigned her Sponsorship. However, like Miss Jameson and Captain Mumford, she remained a pacifist until the summer of 1940, when the Nazi breakthrough convinced many humanitarian pacifists that they had been calculating the balance sheet of suffering on the false assumption that what should be weighed in the scales against the cost of war was the sacrifices that would have to be made in a 'reasonable' negotiated settlement rather than the price of submission to an unreasonable tyranny.

Bertrand Russell, the brilliant logician and philosopher, who in the early summer of 1940 was also to recant, believed that he had computed every possible factor *before* finally choosing pacifism in the autumn of 1936. As early as the summer of 1935 he had a strong presumption that, because a League war against Italy would not be justified on utilitarian grounds, no modern war would ever be; but he nevertheless felt the need to prove this proposition to his own satisfaction by devoting a book to it. As late as August 1936 he was still not ready to join the P.P.U.; but on 30 October of that year, when his *Which Way to Peace?* was published, he wrote to Ponsonby: 'When some time ago you sent me the Peace Pledge, I thought I had better write my book before signing it, so as to make sure what my opinions are. I am now prepared to sign it, and so is my wife, but foolishly we have mislaid the forms sent before,'[2] New forms were duly sent and Russell was soon made a Sponsor.

---

[1] Cited in Constance Babington Smith, *Rose Macaulay* (1972), p. 140; see also Mary Agnes Hamilton, *Remembering My Good Friends*, p. 139.

[2] A.P.

Which Way To Peace? Analysed the different policies for war prevention—including isolationism, alliances, collective security, and the 'policy of expedients' favoured by the British Government—in the light of both the existing political situation and the nature of warfare. Russell's perspective was essentially the same as the year before:

If an international government existed and were possessed of the only legally permitted armed forces, I should be prepared to support it in suppressing rebellions, since I should regard this as the only means of making peace secure. The evil of war is quantitative, and a small war for a great end may do more good than harm.[1]

But while modern sovereign states existed Russell was convinced no war could survive the medieval test of the Just War which, as updated by Russell into twentieth-century terms, involved satisfying five conditions: it had to be winnable; its cause had to be worth dying for; worth killing for; and also worth 'exterminating large parts of the civil population for'; and—most difficult of all, he believed—'the cause must be secured by victory'.[2] It was after applying these tests that Russell concluded: 'What is right and what is wrong depends, as I believe, on the consequences of actions, in so far as they can be foreseen; and I cannot say simply "war is wicked", but only "modern war is practically certain to have worse consequences than even the most unjust peace".'[3] However, in his utilitarian calculation of the consequences, Russell depended on three assumptions which explain his subsequent discovery, which he made public in 1940, that he had been wrong. The first was a vision of the next war which was so exaggerated that in practice the scales were excessively loaded on the debit side: for example, in April 1932 he had predicted that 'of Europe almost certainly very little will be left, and it is to be expected that anywhere from 50 per cent to 90 per cent of its inhabitants will perish';[4] and in 1936, arguing about pacifism with Gerald Brenan, he forcefully reiterated these views.[5] The second assumption was an over-

---

[1] Russell, *Which Way to Peace?* (1936), p. 151.
[2] Ibid., pp. 118–19.
[3] Ibid., pp. 221–2.
[4] *NW*, Apr. 1932.
[5] Gerald Brenan, *A Personal Record 1920–72* (1974), pp. 271, 329.

optimistic view of the Nazi regime, which enabled him to make exaggerated claims for economic appeasement, insisting: 'With the fear of war removed bullying would soon lose its charm, and a liberal outlook would become common. To think otherwise is to attribute to original sin faults which are in fact attributable to the Treaty of Versailles.'[1]

It was, however, his third assumption, his exaggerated picture of the infringement of liberties which even a victorious war fought by a democratic power would entail, which provided the coping stone for his pacifism. As he expressed it on 3 March 1937, in reply to one of Gilbert Murray's persistent attempts to win pacifists back to support for collective security:

You feel 'They ought to be stopped.' I feel that, if we set to work to stop them, we shall, in the process become exactly like them, and the world will have gained nothing. Also, if we beat them, we shall produce in time someone as much worse than Hitler as he is worse than the Kaiser.[2]

Not only did this argument enable Russell to pre-empt objections of the sort which had been made to Joad's and Nichols's earlier attempts at 'utilitarian' pacifism, by showing that it was not just hedonistic or materialistic but was concerned for social and spiritual values, it enabled him also to conclude that no modern war could fulfil the fifth of his criteria for a Just War. Any cause for which it was worth contemplating war would, he believed, inevitably be negated by the totalitarianism necessitated by modern defence measures.

Having arrived at this conclusion during the Spanish Civil War, Russell seems to have assumed that his pacifism could have no more exacting test to meet. According to his utilitarian analysis he accepted that any Government had a reasonable chance of imposing its will within its frontiers, and he therefore felt able, without compromising his pacifism, to agree that 'the Spanish Government is obviously right to resist its rebels.' Outside intervention would, however, do more harm than good, though he admitted that British military support for the Spanish Government would be 'a thousand times' more justifiable than resort to arms in

[1] Russell, *Which Way?*, p. 143.
[2] G.M.

defence of the British Empire.[1] When Murray attempted
to suborn him, it was in the hope that Spain would be the
weak spot in his armour; but Russell was unmoved by his
probing: 'Spain has turned many people away from pacifism.
I myself have found it very difficult, the more so as I know
Spain . . . and I have the strongest feelings on the Spanish
issue.' But he was adamant that 'having remained a pacifist
while the Germans were invading France and Belgium in
1914, I do not see why I should cease to be one if they do
it again.'[2]

But it was to be exactly while the Germans were again
invading France and Belgium that Russell announced that
fighting the Germans was a lesser evil than submitting to
Hitlerism. He had been privately convinced of this since the
Nazi–Soviet pact, and even before that he had experienced
doubts which he did not admit even to himself. Although he
normally allowed his books to be reprinted even when they
no longer represented his opinions, he made a significant
exception for *Which Way to Peace?*, admitting later, in his
autobiography, that it was 'unconsciously insincere' even at
the time of writing.[3] This insincerity was, it may be surmised, his denial of the fact that the basis of his pacifism had
been humanitarian, or even spiritual, rather than rational. As
his autobiography also revealed, his initial conversion in 1901
had resulted spontaneously from an overwhelming mystical
insight into human suffering when he witnessed the wife
of A. N. Whitehead, his Cambridge colleague,—a woman with
whom there is, according to a recent biography, 'considerable
though circumstantial evidence' that his relationship was
more than one of affectionate friendship[4]—racked by an
agonizingly painful heart-attack.[5] His presentation of pacifism in the form of a utilitarian analysis drawn from empirical
observations of the effect of modern war, was, in effect,
an attempt to disguise his unconscious dependence on the
same aversion to pain which had explicitly moved Nichols

---

[1] Russell, *Which Way?*, pp. 57, 152.

[2] Russell to Murray, 3 May 1937, G.M.

[3] Russell, *Autobiography*, ii, p. 191; see also Katherine Tait, *My Father Bertrand Russell* (1975), p. 119.

[4] Clark, *Russell*, p. 85.

[5] Russell, *Autobiography*, i, p. 146.

and Joad. Thus although he had liked to characterize himself, for example in the satirical obituary he published of himself in 1937, as a thorough-going utilitarian whose 'mathematical studies had caused him to take a wrongly quantitative view which ignored the question of principle involved' in the Great War, and whose 'lack of spiritual depth' was 'painfully evident'[1] in his pacifism, he had, as he later admitted, 'allowed himself more of a creed than scientific intelligence can justify.'[2] It was the realization of that fact which enabled him to recant his pacifism.

Those whose humanitarian pacifism proved more durable were those like Heard and Huxley who, while initially hoping that it would prevent war, were also aware from the start that it was a creed. To Gerald Heard, who had emerged with Huxley as an active pacifist campaigner in the autumn of 1935, the mystical tendencies which were later to lead him to Buddhism seemed, even by 1936, more important than the practical business of converting the masses—as Sheppard discovered when he made the mistake of asking him to write a P.P.U. pamphlet 'and to be as simple as he ever could, but obviously that is beyond him'.[3] Early in January 1937, moreover, Heard published a daunting book which urged men to 'resensitize their awareness' by 'mind-body' training based on strict attention to diet, physical demeanour, and respiration.[4]

Although by contrast Huxley was less frighteningly abstruse and more politically aware, even he could write to a friend during November 1935:

I am . . . talking over ways and means, with Gerald, for getting an adequate pacifist movement onto its feet. The thing finally resolves itself into a religious problem—an uncomfortable fact which one must be prepared to face and which I have come during the last year to find it easier to face.[5]

Since he was later to insist that he was not religious, it seems that here he used the word in its broadest sense. At the time the status of the moral belief on which pacifism rested was

[1] Reprinted in Russell, *Unpopular Essays* (1950), p. 222.
[2] Russell, *Autobiography*, ii, p. 192.
[3] Sheppard to Ponsonby, 31 Aug. 1936, A.P.
[4] Gerald Heard, *The Third Morality* (1937).
[5] Huxley to Ocampo, 19 Nov. 1935, in Smith (ed.), *Letters*, p. 398.

less important to him than its efficacy: his energies were
mainly devoted to probing the ideas of the American Gandhiphile Richard B. Gregg, who advocated a form of non-violent
training for pacifists. By 1936 Huxley was highly optimistic,
and in the first and most famous pamphlet ever published by
the P.P.U., *What Are You Going To Do About It?: The Case
for Constructive Peace*, he claimed boldly that pacifism

has the double merit of being not only morally right, but also strictly
practical and business-like. Guided by the moral intuition that it can
never in any circumstances be right to do evil and by the two empirically verified generalisations, first, that means determine ends and,
second, that by behaving well to other people you can always in the
long run, induce other people to behave well to you, he lays it down
that the only right and practical policy is a policy based on truth
and generosity.[1]

Like Russell's own 'empirically verified' utilitarian case for
pacifism, however, Huxley's claim held good only if ends
were defined in spiritual rather than political terms. If Russell
had not appreciated this fact at the time, and Huxley did not
make it explicit, it was not surprising that less intelligent
humanitarian pacifists began to confuse moral and practical
judgements. Characteristic of much Huxley-influenced early
P.P.U. propaganda was Mumford's assertion that 'war . . . as
political policy is morally wrong, and consequently will never
produce good results'; or that 'security for nations, ideals or
personal freedom can be obtained only by non-violent
resistance, by mental and not physical struggle—in other
words, that the power of mind over matter, universally
accepted in theory, has practical significance.'[2] When it came
to be understood that humanitarian pacifism was not guaran-
teeing the worldly triumph of 'mind' over 'matter', but was
merely arguing that 'matter' divorced from 'mind' was
illusory and ultimately futile, it suffered more defections
than any other pacifist inspiration.

But even though the tide of humanitarianism which had
characterized the P.P.U.'s rapid growth during 1936-7 thus
began to ebb, it left an indelible mark on the pacifist movement. 'Of genuine pacifism, outside the Christian church', the
Revd A. D. Belden noted in July 1938, 'the greater part is

[1] p. 26.
[2] Mumford, *An Introduction to Pacifism*, p. 15.

motivated simply by humanitarianism';[1] and a question-naire sent to new members joining the P.P.U. in 1938 revealed that by far the most frequently cited influence impelling them towards pacifism was still Huxley's pamphlet.[2] The humanitarian tinge of the C.O. movement—particularly among the better educated—was widely noted: the Oxford don Maurice Bowra, for example, was impressed not only by the quality of the undergraduates who declared themselves pacifists at the start of the war but also by the fact 'that their motives were usually not Christian, but humane';[3] while Denis Hayes, himself a C.O. and historian of the 1939-45 movement, emphasized that 'the typical P.P.U. objector was broadly humanitarian, broadly moral, broadly ethical'—rather than strictly religious or political.[4]

In contrast with the Great War, when the difference of outlook between Christian and socialist pacifism had been acute—or even in contrast with the twenties and early thirties when Ponsonby, Nichols, and Milne had felt themselves to be defining a new and distinctive inspiration—it was hard in the Second World War, as Vera Brittain noted in 1942,[5] to fit many C.O.s into any single category at all. By the outbreak of war the different inspirations had converged, as it came to be accepted that their assumptions about the value of the individual and the unity of mankind amounted to a common creed. Just as political pacifists had been forced to accept that their conception of socialism was spiritual, and Christian pacifists that their conception of Christianity was a liberal or even 'humanist' one, so humanitarian pacifists had come to accept—albeit more slowly—that their position was, in Hayes's words, 'an idealism that was as much a matter of faith as the creed of the religious'.[6]

---

[1] *PN*, 23 July 1938.
[2] *PN*, 31 Mar. 1939.
[3] C. M. Bowra, *Memories 1898-1939* (1966), p. 352.
[4] Hayes, *Challenge of Conscience*, p. 28.
[5] Vera Brittain, *Humiliation With Honour* (1942), p. 28.
[6] Hayes, *Challenge of Conscience*, p. 29.

12

ACTIVISTS AND SYMPATHIZERS

As late as 10 December 1935, Sheppard had been unsure how to develop his pacifist campaign, inquiring of Laurence Housman: 'What are we to do with our 100,000 men in the New Year—other than teach them the strength of their case and the discipline that the Cause requires?'[1] Just as it seems to have been the first signs of the Abyssinia crisis which impelled him in July 1935 to call together the signatories of his original letter of nine months before to form the Sheppard Peace Movement, it seems to have been the events of the early months of 1936 which led to the foundation, on a more formal basis, of the Peace Pledge Union. Early in May 1936 he was approaching possible Sponsors; and the P.P.U. was officially launched on the 22nd of that month at a meeting of Sheppard, Ponsonby, Storm Jameson, Soper, Hudson, Raven and Crozier.[2] Offices, formerly provided at Crozier's home, were taken in Grand Buildings, Trafalgar Square, until on 1 August 1936 the P.P.U. moved to larger premises on the fifth floor at 96 Regent Street, where it remained until March 1939 when, with the proceeds of the memorial fund for Sheppard, it purchased No. 6 Endsleigh Street, christening it Dick Sheppard House. Owning premises is perhaps the major factor ensuring the survival of a cause group even when in decline (since no rent, which increases with inflation, has to be paid out of dwindling subscriptions), which helps to explain why the P.P.U. still survives in the same building today in much reduced circumstances.

With hindsight, the P.P.U.'s claim to lasting fame was the quality of its leadership in the thirties. This was despite the fact that its original aim had been simply to attract a mass membership (as the next chapter will show) and despite the

[1] Housman (ed.), *What . . . ?*, p. 244.
[2] P.P.U. Sponsors, 22 May 1936; see also Sheppard to Ponsonby, 7 May 1936, A.P.

fact that, whereas no previous pacifist society had ever broken into five figures, its membership total was to reach 136,000 in April 1940. But this was little more than a quarter of the number of signatories of his pledge which Sheppard had originally predicted in November 1934 and only just over a half of the target which nine months later he had set for Christmas 1935:[1] the P.P.U. had thus fallen well short of building up the political muscle it had originally sought. However, its membership contained many gifted individuals, ranging from public figures such as Osbert Sitwell, J. D. Beresford, Reginald Sorensen and the Revd A. D. Belden, to as yet unknown young men such as D. S. Savage, Henry Pelling, and even T. Dan Smith.[2] In particular, the Sponsors, as its collective leadership was known, comprised perhaps the most intellectually distinguished committee ever assembled by a controversial British pressure group. A survey of the individual Sponsors not only reveals a complete cross-section of the various strands of inter-war pacifism, it also gives an indication of the nature of Sheppard's achievement in attracting and co-ordinating so heterogeneous a group.

Although the informality of the P.P.U.'s organization makes a definitive list hard to establish, it seems that up to the start of the war, thirty-six pacifists were given the title of Sponsor.[3] These included a remarkably high proportion of established pacifist leaders, the major *exceptions* being the Quakers (except for Sheppard's old friend Housman, Humphrey Moore, the founder of *Peace News*, and Maurice Rowntree, who became a Sponsor after being appointed treasurer in 1939—a post which, as already noted, most societies liked to have in Quaker hands); certain Christian pacifist intellectuals, such as Richards, Macgregor, Cadoux, and George M. Ll. Davies who were based outside London and also worked mainly through the F.o.R.; a number of parliamentary pacifists, such as Cecil H. Wilson who had resigned from the F.o.R.'s General Committee in March 1936, pleading overwork[4] and may simply have lacked the

---

[1] *The Times*, 20 Aug. 1935.
[2] *Observer*, 28 Apr. 1975.
[3] See Appendix II.
[4] F.o.R., G.C., 9–10 Mar. 1936.

the time; and some well-known individuals, such as Brockway, Reynolds, Joad, Nichols, and Milne, who, despite their
public reputation as pacifists, had already started to modify
their former absolutism. In addition to mobilizing established
pacifists—even those who, like Plowman, had previously been
highly sceptical about pacifist campaigning—the P.P.U.
also attracted most of the best-known recruits to pacifism
from 1936 onwards.

The thirty-six Sponsors represented every pacifist inspiration. Christianity was represented by (as well as the three
Quakers mentioned) a number of leading clergy: Sheppard
and his fellow Anglican Canons, Morris and Raven; Metho-
dists such as Soper and Carter; the Presbyterian Gray; and the
Revd George Macleod, founder of the Iona Community and
future Moderator of the Church of Scotland who had won a
Military Cross in the Great War. Others preferred to describe
themselves as Christian socialists: Lansbury, Hudson, Salter,
Barr, and Alex Wood; also in this category were Vera Brittain
and two recruits from the N.M.W.M., Runham Brown (although his Christian faith was weakening) and Wellock.
Socialist pacifism proper was confined to Bing (also of the
N.M.W.M.), Plowman, Ellen Wilkinson, and—until he
embraced Christianity—Murry. By far the largest group were
humanitarian pacifists: Crozier, Ponsonby, Huxley and
Heard; also most of the converts of 1936: Mumford, Rose
Macaulay, Storm Jameson, and Russell; and three who were
well known for their (often anti-war) art: the poet and
writer Siegfried Sassoon (the one Sponsor whose membership
was entirely nominal), the cartoonist and illustrator Arthur
Wragg (1903–76), and Mrs Ursula Roberts, who wrote novels
and poetry under the name Susan Miles. All the above can
be described as public figures, apart from Moore, Rowntree,
Brown, and Bing; the other exceptions also owed their
position to the practical help they gave to the P.P.U.: Elizabeth
Thorneycroft, a barrister who was active in the Hampstead
Group as well as at Headquarters, John Barclay, a Christian
pacifist who resigned his job with the London Cooperative
Society to become the P.P.U.'s National Group Organiser,
and Mary Gamble, whose energetic pacifist campaigning
obliged her to stand down as prospective Labour candidate

for Tamworth because the local party disliked her views,[1] but enabled her, at a P.P.U. meeting in Oxford, to meet Murry, whom she married after the death of his third wife.

The coming together of most leading pacifists in one organization provides a good opportunity to attempt a judgement on the sort of person attracted to the pacifist movement in the thirties. Although, as already noted, the historical data are insufficient to attempt a sociological analysis as systematic as that applied by Dr Parkin to the Campaign for Nuclear Disarmament, a comparison with his important study serves to elucidate several important features of pacifist support.

In particular, it emphasizes the need to make a distinction in the structure of that support between activists and sympathizers. Those willing to face the psychological and social pressures implied by activism will tend to exhibit common characteristics in a way that those prepared merely to express sympathy with the activists' particular remedy will not. Though all movements need a core of activists, the extent to which they also acquire a wider circle of sympathizers depends on the extent to which the issue on which they are pressing for reform worries the public mind. In analysing C.N.D., Parkin's task was simplified by the fact that 'the bomb' was never a matter of pressing public concern during its heyday—except perhaps during the Cuban missile crisis of November 1962 which, revealingly, helped to undermine the movement. People who believed the bomb to be an issue were thus activists by definition, and their interest in it can in part at least be explained with reference to their wider outlook and their personality. As Parkin observed, C.N.D. 'served as a rallying point for groups and individuals opposed to certain features of British society which were independent of the issue of the bomb.'[2] They were gaining the satisfactions of activism through what was, in effect, a symbolic protest.

Parkin's thesis that many C.N.D. activists were engaging in expressive rather than instrumental politics is of some value in understanding pacifist activism in the twenties. In

[1] Interview, 4 July 1977.
[2] Parkin, *Middle Class Radicalism*, p. 5.

the calm of that decade, the pacifist movement had relatively few sympathizers who felt driven to support the movement because they accepted its strategy as the best solution to an urgent crisis. Like C.N.D. it could be said to be a movement of activists 'in which "progressive" values were fully re-presented in their pure form'.[1] It had the same strong links with left-wing Labour politics and with movements to re-vitalize the Churches; and, if its progressive characteristics differed in certain details from those of C.N.D., this merely reflected the social changes over the intervening three decades: in the twenties, for example, the youth culture which was so marked a feature of the sixties was as yet un-known, and religious feeling was far stronger.

During the thirties, however, war became a real fear and, therefore, a genuine issue which no one could ignore. As a result pacifism ceased to be a movement of symbolically-protesting activists only, and attracted sympathizers—people who, forced to make up their minds on how best to prevent war, gave serious consideration to pacifism, and even tried the idea on for size (normally, however, without becoming activists themselves). The P.P.U. had deliberately set out to appeal to sympathizers as well as activists: at the first meeting of the Sponsors J. H. Hudson had 'urged that we should aim at getting the ordinary people who do not usually come out but who are with us';[2] and no membership requirement was imposed beyond willingness to sign the pledge. This doctrinal permissiveness paid dividends: as a reader of the *New States-man* noted two months later, the P.P.U.'s rapid early growth in comparison with that of all previous such societies was due to its success in appealing 'not only to the convinced absolute pacifist but to the large number of people with only slight political knowledge but with a recent realisation of the fearful imminence of war, who are fascinated by the direct simplicity of the crusade.'[3] Quantity was thus achieved at the expense of quality. An eighteen-year-old waiting to go up to Cambridge was one of the purely nominal members attracted by the absence of strings attached to the pledge:

[1] Ibid., p. 39.
[2] P.P.U. Sponsors, 22 May 1936.
[3] *NS*, 18 July 1936, p. 83.

I signed a card on which was printed the sentence 'I renounce war and never again will I support or sanction another'. This did not require much effort. I simply signed my name and posted the card to Dick Sheppard's headquarters; nothing more was asked of me. I then dived back into the pleasures of life, and wished politics to hell.[1]

In the event, the Spanish Civil War broke out almost at once, undermining his 'pacifism' and helping to convert him to Marxism; it seems probable, however, that his card remained on the P.P.U. file.

Since even the P.P.U. itself was unclear, as will later be seen, whether or not signatories who never followed up their original card—Henry Pelling was another example—should be regarded as members, it is meaningless to talk about the 'typical' pacifist without specifying whether one is referring to the sympathizer or the activist. The sympathizer may well, particularly in 1936-7, have been more typical in the sense that he was more numerous; but he did not constitute a type. The radicalism of his stand on war was often in marked contrast to his conformist attitudes on other issues, as was shown by the considerable suspicion felt in the N.M.W.M. at the 'bourgeois' nature of the P.P.U., even at the point of agreeing to merge with the latter; and also by the tendency for activists to keep reminding all pacifists not to 'isolate' war from other social evils. As one expressed it in *Peace News*: 'The Peace Pledge Union has been called a middle-class movement. Let us prove we *are* willing to put an end to the economic differences which lead to class distinctions.'[2]

The activist hardcore of the movement did, however, constitute a recognizable type in the sense that its pacifism, like support for C.N.D., was a 'capsule statement of a distinctive moral and political outlook'.[3] This, as already noted, had been the case in the twenties too, but the 'capsule' had been significantly modified by the events of the thirties. No longer was it part of the mainstream of progressive values—in the thirties this became increasingly anti-fascist and, therefore, hostile to pacifism. The expressive satisfactions which, Parkin

---

[1] Mark Holloway, in Clifford Simmons (ed.), *The Objectors* (Isle of Man, 1965), p. 126. (Unusually, however, Holloway was to return to pacifism—in Dec. 1940, even though he was by then serving in the Navy.)

[2] *PN*, 24 Sept. 1938.

[3] Parkin, *Middle Class Radicalism*, p. 3.

believes, C.N.D. provided for youthful idealists amid the political apathy of the sixties, and which pacifism had also provided in the not wholly dissimilar conditions of the twenties, were provided in the thirties not by pacifism but by Marxism and by such causes as the hunger marches and the fight against Franco. By the later thirties, therefore, pacifist activists were swimming against the main tide of progressivism. They were doing so for one of two reasons: either they were survivors of an older political tradition which had suddenly been engulfed by the new tide; or they were deliberately pioneering an alternative mode of political dissent.

The first, mostly older and less educated pacifists, were cast in the stern mould of traditional Nonconformity. Joad believed, with evident distaste, that the 'ordinary pacifist' was a non-smoking, non-drinking vegetarian.[1] The extent to which this was in fact the case is hard to establish, although the articles and, especially, the advertisements in pacifist publications, and the testimony of P.P.U. staff members who regularly visited local groups, confirm that there was a sizeable element in the movement fitting Joad's description. 'At the first Peace Pledge Union camp at Swanwick', one member later recalled, '. . . there was a large table for vegetarians and as the days went by the number of people at the vegetarian table grew steadily . . . until the crowd was almost equally divided.'[2] (The two camps eventually played each other at cricket.) Obituaries in pacifist journals—a sample biased, it must be admitted, towards those who remained active pacifists until their death and towards memorable characters—reveal a considerable proportion of vegetarians, esperantists, and members of small sects, and also of eccentric personalities. For example, the obituary of Harold Hutchins, who joined the P.P.U. in 1936, stressed his extreme absent-mindedness and unworldliness;[3] Alf Mashford's noted his life-long campaign of harassment against Life Assurance companies which resulted in his imprisonment on a number of occasions;[4] while that of Laurie Hislam,

[1] C. E. M. Joad, *Journey Through The War Mind* (1940), p. 98.
[2] Roy Walker, *PN*, 21 Sept. 1947.
[3] *Pacifist*, Apr. 1965.
[4] Ibid., July–Aug. 1969.

a long-serving member of the P.P.U. National Council and later active in the Committee of 100, told the story of his arrest for panicking the crowd which had gathered in Downing Street on the eve of war in September 1939 by lobbing tennis balls—which were mistaken for hand-grenades—into its midst as a means of demonstrating the horror that war would bring.[1]

But in addition to the survivial of what might be called pacifism's puritan activist—occasionally quietist but with a tendency to overbalance into self-righteousness and minority-mindedness of the kind exemplified by the N.M.W.M.—there was in the thirties a newer type, associated with the minority of socialists whose views were akin to non-violent anarchism and whose pacifism therefore survived or was stimulated by the Spanish Civil War, and with the increasing numbers of humanitarian pacifists. This type can be called the libertarian activist: it was less sharply defined, but in so far as it exhibited a characteristic approach to life it was secular and bohemian. Its inspiration was a conception not of morally correct behaviour, but of individual liberation from unjust restraints. This impulse was perceptively described by Ethel Mannin (1900–), shortly after becoming a political pacifist in January 1939. A novelist known for her bohemian life in the twenties, she had joined the I.L.P. in 1932 before living with and later marrying Reginald Reynolds. Like her husband she abandoned anti-militarism in her enthusiasm for the Republican cause in Spain, but was soon reconverted, this time to strict pacifism. Despite these apparent changes of course, she came to believe that her life had been dedicated consistently to a 'passion for liberty' which had finally led her to pacifism. In the twenties, it had 'asserted itself in a completely hedonistic attitude to life; in the last few years I have been absorbed in this idea of human liberty which can only be achieved in a free social order.'[2]

Humanitarian (as distinct from political) pacifists did not see this freedom as being so explicitly a product of the social structure; they emphasized the right of the individual to

[1] Ibid., Sept. 1966.
[2] Ethel Mannin, *Privileged Spectator: A Sequel to 'Confessions and Impressions'* (1939), p. 28.

think for, and to enjoy, himself. The new atmosphere could be seen at the P.P.U.'s second summer camp held in 1938 at Langham (Murry's former Adelphi Centre which the P.P.U. took over after he became a Sponsor) where, according to *Peace News*, 'the gregarious had their fill of human society in the bedrooms and bathrooms—the latter being responsible for a wholesale breaking down of inhibitions about taking one's bath in public.'[1] At times there was tension between the two strains: Richard H. Ward (1910–69), a struggling young actor and writer who later founded the Adelphi players (a pacifist theatre group), was not the only one of the junior workers at Headquarters to be involved in affairs which outraged the Nonconformists Sponsors[2]—Salter and Hudson were later to resign on such an issue[3]—and which made the London Quaker community chary about backing the P.P.U.[4] Even Nonconformity, however, was responding to the Freudian revolution and it was noteworthy that two pacifist converts among its ministry, Leslie Weatherhead and, more especially, Herbert Gray, specialized in preaching a more progressive attitude to sexual problems.

The libertarian type was commonly a member of the younger generation of progressives which dissented from what it considered to be the bellicosity and materialism which had come to dominate the anti-fascist, Marxist-tinged mainstream of left-wing thought. The generational aspect of the difference must not, however be exaggerated. The libertarian strain in progressivism was not new: older pacifists, such as Russell and Joad, had already exemplified it; and an intensity reminiscent of their absolutist predecessors in the Great War could still be found among younger pacifists such as Roy Walker, a young P.P.U. activist who was to go on hunger-strike in prison in the Second World War and, later, to become a keen vegetarian. Yet an examination of the young idealists who devoted their main energies to pacifism, in many cases working for a time at P.P.U. head-

---

[1] *PN*, 6 Aug. 1938.
[2] Nancy Browne to Dorothy Plowman, undated letter, early 1940, M.P.
[3] According to Brockway, *Bermondsey Story*, p. 236.
[4] Roger Wilson to the author, 19 Aug. 1977.

quarters—Richard Ward and Roy Walker, who have already been mentioned, plus Frank Lea, Ronald Duncan, Nigel Spottiswoode, and David Spreckley—reveals a surprisingly homogeneous type. All were ex-public schoolboys with strong creative leanings. All, except for Ward (1910-69), had been born between 1913 and 1915 and were, therefore, a significant few years younger than the 'King and Country' generation which had been moulded by the war literature of the 1928-30 period but had been strongly influenced towards Marxism by the slump. All had radical political impulses but either found Communism stifling, as in the case of Spottiswoode and Lea, or found the influence of Gandhi or de Ligt stronger, as in the case of Walker, Duncan, and Ward. All, moreover, were influenced by the pacifist literature and propaganda of the middle thirties: Lea was converted by reading Plowman; Walker by reading Huxley; Spreckley by reading A. A. Milne; while Duncan was strongly influenced by reading the American pacifist, Richard Gregg.

Frank A. Lea (1915-77), a Cambridge science graduate whose interests had shifted towards literature and philosophy, had volunteered to serve in Spain; on his conversion he worked instead for the *Adelphi* and for Murry, whom he later succeeded (from 1946-9) as editor of *Peace News*, and whose biographer he became, devoting his subsequent career to freelance writing and lecturing.[1] Duncan, Spottiswoode, and Spreckley had all lost their fathers during infancy—in the latter two cases in the Great War—and rebelled against the values of their conventionally patriotic upbringing. Of part-Indian extraction and a Cambridge pupil of F. R. Leavis, who was later to achieve success as a dramatist, Ronald Duncan (1914-) was impelled by his belief in non-violence to attempt to practise reconciliation in a South Wales strike, to visit Gandhi in India, and to undertake propaganda work for the P.P.U.; he also persuaded Benjamin Britten, also a pacifist, to write a 'Pacifist March' for a grand P.P.U. occasion (which, however, never took place).[2] Nigel Spottiswoode (1915-), Duncan's friend at Cambridge, from where he

---

[1] Interview, 2 Mar. 1977.
[2] Ronald Duncan, *All Men Are Islands: An Autobiography* (1964), pp. 128-42.

was sent down for concentrating not on his mathematics but on film-making of a variety too permissive for the Proctors' taste, joined the P.P.U. staff late in 1936; simultaneously he was attempting to patent a new type of film camera, and shortly before the war retired to live the simple lie in Devon with Duncan and to work on his invention.[1] David Spreckley (1915–   ), who was destined for a naval career until bad eyesight forced him to transfer from Dartmouth to Sandhurst—a comedown socially which crystallized his mounting rebelliousness against the 'respectable' values of step-parents, used his small private income to finance his full-time work for the P.P.U. from late 1936 till he resigned in 1941, frustrated with its lack of militancy. His idealism, which led him to interrupt his pacifist work during 1938 to do social work in Hong Kong, was matched by a zest for life: he was a dare-devil amateur pilot and in the war dodged arrest for eighteen months during which time he worked pseudonymously as an actor. After the war he attracted notice for turning the private business he had started into a co-operative.[2] Roy Walker was, as already implied, the odd man out of this group, being regarded by the others with some trepidation on account of the relentless intensity of his personality and his energy: in many respects he was a strict-pacifist version of Reginald Reynolds, sharing also his enthusiasm for Gandhi. Having resigned from his office job in 1937 to give his services free to the P.P.U., he was taken on to the payroll and was the driving force behind many of its campaigns; his post-war career as a critic and author was handicapped, however, by mental illness.[3] Taken as a whole the younger generation of thirties pacifists represented within the British tradition of dissent a transitional stage between the Nonconformist conscience and the beatniks.

The existence of two activist generations meant that the pacifist movement lacked a distinctive age profile. Some pacifists felt that the movement appeared too elderly; for example, a discussion on the letters page of *Peace News* on how the P.P.U. might improve its image in public demonstrations

[1] Interview, 6 Sept. 1977.
[2] Interview, 26 June 1977.
[3] Roy Walker to the author, 28 July, 12 Aug., 10 Oct. 1977.

included a plea in the 13 August 1938 issue that those taking part should 'be definitely *selected* by the organisers' as being neither 'too odd' nor 'too old'. But in the few cases where the percentage in different age groups claiming conscientious objection at approximately the same stage of the Second World War can be compared, the figures suggest that the younger were the more pacifist. The only significant exception to the steady wartime decline in the percentage registering as C.O.s occurred between January and June 1941 when the two batches born in 1921–2 had a higher rate of registration (0.57 per cent and 0.47 per cent) than the three oldest groups to be conscripted for military service through-out the war, between which they were sandwiched—those from the pre-Great War generation born in 1900–4 (0.36 per cent, 0.38 per cent, and 0.36 per cent).

The sex ratio was more clear-cut. Although it was widely believed that women were the more strongly attracted to pacifism—the *Peace News* reader just quoted warned also against pacifist demonstrations being 'too predominantly female'—the P.P.U.'s membership was more than two-thirds male,[1] and Sheppard's opening of the pledge to women in July 1936 met with a disappointing response. The peace movement had from the Great War onwards undoubtedly given many women their first public platforms and organiza-tional opportunities outside the feminist cause, and this fact may explain why the public mind exaggerated their role within it. Another possible explanation is that the P.P.U. had many female sympathizers who felt it inappropriate for them to join since they were not, in practice, going to be asked to fight (although the pledge referred to supporting war, not to taking part in it).

In terms of class there is little difficulty: both at the time and with hindsight pacifism appears mainly middle-class, as Parkin's detailed occupational analysis found was also the case with C.N.D. But this is scarcely surprising: joining cause groups is a middle-class activity dependent on leisure, education, and economic security. Thus although the P.P.U.

[1] Vera Brittain, *Letters to Peace Lovers* (1940), p. 55; interview with Sybil Morrison, 13 Oct. 1976.

attracted a number of working-class sympathizers—such as John Wanstall, an East End-born skilled maintenance engineer, who signed the pledge but did no more[1]—the patchy evidence about Second World War C.O.s suggests that it failed to mobilize even such working-class pacifist feeling as there was. The working class (and, more especially, the unskilled) was underrepresented among objectors, and its pacifism seemed to derive from two main traditions (leaving aside, of course, the *pacificist* tradition of militant socialism which helped to swell working class representation among C.O.s) both of which were on the wane by the thirties. These were: the 'Lansbury tradition', which saw pacifism as an organic part of socialism; and the tradition of Nonconformist pacifism which seemed increasingly to be confined to the workers of Wales (where both the Peace Ballot and conscientious objection statistics revealed a slightly higher level of pacifism than elsewhere). Even within the middle class, the P.P.U.'s leading activists—for example, its public school 'libertarians' already mentioned—were probably more elevated socially than most of its supporters. Its 'puritans' tended to be lower-middle-class, and the C.O.s of 1939–45 have been described as predominantly 'black-coated' and 'white-collar', although the occupational category which produced the most objectors in relation to its size was, according to one limited survey, 'Professional and Civil Service'.[2] As Parkin also found, those working in commerce or business were uncommon; and his stress on the importance of the 'welfare and creative' occupations is also strongly borne out by an analysis of the P.P.U.'s leadership. No less than twelve Sponsors lived primarily by their pens, and seven were clergymen, although not all leading pacifists in holy orders had become Sponsors.

While no systematic consideration can here be given to the general problem of the nature and direction of the causal connection between certain occupations and commitment to radical ideologies, a few comments can be offered.

[1] Interview, 4 May 1975.

[2] Cited in Rachel Barker, 'Conscientious Objection in Great Britain, 1939–45' (Ph.D. Thesis, Cambridge, 1978), pp. 79–80; see also Hayes, *Challenge of Conscience*, pp. 201–2.

In the case of clergymen the connection would appear to be self-evident. So too would the practical advantages enjoyed by writers: in addition to the considerable economic security they enjoyed in the thirties—stable prices and comparatively generous fees from the plethora of journals and papers enabled even a lazy writer of no private means like Plowman, whom his wife admitted to have 'had a lifelong quarrel with his pen',[1] to live in modest comfort in Hampstead Garden Suburb—writers always possess freedom, both to devote time to pacifist activities and to escape the institutional pressures which accompany support for minority viewpoints. This pressure to conform was stronger in the thirties than in the more liberal sixties, and this may explain why schoolteachers, one of C.N.D.'s largest occupational categories, seem to have played less of a role in the P.P.U., and why, although pacifism was no handicap for junior clergy, there was only one pacifist bishop: E. W. Barnes, whose pacifism dated from his former career as a mathematics don at Trinity College, Cambridge (where he had been a friend of Russell's),[2] and who did not become a Sponsor. Although pacifist writers, notably Russell and Huxley, enjoyed outstanding critical and intellectual acclaim, few pacifists in other careers attained advancement of any kind. The exceptions were: Lansbury, whose rise to the leadership of his Party was fortuitous and not achieved until well into his seventies; and those Christians who achieved the success unattainable in their Churches in the more tolerant atmosphere of academic life: Macgregor, Cadoux and, in particular, Raven who added to his Regius Professorship at Cambridge both the Mastership of Christ's College in 1939[3] and, later, the Vice-Chancellorship. On the subject of institutional pressures it can finally be noted that several Sponsors escaped them in ways other than through being writers or academics: through being retired, as were Mumford, Herbert Gray, and Crozier; through being self-employed, as were Elizabeth

[1] D.L.P[lowman] (ed.), *Bridge*, p. 6.

[2] G. H. Hardy, *Bertrand Russell and Trinity* (1942; facsimile edn., Cambridge, 1970), p. 31 n.

[3] He had been passed over three years previously in the election on which C. P. Snow based the defeat of the gifted but emotional 'Paul Jago' in his novel *The Masters*: Dillistone, *Raven*, p. 192.

Thorneycroft (the only representative of the professions unless Salter is counted as a doctor rather than a politician) and Runham Brown (the only businessman); or through possessing private means, as did Ponsonby and Mary Gamble.

Freedom may explain why cause group work was taken up, but it cannot itself account for the particular cause chosen. Unlike C.N.D., which existed almost in an ideological vacuum, the P.P.U. was just one of many competing progressive campaigns. In trying to find out what was the distinctive appeal of pacifist activism in the thirties the historian cannot explore his own hunches and generate his own evidence by opinion surveys (as Parkin has done); his subjects are mostly dead and the survivors, even if their memories are reliable, cannot be questioned on a statistically significant scale. Yet he has one compensating advantage: he has in many cases fuller biographical details about the dead, and is not dependent on information they themselves have volunteered. On the admittedly impressionistic basis of the random sample whose motives and characteristics can be examined, tentative suggestions will be offered concerning the personal circumstances of pacifist leaders which may help to explain why they exposed the cause they did.

All social movements are, in a sense, urging society to gamble: they are advocating what are, to a greater or lesser extent, leaps into the unknown, based on the hope that what has come to be regarded as normal human behaviour can be changed for the better. Pacifism is unique not only because it expects this change to be fundamental—the same can be said of anarchism—or because it involves risk for itself—many revolutionary movements risk persecution—but because it demands that the whole of society stakes everything, all at one throw, on its creed. One of the characteristics of a number of those prepared to take responsibility for recommending society to take this gamble in the thirties was, not surprisingly, a high degree of confidence in their own judgement even in the face of opposition and incredulity. Murry was an extreme example, telling his son shortly before his death in 1957: 'True I have incessantly been mistaken. But since I have tried to keep myself open to experience my mistakes haven't worried me. I have been able to accept them

as minor revelations';[1] his post-war belief, remarkable for a
recent ex-pacifist, in a pre-emptive nuclear strike against the
Soviet Union in certain circumstances, was also shared by
Russell, who, like Joad, was noted both for the confidence
with which he delivered controversial opinions on a wide
range of social and moral issues and for the frequency with
which he changed them. Barclay's 'boundless optimism' was
'too much' for at least one of his P.P.U. colleagues;[2] Soper,
whose Christian faith and political optimism proved no less
serene but far more consistent, possessed the confidence in
non-violence to deter by force of personality a ruffian with
a knife who threatened to attack him on his soap-box;[3]
and Wellock, like Bing and Brown an absolutist C.O. in the
Great War, devoted his life to the ideal of self-sufficiency
long before it became fashionable. With self-confidence
went a considerable independence of mind and willingness
to take unorthodox ideas seriously: Lansbury became interested in Theosophy; Heard, 'a dress fetishist favouring
purple suede shoes and leather jackets with leopard-skin
collars', had an unusual fascination with 'paranormal phe-
nomena',[4] and, though a professional man of science, became
a doctrinaire Buddhist; Huxley, as already noted, also readily
suspended his critical faculties in his enthusiasm for a number
of unorthodox medical remedies; Plowman was (wrongly)
convinced that he possessed the healing power to nurse
Murry's tubercular second wife, Violet, back to health;[5]
and Leslie Weatherhead's 'uncommonly broad credibility for
the uncanny' led him to frequent spiritualist seances at
which 'he suspended his disbelief'.[6] Even Ponsonby, who
liked to present his pacifism as a question of blunt common-
sense, had a curious obsession with the phenomenon of
time: in 1936 he published a book which appeared to argue
that the observable fact that our perception of the rate at
which time passes is subjective was somehow connected with
his own inability to comprehend the concept of eternity and

---

[1] Colin Middleton Murry, *Clapping*, p. 139.
[2] *PN*, 25 Sept. 1942; and interviews with David Spreckley, Frank Lea.
[3] Donald Soper, *Question Time on Tower Hill* (1935), p. 40.
[4] According to P. N. Furbank, *E. M. Forster: A Life*, ii (1978), p. 136.
[5] Plowman to Murry, 'Christmas Day, 1930', M.P.
[6] Weatherhead, *Kingsley Weatherhead*, p. 129.

immortality, and that, taken together, these factors meant
that the individual should at once urge the immediate adoption of the policy he knew to be right.[1] Others were, it
should be noted, much less self-confident: Rose Macaulay's
doubts led her to resign her Sponsorship as early as March
1938 although she remained a pacifist for two further years;
and Sheppard's perpetual agonizing has led to speculation
about how he would have behaved had he lived beyond
October 1937.

Being not so much a policy for war prevention as an act
of faith, pacifism may have had a psychological appeal for
those undergoing personal stress which alternative policies
did not. This hypothesis is suggested by another characteristic of those leading pacifists whose private lives can be
examined: the high proportion who were experiencing
difficulties of one sort or another at the time of conversion.
This may have helped to break down the normal inhibitions
towards exposing 'extremist' views—as was later admitted
by an ordinary P.P.U. member, Sydney Carter, to have been
true of his own conversion. (Though attracted by the ideas
of Huxley and Gregg, he was not pushed over the edge until
he was jilted: 'Somehow the tie between me and the community that I was part of snapped. The moth-like solitude
that awaited the conscientious objector, which I had so
dreaded, now seemed endurable.')[2] Emotional and sexual
difficulties also affected a number of leading pacifists.
Russell's initial commitment to pacifism in 1901, which
thereafter he sought to rationalize in utilitarian terms, dated,
as already noted, from his intense sympathy for Mrs Whitehead, with whom he was emotionally involved. Sheppard, as
will shortly be noted, had an unhappy marriage: for him, as
for Murry whose adoption of pacifism has been interpreted
as a corollary of the decision to return to his violent third
wife, pacifism implied also a very personal commitment to
love and reconciliation. Although the details of Morris's and
Mumford's conversions remain obscure, they led somehow to
the break-up of their marriages: Morris's decision to become

[1] Arthur Ponsonby, *Life Here and Now: Conclusions Derived From An
Examination of the Sense of Duration* (1936).
[2] Simmons (ed.), *The Objectors*, p. 54.

P.P.U. Travelling Secretary and later to work full-time at headquarters in London may, like his decision to leave the Church in 1939, have been connected with his leaving his wife (who disapproved of his pacifism) and three children; while Mumford's affair with Margery Rayne forced her to resign as office secretary.[1] Several of the female Sponsors led private lives that contained a large measure of unhappiness and frustration. Maude Royden, a later recruit to the P.P.U., in 1938, found herself, as has already been mentioned, in a platonic *ménage à trois*; Rose Macaulay's lover, the novelist and lapsed Catholic priest Gerald O'Donovan, was also married.[2] Though Vera Brittain's marriage to George Catlin proved, after a difficult start, very successful, it was an unusual one, being based on long periods of voluntary separation while both parties concentrated on their own careers;[3] while Mary Gamble, though finding happiness after July 1939 with Murry, whom she later married, has described the frustrations of a spinster's existence in the thirties.[4] That pacifist activism could be a response to private dilemmas is also suggested by the career of Sybil Morrison (1893–), a former suffragette and pillar of the post-war P.P.U. who had started as an active pacifist speaker in the late thirties, being elected to the first National Council when it replaced the Sponsors in May 1939: 'Bewildered by . . . her own sexual ambiguity'—she had only slowly come to realize she was a lesbian—'she found salvation in the pacifist movement', as she was later, with characteristic honesty, to acknowledge.[5] In addition, Nichols was homosexual; while the compulsiveness of Joad's womanizing was remarked upon by many of his acquaintances.

In several cases the personal difficulty was compounded by nervous or physical infirmity. Sheppard was converted at a time when asthma had prostrated him; and Maude Royden's inspiring Christian socialist preaching of the power of good to overcome worldly obstacles may have owed something to

[1] Interviews.
[2] See Constance Babington Smith, *Rose Macaulay*, pp. 89–91, 96–7.
[3] Brittain, *Testament of Experience*, pp. 37–42.
[4] See Mary Middleton Murry, *To Keep Faith* (1959), pp. 14–28.
[5] 'Miss Sybil Morrison Talks To Jilly Cooper', *Sunday Times*, 2 July 1978.

her own lameness. The connection between pacifism and an acute sensitivity bordering on nervous illness was even more common. Just as veteran pacifists Davies and Hobhouse, both of whom supported the P.P.U., had initially embraced pacifism following breakdowns, so too Huxley espoused it as part of the process of conquering his insomnia. Not all pacifists solved their problems: Roy Walker's courageous post-war struggle with mental illness has been mentioned;[1] and both Mrs Swanwick, whose isolationist views were indistinguishable from pacifism by the mid-thirties, and Ellen Wilkinson, whose pacifist phase was brief and troubled, were later to commit suicide.[2]

Also, in a few instances, pacifism can be linked with career disappointments—particularly in the case of those who seemed most temperamentally out of sympathy with the more extreme of their new colleagues. A clear case was Crozier, whose dislike of pacifist faddishness and indiscipline was unconcealed and whose enforced retirement with a grievance against the army accounts to a considerable extent for his pacifism. Sheppard, who, like his fellow ex-chaplain Raven, was never able to believe conscientious objectors to have been as noble as the soldiers he saw sacrifice their lives in the Great War, embraced pacifism at a moment of, not just illness, but also extreme disillusion with the Church and despair at his future career—though his later treatment from the ecclesiastical authorities proved generous. Raven's espousal of pacifism after he had perceived the tide of opinion turning in its favour may—for his critics saw him as a vain and histrionic performer, and one at least of his clerical colleagues in the P.P.U. doubted his 'moral seriousness'[3]—have been a bid to recapture the limelight he had enjoyed during C.O.P.E.C. but not subsequently. In the event, however, as already noted, his failure to achieve rapid ecclesiastical preferment was compensated for by academic success.

---

[1] See also his letter to *The Times*, 9 Oct. 1971, on the difficulties of the long-stay mental patient.

[2] Respectively: in Nov. 1939 (see Brittain, *Testament of Experience*, p. 226; Keith Robbins's unwitting comment that 'she was happy in the occasion of her death'—i.e. at the start of the war—is thus unfortunate: *Abolition*, p. 204); and on 6 Feb. 1947 (see Donoughue and Jones, *Herbert Morrison*, p. 392).

[3] Interviews. For his ecclesiastical disappointment and his conception of 'dramatic, charismatic' leadership, see Dillistone, *Raven*, pp. 255, 405.

These suggestions about pacifist motivation are, it must be repeated, tentative. It may well be argued that similar beliefs and predicaments are found among non-pacifists, and that support for pacifism should be explained purely on its merits as a wholly rational option to choose in view of the expectations about modern war held in the thirties, or of the powerful theological arguments for believing that it was the only Christian policy. Indeed an example can be given of the dangers of interpreting support for pacifist policies in terms of a particular 'type'. After Munich the P.P.U. became interested in personal acts of reconciliation on a mass scale and discussed 'the suggestion that members of the P.P.U. should ask German visitors to stay with them'.[1] Before, however, one is tempted to interpret this faith in citizens' diplomacy as revealing a characteristic outsider's view of politics it should be considered that no less an embodiment of realistic governmental thinking than Maurice Hankey, Cabinet Secretary from the creation of the post until July 1938, wrote and circulated a draft letter to *The Times* on 29 August 1939 suggesting that 'the innumerable bodies of all kinds in this country which have established contacts with some corresponding body in Germany' should send letters to their opposite numbers urging a peaceful solution to the Danzig crisis.[2] Nevertheless it can scarcely be denied that the leading pacifists were a collection of memorable and unusual personalities—in the words of the self-confessed 'baby' of the Sponsors, Lord Soper, 'an odd lot'.[3] This makes it remarkable that the P.P.U. managed to function at all with the unwieldy committee of idiosyncratic Sponsors as its main decision-taking body, and also that it managed to attract so many sympathizers and even activists from among those previously suspicious of pacifists as cranks. Fear of war is clearly a major part of the explanation; but any consideration of the P.P.U. as an organization must begin by recognizing the importance of its founder's simple appeal and of his ability to generate a sense of harmony among so many strong individualists.

---

[1] P.P.U. Management Committee, 7 Nov. 1938.
[2] Stephen Roskill, *Hankey: Man of Secrets*, iii (1974), pp. 414–16.
[3] Interview, 28 Oct. 1976.

13

THE PEACE PLEDGE UNION UNDER SHEPPARD, 1936-7

(i) Führerprinzip

The extent to which the P.P.U. depended on Dick Sheppard during his lifetime can scarcely be exaggerated. At the first meeting of the Sponsors: 'It was generally agreed that the direction should rest largely in one man's hands, at any rate for a time.'[1] Sheppard was thus, on a business analogy, managing director as well as chairman of the board; but even with a growing staff of secretaries and volunteers, led by the capable Margery Rayne, it was soon clear that he could not cope with the large intermediate area of operations which fell between the Sponsors' philosophical and strategic guidelines and the purely routine work of the office clerks. However, the attempts to relieve him of some of this work served only to confuse the constitutional structure of the P.P.U. and led to greater pressure on Sheppard on that account. In July 1936 it was decided that Morris, Crozier, and Mumford should share responsibility with Sheppard for overseeing the day-to-day business;[2] and as the P.P.U. continued to grow two full-time officers were appointed: Morris became Travelling Secretary in October, and John Barclay National Group Organiser in November. But since only the frequently ill or indecisive Sheppard could take decisions between the monthly meetings of the Sponsors—the sovereign body—chaos often resulted which irritated Crozier (who yearned for the greater efficiency, as he saw it, of the Peace Army and the Sheppard Peace Movement) and created difficulties whenever Headquarters was asked by local Groups for rulings about policy. In particular the difficulty, noted in the next chapter, of knowing whether Gregg's ideas about non-violence constituted official policy,

[1] P.P.U. Sponsors, 22 May 1936.
[2] Ibid., 29 July 1936.

which coincided with one of Sheppard's bouts of ill-health in December 1936, led to an overdue strengthening of the headquarters machinery. An Executive Committee was formed, holding its first weekly meeting on 10 February 1937, consisting of the senior office staff and those Sponsors who were prepared to take an active interest in routine work. And when, also in February, Miss Rayne resigned, for personal reasons but using her resignation to protest at the frustrations caused by the P.P.U.'s constitution, Sheppard was able to persuade Plowman to become full-time General Secretary, a post he took up in March. This change created new tensions, however. The Executive, which reflected Headquarters' vested interest in active campaigning, was a rival authority to the Sponsors—a body whose powers Miss Rayne had wanted to curtail—and became frustrated with that more occasional body's powers of veto. And Plowman, completely out of sympathy with his activist colleagues on the Executive, gave up his post after only a year.

The task of keeping the Executive in step with the Sponsors as well as of keeping the members of both bodies in step with each other was, however, achieved by Sheppard in his lifetime, though not without considerable strain. 'The complications, dear Arthur', he confided in a letter to Ponsonby in the summer of 1936, 'of keeping Gerald, Crozier and others in step are at times more difficult than I can say.'[1] 'I loathe the P.P.U.,' he was heard to exclaim, only half-jokingly, on his way to one Sponsors' meeting; while his cry on the way back from another was: 'What we want is a bloody massacre.'[2] Although his decision to launch his pacifist campaign had been a response to better health, he was far from cured. He was physically unable to speak for more than fifteen minutes when giving a lunch-hour lecture at Friends' House in December 1935,[3] and he tended to work himself to the point of collapse: this happened in July and December of 1936, and again in the early summer of 1937 after a gruelling and disappointing fund-raising trip to the United States. His fatal heart attack on 31 October 1937, at the age of fifty-seven,

---

[1] Sheppard to Ponsonby, 31 Aug. 1936, A.P.
[2] Roberts, *Sheppard*, pp. 285-6.
[3] *Friend*, 13 Dec. 1935, p. 1182.

came as a shock but was scarcely a surprise to those aware
of his penchant for working twenty-hour days.[1] He was
under emotional strain, moreover. His time as Canon of St.
Paul's was, a colleague later wrote, 'a Gethsemane and nothing else',[2] and he brooded about leaving the Church. Also,
shortly before his death, his wife Alison—the spoilt child of
rich parents who faced the unenviable task of living with a
man widely regarded as a saint, and a man who was, moreover, physically incapacitated by asthma for most of their
married life—had left him for their next door neighbour,
Archy Macdonnell, a former member of the L.N.U. staff
who had become a successful humorous writer.[3] Yet Sheppard carried bravely on: his dependable social secretary,
Nancy Browne, who had become almost a member of the
family, deserves some of the credit, but even at the depths of
his domestic troubles Sheppard's personal gift of communi-
cating more than routine parsonlike bonhomie never left
him—the sense of individualized concern he radiated to everyone he met being, by all accounts, astonishing. For example,
all the many descriptions of the P.P.U.'s first summer camp
at Swanwick, only a few months before his death, agree that
it was made memorable almost entirely by Sheppard's
infectious gaiety.[4]

All accounts of his role in the P.P.U. emphasize its charismatic quality. To Murry, Sheppard was a 'great democratic
and Christian *leader*';[5] while as early as July 1935 Kingsley
Martin had written of Sheppard as potentially 'the Führer
of a really formidable peace army'[6]—a metaphor which
occurred later to both Max Plowman and the Dean of St.
Paul's.[7] Rose Macaulay, Murry, Huxley, Kingsley Martin,
and Richard Ward were among those who acknowledged
that, despite their considerable initial suspicion of his

[1] Roberts, *Sheppard*, pp. 240–1.

[2] W. H. Elliott, *Undiscovered Ends* (1951), p. 138.

[3] Sheppard to Ponsonby, dated 'Sunday' (1937) A.P.; Scott, *Dick Sheppard*,
pp. 232–4.

[4] See e.g. *Dick Sheppard By His Friends* (1938), pp. 104–10; D.L.P(lowman)
(ed.), *Bridge*, pp. 608–9; Roberts, *Sheppard*, p. 404.

[5] Cited by Lea, *Murry*, p. 247.

[6] *NS*, 30 July 1935, p. 88.

[7] *Dick Sheppard By His Friends*, p. 22; *Adelphi*, Mar. 1939, p. 261.

sentimental and sugary public persona, they fell under his spell immediately they met him in person. In their company he liked to exaggerate his feelings of intellectual awe—telling Ward on one occasion about a car journey spent in the company of Huxley and Heard throughout which they talked 'on a level of such extraordinarily elevated intellectuality, about such abstruse matters, and in words so remote from ordinary conversational usage, that he could understand nothing that was being said'.[1] Yet, as Rose Macaulay candidly put it in a private letter, 'he has won the respect of his intellectual superiors.'[2]

The secret of his appeal to his fellow Sponsors seems to have been twofold. Firstly, he had an aristocratic manner which, though embarrassing to the younger activists who felt he should live more austerely, enabled the pacifist message to be given a hearing in circles suspicious of left-wing movements. The Sponsors were aware of this and some were also impressed by his common touch: Raven, for example, himself a product of a class-conscious professional family, was so impressed by Sheppard's friendly and concerned relationship with the middle-aged waitress at the London club where they first met for lunch in 1916, that a quarter of a century later he was still describing it as 'a revelation'.[3]

His second asset was his intellectual humility. Plowman, who had certainly been surprised (and was probably flattered) by being rung up out of the blue by Sheppard and asked whether he should quit the Church,[4] later believed Sheppard's strength lay in being 'the living contrary of the modern intellectual. He was a brilliantly perceptive and imaginative man whose active love of persons prevented him from any intense concern with intellectual abstractions.'[5] The extent to which Sheppard's mind was indeed intuitive and imaginative rather than analytical and theoretical can be illustrated by quoting one sentence from his speech to an Armistice Day peace meeting in 1935:

[1] Ward, *Names and Natures*, p. 117.
[2] Constance Babington Smith (ed.), *Letters to a Sister from Rose Macaulay* (New York, 1964), p. 78.
[3] Charles Raven, *The Starting Point of Pacifism* (P.P.U., 1940), p. 12.
[4] Plowman to Murry, 20 Oct. 1936, M.P.
[5] *Adelphi*, Oct. 1938, p. 3.

You and I who were sensitive to our world in 1914, we who are 40, 50 or more, to-day, in the silence of those moments when the veil that hides us from the other world kind of wavers like gossamer in a slight breeze; we who look back into the faces of those we know and those we loved, and whom, before God, we still look upon as martyrs for peace because they died to end war, we cannot easily to-day, I say, forget what it cost them to do what they did, believing they were doing so to save us from that hell, nor can we forget the terrible, ghastly, awful way in which we are failing them, because it does look, doesn't it, I speak not only to you but to myself—that we are not to be depended on.[1]

Equally characteristic was his attempt to define his spiritual beliefs in a note to Ponsonby on 14 May 1936: 'As to my own religious faith, I am blowed if I know exactly where I stand. I am mostly a Quaker these days but Jesus Christ, man or God, (I have never wished to define him) is the hero I would wish to follow.'[2]

It was Sheppard's brilliant achievement to turn into a positive asset this notable weakness as an abstract thinker. With the Sponsors divided over what policy the P.P.U. should adopt, Sheppard's lack of defined views enabled him to devote his energies to teasing out what he thought to be their general will. Such positive opinions as he held, moreover, were middle-of-the-road: he was opposed to adopting either a collaborative orientation towards collective security, as he made clear in *We Say 'No'*, or a position of sectarian quietism, as when he whispered to Kingsley Martin, one of the guests invited to his flat to meet Gregg on 17 July 1936: 'Can't you get up and tell them that we haven't time for all this intensive cultivation and that our job is to stop the next bloody war.'[3] Indeed, essential to his Christianity was his faith that a middle position could be occupied that was sufficiently pure and idealistic to stand outside the self-defeating compromises of politics while at the same time sufficiently relevant and practical to have wide-ranging regenerative power. Just as he had always called for a Church 'that was in the world but not of it',[4] he was still calling a fortnight before his for support for pacifism

---

[1] *Rec.*, Jan. 1936, pp. 13–14.
[2] A.P.
[3] *NS*, 6 Nov. 1937, p. 718.
[4] H. R. L. Sheppard, *If I Were A Dictator* (1935), p. 20.

from those who have hitherto had hopes that a way of avoiding war might have been discovered through social and political means which did not entail their complete personal devotion and severance from the so-called 'order'. Pacifists must live within that 'order' not as baffled idealists but debonair and courageous—as rebels against the world as it is.[1]

But which would Sheppard have chosen if he had lived to face a wartime choice between almost complete 'severance' from the 'order' as a pacifist or accepting that 'the world as it is' required some compromises? Would he have come to believe, as were many P.P.U. members, that he could maintain this middle way by an uncompromising pacifism which stressed its commitment to serving the community in non-violent ways? Mary Gamble recalls asking Sheppard what he would do if war came and receiving the answer: 'Nothing; our duty is to prevent war';[2] and on 24 March 1944 *Peace News* quoted him as having once said: 'If war comes we shall have failed.' A number of P.P.U. members came to believe that Sheppard would have abandoned or modified his pacifism in 1939 or 1940.[3] It is not necessary to base this hypothesis on a view of Sheppard as lacking the courage to face real unpopularity. More objective factors can be cited: his private lack of self-confidence about his pacifism, and his waverings on minor but revealing questions of theory and practice in *We Say 'No'*; his 'emphatic' insistence that the P.P.U. 'could not ask others to make sacrifices involving their livelihood without becoming responsible for their support'[4]—which in peacetime meant allowing members to retain jobs in munitions factories and in war might have led to greater concessions; and his belief about the Great War that the self-sacrifice of the soldiery was greater than that of the conscientious objector. It is possible, therefore, that he would have modified his views in the way Cecil Cadoux was to: by resort to the collaborative orientation to argue that all pacifists had said before about the evil of war was correct, that they were bound by their conscientious inability to

[1] *NS*, 16 Oct. 1937, p. 600.
[2] Interview, 4 July 1977.
[3] Interview with Frank Lea, 2 Mar. 1977.
[4] *Report*, P.P.U., A.G.M., M.P.

fight, but that they had to admit that one side had the better cause and should not be obstructed.[1]

Against this it should be pointed out that Sheppard was so committed to pacifism that any modification of his views would have raised embarrassing accusations of expediency. Most P.P.U. members believed Sheppard would not have wavered but would have shown the courage of the Revd Robert Carbury, hero of Vera Brittain's post-war novel *Born 1925*, a fashionable West-end parson and pacifist leader who was undeterred by the war and who, though somewhat idealized—he was an Etonian, a Great War V.C. and Cambridge First—was based on Sheppard.[2] When Mary Gamble repeated her conversation with Sheppard to Raven, he refused to believe that Sheppard could have said it.[3] All that can be said for certain, however, is that Sheppard's sudden death in October 1937 saved him from a dilemma which could only have been distressing for a man so lacking in dogmatism, so respectful of the opinions and instincts of the man in the street, and so anxious to forestall the outbreak of another war.

(ii) The Power of Non-Violence

How did pacifists expect their faith to prevent a second world war? Faced with the crises of 1936 many seem to have felt that their very presence might calm the public mind at a time when Europe was poised on the brink of an arms race, if not of war itself. Warning in May against rearmament, Leyton Richards insisted that 'when people are "badly frightened" they do silly things and hit out blindly and this seems to be precisely what the British public is being induced to do today.'[4] The widely-held view that the next war would be started and completed by a single air raid also encouraged the belief that abstaining from air rearmament would, by removing all provocation, eliminate the danger of annihilation by a pre-emptive enemy air strike. The more

[1] See below, p. 298.
[2] Vera Brittain, *Born 1925: A Novel of Youth* (1948).
[3] Interview with Mary Middleton Murry, 4 July 1977.
[4] *Spectator*, 29 May 1936, p. 981.

optimistic pacifists believed that avoiding provocation would also encourage a positive response; for example, Soper was insisting in May 1936 that a 'real yearning for peace' could be found, 'not least of all in countries like Italy and Germany'.[1] And even those more pessimistic about European passions could hope for isolationism at least; Wellock, for example, had the previous month stated: 'It may be that the catastrophe of a Second World War is unavoidable, but should it occur I think it is supremely important that this country should not be involved in it.'[2]

The founding of the P.P.U. on 22 May 1936 meant, as was generally recognized, that further thought would be necessary on this point. Announcing the new organization in *Reconciliation* for June 1936, Soper admitted: 'It is quite obvious to everybody, not least those at Headquarters, that a policy must be formulated and a great campaign begun.'[3] But since the first meeting of Sponsors had agreed to leave policy to Sheppard himself, no strong guidance was offered and no explicit policy statement, beyond the simple pledge he had first used in his letter of 16 October 1934, was issued by the P.P.U. in his lifetime. Sheppard merely attempted to respond to what he saw as the consensus of views among his colleagues. As a result he followed the lead of the most active of the early Sponsors—Soper, Huxley, Crozier, and Ponsonby—all of them highly optimistic advocates of the efficacy of non-violence, and committed the P.P.U. to the belief that 'non-violent resistance' would prevent war. Thus when on 11 June 1936 Rose Macaulay had, in the course of the discussion in which Sheppard persuaded her to become a Sponsor, asked how pacifism could deal with international bullying, she learned from him (as she afterwards informed her sister) that 'there seems to be something called non-violent resistance (see Aldous Huxley enclosed) which they think would work.'[4] The following month Sheppard, in formally opening the P.P.U. to women members, exhorted them

[1] *Rec.*, May 1936, p. 117.
[2] *PN*, 10 Apr. 1936.
[3] p. 164.
[4] Babington Smith (ed.), *Letters to a Sister*, p. 76.

'to train themselves locally in the technique of non-violence.'[1]

The upsurge of interest in non-violence—which now tended, significantly, to concentrate on the efficacy of passive resistance to an invading army rather than the possibility of morally deterring aggression in the first place—was due to the failure of most other painless policies, such as economic sanctions, and also to the discovery of an appealing new formulation of the strategy of passive resistance by the colleague of whom Sheppard was then most in awe, Aldous Huxley.

Interviewed during the Abyssinia crisis, Huxley had stressed his conviction 'that the only practical way of dealing with the problems of war is the organisation of what Gregg in his recent book on the subject calls Non-Violent Coercion—the method of Gandhi and so many others.'[2] The book in question, first issued by an American publisher in 1934 and overlooked in Britain until an astutely-timed new edition appeared in September 1935, was The Power of Non-Violence by an American Gandhiphile, Richard B. Gregg. Gregg, a labour lawyer who became interested in non-violent techniques after becoming involved in a railway strike, had travelled to India to meet Gandhi and had spent four years there, developing his psychological theory.[3] His book began by rehearsing the best-known historical examples of successful non-violent action—such as Magyar resistance under Deak to the Habsburgs before 1869, Gandhi's work in South Africa before the Great War and in India after 1930, and a sit-in strike by Hungarian miners at Pécs in October 1934. Since these examples were for the most part familiar from other books on the subject,[4] repetition of them risked implying not the diversity of historical applications of non-violence but, rather, the limited extent of its success. Gregg's originality was to add to these conventional historical and spiritual arguments a psychological conflict-theory of 'moral

[1] NS, 10 July 1936, pp. 661–2.
[2] Johnson, Peace Offering, pp. 154–5.
[3] Chatfield, For Peace and Justice, p. 204.
[4] For similar works, see Brockway, Non-co-operation in other Lands; Ruth Fry, Victories Without Violence (1930), More Victories Without Violence (1938); Bart. de Ligt, The Conquest of Violence (1937).

mechanics' or even 'moral jiu-jitsu'. His thesis was that a trained corps of resisters could inhibit and embarrass the soldiers ordered to deal with them. If the soldiers assaulted them nevertheless, or if gas and bombs were used to evade a face-to-face confrontation in which non-violent resistance could take place, this action would win widespread support for the resisters from within their own people, and 'a very complete and effective trade boycott and strike of domestic or industrial work could be organised'.[1]

But 'Greggism', as it came to be known in the P.P.U., was open to the same objections already noted in the context of earlier enthusiasm for Gandhi's ideas. As non-pacifists pointed out, it was designed for use against a domestic or imperial oppressor rather than an international bully. If adapted to the international sphere it made tacit assumptions about its standard of morality only slightly less optimistic than those of the 'extreme' pacifists of 1931–2. The surprisingly few explicit pacifist discussions of the consequences of invasion revealed how far believers in non-violence continued to base their calculations on expectations of 'reasonable' behaviour from aggressors. Sheppard, for example, found it 'impossible to believe' that enemy soldiers could bring themselves 'to gas, to bomb, to shoot, to crush and conquer' an unarmed people, and believed they would refuse to obey their dictators' orders.[2] Soper, however, wanted to

face the worst. Perhaps the nation which renounced violence will suffer crucifixion, it is a possibility, though I think today a small one. But though there is little chance that its women and children will be butchered, the people of any country might have their lives seriously restricted and their outward freedom denied them. That is I think a real prospect if such an invasion were to come from a so-called civilised power . . . I cannot believe that it would involve any loss of life.[3]

If such was assumed to be 'the worst'—with no mention, for example, of the victimization of British Jews—then it was less surprising that non-violence was considered an acceptable risk by pacifists. It should be remarked too that the British public generally seemed less prone to alarms about the possibility of invasion (until the summer of 1940) than it

[1] Richard B. Gregg, *The Power of Non-Violence* (1935 edn.), p. 53.
[2] H. R. L. Sheppard (ed.), *The Root of the Matter* (1937), pp. 323–4.
[3] *Rec.*, May 1936, p. 119.

had been in the years before 1914—a strangely complacent
attitude which may have resulted from its obsession with air
attack.

The second objection was that non-violence was no less a
form of coercion than violence. It was here that Gregg
thought he had the answer, but the arguments he adduced
merely raised new difficulties. Gregg's 'moral mechanics'
interpreted the human personality as a force-field of emotions which his technique could bring into harmony by 'using
in a moral sphere the principle of the resolution of forces
. . . instead of the wasteful principle of direct opposition and
consequent waste of energy and unsatisfactory and only
temporary results.'[1] In these terms the invader was not
crushed by 'moral jiu-jitsu' but set at peace with himself.
But though the theoretical dilemma was resolved, Gregg's
psychological technique required considerable training; as
Huxley admitted, it 'would have to be as efficient in its way
as the organisation and discipline of an Army.'[2] Recognizing
this fact, the P.P.U. formed its members into local 'Groups',
as Gregg had recommended, and published for them a manual,
Training for Peace, which went into detail about the merits
of meditation, singing together, and folk-dancing, as a means
of attaining the communal spirit necessary to practice non-
violence, and even suggested: 'Spinning or knitting clothes
for one's family or for others, if undertaken by the members
of the P.P.U., would provide significant work for the inarti-
culate, for mothers who cannot easily go to meetings or old
people who cannot go out.'[3]

But this programme risked convincing the pacifist movement's newly won sympathizers that it was, after all, a
movement of cranks. The fact, moreover, that so devoted
a Gandhiphile as Reynolds found Huxley and Heard's training too oppressive to persevere with;[4] that a mystic like
Plowman likewise experienced 'an unconscious resistance

[1] Gregg, *Non-Violence*, p. 53.

[2] Johnson, *Peace Offering*, p. 155.

[3] Richard B. Gregg, *Training for Peace: A Programme for Peace Workers*
(P.P.U., n.d. [1936]), pp. 101–2, 23.

[4] Reynolds, *My Life*, p. 109.

to intensive Study Groups and all Yogi-Bogie exercises';[1] and that Sheppard himself became impatient with 'all this intensive cultivation',[2] showed that even the most convinced pacifists baulked at it. Far from generating an effective mass movement Gregg's training methods seemed to produce an élite of mystics. After a few months experience of the P.P.U.'s Bradford Group, Margery South was protesting late in 1936 'with all my heart against the healthy and natural hatred of war being used to build up a "precious" doctrine which has as its objective the regeneration of the individual rather than the prevention of war.'[3]

As a result of growing criticism of this kind—and of an offer from a hundred East-Enders to volunteer for such training, which the Sponsors had to consider in November 1936—the P.P.U. was forced to reappraise its attitude to 'non-violent resistance'.[4] The Sponsors sought the advice of Ronald Duncan, who had sent in an essay on the subject; he told them that non-violence could be practised, without 'any form of conscious psychological training', by a small nucleus 'whose function it would be to attempt to give a pacifist lead wherever there might be any trouble such as a strike or riot'. The sole prerequisite would be 'a knowledge of pacifism and the development of a feeling of unity with those with whom they would be associated.'[5] The Sponsors discussed this view at length without being able to reach a decision, a stalemate reflected in the fact that the draft pamphlet which Duncan had originally sent in was published, with Sheppard's blessing and circulated with P.P.U. literature, though it did not bear the P.P.U. imprint itself.

Appearing early in 1937 as *The Complete Pacifist*, this pamphlet which Duncan had originally sent in was published, with Sheppard's blessing and circulated with P.P.U. litera-to be based merely on a reiteration of the arguments made familiar in Angell's *The Great Illusion*, to the effect that no nation could benefit by conquering another, with the added

---

[1] Plowman to West, 21 Oct. 1936, D.L.P(lowman) (ed.), *Bridge*, pp. 578-9.

[2] Quoted in *NS*, 6 Nov. 1937, p. 718.

[3] South to Rayne, 28 Dec. 1936 (copy), A.P.

[4] P.P.U. Sponsors, 12 Nov. 1936.

[5] Ibid., 25 Nov. 1936; Duncan to the author, 5 Aug. 1977.

[6] Ronald Duncan, *The Complete Pacifist* (1937), p. 17.

assumption (which, contrary to popular misconception, Angell had *not* made) that every nation would be capable of rational behaviour. The more original and interesting part of Duncan's case was where he explained his strategy for gradually converting the population to pacifism by means of small 'cells' of pacifists, organized like a religious order. These nuclei of pacifists would not escape into ivory towers but go out and practise non-violence in the slums and factories. Duncan was optimistic about the prospects of their missionary role: 'If they are integrated, convinced, certain of themselves, their poise will be secure and their balance safe.'[1] When, however, Duncan himself attempted to preach non-violence to the striking miners of the Rhondda valley he had, as he later admitted, his poise and balance upset by the hostility of the local Union Secretary, a Communist.[2]

Although it eschewed many of Gregg's faddist incidentals, *The Complete Pacifist* helped to bring to a head the growing fear that Greggism was endangering the P.P.U.'s whole future development. On 7 January 1937 Crozier let off steam in a nine-page letter to Ponsonby replete with nostalgia for the days before, as he saw it, 'cranks' had waylaid the movement:

It has become obvious for some time to me that the Gregg theory might well split the Union, if the Gregg cranks were allowed to take control. During the period that the Sheppard Movement, as it was then called, was here we kept a very strict and firm hand on cranks and others who wished to argue about or depart from the pledge, which was open to signature . . . Miss Rayne was not a pacifist in the complete sense nine months ago. Captain Mumford has only become a Greggite more recently. Up to about eight months ago he was a believer in Collective Security and it is obvious from his book published in the Spring of 1936. Canon Morris unburdened his soul in the pulpit to his congregation three or four years ago, and has since, I may say quite recently fallen for Gregg.[3]

Simultaneous symptoms of this discontent included: Margery South's new-found wistfulness, in her letters of complaint about Greggism, for the relatively unpretentious N.M.W.M. (which she had abandoned to join the P.P.U.);[4] the insistence of the Chairman of the Oxford University Pacifist Association

---

[1] Ibid., p. 25.
[2] Duncan, *All Men Are Islands*, pp. 128-30.
[3] A.P.
[4] South to Ponsonby, 10 and 12 Jan. 1937., A.P.

that 'for the moment the acquisition of members is more important than the training of small groups on Gregg's lines';[1] and the satirization of Greggism in a private revue put on by London P.P.U. members.[2] By 2 February 1937 Sheppard, back from a period of illness, was privately admitting to Ponsonby that 'a bloomer was made over "The Complete Pacifist" ' and claiming that 'the Greggism' in it had been intended only 'for certain people for whom that line of approach might be useful', and that it was not an official P.P.U. pamphlet.[3]

But this did not answer the question of whether Greggism in general was official P.P.U. policy, as Sheppard himself had earlier implied when he had described *The Power of Non-Violence* as 'the text-book of our movement'.[4] Gregg's work had strong support among the newly formed groups, being 'the "bible" of constructive pacifism', in the opinion of the Wembley Group, which also considered that 'above all, the P.P.U. stands for the method of non-violent resistance'.[5] It was the administrative implications of this confusion over policy revealed during Sheppard's illness, about which Margery Rayne's Parthian Shot complained,[6] which led to the creation in February 1937 of an Executive Committee and the appointment of Plowman as General Secretary; but on the policy issue itself nothing was done. By April, in consequence, a campaign to rid the P.P.U. of Greggism had become apparent. The Chairman of Oxford's student pacifists again complained: 'We have gossiped about vegetarianism and knitting and Indian ahimsa, when we ought to have pondered economics and Parliament and Spain';[7] while Ponsonby, ever concerned to dissociate pacifism from cranky tendencies, lent his authority to the view that, although initially presented to the P.P.U. as a practical policy, Greggism had in practice proved a sectarian distraction from

[1] *PN*, 30 Jan. 1937.
[2] Interview with Sybil Morrison, 13 Oct. 1976.
[3] A.P.
[4] *PN*, 25 July 1936.
[5] *Peace Front: Review of the Wembley Group*, 7 Nov. 1936.
[6] Rayne to the P.P.U. Sponsors, 5 Jan. 1937, A.P.
[7] *PN*, 17 Apr. 1937.

the urgent business of war prevention.[1] Kingsley Martin had
warned against this danger from the start: at the gathering
of prominent pacifists at Sheppard's flat on 17 July 1936 to
meet Gregg, he had 'brisked things up by asking if we were a
set of quietists or a political organisation';[2] and in the *New
Statesman* for 8 May 1937 he again insisted:

If the Peace Pledge Union merely stands for disciplined non-violent
resistance in war time it will quickly fizzle out. The question is whether
it can do anything before war comes. When the bombs are falling the
difference between a man who is standing with his hands folded and
one who is gesticulating with a rifle will scarcely be noticeable.[3]

In May 1937, despite an attempt by Gregg to justify
'faddism',[4] his manual was withdrawn as an official P.P.U.
document—although it was characteristic of the P.P.U.'s
consistent policy of tolerating all forms of pacifism that it
continued to be available for those who wanted it.[5] From
this point onwards advocates of non-violence were noticeably
embarrassed by its Greggist connotations. Richard Ward, for
example, admitted in a pamphlet on the subject in 1938: 'I
am sure that some of you will expect me to advocate . . .
every conceivable crankiness. We are on the dangerous
ground marked "training for peace", obviously the next
thing is for us to talk about knitting, navel-gazing, morris
dancing, and a diet of nuts.'[6] Instead, Ward emphasized his
preference for Bart. de Ligt's anarchist approach to non-
violence, which saw it as a form of long-term education of
the ordinary worker's social consciousness.

The main consequence of Greggism, however, was not that
the P.P.U. received bad publicity but that it was distracted
from considering the central problem of non-violence: would it
prevent war? A P.P.U. member wrote to Ponsonby agreeing
strongly with his strictures on Greggism 'because we have
just been having a good dose of Gregg and one can't help
feeling the danger of the P.P.U. becoming "a refuge for

---

[1] *PN*, 1 May 1937.
[2] D.L.P(lowman) (ed.), *Bridge*, p. 573.
[3] p. 763.
[4] *PN*, 24 Apr. 1937.
[5] P.P.U. Sponsors, 5 May; E.C., 3 May 1937.
[6] R. H. Ward, *What Is Non-Violent Technique?* (Pacifist Publicity Unit,
1938), p. 10.

faddists" ' but also asking pertinently: 'isn't non-violent resistance the pacifist's only substitute for war-like resistance?
Surely we can't just give in and knuckle under to, say,
fascism? and if we won't fight, isn't the Ghandi [sic] stuff the
only alternative?'[1] On the non-Greggist aspects of non-
violence the P.P.U. was surprisingly vague. Sheppard's
comments on war-prevention tended to be visionary rather
than instructive; for example, he told a Manchester peace
meeting in the spring of 1937: 'Last night I had a dream. In it
George Lansbury and I were playing tennis against Hitler and
Mussolini. George had a game leg and I was asthmatic but we
won six–love.'[2] Murry, who with the enthusiastic certainty
with which he embraced each new idea had become one of
the P.P.U.'s most confident believers in moral deterrence, was
scarcely more precise. In the spring of 1937 he was asserting
that it was 'probably as near to a certainty as human reckon-
ing can attain that against a Pacifist England, Fascist Germany
would be completely incapable of making war' (though he
did accept, in contrast with pacifists earlier in the decade,
that it was nevertheless 'necessary to envisage and accept in
imagination the peaceful submission of this country to an
invading army'); but his only explanation for this belief was
his claim, unsubstantiated beyond generalities about the
contradiction between peace and capitalism, that if a pacifist
movement became strong in England 'its repercussions within
the Fascist nations could not fail to be profound.'[3]

Murry was already on the verge, however, of abandoning
his faith in the practicality of pacifism, and was later to
criticize the 'rather superficial idea' that non-violence was a
political idea since, even as understood by Gandhi, it was
'primarily a religious attitude'.[4] Similarly Ward was, late in
1937, describing it as 'action on a spiritual plane', and denying it was a short-term tactic.[5] Humanitarian pacifists were
thus following their Christian colleagues in the discovery that
the triumph of the values of peace and love over those of

[1] Dorothea Haworth to Ponsonby, 7 Mar. 1937, A.P.
[2] Cited in Brittain, *Testament of Experience*, p. 172.
[3] Murry, *Necessity of Pacifism*, p. 114.
[4] *PN*, 23 Feb. 1940.
[5] (R. H. Ward), *H. R. L. Sheppard: A Note in Appreciation* (1937), p. 78.

violence and hatred would be a longer-term process than they
had once hoped, and one in which suffering and material
disaster might play a part. Since the events of 1936 Christian
pacifists had been increasingly willing to accept the view
that, as Vera Brittain was later bluntly to put it, 'from a
worldly standpoint, Christianity was founded on a *failure*—
the death of its leader on the Cross'.[1] G. H. C. Macgregor
wrote in 1936 that a Christian nation should be willing to
'risk everything on the conviction that God's will would
work', and that this involved being 'ready to risk crucifixion
at the hands of its possible enemies.'[2] A statement by the
Society of Friends in May 1937 emphasized: 'Our faith in
disarmament is not based on a plea for safety. The followers
of a crucified Lord could never advocate a "safe" policy;
"safety first" is not a Christian virtue.'[3] And in his book *War
and the Christian*, which appeared in May 1938, Raven was
for the first time explicit that

if the Christian pacifist is challenged with the question 'Do you seriously mean that you would sit still and see your own country invaded?'
he answers that this is the logical outcome of his views, that he believes
it to be a far more fruitful course than war, and that in fact he does
not believe that a thorough-going pacifism would have this result.
Logically, of course, an acceptance of the Cross as the way of salvation involves a belief in the value of unresisting martyrdom as the
supreme instrument for accomplishing God's purpose.[4]

In each case, however, the continuing optimism that this risk
of 'crucifixion' was not an overwhelming one was based on a
belief, not in non-violence, but in Christian appeasement as
a policy which could forestall aggression.

With other ideas to fall back on—appeasement, isolationism, the belief that public panics and arms races alone
caused wars—it seems doubtful whether the lip-service paid
to non-violence was matched by any real belief in it. Indeed
careful analysis of statements of some of its leading exponents reveals a tendency to fall back sometimes even on
orthodox defence thinking. For example, when Einstein

[1] Brittain, *Rebel Passion*, p. 74.
[2] Macgregor, *New Testament*, p. 103.
[3] *Quakers and War* (leaflet issued by Friends' Peace Committee and Northern
Friends' Peace Board, May 1937).
[4] p. 153.

recanted his pacifism in August 1933 on the grounds of Nazi aggressiveness, Ponsonby at once remonstrated vehemently with him, arguing: 'Hitler's methods may be insane and criminal, but I am fairly convinced that he is not such a fool as to think that he could gain anything for Germany by waging war against another country.' The argument he adduced in support of this, however, was not the efficacy of non-violence but, implicitly, that of military deterrence: 'He would have all Europe arrayed against him and utter defeat would be inevitable.'[1] Similarly Crozier was known in unguarded moments to forget his own expressed view that armaments could not bring security. Thus, despite his own debunking of the Great War, he could condemn those pacifists who were 'inclined to turn up their noses at the work of the men who served in the front line who, after all, saved this country from degradation.'[2] Also his book *The Men I Killed*, published in July 1937 (just a month before his death) and described by *The Times* as 'in kindness to him . . . best forgotten', showed exuberant delight in the martial affairs he was ostensibly condemning and tended to denounce the British government more for being 'war-incompetent' (as he put it) than for being war-like. 'His Majesty's Government! Regard them,' he ejaculated at one point. 'Do they look as if they could run a war?'[3]

If the most forthright advocates of the power of non-violence sometimes wavered from its logic, it was not surprising that many signatories of the peace pledge proved to be only 'ninety-nine per cent' pacifists. For example, Ellen Wilkinson (1891-1947) joined the P.P.U. in 1936 'after a prolonged struggle with herself',[4] despite the fact that in 1934 she had co-authored a book criticizing pacifism and still made it clear she had some reservations about the strict pacifist position.[5] Although she came to consider her position

[1] Ponsonby to Einstein, 21 Aug. 1933, cited in Otto Nathan and Heinz Norden (eds.), *Einstein on Peace* (1963), p. 250.

[2] *PN*, 14 Aug. 1937, p. 8.

[3] p. 20.

[4] Brittain, *Testament of Experience*, p. 166.

[5] Ellen Wilkinson and Edward Conze, *Why War? A Handbook for those who will take part in the Second World War* (n.d. [1934]), esp. pp. 2, 5, 48. See also Crozier to Ponsonby, 7 Jan. 1937, A.P.

untenable, and resigned in March 1937,[1] others of similar views felt justified in remaining in the P.P.U. because of their personal record of 'peace' work. For example, Fred Jowett (1864–1944), the veteran I.L.P. anti-militarist who had made it clear since before the Great War that his 'pacifism' did not extend to wars for 'national defence', admitted to Ponsonby on 4 September 1936:

Yes, I have joined the Peace Pledge Union, not as a Non-Resister but as a War Resister. I make this explanation because I want it to be clear to you, who may differ with me on this particular point of view, that I believe people of every race, colour or nationality have the right to resist armed invasion or blockade of their homeland, and, also to resist militarist rebellion, such as, for example, the present militarist rebellion in Spain. I hope you do not think that holding this point of view is inconsistent with membership of the Peace Pledge Union. After careful consideration before joining I felt sure it was not.[2]

Similarly, Reginald Sorensen remained in the P.P.U., to its embarrassment, although he supported rearmament (on the grounds that a majority wanted it)[3] and made no secret of his belief 'that a virile people must defend itself and that there are certainly worse things than war'.[4] With influential figures thus interpreting the pledge loosely it was not surprising that, reporting on the P.P.U.'s progress to the trustees of the old N.M.W.M., Harold Bing 'felt that the pacifism of a large number was of limited quality.'[5] In particular, as non-pacifists often noted,[6] confusion persisted between non-resistance and non-violence (even though the latter was carefully described as non-violent resistance in order to stress this distinction); and many years later Sybil Morrison was bluntly to assert: 'No-one really believed that Hitler could be stopped by non-violent resistance and those who believed in "resist not evil" had no conception of what it would really mean.'[7]

[1] P.P.U., E.C., 22 Mar.1937.

[2] A.P.; for his 'national defence' brand of 'pacifism', see Fenner Brockway, *Socialism Over Sixty Years: The Life of Jowett of Bradford* (1946), pp. 131–2.

[3] See his letter defending his position, *Daily Herald*, 12 Oct. 1937. In Nov. 1937 he stayed away from a P.P.U. meeting in his constituency addressed by Ponsonby and Carter to avoid embarrassment because of his unorthodox 'pacifist' views: (Leyton) *Guardian*, 11 Nov. 1938.

[4] 309 H.C. Deb. col. 2389 (12 Mar. 1936).

[5] N.M.W.M.Trustees, 11 June 1938.

[6] e.g. W. M. Watt, *Can Christians Be Pacifists?* (S.C.M., 1937), p. 77.

[7] *Pacifist*, June 1974.

But at the time most pacifists were highly sensitive to criticisms on these lines, particularly in the spring of 1937 when the P.P.U. was completing its first year of existence with a membership that was well short of earlier expectations and with an increasingly vocal apolitical wing to trouble the majority of practical pacifists. In April 1937 Margery South was complaining that if the ideas of John Barclay (the devout Christian who had become National Group Organiser the previous November) were

to be those generally imposed on the groups—then the P.P.U. is to be a separatist movement incapable of influencing the general life of the nation. As far as we are concerned up here we might as well close down and let the F.O.R. carry on as before. And the F.O.R. is just hopeless...[1]

The following month, which was also the time the Sponsors formally abandoned Greggism, Joad added to the irritations of the practical pacifists by depicting the P.P.U., in a long *New Statesman* article on 'What is happening to the Peace Movement?', as 'religious rather than political in its nature' since it aimed 'at the preservation of individual integrity in the face of war rather than at the prevention of war'.[2] Joad's insistence on political relevance had, as already noted, led him to adopt a collaborative orientation towards collective security even during the Abyssinia crisis and he was not to preach peace at any price until around the time of Munich. His provocative remarks about his fellow pacifists elicited an angry defence of the P.P.U. from Rose Macaulay:

Its aim is to prevent war; its belief, that if a large number of people in all countries refused to abet or contemplate these means of settling their differences war would, in fact, be prevented. The fact that so far the number is necessarily too small for this purpose to be attained is irrelevant.[3]

Yet according to her own logic the number of pledged pacifists was all-important, and her letter betrayed her private fears that pacifism might not be able to prevent war which led her to resign her Sponsorship in March 1938. Once the idea of independent non-violent action by a highly-trained élite of pacifists had been abandoned, then the P.P.U.'s sole hope of political influence (other than remaining a small

[1] South to Ponsonby, 14 Apr. 1937, A.P.
[2] *NS*, 15 May 1937, pp. 802-4.
[3] *NS*, 22 May 1937, p. 845.

propaganda group) was to become a mass movement of such
dimensions no Government could ignore it. This seems to
have been Sheppard's initial strategy. On 14 July 1935 he
had told his Albert Hall audience: 'Send me a million men
like you and then any government must look out'; and the
following month he predicted a membership of 250,000 for
the Sheppard Peace Movement by Christmas of that year.[1]
Although the total had only climbed from 50,000 to 80,000
by the following April, he remained confident that 'the
number is growing so rapidly that the gentlemen in Whitehall
may soon have to take serious note of it and to revise their
ideas.'[2] The official founding of the P.P.U. in May (and its
opening to women two months later) provided further
momentum, and at the very end of July 1936 Raven told
the International F.o.R.'s Conference at Cambridge that
Christian pacifism was now 'in the sphere of practical politics
. . . The practical politicians were in fact taking pacifism
seriously.'[3] In August six figures were reached; by October
membership was reported to be growing at the rate of 4,500
per week; and the following month the Sponsors were talking
of a possible membership of a million. By the end of 1936
the total stood at 118,000—an increase of 15 per cent in four
months and 47 per cent over eight months.[4]

Though to an improvised organization with a staff of
about thirty this was a satisfying and almost overwhelming
rate of expansion, it was less than a third of the current
membership of the L.N.U. in what was for it a year of sharp
decline. Moreover the L.N.U. total was of subscriptions
collected by local branches whereas what the P.P.U.'s total of
pledge cards meant in practice was far from clear. It was an
inevitable consequence of Sheppard's *laissez-faire* approach
that as late as April 1937 Morris could raise so basic a question as 'how far a signatory of the pledge came into the
organisation of the P.P.U.?'[5] The problem was real enough:

---

[1] *Daily Herald*, 15 July; *The Times*, 20 Aug. 1935.

[2] *Rec.*, Apr. 1936, p. 88.

[3] *Rec.*, Sept. 1936, p. 238.

[4] Figures from minutes of P.P.U. Sponsors; these do not always tally with
the figures published in *PN*.

[5] P.P.U., E.C., 14 Apr. 1937.

an early estimate was that 'scarcely a quarter' joined local Groups;[1] and it was significant that a private reappraisal of membership figures in March 1937 by the W.R.I.'s experienced organizer Runham Brown produced an estimated total of only 87,000.[2]

Most disappointing of all, however, was that the rapid growth of even nominal membership was not sustained after 1936. By Sheppard's death in October 1937—at which time the L.N.U. Executive was being reassured that its rival 'seems to be somewhat losing its attraction'[3]—the figure was only 120,000. Thereafter it may even have declined (or been weeded) since at the end of April 1938 the Sponsors were told it was under 118,000, and a few weeks later Viscount Cecil was able to confirm to his Executive that, from what he had recently learned at a conference of the L.N.U.'s regional representatives, 'there was no great ground for apprehension concerning the growth of the P.P.U.'[4] Although the P.P.U.'s membership seems to have begun increasing again from that point, the numbers were small compared with 1936: 700 members per month from the summer of 1938, increasing to 1,200 after the introduction of conscription. Although some of these late converts—especially those, like Maude Royden, who joined as part of the one significant expansion of membership, that caused by Munich—saw pacifism as a last ditch means of averting war, the majority—like those joining the F.o.R. in unprecedented numbers—were increasingly resigned to war. It was after war had started, moreover, that the P.P.U. enjoyed its final surge of recruitment, reaching its maximum aggregate of approximately 136,000 members in April 1940. At the outbreak its total had been 130,000— only 10 per cent above the figure it had been claiming at the end of 1936. The only two ways in which the P.P.U. continued to make progress after 1936 were: increasing the circulation of *Peace News* from 6,000 to a steady 20,000 or more; and increasing the number of local Groups from 300

[1] Margery Rayne in *PN*, 10 Oct. 1936.
[2] P.P.U. Sponsors, 8 Mar. 1937.
[3] Memorandum by Kathleen Courtney and Will Arnold-Forster, 25 Oct. 1937, Add. MSS 51141, R.C.
[4] L.N.U., E.C., 19 May 1938.

in December 1936, to a total of 1,150 by the outbreak of war. Although the number of activists was very small even if all the nominal Groups existed in practice, it seems that as war approached the ratio of activists to sympathizers was increasing. The movement's quality, if not its quantity, was improving significantly.

By the time of Sheppard's death it was thus already clear that membership had reached a plateau stage from which no mass expansion could plausibly be extrapolated. Although as late as 1938 pacifists continued to be optimistic—Raven argued that pacifism was recruiting faster than the armed services,[1] and the newly-formed Hull Group was 'told that the immediate aim of the P.P.U. was to increase the membership of genuine signatories to a million, so that they could use their policy with some effect in affairs of national importance'[2]—pacifists were forced to adjust to being a minority movement without political influence for the foreseeable future at least. The only contribution they would realistically make to preventing war would be as part of the wider movement for appeasement—and in that movement they would not only be a tiny minority but also, since they derived their support for appeasement from a controversial doctrine, a potential political embarrassment. Pacifists were forced to decide, therefore, whether the prevention of war was really the essential motive of their faith. That most were in two minds on this question was illustrated by the appearance, on 15 October 1937, of a pamphlet in which Lansbury made one of his rare attempts to define his pacifism in detail. At first he appeared to be clear that, even if he had no effective pacifist programme for war prevention, 'I should still be an ardent pacifist, doing my utmost to persuade young men and women to have nothing whatever to do with war.' Within a few pages, however, he had contradicted himself by claiming that 'for pacifists who, like myself, feel that our creed can only be justified if it saves civilisation from the horrors that threaten it, there

---

[1] Raven, *War and the Christian*, p. 24.
[2] *Peace Centre Calling* (Hull and District P.P.U.), Mar. 1938.

is a very real problem.'[1] Just sixteen days after Lansbury had made public his dilemma Sheppard's death made its resolution by the P.P.U. more urgent—and more painful—than ever.

[1] George Lansbury, *Why Pacifists Should be Socialists* (*Fact* No. 7, 15 Oct. 1937), pp. 55, 64.

14

AFTER SHEPPARD
(1): CAMPAIGNING FOR APPEASEMENT

(i) 'As Sheep Not Having A Sheppard'.

'So here we are, very literally as sheep not having a Sheppard',[1] Plowman wrote to Murry on 8 March 1938, deeply disillusioned by five months of internal controversy within the bereaved P.P.U. during which he, as General Secretary, had borne a particularly heavy burden. Already Sheppard's death seemed a watershed in the affairs of the P.P.U., but with hindsight this can be seen to have been partly because of its timing. Though occurring within days of Sheppard's remarkable victory over Churchill and J. B. S. Haldane in the election by Glasgow University students of their Rector (a victory which he had welcomed as at last putting pacifism 'on the map'),[2] it came several months after the P.P.U.'s rapid early growth had begun to flag and only a few months before Hitler began redrawing the map of Eastern Europe. The tremendous shock of losing Sheppard—'It was as though the bottom had dropped out of the world . . . I can't take it in—nor begin even to try to estimate what a blow it will be to the pacifist movement . . . ', wrote Vera Brittain immediately on hearing the news[3]—did not create the problems for the P.P.U. which were soon to follow; but it did force a return to first principles, and it removed, shortly before international events were to increase the strain on the pacifist movement, the uniting influence which had managed to conceal unresolved differences, dating from the inception of the P.P.U., about its policies and essential nature.

The widening breach between the war-preventing pacifists

---

[1] M.P.

[2] Morrison, *I Renounce War*, p. 26.

[3] Quoted in Vera Brittain, *Thrice A Stranger: New Chapters of Autobiography* (1938), p. 272.

and the growing number—always a minority of the movement as a whole but strongly represented among the Sponsors— which was coming to see pacifism as apolitical and, in the broadest sense of the word, 'religious' was reflected in tension between two conceptions of how the pacifist movement should be organized. That favoured by practical pacifists was the more conventional; they saw a pacifist society as either a pressure group efficiently manipulating opinion, or as a political movement, mobilizing supporters and reflecting their views in a formal programme arrived at by normal democratic procedures. The model favoured by apolitical pacifists, however, was that of a fellowship of believers, organized not to achieve any political end but to facilitate communion between independent individuals of like mind. The F.o.R., as already noted, saw itself in this way, as did the denominational pacifist fellowships set up after 1933; their common assumption, expressed by *Reconciliation* in August 1935, was that 'the problem of peace is not to be solved by war's devices, close organisation, uniformity of word and action, and mass emotion. Propaganda is not our weapon . . . Organisation is subsidiary.'[1]

Since its inception the P.P.U. had been a hybrid, reflecting Sheppard's desire for a middle way. Its purpose was that of the practical pacifists and Sheppard supported political campaigning and propaganda with zest, being prepared to indulge in a little mild civil disobedience. Thus when Russell proposed at a Sponsors' meeting that members should refuse to pay their income tax to a Government that would spend it on arms, but pay it to the P.P.U. instead, Sheppard was attrracted by the idea even though the P.P.U. Executive had already insisted that 'such resistance would be ineffective and illogical'; as late as August 1937 he was advocating 'seditious' acts that would break through the barrier of press silence and get the P.P.U. into the headlines.[2] But such gestures were impulsive and spasmodic and were largely offset by his dislike of formal organization and of specific policy commitments, both of which he tended to dismiss with the characteristic assertion that 'simplicity was more

[1] p. 201.
[2] P.P.U. Sponsors, 15 Sept. 1937; E.C., 22 Apr., 11 Aug. 1937.

effective than complexity'.[1] On constitutional questions, therefore, he aligned himself with the apolitical wing. The P.P.U. was in theory a collective despotism of the Sponsors' and, in practice, its organizing principle was the *Führer-prinzip*.

However, in arranging the merger with the highly political N.M.W.M. early in 1937 it was agreed to 'democratize' the P.P.U.—a concession somewhat lightly entered into (perhaps because Sheppard was ill and Morris and his fellow negotiators may have confused it with the improvements in decision-taking machinery which were widely accepted as necessary at this time). In the event, no progress was made towards implementing this promise because Sheppard was unenthusiastic and the new General Secretary was passionately convinced, as he wasted no time in telling the Executive Committee, of 'the importance of the organisation of the P.P.U. retaining its revolutionary character and not trying its hands by making its constitution formal and democratic'.[2] Plowman's objections were made admirably clear in a formal statement he made to the Sponsors when they discussed the subject in the summer of 1937:

The P.P.U. is a minority movement. To claim the democratic form for the determination of policy is for it to claim what it has no right to, for upon a democratic basis of government by majority it has no power at all. It must therefore lay its claim to power elsewhere than in the democratic ideal; and this, of course, it does in claiming the supremacy of conscience over the right of majority government . . . We are in fact one body by unanimity of conviction and not upon the ground of majority rule. The P.P.U. is a movement of *consent* not of authority.[3]

The question was allowed to lie dormant in a sub-committee until the death of the Führer necessitated the modification of the *Führerprinzip*. The initial reaction of the Sponsors and the Executive Committee at a joint emergency meeting just three days after Sheppard died was to groom the most likely candidate to step into Sheppard's shoes: 'It was generally felt that Canon Morris must play an increasingly important part in the work of the Union';[4] and Plowman long continued

[1] P.P.U., E.C., 14 Apr. 1937.
[2] P.P.U., E.C., 11 Mar. 1937.
[3] 'Read at Sponsors Meeting abut mid-1937', dated 11 May 1938, M.P.
[4] P.P.U. Sponsors and E.C., 3 Nov. 1937.

to campaign for Morris to be given fuller powers.[1] But no one could take on Sheppard's role as charismatic leader, and a more formalized solution was adopted after a winter of intensive constitutional discussion: Morris became Chairman (and Soper Vice-Chairman) and Lansbury became President, the new hierarchy being approved at the first Annual General Meeting of the P.P.U., held on 2–3 April 1938 at Friends' House, which was attended by over 1,000 people. But the holding of the meeting was as far as democratization then went; for, to secure a compromise between the constitutionalists and anti-constitutionalists, the proposals to adopt a formal constitution were shelved. The Sponsors' authority was reaffirmed, and the Executive Committee was retitled the Management Committee to remove ambiguity on this point.

Even so this was too much for Plowman who, still fulminating against 'the bastard word "democratisation" ',[2] had offered his resignation as General Secretary in February. He was given a month's leave and returned to deliver the annual report to the A.G.M., in the course of which he condemned the constitutionalists and announced that he would be continuing to help at Headquarters only in a voluntary capacity.[3] (The General Secretaryship, left open since February, was not formally filled until Morris took it over in May 1939.) Since, however, he continued to serve on the Management Committee until September 1938, in addition to being a Sponsor, he did not wholly escape the frustrations which had convinced him that half the Sponsors 'are indolently asleep and the other half are rats'. His objection to democratization in principle had been reinforced by his dislike of its proponents in practice. In particular his mystical temperament clashed with what he called 'the Parliamentary crowd' and, more especially, 'the small-time politicians' of the N.M.W.M. 'To be taking instructions from Runham Brown and Bing is not my idea of life,' he informed Murry, to whom he poured out all his troubles, 'but

[1] P.P.U., E.C., 14 Feb. 1938.
[2] D.L.P(lowman) (ed.), *Bridge*, p. 624.
[3] P.P.U., E.C., 14 Feb., Sponsors, 25 Feb. 1938. *Report*, P.P.U. A.G.M., M.P.

they are the people who are most often on the spot.'[1] Runham Brown—to whom he privately referred as 'Run 'em down',[2] in deference to his formidable skills in getting his way in committee—was his particular *bête noire*, largely because of his important role, as the P.P.U.'s sole businessman, on the finance committee; so much did his whole approach seem the antithesis of Sheppard's disinterested spirit that by October 1938 Plowman and Murry were agreed that Brown was 'an evil beast'.[3]

Apart from personalities, Plowman's main objection to 'the Parliamentary crowd'—even to those, like Ponsonby and Hudson, whom he liked—was that 'they want the P.P.U. to go all political'.[4] Plowman himself regarded all political campaigning as a coercion of the individual conscience: his first reaction on hearing of the Sheppard Peace Movement during the Abyssinia crisis had been that he 'wouldn't cross the road to persuade anyone to sign that pledge'—a view he never abandoned.[5] On his arrival at the P.P.U. he opposed all moves to define a policy on which to campaign: 'It is premature to have a policy. We can only desire peace';[6] and his statement to the Sponsors opposing democratization had been adamant that no policy commitment should be required of members:

Acceptance of so-called pacifist policy is not compulsory upon any pledge signatory . . . since no one can acquire by signature of the pledge—by election or any other means—the authority to dictate or even decide policy on behalf of all the other signatories . . . . The P.P.U. must tolerate anything spoken in its name which does not contradict the implications of the pledge.

In Sheppard's lifetime the pledge remained the P.P.U.'s only policy-ruling: the status even of its pamphlets being unclear. Although several Sponsors and most of the Headquarters staff had wanted clearer policy guidelines—on Greggism, on what international policy the P.P.U. recommended, and on what attitude to take to Government

---

[1] Plowman to Murry, 8 Mar. 1938 (see also 6 May 1937), M.P.

[2] Interview with Frank Lea, 2 Mar. 1977.

[3] Plowman to Murry, 24 Oct. 1938, M.P.

[4] Plowman to Murry, 8 Mar. 1938, M.P.

[5] Plowman to West, 29 Oct. 1935, in D.L.P(lowman) (ed.), *Bridge*, p. 539; see also p. 663.

[6] P.P.U., E.C., 3 May 1937.

defence measures involving civilian co-operation—they had
felt unable to challenge Sheppard and, indeed, were not blind
to the crusading radicalism concealed by his aristocratic
manner. After his death, as part of the negotiations for a
more formal constitution, a policy Manifesto was drawn up.
Unveiled on 7 March 1938, it became the basis for an energetic national campaign over the next few months; at the same
time the staff became politically more militant. In the spring
of 1938 they produced a leaflet urging non-cooperation with
air raid precautions to which the Sponsors, reluctant to interfere with individual consciences and to single out one of the
least objectionable aspects of the Government's defence
policy, took exception. To the Management Committee the
Sponsors' insistence on withdrawing the leaflet 'had opened
up the larger question as to the actual position of the Sponsors in relation to the movement as a whole and the office
staff in particular.'[1] A formal meeting between the Sponsors
and the young staff members, Spottiswoode, Ward, and
Walker, had to be held, at which Lansbury produced the
Sheppard-like solution that no formal guidelines should be
drawn up but that the staff should be exhorted to continue
their good work in the spirit of loyalty to the P.P.U.[2] However, even Morris had become concerned at the Union's
increasing political activism. Normally reluctant to align
himself with any faction, he wrote to Ponsonby expressing
his alarm at recent signs 'of a difference as to the essential
aims and purpose of the P.P.U.' While insisting that he fully
accepted 'the necessity of presenting the aim of the P.P.U.
in a "political shape" and of emphasising the fact that we
have a programme for constructive peace making', he felt
that 'there was not wanting some evidence of an attempt
to capture the P.P.U. for what might be called "political
purposes" and set it in a direction other than Dick had in
mind'. He named Salter, Brown and, in particular, Hudson,
as those whose attitude troubled him.[3]

Another bone of contention between the P.P.U.'s
apolitical and militant factions—and one which aroused

---

[1] P.P.U., E.C., 9 May 1938.
[2] P.P.U. Sponsors, 8 June 1938.
[3] Morris to Ponsonby, 6 June 1938, A.P.

Plowman to new heights of fury—was *Peace News*. Founded by Humphrey S. Moore, a Quaker journalist who had formed an F.o.R. study group in Wood Green which then resolved to start a 'peace' newspaper, it had been launched on 6 June 1936 as a weekly 'serving all who are working for peace'. Sheppard liked the paper and from 25 July it became 'The Weekly Newspaper of the Peace Pledge Union', whilst still aiming to provide 'an open forum' for all anti-war viewpoints—including, in its early months, those of the collective security movement. Though it achieved a creditable regular circulation of 20,000 copies, reaching a peak of 35,000 in the week of Munich, many Sponsors felt that, in view of the P.P.U.'s subsidy to (and, after December 1937, ownership of) the paper, it gave insufficient prominence to the P.P.U.'s own views and activities; others objected to the fact it was 'designed after the model of the daily sensational press', whereas they would have preferred it closer in style to the *New Statesman*.[1] Plowman also resented the fact that Moore printed contributions from staff members criticizing the Sponsors, and came to suspect that he was kept on as editor, despite his financial incompetence and the P.P.U.'s galaxy of better-qualified candidates, only because Runham Brown found him so willing to use the paper to publicize and raise funds for his W.R.I.[2] Yet when it was suggested that Plowman take over—by Kingsley Martin who, atoning for his reluctant conversion to supporting military resistance to fascism, took a keen interest in how to improve *Peace News*[3] —Plowman refused.[4] Instead he accepted the editorship of the *Adelphi*, which since Murry had become a pacifist had lost the backing of the wealthy socialist Sir Richard Rees and was available to its seven hundred subscribers only. To these, however, Plowman preached an apolitical pacifism very different from the practical pacifism of *Peace News* but nearer, he was convinced, to Sheppard's own conception.

Though Plowman felt, with some justification, that he was the main guardian of Sheppard's approach, and though he

---

[1] P.P.U. Sponsors, 27 Oct. 1937.
[2] Plowman to Murry, 24 Oct. 1938, M.P.
[3] P.P.U., E.C., 24 Nov. 1937, Management Committee, 3 Aug. 1938.
[4] Plowman to Murry, 23 June 1938, M.P.

liked to advise any fellow Sponsor with whom he found himself in disagreement 'to discover what had been Dick's spirit and to see if he couldn't do his little best to perpetuate it',[1] it was Morris who bore the burden of Sheppard's mediating and uniting role. Plowman, who had wanted Morris to take over Sheppard's position as benevolent despot, was aware of this and would then have agreed with Bing's later tribute to his 'wonderful capacity for perceiving the points of agreement in apparently differing views and expressing them in terms that were acceptable to all.'[2] But as the disagreements in the P.P.U. widened he wondered increasingly how Morris felt able to do this and came to believe that, instead of providing the inspiring leadership which transcends differences, he was merely a diplomat skilled in balancing them—'I'm afraid he's a born wangler', Plowman sadly concluded in May 1939.[3] This was unfair to Morris: even though his burning of his ecclesiastical boats made it harder for him to pursue an issue of principle to the point of resignation, his tireless work for reconciliation and appeasement within the P.P.U. was based not on expediency but on a strong belief that pacifism begins at home.

At the second A.G.M.—'a perfect mixture of nightmare and broad farce' in Plowman's eyes[4]—in 1939 Morris became General Secretary (as well as Chairman); and another step was also taken towards democratization when the Sponsors were abolished as a controlling body (though retained as an honorific rank) and replaced by an elected National Council of national and regional representatives plus a few co-opted members. In addition the Management Committee regained its former title of Executive Committee in recognition of the fact it now possessed real executive authority between the meetings—necessarily infrequent because local delegates had to be summoned—of the National Council.

But the politically-minded did not have it all their own way. The P.P.U. continued to take the attitude it had in January 1939 when it had been urged to condemn the

---

[1] Ibid. (The Sponsor in question was Mumford.)
[2] *PN*, 17 Nov. 67.
[3] Plowman to Murry, 5 May 1939, M.P.
[4] Ibid.

National Register: 'The Sponsors did not think they could
support organized opposition as a body though individuals
would obviously take their own stand.'[1] A No-Conscription
League had been formed in 1938 by Brockway, with Hudson
—who tendered his resignation (later, it seems, rescinded) as
a P.P.U. Sponsor on the issue of the National Register—as
Honorary Secretary and Salter and Wilson among its leading
members.[2] After the start of the war the P.P.U.'s caution
about harassing the war effort, and its formation of an explicitly anti-political Forethought Committee, increased the
frustration of the political militants. What Plowman—who
himself, in the words of close associates, 'did not suffer
fools gladly' and was 'the most unpractical person in the
world'[3]—failed to appreciate was that, if the P.P.U. was not
to split into two bodies tending towards either the F.o.R.
or the N.M.W.M., it had to live with two conflicting conceptions of itself. Sheppard has possessed both the charisma
and the favourable circumstances to fuse both together into
a crusade; but after his death they could coexist only on the
basis of a compromise, loyally managed by Morris throughout the quarter of a century (excepting an enforced three-
year break) in which he held the General Secretaryship.

(ii) Pacifist Appeasement

The Manifesto which the P.P.U. had produced after Sheppard's death revealed that by 1938 its hopes for war prevention
were based on 'economic appeasement and reconciliation'.
Unveiled by Lansbury in the course of his speech in the
Commons on 7 March 1938,[4] the Manifesto reiterated the
ideas which he had been advocating since his 'Plea for a Truce
of God' in August 1935. By the end of 1936, despite the end
of the Abyssinian war which had first stimulated it, the call
for a world conference had established itself as a central

[1] P.P.U. Sponsors, 6 Jan. 1939.

[2] Denis Hayes, *Conscription Conflict* (1949), p. 375; P.P.U. Sponsors, 17
Jan. 1939.

[3] Barclay in *PN*, 13 June 1941; Lea in *Community Broadsheet*, 20 June
1941, p. 8.

[4] 332 H.C. Deb. cols. 1618-19. It is reprinted in Morrison, *I Renounce War*,
pp. 18-19.

part of pacifist propaganda: for example, despite his avowed aim of avoiding the political case for pacifism in his study, published in September, of its theological basis, G. H. C. Macgregor could not resist stating the arguments for appeasement;[1] and when the following month the W.I.L. held a weekend conference on the subject of pacifism, 'The Haves and Have Nots' was the first item on the agenda.[2]

Yet with the P.P.U. absorbed during 1936-7 with non-violence and reluctant to produce any formal international policy recommendations, the pacifist case for appeasement had to be made independently. In the summer of 1936 three Labour M.P.s—Wilson, Salter, and Hudson—founded the Parliamentary Pacifist Group. This attracted the support of a number of Labour politicians, including Lansbury, Barr, Sorensen, Fred Messer, George Hardie, and the socialist peers Ponsonby, Arnold, Faringdon, and Sanderson, who were increasingly aware of being an isolated minority within the Labour Party. In September 1936 the Group issued a National Manifesto for Peace and Disarmament,[3] which was endorsed by a number of prominent pacifists; and in 1937 it followed this up with a series of successful National Conventions to publicize its Manifesto, which were held at Manchester in March, at Birmingham in June, and in London in September.

Lansbury's personal campaign for a world conference was launched before the P.P.U. was officially set up. In April 1936 he left for a gruelling two-month tour of the United States, accompanied by Salter; and in September 1936 he visited Germany. This latter trip raised pacifist hopes to such an extent that Percy Bartlett, the long-serving General Secretary of the F.o.R. who had accompanied Lansbury, promptly resigned in order to become Secretary of the newly-formed Embassies of Reconciliation.[4] This organization, whose leading figures included Raven, Runham Brown, and Ruth Fry, as well as Lansbury and Salter, sponsored Lansbury's European tours in 1937, in the course of which he interviewed Hitler (whom he later described as 'one of the

---

[1] Macgregor, *New Testament*, p. 144.
[2] W.I.L., E.C., 1 Sept. 1936.
[3] *PN*, 26 Sept. 1936.
[4] F.o.R., G.C., 21-2 Sept. 1936.

great men of our time'),[1] Mussolini (whose economic understanding he considered 'sound'),[2] and a number of political
leaders in France and Eastern Europe. His stolid persistence
contrasted with Sheppard's impulsive gestures: the latter's
letter to Hitler asking permission to preach in Germany, like
his declared intention of flying to Spain to intercede personally with Franco, made no headway.[3]

The tacit switch of pacifist hopes from the exclusively
pacifist policy of non-violence to the more broadly-based one
of appeasement forced the P.P.U. to adjust for the first time
to the dilemmas of the collaborative orientation, which included the embarrassment of agreeing with the Government
and with pro-fascists, and of being forced to play down their
own distinctive beliefs.

By the time appeasement became official P.P.U. policy,
the National Government had embarked on a superficially
similar policy. All connection between pacifism and the
Government's policy of appeasement has been strongly
denied by the peace movement,[4] and at the time most
pacifists were careful to dissociate their idealistic plans
for a new international order from what *Peace News* for
20 November 1937 called 'a mere bargaining or bartering
of advantages for the sake of easing the politicians' paths'.
Many saw Chamberlain's policy as a deal with Germany
based on mutual interests: for example, Wellock, who
argued that Eden's resignation 'made it completely clear
that British Imperialism and Fascism are strongly bound
together' (though the Anschluss with Austria forced him
to modify this interpretation).[5] When it was apparent
that Chamberlain's policy had failed Lansbury was able
to comfort pacifists with the thought that it was 'not *our*

---

[1] Lansbury, *My Quest*, p. 141.

[2] Ibid., p. 162.

[3] *PN*, 8 Aug., 14 Nov. 1936.

[4] The University Group on Defence Policy devoted a pamphlet to arguing
that 'appeasement had nothing to do with peace movements let alone with
pacifism': *The Role of the Peace Movements in the 1930s* (Pamphlet No. 1,
Jan. 1959), p. 7. The argument advanced in this chapter is in broad agreement
with David Lukowitz, 'British Pacifists and Appeasement: The Peace Pledge
Union', *Journal of Contemporary History*, 9 (1), Jan. 1974, pp. 115-27.

[5] *PN*, 5 and 26 Mar. 1938.

policy of appeasement through Conference and mutual concessions which has failed. It is appeasement plus the mailed
fist which has failed.'[1]

But pacifists desiring to prevent war could not wholly
dissociate themselves from the Government's policy: Ponsonby supported non-intervention in Spain and, in spite of
criticism, later insisted that 'there was nothing on our side
to be ashamed of' in the Munich settlement;[2] Maude Royden
joined the P.P.U. in September 1938, as she later told Morris,
'in the belief that you were backing up Chamberlain' and that
the P.P.U. was 'the only really big organisation which was
trying to do that';[3] and the first issue of the *Christian Pacifist*
(as *Reconciliation* had restyled itself in January 1939)
argued: 'The policy of "appeasement", though the word has
recently been given a new and less favourable content by its
opponents, is one which in itself deserves our hearty support.
It is an honest and sensible attempt to settle grievances
instead of quarrelling and finally fighting about them.'[4]

It was in the Munich crisis that the P.P.U. enjoyed its last
surge of recruitment from those hoping to prevent war.
Whereas it had attracted only a thousand new members in the
previous three months, in September 1938 it recruited 1,330,
followed by 1,146 in October and 949 in November.[5] One
of these, as already mentioned, was Maude Royden, who as
late as August 1938 was reaffirming her view that the P.P.U.
was too negative, and her preference for the L.N.U. In September 1938, however, she changed her mind and on the
20th of that month tendered her resignation from the L.N.U.
to Viscount Cecil on the grounds 'that I feel more and
more strongly the absolute stupidity of war and have felt
bound to join the Peace Pledge Union.'[6] A week later she
privately circulated a letter to leading policitians, insisting:
'It is not too late to establish *Peace With Honour*. Let us ask
for Justice for *All* . . . What are we British to sacrifice for that
Peace for which we have asked Czechoslovakia to sacrifice

[1] *Christian Pacifist*, May 1939, p. 115.
[2] *PN*, 18 June 1938; *Fortnightly Review*, vol. 146, p. 548.
[3] Cited in *PN*, 13 Oct. 1939.
[4] p. 1.
[5] Figures from minutes, P.P.U. Sponsors.
[6] Royden to Cecil, 8 Aug., 20 Sept. 1938, Add. MSS 51181, R.C.

so much?'[1] The behaviour of the Czechs even enabled pacifists to interpret Munich in religious terms. A message from
Lansbury to Beneš compared their sacrifice to that of Christ
and insisted: 'General war is the worst evil of all. To accept
the German terms *now* may be the greatest, strongest act
possible to statesmanship, releasing new spiritual forces. Not
law now, but only grace, is strong enough. Friendship to
aggression, without limit, is the way of Christ.'[2] Similarly
Leyton Richards, in a 'Crisis Booklet' published in December
1938, claimed that 'the parallel between the action of the
Czechs and the events of Calvary is not too remote for us to
see the redemptive principle at work, even in the relationship of sinful man to sinful man.'[3]

Where pacifists had formerly argued that unilateral disarmament would bring peace, they now implied that unilateral
gestures of economic sacrifice by Britain would have the
same effect. This rested on two questionable assumptions.
The first—with hindsight clearly mistaken—was made explicit
by Raven, writing in 1938: 'Assuming the worst that can be
said of Mussolini or Hitler, it remains true that an intelligent
psychology will approach them fearlessly and without parade
of arms, will strive to understand and discuss their grievances
and ambitions, and will meet their advances with generosity
and "sweet reasonableness".'[4] The second, as expressed by
Herbert Gray, also in 1938, was 'that it will be time enough
to think of action in relation to the injustices for which
other nations are responsible, when we have dealt with those
for which we are responsible.'[5]

But, in fact, Britain had little of her own to offer except
colonies, and to hand their populations over to an avowedly
racist nation was hard to justify in moral terms. Though
pacifists, like many socialists, put forward schemes of international control, they rarely considered whether Germany
would accept this. As with non-violence during 1936–7, it
was unclear how far pacifists believed in their own arguments

[1] Circular letter dated 27 Sept. 1938, in Cripps Papers.
[2] Lansbury to Beneš, 26 Sept. 1939 (copy), Lansbury Papers.
[3] Leyton Richards, *The Crisis and World Peace* (S.C.M. Press Crisis Booklet No. 4, Dec. 1938), p. 50.
[4] Raven, *War and the Christian*, p. 156.
[5] A. Herbert Gray, *Love: The One Solution* (1938), pp. 124–5.

about appeasement, and how far they really hoped that a war postponed might be a war prevented, or that if war broke out, Britain might simply refuse to join in because of the awful destruction it would risk if it honoured its commitments to Eastern Europe. One pacifist who admitted that his views were in part at least based on self-interested isolationism was Joad, who had responded to the Munich crisis by making clear that, while he was not an 'extreme pacifist', he was 'a pacifist in regard to the existing international situation'.[1] In a letter to Frank Hardie on 3 October 1938 he gave as a reason for welcoming Munich the fact that 'it is not our business anyway, and whether Sudeten Germans belong to Germany or Czechoslovakia is a matter not worth the life of a single Englishman.'[2] In a Penguin Special, *Why War?*, published in March 1939, he advanced what Roy Walker described as the 'materialistic' case for pacifism,[3] arguing that a war postponed might be a war averted and endorsed the National Government's policy with the observation: 'ce n'est pas magnifique, mais ce n'est pas la guerre.'[4]

Although Claud Cockburn's radical news-sheet *The Week* is remembered for its 'discovery' of the Cliveden Set, it should be remembered that at the time it was concerned also to attack 'the pacifists and the do-nothing wing of the Labour Party'.[5] Pacifists often came close to exculpating Germany: for example, despite his distrust of political judgements, Plowman believed that 'Germany is what the allies have made her', and was ready to support a campaign for the revision of Versailles;[6] so was Wellock, to whom 'the wonder is that Germany did not challenge the Treaty of Versailles and rearm earlier.'[7] In July 1938 *Peace News* called for concessions to the Sudeten Germans, and the following month it questioned

---

[1] C. E. M. Joad, *A Guide to Modern Wickedness* (1939), p. 188. The preface of this book is dated Dec. 1938.

[2] F.H.

[3] *PN*, 31 Mar. 1939.

[4] C. E. M. Joad, *Why War?* (1939), p. 33.

[5] *The Week*, No. 214 (27 July 1938); see also Patricia Cockburn, *The Years of 'The Week'* (1968), p. 180.

[6] Plowman, *Faith Called Pacifism*, p. 28; Plowman to Murry, 20 July 1937, M.P.

[7] *PN*, 13 Mar. 1937 (see also 7 July).

the claim of Czechoslovakia—or 'Czecho–Germano–Slovako–
Hungaro–Polono–Ruthenia', as it preferred to call it—to be
considered a nation-state at all.[1] Salter was as unswerving and
outspoken in his appeasement as in all other aspects of his
pacifism. In February 1936 his anti-imperialism had made
him sound like an apologist for Mussolini's Abyssinian
adventure:

Can it be expected in view of this unequal and unfair distribution of
the world's resources that these virile, energetic and spirited nations
will continue to sit quiet, restricted in self-development, deprived
of necessities and comforts, and starved or semi-starved, while other
nations, notably ourselves, have everything we need? Why have we
full supplies? Just because we were first into the field in seizing all
the delectable and exploitable parts of the world.[2]

And even after Munich he could still claim, in an article
entitled 'British Aggression': 'The average German will
withdraw his backing from Hitler if we show willingness
to be just.'[3]

This willingness to understand the German case sometimes contrasted with a corresponding willingness to believe
the worst of the British. When in his *Peace News* column for
16 January 1937, Ponsonby repeated—playfully, as he later
claimed—a rumour that the Crystal Palace fire had been a
deliberate ruse to remove a conspicuous landmark by which
enemy bombers could navigate, Laurence Housman—who
had shown a markedly tolerant attitude to German rearmament[4]—wrote to him to say that he had arrived at the same
conclusion and had suggested it to various people: 'One of
the last was a Conservative M.P. who thought that it was a
very plausible theory only our Government did not do such
things, only the Nazis; at which I laughed and said "Don't
they?" '[5] Similarly, the *Christian Pacifist* could ask even after
Prague: 'Why are we so angry with the German government?
Is it really because we care so much for human liberty and
self-determination of people? Then what of our present
policy (God forgive the past) in India, Africa, Palestine,

[1] *PN,* 30 July, 13 Aug. 1938.
[2] *Rec.*, Feb. 1936, p. 46.
[3] *Rec.*, Nov. 1938, p. 352.
[4] See Housman to Sheppard, 19 Mar. 1935, in Housman (ed.), *What . . ?*,
p. 251.
[5] Housman to Ponsonby, 1 Feb. 1937, A.P.

Jamaica? The question must be answered before God.'[1] And, in a statement of his pacifist beliefs drawn up on 21 September 1939, Eric Gill, who had been co-opted onto the P.P.U. National Council in May 1939, insisted that 'the beam in our own eye is not inconspicuous. *We* cannot set up as arbiters. Our hands are no cleaner than anyone else's.'[2] Rare though such extreme views may have been, Cecil Cadoux felt obliged to insist, on the outbreak of war, that pacifists 'render poor service to the peace and well-being of the world by suggesting that the public deeds of the German and Italian Governments are not brutal and murderous, or that the undoubted shortcomings and iniquities of Britain are deserving of equal condemnation', and to warn lest 'we shall display so inadequate a grasp of reality as to forfeit our right to pronounce on the way it ought to be dealt with.'[3]

After Hitler's seizure of Prague in March 1939 most former appeasers became disillusioned (or focused their optimism on the Federal Union movement instead); as a result the P.P.U.'s remaining allies in the dwindling appeasement lobby were for the most part avowed pro-fascists. Mosley was restoring the impetus of his British Union by playing the peace card, while the Marquis of Tavistock (shortly to succeed to the Dukedom of Bedford), having preached social credit and appeasement in pacifist journals and at P.P.U. meetings, had formed an (anti-Semitic) British Peace Party. It was perhaps inevitable, therefore, that allegations began to be made from the spring of 1939 onwards to the effect that the P.P.U. was itself a pro-Nazi movement.[4]

Most pacifists were upset and offended by such accusations, their attitude to Nazism being summed up in Rose Macaulay's exasperated comment: 'Yes d— the Nazis. They are persecuting us all, befuddling our minds and dominating our imaginations and making pacifism impossibly difficult. I hate it.'[5] Nichols, almost the only well-known 'pacifist' to support the British Union of Fascists and the

[1] *Christian Pacifist*, Apr. 1939, pp. 85–6.
[2] Cited in Robert Speaight, *The Life of Eric Gill* (1966), p. 307.
[3] *Christian Pacifist*, Oct. 1939, p. 257.
[4] See *PN*, 21 July 1939.
[5] Babington Smith, *Rose Macaulay*, p. 145.

Anglo-German Fellowship, found himself 'incurring the
odium of many pacifist friends in the past';[1] and a reader
of *Peace News* actually complained that, so far from the P.P.U.
being pro-German, the sole reason he had not joined it was that
he found it so 'bitterly anti-Hitler'.[2]

Yet pacifists did leave a number of hostages to fortune.
They perhaps could not help the fact, revealed by the correspondence columns of *Peace News*, that some of their members
also subscribed to fascist journals; but it was unnecessary and
unwise of the P.P.U., when in May 1939 it published its
highly successful *Peace Service Handbook*, to include the
pro-Nazi organization The Link in its list of societies working
for international reconciliation; even more unwise was Stuart
Morris's decision to join The Link himself.[3] A couple of
Quakers associated with the P.P.U.— Corder Catchpool,[4] the
former absolutist who was to act as its treasurer towards the
end of the Second World War, and Ben Greene (1903-75),[5] a
well-known Labour activist who had spoken at P.P.U. meetings and was to be interned in 1940—tended, for all their
undoubted idealism, to be highly uncritical apologists for
Germany. In addition, the occasional contributor to *Peace
News* deviated from the highest pacifist standards: in August
1939 Ethel Mannin, always prone to see war as the result of
the machinations of sinister vested interests, attacked 'Jewish
racial feeling and Jewish interests vested in Big Business and
the Press' for fomenting hatred of Germany;[6] and during the
war *Peace News* carried articles both by Hugh Ross William-
son, an apologist for the German attack on Poland, and by
the Duke of Bedford, who adduced 'the very serious provocation which many Jews have given by their avarice and arrogance

---

[1] Nichols, *Men Do Not Weep*, p. 23.

[2] *PN*, 21 July 1939.

[3] *NS*, 3 June 1939, p. 852; P.P.U., National Co. 1 July 1939; *PN*, 18 Aug.
1939.

[4] For criticism of Catchpool see Robert Dell, *Germany Unmasked* (1934),
p. 17, and *Friend*, 27 May 1938, pp. 479-80.

[5] For his views see *PN*, 3 Sept. 1938; see also Ben Pimlott's biographical
note in the *Bulletin of the Society for the Study of Labour History*, No. 37
(Autumn 1978), p. 15.

[6] *PN*, 4 Aug. (see also 11 Aug.) 1939. (The I.L.P. journal *Forward* had also
attacked 'Jewish control' of British foreign policy on 3 June: Robert Skidelsky,
Oswald Mosley, p. 439.)

when exploiting German's financial difficulties; by their
associations with organised vice; and by their monopolisation
of certain professions'[1] as reasons for taking a sympathetic
view of Germany's behaviour. The Duke was even elected a
member of the P.P.U.'s National Council.

These lapses by the P.P.U. played into the hands of its
most implacable critics. 'After Dick Sheppard's death British
pacifism seems to have suffered a moral collapse', George
Orwell was claiming in 1941, '. . . many of the surviving
pacifists now spin a line of talk indistinguishable from the
Blackshirts ("Stop this Jewish war" etc.), and the actual
membership of the P.P.U. and the British Union overlap to
some extent.'[2] But such accusations were surprisingly infrequent in view of the fact that the P.P.U. was publicly
criticizing the defence effort at a time of national emergency.
Although widely regarded as mistaken and gullible, the P.P.U.
was not generally held to be seditious or treasonable—in
contrast to the widely-voiced opinion during the Great War
that all peace societies (even those which did not call for a
halt to the war) were pro-German conspiracies. Thus before
the Second World War started the P.P.U. had been able to
establish, by its self-evident integrity, that it was pro-Nazi
only in the sense that, like Soper, its members attempted to
see 'something of God' in everyone, including Hitler and
Mussolini.[3]

But the main reason pacifism was treated tolerantly was,
of course, that it was too weak to be politically significant:
of the first batch of conscripts, for example, who registered
in June 1939, only 1.8 per cent applied for C.O. status.[4]
Even those pacifists who retained their belief in appeasement
right up to, or even beyond, the outbreak of war had increasingly to accept that, by the logic of the collaborative
orientation, they had to be content with at best a minor and
self-effacing role in the wider movement—as was illustrated
when, after its offer to dispatch 5,000 pacifists to the

[1] *PN*, 20 Feb., 30 Oct. 1942.
[2] *Partisan Review*, Mar.-Apr. 1941, cited in Orwell and Angus (eds.), *Collected Essays*, ii, p. 69.
[3] Purcell, *Portrait of Soper*, p. 79.
[4] Hayes, *Challenge of Conscience*, p. 382.

Sudetenland during the Munich crisis had received its inevitable rebuff,[1] the P.P.U. found it could do little except offer
to help with the National Peace Council's petition for a new
world conference on the condition that it could put its own
name on the forms it distributed.[2] Thus although the P.P.U.
had been founded because of a conviction that all existing
peace societies were tainted with compromise and that pacifists had a pure and unique contribution to make, most of
its members came to accept Richards's opinion 'that there
is an increasingly common ground that can be occupied by
pacifist and non-pacifist alike'.[3] From this it was a short step
towards urging that, in the interests of the appeasement
movement, pacifists should avoid stressing their own controversial views. Raven, who believed that a 'common policy
which did not raise the question of armed force' might
unite pacifist and non-pacifist Christians, recommended that
'pacifists ought to shrink from anything that would sharpen
controversy' in order not to 'forfeit their hopes in influencing
their fellow Church-members . . . '[4] A similar approach was
urged by Ponsonby who, in a long memorandum to Morris
in June 1939 about the P.P.U.'s immediate policy, insisted
that its urgent duty was to seek by 'propaganda and letters'
to influence the Government in the direction of appeasement. So convinced was Ponsonby that the sole rationale of
pacifism was to prevent war that, in order to maximize its
influence, he even urged the P.P.U. to soft-pedal its absolutism:

There is no need to flaunt our extreme pacifism or to speak and write
as members of the P.P.U. This only creates a prejudice against everything we may say and prevents editors from accepting letters. We must
remember the great number of sensibly minded people who do not
subscribe to our extreme doctrine and encourage and support them
when they turn in the right direction.[5]

For Ponsonby, formerly the most outspoken critic of the
collaborative orientation and the scourge of all 'half-way
houses', to recommend a dilution of policy in this way was

[1] P.P.U. Sponsors, 6 Oct. 1938.
[2] P.P.U. Management Committee, 12 Oct. 1938.
[3] Richards, *Crisis and World Peace*, p. 9.
[4] Raven, *War and the Christian*, pp. 168, 174.
[5] Memorandum, P.P.U., E.C., 12 June 1939.

a clear illustration of the demoralization of practical pacifism in the exceptional circumstances of the late thirties. Thus it was apolitical pacifism which, though still a minority taste in the pacifist movement as a whole even in the late thirties, attracted unprecedented and growing support among leading pacifist thinkers.

15

AFTER SHEPPARD (2): RETREATING FROM POLITICS

Throughout the inter-war period a minority of pacifists had consistently claimed that, however effective pacifism might be as a means of preventing war, its real justification was independent of politics and that true pacifists should be prepared, in a last resort at least, to adopt a sectarian orientation. Most of those taking this position were, like George M. Ll. Davies and other members of the F.o.R., Christian quietists; only the very unusual socialist pacifist, such as Plowman, did so; and those of humanitarian inspiration were even scarcer. However, once the appeal of first non-violence and then collaboration with appeasement began to wane, even practical pacifists—that is, those who did not recant their pacifism altogether—showed an increased enthusiasm for the one remaining orientation. To opt out of politics was the logical corollary of what Murry called 'this natural progression (as I believe it to be) of rational pacifism to religious pacifism'[1] which began after the optimism of 1936 had subsided.

One way of opting out was to retreat to America as did the P.P.U.'s three most formidable intellectuals: Russell, Huxley, and Heard. Russell was inquiring about a teaching post in the United States as early as December 1936, giving as his reason the fact that England 'is no place for children, with the imminent risk of war . . .';[2] but it was not till the Munich crisis that he crossed the Atlantic, still claiming to be 'an extreme pacifist' but giving signs of growing doubts in his comment to the American press on arrival that he realized there were occasions 'when it is very difficult to keep out of war'.[3]

[1] J. Middleton Murry, *The Pledge of Peace* (1938), p. 10.
[2] Russell to Norton, 28 Dec. 1936, in Feinberg and Kasritz, *Bertrand Russell's America*, i, p. 127.
[3] Ibid., p. 127.

Huxley had preceded him in April 1937, on a lecture-tour which was to turn into a sojourn of twenty-five years. It was during his first summer there that he finally completed his pacifist magnum opus in which he had set out to prove to his own satisfaction his two-year-old working hypothesis that bad means could not produce good ends. Published in November 1937, *Ends and Means: An Inquiry into the Nature of Ideals and into the Methods Employed for their Realisation* was at that time by far the most serious and ambitious of his books. Its central thesis was that 'if the ends we all desire are to be achieved there must be more than a mere deflection of evil; there must be suppression at the source, in the individual will. Hence it follows that large-scale political and economic reform is not enough.' In locating the problem in the individual will and in seeking to purge it of selfish impulses Huxley was drawn to the ideal, common to Buddhist, Confucian, and Hindu philosophy, of 'non-attachment': a state of freedom from all egoistical desires which could be achieved by meditation. Oriental mystics had shown, Huxley believed, 'that it was possible for individuals to transcend the limitations of personality and merge their private consciousness into a greater, impersonal consciousness underlying the personal mind.' He had not completely abandoned his belief that 'quite apart from the validity of its philosophical basis . . . non-violence can prove its value pragmatically—by working'; and he also recommended the 'one short-term policy which every individual can adopt—the policy of war-resistance'.[1] But, compared with his earlier pacifist writings, the emphasis of his thinking had shifted away from the short-term and the practical towards the long-term and the mystical. The rumour which reached Kingsley Martin in 1938 to the effect that Huxley and Heard were actually setting up their own religious community was not, therefore, wholly implausible. Replying to Martin to deny the rumour, Huxley admitted that he had become very interested in such experiments: 'for I become more and more firmly convinced that it is completely pointless to work in the field of politics . . . '. He was also critical

[1] pp. 24, 295, 140.

of religious people 'who think they can go into politics and transform the world' but who always 'end by going into politics and being transformed by the world'. His conclusion was that sectarianism was the only solution for those impelled by religious feelings: 'Religion can have no politics except the creation of small-scale societies of chosen individuals outside and on the margin of the essentially unviable large-scale societies . . . '[1]

This view was also—at some length—put into the mouth of Propter, one of the leading characters in Huxley's novel *After Many A Summer*, which he wrote in the spring and summer of 1939. Huxley's partial detachment, however, from Propter reflected the impasse which his pacifist thought had reached soon after his arrival in America, and which accounted for his retirement from active pacifist campaigning after the publication of *Ends and Means*, even though he remained a Sponsor of the P.P.U. for the rest of his life. Though he had come to see the difficulties of political action, he could arouse little enthusiasm for what he recognized to be the only alternative, preferring in later life to develop his mysticism by the more self-indulgent means of mescalin. At the same time he began to deny that his pacifism was in any strict sense religious, insisting that it was philosophical; in 1953 he was adamant on this point even though it was a possible obstacle to securing the United States citizenship for which he had applied.[2]

In this he and Heard, who had accompanied Huxley to America and continued to live near him, came to disagree. Heard took sectarianism seriously: Maria Huxley recorded late in 1938 that he 'thinks that we are seeing far too many people and are not confining ourselves to those who want to save their souls'; and she was irritated by the way his daily routine was inflexibly constructed around his periods of meditation.[3] He also became more religious, not less, becoming a Buddhist and founding his own community during the Second World War.

Pacifists did not have to go to America to opt out,

---

[1] Cited in Bedford, *Huxley*, i, p. 376; Martin, *Editor*, pp. 203–4.
[2] Bedford, *Huxley*, ii, pp. 150–1.
[3] Bedford, *Huxley*, i, pp. 367, 371.

however. Murry, for example, stayed put in East Anglia but moved from practical, socialist pacifism towards Christianity and sectarianism. The first sign of his new piety came in the epilogue of what was otherwise a secular statement of the non-violent orientation, *The Necessity of Pacifism*, published in the spring of 1937. The gradual change in his outlook, which led him to join the Anglican Pacifist Fellowship (from which, however, his irregular liaison with Mary Gamble from 1939 onwards forced him later to resign), can be traced through his regular contributions to *Peace News* and *Adelphi*, which were collected together and published in September 1938 under the title *The Pledge of Peace*. In his preface Murry noted how other sceptics like Huxley had 'completely changed, under the urgency of pacifism, to a religious mysticism' and how 'the signing of the Peace Pledge has meant for me a gradual passing into an entirely new sense of the reality of Christian Communion.' And he acknowledged that his conception of pacifism had, as a result, ceased to be practical and had become sectarian:

The real business of a Pacifist movement is to bear its witness against the total dehumanisation of humanity that is necessitated by modern war. If once Pacifists succumb to the view that the validity and value of their movement depends upon its success in preventing war, they have surrendered everything, and their movement is bound to fail. It is manifest that there is not going to be, as facile optimists imagine, a vast upsurge of national opinion against war . . . The Pacifist cause will be won, if it is won, by those who have come to see that winning is a secondary affair. What matters is that men and women should bear their witness—and bear it, if need be, to the end.[1]

The new activists rallying to the P.P.U. in 1939 included a number attracted by this despairing view of politics; the best known was Eric Gill who, as already noted, had joined the National Council in May. A classically bohemian figure in his habitual smock, full beard and steel-rimmed spectacles, Gill combined a sensual artistic zest (his particular forte was erotic engravings) with a yearning for spiritual truth which had led to his conversion to Catholicism in 1913. Although already professing socialism, his reaction to the Great War was merely, as earlier noted, that it was an interruption to his work—although, ironically, it was soon to provide him with

---

[1] Murry, *Pledge*, pp. 10, 11–12.

lucrative post-war commissions for carving war memorials.[1] His grounds for opposing his call-up, which he managed to postpone until two months before the end of the war, were not conscientious, and it was only in retrospect that Gill fitted the war into his increasingly hostile critique of industrialism. As he later acknowledged in his *Autobiography*: 'I hadn't connected in my mind the business of industrialism and the business of war-making . . . I was not a pacifist in the specific sense of the word, still less a "conscientious objector".'[2] The views which he propounded with increasing intensity after 1918—and most notably in his book *Money and Morals*, published in 1934—combined elements of William Morris, Belloc and Chesterton, and were clearly rooted in the craftsman's hostility to a mass-produced civilization. At first his anarchism got the better of his pacifism. He was, for example, one of the most outspoken Catholic supporters of the Republican cause in Spain; and throughout the rest of his life (he died suddenly in November 1940) even when addressing an explicitly pacifist audience—such as the F.o.R. in 1939—he would not mitigate his calls for 'the subordination of the man of business and the dealer and the money lender' at whose doors he laid much of the blame for war.[3] But though his critique never changed, he became increasingly sceptical about political action to rectify matters; by April 1940 he was admitting in a private letter that 'politics are not my affair and Neville C. and Adolf H. seem to me like Tweedle Dumb [*sic*] and Tweedle Dee.'[4] In his *Autobiography*, published a few months later, he concluded: 'I must keep clear of politics—politics as the word is understood in our time and in what are called democratic countries . . . "Religion is politics, politics is brotherhood", said William Blake, and, I may add "Brotherhood is poverty and poverty is peace". That is where I found myself and that is where I shall remain.'[5] Pacifism appealed to him because it appeared to provide the mystical sense of brotherhood he

[1] Speaight, *Gill*, p. 89.

[2] Eric Gill, *Autobiography* (1940), p. 201.

[3] Eric Gill, *Last Essays* (1942), p. 53.

[4] Gill to O'Connor, 2 Apr. 1940, in Shewring (ed.), *Letters of Eric Gill*, p. 445.

[5] Gill, *Autobiography*, p. 260.

had sought by living during most of the inter-war period
in a succession of small craft communities and by becoming
a Tertiary of the Order of St. Dominic. As he insisted in a
pamphlet published early in 1940: 'The P.P.U. has not failed
because it has failed to prevent war . . . Its primary and real
work is the preparation of peace, the rediscovery of the
foundations of human order and the winning of men to build
on them . . . '[1]

Pacifists were thus arriving in increasing numbers at the
conclusion which Plowman had long since reached. Arguing
with a Marxist friend in December 1935 he had written:
'You say "after all the problem is to stop war". I say it's
not. There's no such problem. The problem is how to live
like a human individual in order that you may live socially
and communally.'[2] The paradox contained in the last part
of Plowman's formulation was revealing. Pacifists derived
their faith from an extreme individualist belief in the sovereignty of each conscience; but they were also for the most part
aware of the danger of seeming to adopt a quasi-pacifist
unconcern for those whose consciences were less exigent.
They therefore insisted that their opting out was an act of
real concern for the health of society as a whole. Christians
like Morris talked of pacifists as a 'redemptive minority'[3] wit-
nessing to the ideals which would eventually enable society
to advance spiritually. Humanitarian and, more especially,
socialist pacifists were even more concerned to emphasise
that pacifism was a revolutionary social faith; Ethel Mannin,
for instance, wrote at the time of her conversion: 'Graduating
through Marxism to anarchism, pacifism is only one step
further on.'[4]

But, as with anarchism, it was always hard to specify a
political model for helping a society whose political system
had to be rejected. In the later thirties many pacifists felt
they had discovered the answer in the idea of the small
self-selected community in which individuality could find

---

[1] Eric Gill, *The Human Person and Society* (P.P.U., 1940), pp. 6–7.
[2] Plowman to Jack Common, 1 Dec. 1935, in D.L.P(lowman) (ed.), *Bridge*,
p. 547.
[3] *Listener*, 22 Jan. 1936, p. 145.
[4] Mannin, *Privileged Spectator*, p. 304.

expression while also helping to create the nucleus of a new
social order. Whereas in 1936-7 talk of non-violent training
had enjoyed a vogue among pacifists, by March 1938 a contributor to *Reconciliation* was commenting: ' "Community"
is becoming one of those hard-worked words';[1] and by July
Mumford, who six months previously had been vexed at the
danger to the unity of the P.P.U. from an excessive preoccupation with 'politics', had started also to complain about
a similar obsession with 'community'.[2] By the beginning of
1939 'a steady growth in Community interests up and down
the country' was being recorded. 'Men and women everywhere are feeling impelled by the menace of our times to
all sorts of cooperative activities.'[3] This was certainly true
of several P.P.U. members: George Macleod had launched his
partly pacifist Christian community on Iona in 1938 with
Macgregor's help and Raven's enthusiastic encouragement;[4]
Richard Ward, having expressed his conviction that 'the way
to peace is a personal responsibility rather than a matter for
governments, pacts and conferences' and therefore 'requires
an inward before an outward revolution', lived for a while
in an income-pooling community in London (before it dis-
integrated);[5] and in June 1939 Ronald Duncan and Nigel
Spottiswoode set up their own agricultural community in
Devon. By the summer of 1939 this tendency had become
sufficiently pronounced for anti-militarists of strong Marxist
leanings to express concern at this retreat from the political
struggle.[6]

The fact that pacifists were abandoning political claims
for their beliefs made it easier for non-pacifists to recognize
the moral legitimacy of pacifism, and during 1938-9 discussion of pacifism was marked by a greater tolerance than
five or so years earlier. Among the new dispassionate assess-
ments of pacifism emanating from the political left were: a
Political Quarterly article by Kingsley Martin in April 1938,

[1] *Rec.*, Mar. 1938, p. 79.
[2] *PN*, 2 July 1938.
[3] *Christian Pacifist*, Jan. 1939, p. 16; see also *Friend*, 6 Jan. 1939, p. 18.
[4] Dillistone, *Raven*, p. 284.
[5] R. H. Ward (ed.), *Ten Peace Plays* (1938), p. xi; Ward, *Names and Natures*,
pp. 208, 217-18.
[6] See e.g. Alexander Miller, *Pacifism, Revolution and Community* (1939).

prompted by Huxley's *Ends and Means*; John Lewis's Marxist study, *The Case Against Pacifism*, which was written early in 1938 (though held up by Gollancz's latent pacifism until 1940 when it appeared under another imprint);[1] and the 1939 Burge Memorial Lecture by A. D. Lindsay, Master of Balliol. In each case the message was the same: impatience with (in Lewis's words) 'those who believe that pacifism is not only right in principle but bound to produce desirably results immediately',[2] and with (what Lindsay called) the 'sham pacifism' which 'converts the sincere view of the doctrinaire pacifists that we ought to abjure war into the view that what matters about war is that we should keep out of it.'[3] But as a corollary there emerged a new respect for the 'doctrinaire' absolutist who recognized the dogmatic and sectarian basis—and, therefore, the limited appeal—of his position. For (as Kingsley Martin pointed out): 'These arguments do not dispose of pacifism. They merely suggest that the pacifist is wise to base his argument on ethical and not on political grounds. If he wishes to do public work in present society, he must confine himself to those types of social service and propaganda which Quakers have long made peculiarly their own.'[4] To a considerable extent the pacifists of the Second World War were themselves to accept this wisdom.

[1] John Lewis, *The Left Book Club* (1970), p. 104.
[2] John Lewis, *The Case Against Pacifism*, p. 42.
[3] A. D. Lindsay, *Pacifism as a Principle and Pacifism as a Dogma* (Burge Memorial Lecture, 1939), pp. 19-20.
[4] Kingsley Martin, 'The Pacifist's Dilemma Today', *Political Quarterly*, Apr.-June 1938, pp. 168-70.

16

WAR AND SECTARIANISM, 1939-45

It took the military perils of the Second World War—or, to be more precise, of the period from May 1940 until the end of 1942—to confront the pacifist movement as a whole with the truths at which its leading thinkers had arrived by the late thirties. It is probable that, despite increased support for sectarianism, the majority of pacifists hoped right until the last to prevent war by collaborating with the movement for appeasement; and, when war was declared, most of them simply transferred their allegiance to the movement for a negotiated peace. Since the Danzig crisis added little to the case for fighting Nazism (which had already been effectively established by Prague), and since Britain was in no immediate danger, there were few defections from pacifism at the outbreak of war. Those immediately reneging were for the most part simply formalizing long-standing doubts. In this category were a number of socialist pacifists such as Lucy Cox[1] and Leslie Paul who, long convinced of the evil of fascism, 'discarded the remnants'[2] of their pacifism. So too were those who had come to realise that they had never been more than 'ninety-nine per cent' pacifists: Maude Royden, for example, who resigned from the P.P.U. in September 1939 just twelve months after joining, confessing to Morris: 'I feel that I owe you an explanation for having joined the P.P.U. last year rather than for leaving it this. I ought not to have joined';[3] and Leslie Weatherhead who confessed in a book completed in November 1939 that he had never really been a pacifist and his signing of the peace pledge had been 'a refusal to think'.[4] They were more than compensated for by an influx of converts: the proportion of conscripts registering as C.O.s

[1] Interview.
[2] Paul, *Angry Young Man*, p. 284.
[3] *PN*, 13 Oct. 1939.
[4] Leslie Weatherhead, *Thinking Aloud In Wartime* (1939), p. 22.

increased from the pre-war 1.8 per cent to the 2.2 per cent of the first wartime batch in October 1939; and the P.P.U. gained 2,435 members in September and 2,280 the following month. These recruits to the pacifist movement included young writers, musicians, and thinkers such as Alex Comfort, Michael Tippett, and Edward Blishen; while some older luminaries became Sponsors of the P.P.U. for the first time after the war had begun, including Dame Sybil Thorndike (1882-1976), Sir Arthur Eddington (1882-1944), a Quaker who had been Professor of Astronomy at Cambridge since 1913, Eric Gill, and George M. Ll. Davies.

The issues and alignments in the pacifist movement remained broadly the same between Prague and Dunkirk, the main effect of the outbreak of war being simply to intensify them. Those who had formerly called for negotiations with Hitler did so with even more urgency than ever (and were joined by Murry whose sudden conversion to this idea can be connected with his simultaneous attempts to negotiate a peace between his wife and Mary Gamble once the former had discovered about his liaison with the latter);[1] and those who had campaigned against conscription were also keen to step up their campaign. On the other hand, apolitical pacifists like Plowman were more than ever convinced that practical pacifists—'pacifists typified by Ponsonby', as he put it—were 'rendered absolutely futile by their simple cleavage between peace and war.' Himself on the point of moving into the old Adelphi Centre to form a pacifist community with Murry, Lea, and others, Plowman insisted that it was a matter of 'life or death for the P.P.U. whether they—as a corporate body—make some actual attempt at social living at this time.'[2]

The P.P.U.'s increasing difficulties in steering its middle course between these two poles were reflected in the formation of two ginger groups within it: the Forethought Committee, which was, in effect, a reconstituted committee of Sponsors, dominated by religious-minded advocates of community-living including Murry, Plowman, Raven, Vera

---

[1] Lea, *Murry*, p. 305.
[2] Plowman to Murry, 23 Dec. 1939, M.P.

Brittain, Mary Gamble, and Wellock; and the Forward Movement formed soon afterwards by the militant young activists who by January 1940 were publicly urging the P.P.U. 'to be more active in stopping the war'.[1] Responsibility for holding these two factions together fell, of course, on to Morris's shoulders but also, increasingly, on to those of Alex Wood, who became Chairman following the former's relinquishing of that position (though not of the General Secretaryship) in November 1939 because of his divorce. Though Wood's personal approach was strongly inclined towards the thinking of the Forethought Committee, his humility and integrity earned him respect even from those of more militant inclinations. One feature of the P.P.U.'s middle course was its reluctance to interfere with conscription: it issued a leaflet informing C.O.s of their rights but refused—in so far as it could control its activists—to picket the Labour Exchanges where registration was being carried out; and Morris attempted to scotch allegations that its policy was seditious by insisting: 'So far as the Peace Pledge Union is concerned there has never been any attempt to force a man's conscience or to find it for him.'[2] But at the same time it committed itself to calling for an immediate negotiated peace, organizing a special Women's Peace Campaign, led by Mary Gamble and Sybil Morrison, which reached its crescendo in March 1940.

It was the German military breakthrough in the spring of 1940 which proved a watershed for pacifism. With their country in acute danger, many pacifists realized that they had confused pacifism with isolationism by tacitly assuming that there could be no genuinely defensive continental war. The proportion registering as C.O.s, which had already declined slightly with each new batch since October 1939, fell by a further half during May and June 1940, reaching 0.5 per cent in July. Similarly the membership of the P.P.U., having passed the 136,000 mark in April 1940, suffered its first ever net loss in May, when 627 resigned and 210 joined. Resignations included three Sponsors—Russell, Mumford, and

[1] PN, 12 Jan. 1940.
[2] PN, 1 Mar. 1940.

Storm Jameson—and other leading pacifists publicly re-
canting at this time included Joad, Rose Macaulay, Milne,
and J. D. Beresford. Even the F.o.R. (which, sectarian in
orientation, was best prepared for the crisis and able to
expand throughout the war) suffered 200 resignations during
the summer of 1940 and saw its rate of recruitment reduced.
The shock to the movement, and its realization that it was
facing its extreme test, was evident on 14 June 1940 in John
Barclay's regular *Peace News* column on P.P.U. Group activity:

During the last few weeks I have had letters from old friends, men and
women who I should have been ready to 'back my shirt on', who have
written to say that they can no longer hold to their pledge of personal
renunciation of war . . . Unless we have really faced up to the possibility of military defeat we cannot claim to have examined the faith
called pacifism. If at the back of our minds has always been the comforting thought that in the end the Allied Forces would win, our
pacifism has never been more than an academic philosophy. I believe
that is is this possibility of military defeat that has come as a terrible
shock to so many people. Pacifism faced by military dictatorship and
no longer sheltering behind it—this is something that may cause complete renunciation of previously held convictions.

As Storm Jameson pointed out, in a pamphlet renouncing
her previous convictions which took her three months of
painful introspection to write, the assumptions underlying
the call for a negotiated peace had been proved to be invalid:

A pacifist who says, 'Come let us reason together' is guilty of a deep
refusal of honesty. The way of reasoning together is not open to us.
What is open to us is submission, the concentration camp, the death of
our humblest with our best, the forcing of our children's minds into an
evil mould. If he says 'I would choose this rather than war', he is
using the right accorded him by our civilisation to make a moral choice.
But he must choose, not evade the implications of his choice . . . When
my reason forced me to see the choice in these terms I was unhappy.
But I could not choose submission.[1]

Roy Walker also insisted that a negotiated peace would itself
involve evil and injustice—such as agreeing to hand over
political refugees to the Nazis as the French had been obliged
to—and that a pacifist willing to accept one would, just like
the militarist, 'be doing evil that good may come of it'. Yet
he retained his pacifism and pointed out that pacifists were

[1] Storm Jameson, *The End of This War* (P.E.N., 1941), p. 25; see also her
Journey, ii, p. 95.

logically committed to believing that this was better than a continuation of the war. Murry, who in July 1940 agreed to take over as editor of *Peace News* in its hour of need, was also convinced that, while pacifism was a social and spiritual faith which must not be confused with a purely political movement such as a stop-the-war campaign, a pacifist had nevertheless to accept 'that, in the world today, any peace is better than any war . . . '[1]

A considerable number, however, were reluctant to admit this: Sybil Thorndike later recalled being advised by Lansbury shortly before his death that 'it would be better to be over-run by the Germans than to fight'; she, however, 'couldn't go as far as this' yet still considered herself a pacifist.[2] A sufficient number of others thought the same way for Mary Gamble, writing in August 1941, to deplore the fact that, whereas in the early months of the war 'the vast majority of the movement' would have backed any peace offer 'from whatever quarter', this was no longer true because many pacifists now 'appear to think that because they "can't trust Hitler" a continuation of the war is better than a peace negotiated with the German Govenment.'[3] Some, including Sorensen and Cadoux, accepted the political case for the war and, in effect, argued that a collaborative pacifist should support the war effort. The former, as already noted, had felt able to endorse rearmament in 1937; the latter, however, concluded a painful process of rethinking his Christian pacifism when, late in 1940, he published a major work which argued that the war was 'relatively justified' and that pacifists should

admit that it is better that it should be victoriously carried through than that it should be discontinued before the undertaking is completed. I cannot refuse to make that admission; and I make it without the consciousness, in doing so, of betraying my pacifism or forfeiting my right to propagate it.[4]

Most pacifists, however, abandoned the collaborative orientation and accepted that, unless they reneged, the only choice was between non-violence and sectarianism. If they

[1] Walker, *PN*, 10 Oct., 1941; Murry (editorial) *PN*, 18 July 1941.
[2] Cited in Elizabeth Sprigge, *Sybil Thorndike Casson* (1971), p. 230.
[3] *PN*, 22 Aug. 1941.
[4] Cadoux, *Christian Pacifism Re-Examined*, p. 216.

still saw pacifism as a practical policy, they had openly to adopt the non-violent orientation of urging peace on any terms; but since it was clear that no mercy could be expected from Hitler, and since only the Norwegians had explored the possibilities of passive resistance, this policy aroused the enthusiasm of only the most resolute and militant of pacifists, such as Walker. Most pacifists were extremely anxious not to be thought to be obstructing the war effort, particularly in the summer of 1940 when fear of fifth columnists was at its height. Thus when, for example, in May 1940 the P.P.U. was prosecuted under Defence Regulation 39A for its poster 'WAR WILL CEASE WHEN MEN REFUSE TO FIGHT. WHAT ARE *YOU* GOING TO DO ABOUT IT?', it at once agreed to withdraw the poster, Morris insisting in court that it was two-year-old stock and 'inappropriate at the present time. It was no part of the Union's policy to promote disaffection in the Forces. Two of his sons-in-law were in the Army and he respected the decision they had made.'[1] And when members of the Forward Movement disagreed with this approach and got themselves arrested, a number of leading pacifists were unsympathetic. Nor did Vera Brittain disguise her dislike of 'belligerent pacifists, incurable minoritarians with a passion for unpopularity . . . They feel that the sole test of their sincerity is the extent to which they can embarrass the Government.'[2] Similarly Roger Wilson (1906–), a Quaker who had been Oxford's leading undergraduate pacifist in the twenties and a speaker for the P.P.U. in the late thirties, experienced while a C.O.

a far deeper sense of spiritual unity with those of my friends in the fighting services who, though detesting war as deeply as I did, yet felt that there was no other way in which they could share in the agony of the world, than I had with those pacifists who talked as if the suffering of the world could be turned off like a water tap if only politiciaians would talk sensibly together.[3]

Privately at least many pacifists would have agreed with George Orwell, who, with all the enthusiasm of a recent convert to the view that to fight Nazism was not merely an act

[1] *The Times*, 24 May 1940.
[2] Brittain, *Humiliation With Honour*, p. 49.
[3] Roger Wilson, *Authority, Leadership and Concern: A Study in Motive and Administration in Quaker Relief Work* (1949), p. 9.

of imperialist rivalry, was insisting: 'In so far as it hampers the British war effort, British pacifism is on the side of the Nazis.'[1]

Making the best available reply to Orwell's taunt, the pacifist poet D. S. Savage argued that Orwell was thinking as a politician: 'He consequently sees pacifism primarily as a political phenomenon. That is just what it isn't. Primarily it is a moral phenomenon . . . Pacifism springs from conscience—i.e. from within the individual human being.'[2] The only tenable position for most pacifists, particularly after the summer of 1940, was the sectarian orientation of abandoning any attempt to recommend pacifism as a practical policy. Many accepted this only implicitly: for example by switching to *pacificist* causes such as food relief or the campaign against indiscriminate bombing which they had formerly tended to dismiss as focussing on symptoms rather than causes. Sectarianism is far from easy, of course, to accept explicitly unless the pacifist feels alienated from society and is fully confident of the righteousness of his own creed. The absolutists of 1916–19, in particular, had felt certain that the war and the state which was prosecuting it were both cruel and evil, and the N.-C.F. had thus 'gained in inner spiritual strength and in intensity of support from the persecution which it had to meet.' Pointing this out at the second annual conference of its Second World War equivalent, the Fellowship of Conscientious Objectors, Fenner Brockway admitted that this contrasted with the 'sincere doubts and perplexities' of opponents of the war against Nazism.[3]

He might also have mentioned another contrast between the two wars, namely the isolation of pacifism from progressive opinion between 1939 and 1945. In the Great War pacifists had drawn strength from the liberal tradition of opposition to conscription; but the price they had paid for the general acceptance over the two subsequent decades of

[1] *Adelphi*, Oct. 1941, cited in Orwell and Angus (eds.), *Collected Essays*, p. 196.

[2] *Partisan Review*, Sept./Oct. 1942, cited ibid., p. 255.

[3] Fenner Brockway, *The C.O. and the Community* (n.d. [1941?]), pp. 3,4; for Brockway's own personal dilemma, see his *Outside the Right* (1963), pp. 18, 26, 32.

the right of conscientious objection was the simultaneous acceptance of the legitimacy of 'National Service'. The libertarian position taken in 1916 even by so orthodox a Liberal cabinet minister as Sir John Simon was now virtually confined to anarchists, such as Ethel Mannin who volunteered for fire-watching but would have refused had it been compulsory.[1] In addition, apart from the tiny handful of anarchists (who included Reginald Reynolds), plus the dwindling I.L.P., and, until June 1941, the largely discredited Communist Party, there were few *pacificists* in the ranks of the C.O.s. The anti-war movement was almost exclusively pacifist; and where the N.-C.F. had seen itself as part of a wider crusade for liberty and socialism, the Fellowship of Conscientious Objectors was quietist, and the Central Board for Conscientious Objectors purely a welfare body. Thus although the total of objectors, at almost 60,000, was nearly four times that of the Great War, their public impact was considerably more muted. By the end of the war, only 0.2 per cent of new conscripts were seeking exemption, and some earlier objectors had abandoned their pacifism.

Simply from the point of view of a strategy for containing a dissident minority, the Government's liberal policy was thus highly effective. It was not merely the P.P.U.'s genuine respect for the individual conscience which made it reluctant to obstruct the conscription machinery: it was also the sensitivity of pacifists such as Lansbury to the fact that 'we possess rights and privileges such as no other nation allows pacifists in wartime'[2]—one Welsh pacifist was made 'proud to be British' by the behaviour of the Cardiff tribunal.[3] Although the Great War's tribunal system was retained, its members were no longer drawn narrowly from local notables, and the uniformed War Office representative who had often acted like a prosecuting counsel had been replaced by an official of the Ministry of Labour acting impartially, like a clerk of the court. In addition the four most contentious features of the Great War's procedure for granting exemptions had been considerably modified. Firstly, there was clear acknowledgement that tribunals were

[1] Mannin, *Brief Voices*, p. 35.   [2] Cited in Postgate, *Lansbury*, p. 323.
[3] E. C. Haigh: *PN*, 18 July 1941.

empowered to exempt unconditionally: as they did in the case of Benjamin Britten, for example, and of 4.7 per cent of objectors in all—double the percentage of the Great War. Secondly, it was acknowledged, after only a brief hesitation, that political beliefs might be 'conscientious'. Thirdly, offers of alternative service were made more flexible: this helps to explain why only 3 per cent of objectors went to prison because of inability to comply with their tribunal's decision, compared with roughly 30 per cent who were incarcerated for periods long or short during the Great War. And, fourthly, for this 3 per cent, which included Walker and Tippett, and for those who came into conflict with army discipline, treatment was more humane: even in the much-publicized case of Kenneth Makin, a Christadelphian who became the first pacifist to be courtmartialled, the complaints against the army for maltreatment in a Glasgow military prison concerned what *Peace News* admitted to be 'petty annoyances' like being served tea in a soapy shaving mug.[1]

These reforms undoubtedly helped to reduce both the size of the absolutist minority and its ability to dramatize the C.O. position as it had done so effectively in the Great War. Yet it would be wrong to assume that the 'reformed' tribunals produced decisions more favourable to the objectors —indeed, since their greater tolerance had encouraged marginal pacifists (as well as the sincere but diffident) to come forward in greater numbers than in 1916, they had to be stricter. Almost 30 per cent of all registered C.O.s had their applications for exemption refused outright, nearly *double* the Great War proportion;[2] and nearly as many again were subjected to conditions to which they had initially objected. The effect of the reforms was thus mainly psychological: they increased the moral authority of the tribunals as embodiments of the general will. As a result less than 7 per cent (just over 4,000) pressed their disagreement with their tribunal's decision to the point of incurring prosecution or court martial; the rest meekly accepted it.

---

[1] *PN*, 12 Apr. 1940. It should be noted nevertheless that Makin suffered a nervous breakdown.

[2] I have never seen this surprising contrast noted; for the statistics of 1939–45 see Hayes, *Challenge of Conscience*, esp. pp. 69–71.

The paradox of the C.O. movement of 1939-45 is that the 'great respect and kindness'[1] which it admitted was shown to it throughout the war (except for the panic during the summer of 1940) made life in several respects harder than for its predecessors who had been confirmed in the rightness of their stand by their harsh treatment and by their sense of political relevance. Only two types of objector seemed unembarrassed by the absence in the Second World War of these psychological aids to dissent: members of esoteric religious sects; and the incorrigibly minority-minded. Although the former seem to have constituted a smaller proportion of C.O.s than a quarter of a century before, many intelligent pacifists were nevertheless disturbed by the number basing their conscientious objections on an all too often uninformed Biblical literalism.[2] Thus Edward Blishen (1920-), a pacifist troubled both over the correctness or otherwise of his position and by its 'obscure discomfort', found himself doing land work in the company of 'an odd rabble' of self-confident quasi-pacifists, 'cussed adherents of strange varieties of Puritanism: Christadelphians, Plymouth Brethren, Elimites, Particular People. Some of these were not so much pacifists as (I uneasily felt) complacent spectators at what they took to be Armageddon.'[3]

The minority-minded pacifist, a type ever present within the movement, had become increasingly conspicuous following the introduction of conscription. Classifying the C.O.s who had worked as guinea pigs for medical research into scabies during the Second World War, a non-pacifist doctor noted two main types: religious pacifists; and 'aggressive' types 'whose real objection is not so much to violence as to being in a position where at any moment they may be ordered around by someone for whom they have no real respect and be ordered to carry out some duty they think futile or unnecessary' and whose 'bloodymindedness' was their defining characteristic.[4] Leslie Paul took the same view. One of the factors causing him finally to renounce

[1] *Christian Pacifist*, Aug. 1939, p. 199.

[2] See Field, *Pacifism and Conscientious Objection*, p. 5; *PN*, 23 Feb. 1940, 3 Jan. 1941.

[3] Edward Blishen, *A Cackhanded War* (1972), p. 24; see also pp. 15-16.

[4] Kenneth Mellanby, *Human Guinea Pigs* (1945), p. 83.

pacifism was his awareness 'that, since exemption had
become so easy and involved no martyrdom of any kind, it
was necessary to be quite sure that a desire to escape military
service was not prompted by something quite different from
"principles".' This made him suspicious of many of the pacifists he met, many of whose 'pacifism' seemed to him merely
'a variant of nihilism, an aggressive refusal to accept *any* of
the burdens of living in a society, and only too often the fruit
of an unadmitted neurosis.'[1] But even the unashamedly
minority-minded found the liberal climate frustrating; one
went so far as to complain that

the State has been more ingenious than we ever imagined it could be.
British totalitarianism has found a way of assimilating pacifists! . . .
So far has the State encroached on our personal liberties that it pre-
sumes to underwrite them, making them valid. This is an extraordinary
extension of totalitarianism . . . the conscientious objector finds himself not too unpleasantly enmeshed in the Authoritarian State. There
is a feeling that somehow we have been diddled . . . [2]

The majority of pacifists found it rather harder, however,
to think in terms of that conveniently impersonal entity 'the
State'; instead C.O.s had to recognize that their quarrel was
with their fellow members of society. The discrimination
which they found hardest to bear arose from unofficial prejudice: *Peace News*, for example, was never banned but
suffered after May 1940 from a boycott by wholesale news-
agents; pacifists who were exempted by their tribunals on
condition that they remained in their present jobs were sometimes immediately sacked by their employers, and when
required to do work of national importance they often found
that other workers—for example, firemen—refused to allow
them to be taken on.[3] For the first part of the war at least,
the ordinary pacifist's commonest predicament was thus to
find himself, as Plowman had predicted in December 1939,
'not in gaol for the govt. [*sic*] won't put him there, but in
the void, upon air' and without a job.[4] Finding employment
was an important task undertaken by the Pacifist Service
Bureau, operating from Dick Sheppard House, and it was to

---

[1] Paul, *Angry Young Man*, p. 284.
[2] Frank Hancock: *PN*, 5 Apr. 1940.
[3] Barker, Thesis, pp. 38–44.
[4] Plowman to Murry, 23 Dec. 1939, M.P.

provide jobs as well as opportunities for a constructive social contribution that the successful Christian Pacifist Forestry and Land Units were organized by Henry Carter.[1] But few pacifists felt justified in expressing resentment at their treatment; as was pointed out by a writer in *Peace News* on 21 February 1941 most of them found it hard 'to avoid the feeling that they are in the wrong with society and because of this to prevent a cautious, even diffident, manner from creeping into their relations with others'. This diffidence was sometimes pressed almost to its logical conclusion: one group of pacifists went on a five-day starvation diet 'to aid seamen';[2] and Herbert Gray admitted that he found the pacifist dilemma 'almost intolerable' and that the 'only perfectly logical thing to do is suicide. Unfortunately, however, this is the path of cowardice and retreat.'[3]

Acutely aware that they had been granted special privileges of a sort traditionally granted only to the Society of Friends, most pacifists responded with the characteristic Quaker desire to repay their debt by social service. As early as the second week of the war the P.P.U. National Council had 'decided that the demand for opportunities of service to their fellows be met',[4] having already been inundated with 900 enquiries about the Pacifist Service Corps (later, Bureau) which it had just formed to undertake humanitarian work. The characteristic outlook of 'the new generation' of C.O.s was summed up by Alex Wood early in 1940:

The absolutists are relatively less numerous now than in the last war. Their contribution is as important as ever but of the young men who appear before our tribunals, the great majority are so sensitive to the claims of the community on their service that they are eager to find some positive and constructive work to do which is not primarily war work.[5]

After the fall of France this eagerness was intensified and the pacifist conception of what was 'not primarily war work' became, it appears, more flexible. Those who had denounced A.R.P. in peacetime welcomed the dangers of the Blitz as

---

[1] Hayes, *Challenge of Conscience*, p. 208.
[2] *PN*, 8 May 1942.
[3] *PN*, 19 Dec. 1941.
[4] P.P.U., National Co., 16 Sept. 1939.
[5] *PN*, 2 Feb. 1940.

an opportunity to show that pacifists were neither cowards
nor fifth columnists, and Pacifist Service Units served refresh-
ments in air-raid shelters and helped to dig victims out of
the rubble.[1]

Whereas in the First World War non-absolutists (who were
a majority, of course) were known as 'alternativists', with
the strong implication that they had compromised their
principles by accepting alternative service, in the Second they
were often described as 'humanitarians', thereby emphasizing
that their motivation was a positive one. Although some
absolutists such as Wellock 'deprecated the proposal that the
P.P.U. should devote itself to relief and restorative work,
and said that its main task would be in the spiritual sphere',
the polarization of the pacifist movement against which
Peace News had been warning[2] never materialized. Although
suspicious that some of this desire to serve the community
amounted to a currying of favour and an escape from recognizing the full implications of pacifism, the most absolute
and intransigent of pacifists also accepted the case for humanitarian action. Plowman privately admitted, shortly before
departing for Langham, that 'what I *really* want to do is my
old job of Ambulance "Waggon Orderly" on A.R.P.';[3]
Walker, a critic of the view that a cup of tea handed out by a
pacifist was in some ways more significant than one dis-
pensed by a non-pacifist, and himself an absolutist who went
on work- and hunger-strike in prison, was also the energetic
secretary of a campaign to urge the Government to organize
controlled food relief for the Belgians, Dutch, and other
suffering nations;[4] and Reynolds, still intransigent enough
to go to prison in 1940 rather than pay a fine for riding a
bicycle without lights, trained as a Quaker relief worker
and did A.R.P. work.[5] The issue which most sharply exposed
the tension between the minority which desired to resist the
war effort and those anxious to serve the community came in

---

[1] For the satisfactions of thus 'making some contribution to mitigating the
effects of the war', see Simmons (ed.), *The Objectors*, p. 16.

[2] P.P.U. National Co., 16 Sept. 1939; *PN*, 27 Sept. 1939.

[3] Plowman to Nancy Browne, 11 Sept. 1939, in D.L.P(lowman) (ed.), *Bridge*,
p. 684.

[4] *PN*, 2 May 1941; Walker to the author, 28 July 1977.

[5] Mannin, *Brief Voices*, pp. 21, 29; Reynolds, *My Life*, pp. 171, 189.

1940 when firewatching was made compulsory. Only a minority of pacifists took a stand on this issue, and, of those who did, most—like the scientist Kathleen Lonsdale[1]—were anxious to stress that the objection was to compulsion, not to the work as such.

For most pacifists social service was a means of atoning for being a tolerated sect without a political solution to offer. In their keenness to help, their outlook became in some cases almost apologetic. Admitting in a *Peace News* editorial on 28 November 1941 that 'it must be a good thing to commend pacifism, by its obvious works, to the average man', Murry warned that it was easy 'to succumb, without quite knowing what is happening, to the desire to be respectable. A great deal of pacifism, today, is intensely respectable'. But Murry, an opponent of minority-mindedness, had no wish to advocate quietism: in common with the other apolitical pacifists of the later thirties who came together after the outbreak of war in the Forethought Committee, he was adamant that sectarian pacifism should not wash its hands of society. Pacifists, he insisted in his editorial, 'must form some concrete image of a possible society of peace'. That pacifism, defined as a social faith, was akin to anarchism was coming increasingly to be understood. It was recognized implicitly early in 1940 by Raven who argued in an influential P.P.U. pamphlet: 'The practical task of pacifism is the achievement of a human way of living';[2] and also by the Forethought Committee which produced four 'Affirmations' which 'though not be regarded as binding on any individual member express in the opinion of the National Council the corporate mind of the Peace Pledge Union'. In contrast with the P.P.U.'s one previous attempt to expand on the pledge—its Manifesto of 1938—these Affirmations had nothing to say about international policy but sought to give guidance on 'the pacifist way of life' and in particular on the pacifist's 'right relationship' to his fellow citizens.[3] By 1941, moreover, the identification with anarchism was being made explicit by

---

[1] Morrison, *I Renounce War*, p. 54. Lonsdale, one of the first two women to become a F.R.S., was a Quaker convert.

[2] Raven, *Starting Point*, p. 10.

[3] The Affirmations are reproduced in Morrison, *I Renounce War*, pp. 101–2.

philosophically-minded younger pacifists, such as Frank Lea and Maurice Cranston.[1]

In the most depressing phase of the war, therefore, enthusiasm for community living reached a peak as pacifists searched for a practical expression of their non-violent social philosophy. 'If the courage of two friends together greatly exceeds their individual braveries,' Raven wrote in November 1940, 'so the creative power of community displays resources literally limitless. To transform collective activity into community life is the chief task of the pacifist movement.'[2] On 14 March 1941 *Peace News* launched a monthly supplement entitled 'Community', in the belief that 'so soon as the grim period of war is over, it will be revealed as the forerunner of the new society'. To a considerable extent the community movement was thus launched to justify an abstract and theoretical belief: that sectarianism can be socially efficacious. Experience showed, however, that communities tended to be microcosms of the 'old' society; and many of the idealistic experiments ran into difficulties within a few years. Plowman's, initially based at the former Adelphi centre, suffered from the fact that, though loved for his personal integrity, its leader was organizationally incompetent to a degree. It fared better for a time after his death in June 1941 under the guidance of Joe Watson, an ex-miner of remarkable personal gifts, but enthusiasm waned and by 1942 even the dedicated Frank Lea had left to take up school-teaching.[3] The personality clashes at Langham, however, were far less serious than those on the farm set up by Duncan in June 1939 at Welcombe, Devon, and the larger one launched by Murry at Thelnetham, Norfolk—as both leaders have entertainingly described.[4] Being owners of their communities' farms, and thus concerned to avoid financial losses, both Murry and Duncan were turned away from their former beliefs in socialism by conflicts with undisciplined and radical pacifists whom they often suspected of joining their

---

[1] See *PN*, 3 Jan., 7 Feb., 18 Apr. 1941.

[2] *PN*, 15 Nov. 1940.

[3] Interview.

[4] Ronald Duncan, *Journal of a Husbandman* (1944); and J. Middleton Murry, *Community Farm* (1952).

communities mainly to secure exemption from conscription. By October 1942 when Spottiswoode departed (and, with the all-or-nothing attitude towards the war which characterized many of the younger pacifists, joined the R.A.F.), Duncan's community had managed to shed every one of its members. Spending half the week in London as editor of *Peace News*, and being so strongly committed to the theory of the 'religious' community, Murry took longer to be 'made sick of young pacifists' but was himself eventually driven to the conclusion: 'Individualism must remain the chief social ethos.'[1] Although Murry's change of heart can in part be attributed to his increasingly pessimistic reading of the international situation and to his decision finally to break off all dealings with his third wife and concentrate on his happy life with Mary Gamble, it was clear that his new belief in individual freedom, which led him to end his life voting Tory, owed much to the lessons he had learned at Thelnetham.

Well before some of its leading advocates had become disillusioned with their practical experiences, however, it was clear that community living, even more than active social service, was a practical proposition for only a minority of pacifists, mainly the young men of military age, and could not provide for the ordinary activist the expressive satisfactions which, before the 1940 crisis, he had gained through normal pressure-group campaigning. Pointing this out in *Peace News* on 28 February 1941 one pacifist admitted:

I have found it rather difficult to adjust myself to a pacifism with no poster-parades, no street-corner meetings, no mass demonstrations; for these strivings were an essential part of our movement . . . Mere doctrinaire discussion, with a dash of social service, as we know it, is not enough to weld together the mass of pacifists and like-minded people, who must feel they are taking part in a crusade.

A few months later David Spreckley, newly elected to the P.P.U.'s National Council and frustrated by its inability since the start of the military crisis to define any active role for itself or its members, suggested that the Union should disband itself. When it refused, he resigned[2]—although, despite walking into R.A.F. recruiting offices on three

[1] Cited in Lea, *Murry*, pp. 309, 323.
[2] *PN*, 11 July 1941.

occasions during the war,[1] he remained a pacifist. For a few, however, the C.O.'s position had become unendurable; as one recipient of an unconditional exemption later recalled: 'The inactivity of my pacifist role became increasingly irksome. I still believed that the position of the pacifist was ultimately right but I was beginning to realise that, at the same time, I could not stand aside from the struggle which was engulfing my contemporaries.'[2] In May 1942 he joined up.

Although the turning of the tide in the war at the end of 1942 ended this phase of maximum guilt and uncertainty, the confidence of the pacifist movement had been too shaken for it to take full advantage of better conditions. The growing likelihood of an eventual Allied victory enabled the P.P.U. to recover its voice in support of an immediate armistice— a policy to which, as Murry and others had pointed out, it was logically always committed but about which it had been, in practice, less than enthusiastic as long as the Allies were in no position to negotiate reasonable terms. Yet, despite the P.P.U.'s campaign, pacifists were much less sure of their right and ability to pronounce upon the political requirements for a just and lasting peace than had been their forerunners in the Great War. In addition Murry himself, whose stimulating editorials had enabled *Peace News* to survive the war with a circulation (laboriously rebuilt through its own distribution network) not far short of 20,000, had by the autumn of 1944 become doubtful about whether Germans could ever be trusted to make democracy work unaided.[3] He had thus started to abandon his pacifist faith in the goodness and reasonability of man; others, it may be surmised, did the same after the Nazi extermination camps were discovered.

At the end of the war, therefore, pacifism had lost most of its political optimism and had failed to create the nucleus of a new society; and, although its most successful constructive activity, relief work, had won its practitioners a measure of respect, it had done nothing to cause supporters of the war to question their own position. As early as 1941 Brockway

---

[1] Interview.
[2] Clifford Simmons, in Simmons (ed.), *The Objectors*, pp. 15–16.
[3] *PN*, 20 Oct. 1944.

had detected 'a tendency today to idealise the No-Conscription Fellowship . . . and to regard the C.O. movement in the present war as a falling away from it.' In some respects this tendency was justified: in particular, a number of nominal pacifists were guilty of intellectual evasion in refusing to admit that, in so far as pacifism could be translated into national policy, it could only be that of peace at any price; as Murry's *Peace News* editorial on 7 April 1944 admitted, they had given 'all sorts of equivocal answers to the plain question: "Are you calling upon us to lay down our arms and let the enemy do his will?" The pacifist has or should have only one answer to that question: a plain "Yes". A plain "Yes" but not an easy one.'

But Brockway had rightly gone on to argue that much of this decline in confidence was due not to a failure of intellect or nerve but to a greater awareness of the real basis of the pacifist position. In marked contrast to the contempt he had formerly shown for any pacifism that was not practical he now admitted that only 'those anchored deeply in religious conviction or reasoned philosophy or political principles can be expected to stand out' against the evils of war. Though he had come privately to realize that he was himself an extreme *pacificist* rather than a pacifist, he was prepared to accept the C.O. movement's value as 'a witness to peace rather than as an immediate instrument of peace.'[1] Many clear-minded pacifists—for example, Ralph and Frances Partridge[2]—who were sceptical about the practicality of pacifist communities but anxious to help their fellow citizens in so far as they could, found themselves regarded by neighbours and friends with suspicion and accepted that they had no alternative but to accept the sectarian orientation even if it seemed to others mere quietism or selfish escapism. In the language Murry liked to use, their 'illusions' about pacifism had been 'purged': yet they still maintained their convictions.

The existence of stoical pacifists who stood by their faith even though they had accepted that it had no immediate

---

[1] Brockway, *C.O. and Community*, pp. 3, 4, 7.
[2] See Partridge, *Pacifist's War*, pp. 80, 142–3, 163.

political or social application explains why at the end of the
war the P.P.U., though unable across the whole country to
muster even 4,000 voters in its National Council elections,
still had 98,414 pledges in its 'live' membership file[1]—over 70
per cent of its peak membership total early in 1940. After
the defections of 1940, it had suffered no major losses except
through death: Lansbury and Gill had had died in 1940;
Plowman in 1941; and Maurice Rowntree in 1944. It had,
however, undergone a number of changes at headquarters,
some of which had been painful. The dismissal of the enthusiastic but unsystematic John Barclay in June 1942 offended
many members; so too did the temporary departure of Stuart
Morris (who was replaced as General Secretary for three
years after 1943 by the Revd Patrick Figgis) following his
imprisonment for nine months under the Official Secrets
Act. He had on several occasions been supplied, by a Civil
Servant who first approached him at a public meeting, with
confidential Government documents concerning contingency
plans for dealing with rebellion by Gandhi in India;[2] and
although the judge publicly acknowledged after the trial
(held in camera, with no detail of the charge disclosed) that
his motives were above suspicion, Alex Wood insisted—to the
point of resignation when the National Council initially disagreed with him—that Morris's resignation be accepted.[3] Yet
the P.P.U. managed to survive these upheavals; as the first
generation of staff members departed, often for personal
and career reasons, others took their place, and morale remained good throughout the war.

It was only when peace came, that the lessons of the war
fully sank in. Admitting, in the P.P.U.'s official history published in 1962, that the 'end of the war left everyone exhausted
and flat; a focal point had been removed and the sense of
urgency had departed', Sybil Morrison detected 'a strange
paradox apparent in the affairs of pacifists, which seem to
make waging peace an easier undertaking when others are

---

[1] Morrison, *I Renounce War*, p. 62; *PN*, 4 May 1945.
[2] For details of the charge, not previously made public, I am grateful to Mrs
Hilda Morris's letter of 12 Feb. 1979.
[3] *The Times*, 17 Feb. 1943; *PN*, 5 Mar. 1943.

waging war'.[1] But, according to the analysis advanced in this study, this paradox was not strange but inherent in the sectarian orientation. By the middle of the Second World War most pacifists had realized that pacifism was essentially an apolitical creed which could not easily be translated into pressure group terms. While the war was being fought pacifists had 'developed a very great sense of loyalty to the unpopular group they formed',[2] as Edward Blishen later put it, and felt the need for an organization to express their sense of shared predicament. But the end of the war left the P.P.U.—like the F.o.R. in 1919 when it had seriously considered winding itself up—with no obvious organizational purpose even in the eyes of many sincere and unshakeable pacifists. This was despite the existence of political conditions which might have been expected to inspire a strong pacifist movement: the continuation into peacetime of conscription; the Cold War; and above all the invention of nuclear weapons of a destructive potential which greatly strengthened the 'utilitarian' argument for pacifism.

Since 1945 the P.P.U. has been forced to face up to the contradiction inherent in any attempt to organize pacifism: that whereas pacifism is a matter of individual conscience which, except in extremely unusual circumstances, will have little political relevance, organizations tend to attract the politically-minded. Thus though the P.P.U.'s considerable achievement had been to demonstrate that pacifism transcended short-term practical considerations, its post-war recruits have often been activists hoping that pacifism could be a lever for radical reforms. Because many apolitical pacifists opted out—the P.P.U.'s membership and *Peace News* sales sagged sharply soon after the end of the war—the P.P.U. has been easily dominated by successive waves of political militants. In 1947, when only 16,000 members remained, the annual general meeting—at which the 'attendance was notably small compared with previous years and many well-known faces were conspicuous by their absence'[3]—committed the Union in such extreme terms to 'destroy completely' the

[1] Morrison, *I Renounce War*, p. 65.
[2] Blishen, *Cackhanded War*, p. 229.
[3] *PN*, 25 Apr. 1947.

National Service Act that Murry, Wood, Soper, Raven, Wellock and Wragg all resigned—though a special general meeting five months later modified the policy, persuading some of these to return.[1] Within a few years, however, serious new disagreements had been provoked: over tactics, by the advocates of civil disobedience, which many pacifists understandably regarded as a form of coercion; and over policy, by those who insisted that pacifists focus their attention exclusively on nuclear weapons. The capture, by militants on these questions, of *Peace News* even forced the P.P.U. to sever its connection with the paper; though its own, much less successful, replacement from 1961, the *Pacifist*, was soon complaining that members of the public were ignorant about pacifism 'and even if recently they have heard the word think it means nuclear disarmament'.[2] If they continued reading either *Peace News*, or the *Pacifist* however, they could have been forgiven for thinking that the word meant alternatively civil liberties, colonial liberation, opposition to apartheid and to racial discrimination, American withdrawal from Vietnam, British military withdrawal from Northern Ireland, or the safeguarding of the environment and ecosphere.

There were two reasons for this diffusion of pacifist interests. One was that pacifists, aware of social issues more immediately pressing than the prospect of another world war, were anxious not to 'isolate war' as they believed their forerunners to have done. More important, however, was that non-violence as a *tactic* became popular among those who were not really pacifists although, because they had a preference for non-violent political methods, they believed themselves to be. Faced eventually with a choice between political effectiveness and strict pacifism they normally opted for the former, often expressing frustration with the P.P.U. for being 'old, out of date, behind the times, redundant' and 'a laughing stock in the peace movement'.[3] As this happened membership dwindled: by the late sixties it was polling less than 600 votes in its National Council elections (representing a tenth of the number of ballot papers distributed to members).

[1] Morrison, *I Renounce War*, pp. 73–4; *PN*, 10 Oct. 1947.
[2] *Pacifist*, June 1961.
[3] Ibid., Dec. 1974, Apr. 1975.

With a flow of mostly young radicals passing through the post-war P.P.U., its continuity and survival has been assured only by the fact of owning freehold premises and by the devoted efforts of wholehearted individuals such as Morris (until his retirement as General Secretary in 1964), his second wife, Hilda, Sybil Morrison, Myrtle Solomon, John Hyatt, and a relatively small number of others. While these have been confident that the peace pledge 'opens up an unlimited field to individual and corporate action of a non-violent nature',[1] they have criticized 'the "I want it now" syndrome'[2] of expecting quick results before mankind has been educated to a higher standard of social and international behaviour; as Sybil Morrison expressed it in the concluding section of her official history of the P.P.U.:

The pacifist movement is very very young; its age, when set against the thousands and thousands of years in which war has been accepted as justifiable and right, is to set it in the womb, not yet fully formed, not born, and it still has far to go in understanding and in planning for the new world in which war will have no place.[3]

It is a tribute to the moral courage of most of those who, since 1940, have sustained the pacifist movement that they have done so without benefit of comforting illusions that it is a political idea or that it is anything other than an exacting personal faith. The inspiration and discipline of the faith called pacifism to which they have dedicated themselves was definitively stated by Vera Brittain, herself an undismayed believer right to the end, during the darkest days of the Second World War:

Pacifism is nothing other than a belief in the ultimate transcendence of love over power. This belief comes from an inward assurance. It is untouched by logic and beyond argument—though there are many arguments both for and against it. And each person's assurance is individual; his inspiration cannot arise from another's reasons, nor can its authority be quenched by another's scepticism.[4]

---

[1] According to the rubric carried in each issue of the *Pacifist* in the early 1970s.

[2] In the words of Mrs Hilda Morris, in a letter to the author, 24 Feb. 1979.

[3] Morrison, *I Renounce War*, p. 65.

[4] Brittain, *Humiliation With Honour*, p. 8.

APPENDIX I:

THE PEACE MOVEMENT

The following is a guide to the peace societies mentioned in the text, including non-pacifist organizations (but excluding groups within the Christian denominations):

British Anti-War Movement (or Council) (B.A.-W.M.): socialist *pacificist*; Communist-controlled, founded after World Anti-War Congress in Amsterdam, Aug. 1932; renamed British Movement Against War and Fascism in 1934, when the Communist line changed. From 1936 the Communists followed a popular-front strategy of working through local Peace Councils and the B.A.-W.M. faded away. No individual members.

'Christ and Peace' Campaign: Loosely organized *pacificist* campaign within Christian churches Oct. 1929–Apr. 1931. Its major success was the Lambeth Conference declaration of 1930.

Council of Christian Pacifist Groups (C.C.P.G.): founded late 1933 to co-ordinate the denominational pacifist groups.

Fellowship of Reconciliation (F.o.R.): Christian pacifist; founded Dec. 1914; quietist; British section of the International F.o.R., established 1919. Membership 3,300 from late 1920s to mid 1930s, rising to 9,813 in 1939. Still in existence.

League of Free Nations Association: internationalist; founded some time early in 1918 to campaign for the immediate formation of a League based on the existing military alliance against Germany. Merged with League of Nations Society in Oct. 1918 to form L.N.U.

League of Nations Society: internationalist; established May 1915 to study proposals of a League of all nations; contained many influential liberals and radicals. Merged with League of Free Nations Association in Oct. 1918 to form L.N.U.

League of Nations Union (L.N.U.): internationalist; founded Oct. 1918 as a merger of the League of Nations Society and the League of Free Nations Association; the largest and most influential peace society after the mid-twenties, reaching its peak in 1931 when 406,868 subscriptions were collected. Organized successful Peace Ballot in 1934–5, but lost support after 1936, collecting 193,266 subscriptions in 1939. Refounded as United Nations Association.

National Peace Council (N.P.C.): set up 1904 (on a more permanent basis, 1908) to organize annual National Peace Congresses and co-ordinate the peace movement (which prevented it from discussing any controversial issue, such as sanctions); organized a petition on appease-ment 1938–9. No individual membership. Still in existence.

New Commonwealth Society: internationalist, set up Oct. 1932 by David, Baron Davies of Llandinam, to campaign for an International Police Force, which would enforce the decisions of an International Equity Tribunal. A small pressure group within the L.N.U.; its member-ship was nearly 3,000 in 1939. Still in existence as the David Davies Memorial Institute of International Studies.

No-Conscription Fellowship (N.-C.F.): pacifist (mainly I.L.P.); founded Nov. 1914 by Fenner Brockway to oppose conscription; after its intro-duction became a welfare body for all C.O.s; wound up when conscription ended in 1919 (but some of its members form the N.M.W.M. and the No-Conscription League.)

No-Conscription League: set up in 1938 by ex-N.-C.F. members to fulfil a similar task, because of the P.P.U.'s reluctance to campaign poli-tically against conscription. Negligible impact.

No More War Movement (N.M.W.M.): pacifist (mainly socialist); set up Feb. 1921 by the *Crusader* group and other ex-N.C.F. members; claimed 3,000 members 1927; thereafter quoted only in number of branches (150, dropping to 83 in 1936). British section of W.R.I. Wound up Feb. 1937 (merged with P.P.U.), except for Birmingham branch and for its Trustees (who constituted themselves the Pacifist Research Bureau, Oct. 1938).

Peace Pledge Union (P.P.U.); pacifist (all inspirations); founded in May 1936, out of the Sheppard Peace Movement, set up July 1935 after a meeting of signatories of the pledge launched by Sheppard's letter, 16 Oct. 1934. Swallows N.M.W.M., Feb. 1937, becoming British section of W.R.I. Peak membership 136,000 in Apr. 1940. Still in existence.

Peace Society (sometimes called International Peace Society): ori-ginally Christian pacifist, but after 1840s increasingly *pacificist*; founded 1816 as the Society for the Promotion of Permanent and Universal Peace; loses influence in 1914 because of failure to condemn war. Mori-bund from 1920s onwards, though claiming a static figure of 5,000 members until 1936. Still in nominal existence.

Sheppard Peace Movement: pacifist; formed July 1935, basis of P.P.U. May 1936. Attracted 80,000 pledges.

Society of Friends ('Quakers'): pacifist but with a growing *pacificist* element. Sect founded mid-seventeenth century. Friends Peace

Committee (est. 1888) and Northern Friends Peace Board (est. 1913) actively participated in peace movement.

Union of Democratic Control (U.D.C.): radical; established immediately after the outbreak of the Great War by neutrality campaigners. Though supporting a League, its belief that democratic control of foreign policy would keep Britain out of wars showed an isolationist attitude; it was the leading *pacificist* society from 1914–24, through its influence in labour and radical circles rather than membership size. Claimed 2,000 members in 1927; thereafter no figures given. In 1930s it was turned into an anti-fascist research and propaganda body by Dorothy Woodman.

Women's International League (W.I.L.): *pacificist*, but no clear policy and with a strong pacifist element; founded at International Women's Conference at The Hague, Apr. 1915, by ex-suffragists; British section of Women's International League for Peace and Freedom. Claimed 3,500 members in 1930s. Still in existence.

War Resisters' International (W.R.I.): founded at an anti-militarist congress at The Hague, Mar. 1921 under the name 'Paco' to co-ordinate socialist pacifism; moved to Enfield in 1923 and name changed to W.R.I., becoming an information service about the fate of C.O.s. Still in existence.

APPENDIX II:

THE P.P.U.'S SPONSORS

An authoritative list is hard to establish. The notepaper in use early in 1937 carried the names of the following 20 Sponsors: Sheppard, Lansbury, Crozier, Morris, Huxley, Rose Macaulay, Storm Jameson, Bing, Mumford, Hudson, Ponsonby, Russell, Raven, Sassoon, Brown, Wragg, Vera Brittain, Wellock, Soper, and Wood. The first A.G.M. in April 1938, which elected Lansbury president, Morris chairman, and Mumford treasurer, re-elected all the previous Sponsors (except for Sheppard and Crozier, deceased, and Rose Macaulay, resigned), plus the following eleven names not on the early 1937 list: Murry, Mary Gamble, Gray, Salter, Barclay, Carter, Housman, Macleod, Plowman, Elizabeth Thorneycroft, and Barr, making a total of 25, plus the three officers. When Barr announced he could not attend meetings he was replaced by Moore, and when Rowntree took over the treasurership he also became a Sponsor. The Sponsors as an executive body met for the last time on 10 May 1939, being replaced by the National Council ten days later. Including all those appointed or elected up to this time, even if they soon withdrew, the total of Sponsors was thus at least 33. In addition Heard and Ursula Roberts had attended meetings but were omitted for some reason from the early notepaper; and it also seems from other evidence that Ellen Wilkinson was a Sponsor in 1936. *Thus the most likely peacetime total is 36.* This excludes prominent pacifists such as Beresford, Reginald Sorensen, and Maude Royden whose exact status in the P.P.U. is unclear. It also excludes those who became Sponsors after May 1939, when it was an honorific title only: these included Gill, G. M. Ll. Davies, Sybil Thorndike, and, after 1942, Eddington. The list of Sponsors, which *Peace News* began publishing regularly during 1940, was, however, considerably attenuated. Several less publicly-prominent figures who had not renounced their pacifism, including Barclay, Bing, Brown, Carter, Mary Gamble, and Moore, had disappeared from it; as well as Lansbury, who had died in May 1940, and Russell, Mumford, and Storm Jameson after they resigned. In September 1940 it contained only 18 names: Wood (chairman), Morris (general secretary), Rowntree (treasurer), Vera Brittain, Davies, Gray, Housman, Huxley, Murry, Plowman, Ponsonby, Raven, Salter, Soper, Sybil Thorndike, Wellock, Wragg, and Gill.

The National Council which took over from the Sponsors on 10 May 1939, consisted of a representative of each local 'area', plus 20 nationally elected members, and a few co-opted members. Its membership was fluid, but the first meeting was attended by (or received apologies from) the following Sponsors who had been elected to it: Salter, Barclay, Raven, Vera Brittain, Mary Gamble, Wood, Wellock, Bing, Brown, Ponsonby, Plowman, and Murry. New names were: Thomas Large, J. R. Purling, W. J. Parkin, Andrew Stewart, Charles Baldwin, Leslie Kirkley, H. O. Evans, G. C. Seagar, J. N. Whale, Herbert Whatley, Denis Riley, Sybil Morrison, Ruth Fry, George M. Ll. Davies, Lady Artemus Jones, Vincent Williams; and, in addition, two members were co-opted: Gill and Moore.

SELECT BIBLIOGRAPHY

This is neither a complete nor fully-itemized bibliography of works consulted. (Scholars wishing more detail should consult my thesis, 'Pacifism in Britain 1931-1939' (D. Phil, Oxford 1976), pp. 383-406.) Section I is a list of unpublished sources; sections II and III respectively bring together for ease of reference the peace journals and other works which have already been cited in the text and footnotes; and section IV lists selected secondary works on the peace movement. (Unless otherwise stated, the place of publication is London.)

I. UNPUBLISHED SOURCES.

(a) Private Papers.

Vyvyan Adams Papers: British Library of Political and Economic Science.

Baldwin Papers: Cambridge University Library.

Bishop Bell of Chichester Papers: Lambeth Palace Library.

Reginald Bridgeman Papers: a small collection in the possession of Mrs Olwen Bridgeman.

Cecil of Chelwood Papers: British Library Reference Division.

Duff Cooper Letters (received on his resignation in Oct. 1938): consulted by courtesy of Mr Martin Gilbert; now deposited in Bodleian Library.

Cripps Papers: Nuffield College.

Davies of Llandinam Papers: National Library of Wales.

Gwilym Davies Papers: National Library of Wales (kept with the Davies of Llandinam Papers).

W. H. Dickinson Papers: Bodleian Library.

Gainford Papers: consulted in Nuffield College.

Lloyd George Papers: House of Lords Record Office.

Frank Hardie Papers: in his possession.

Lansbury Papers: British Library of Political and Economic Science.

Lytton Papers: in the possession of Lady Cobbold.

Kingsley Martin Papers: University of Sussex.

Gilbert Murray Papers: Bodleian Library.

Noel-Buxton Papers: in the possession of the Hon. Mrs J. C. Hogg.

Max Plowman Papers: University College, London.

Ponsonby Papers: consulted in Nuffield College; now in the Bodleian Library.

Rennie Smith Papers: Bodleian Library.

Reginald Sorensen Papers: House of Lords Record Office.

J. A. Spender Papers: British Library Reference Division.

Leonard Woolf Papers: University of Sussex.

(b) Archives of Peace Societies.

'Christ and Peace' Campaign: with the Fellowship of Reconciliation Papers.

Fellowship of Reconciliation: British Library of Political and Economic Science.

League of Nations Union: consulted at United Nations Association; now in British Library of Political and Economic Science.

National Peace Council: consulted at its office; now in British Library of Political and Economic Science.

New Commonwealth Society: National Library of Wales (part of Davies of Llandinam Papers).

No More War Movement: in the possession of Mrs Mabel Eyles Monk.

Peace Pledge Union: consulted at its offices.

Society of Friends: Friends' House Library.

Union of Democratic Control: Hull University.

Women's International League: British Library of Political and Economic Science.

II. PEACE JOURNALS CITED

Christian Pacifist (F.o.R.; 1939–).
Friend (Society of Friends).
Headway (L.N.U.).
New World (N.M.W.M.; 1930–3).
No More War (N.M.W.M.; 1922–30, 1935–7).
Pacifist (P.P.U.; 1961–).
Peace (N.P.C., 1933–41).
Peace News (P.P.U.; 1936–).
Peace Review (N.P.C.; 1931–2).
Reconciliation (F.o.R.; 1924–38).
War (B.A.-W.M.; 1932–4).
War Resister (W.R.I., 1926–38).

III. OTHER WORKS CITED.

Alexander, F. Matthias, *The Use of the Self: Its Conscious Direction in Relation to Diagnosis, Functioning and the Control of Reaction* (n.d. [1931]).

Angell, Sir Norman, *After All* (1951).

Bellerby, J. R., *World Order Without Arms* (1933).

Babington Smith, Constance (ed.), *Letters to a Sister from Rose Macaulay* (New York, 1964).

—— *Rose Macaulay* (1972).

Bedford, Sybille, *Aldous Huxley: A Biography*, 2 vols. (1973–4).

Blishen, Edward, *A Cackhanded War* (1972).

Bowra, C. M., *Memories 1898–1939* (1966).

Brenan, Gerald, *A Personal Record 1920–72* (1974).

Brinton, Henry, *The Peace Army* (1932).

Brittain, Vera, *Born 1925: A Novel of Youth* (1948).

—— *Humiliation With Honour* (1942).

—— *Letters to Peace Lovers* (1940).

—— *Testament of Experience: An Autobiographical Story of the Years 1925–1950* (1975).

—— *Testament of Friendship: The Story of Winifred Holtby* (1940).

—— *Testament of Youth: An Autobiographical Study of the Years 1900–1925* (1933).

—— *Thrice a Stranger: New Chapters of Autobiography* (1938).

Brockway, A. Fenner, *Bermondsey Story: The Life of Alfred Salter* (1947).

—— *The Bloody Traffic* (1933).

—— *The C.O. and the Community* (n.d. [1941?]).

—— *Inside the Left: Thirty Years of Platform, Press, Prison, and Parliament* (1942).

—— *Non-Co-Operation In Other Lands* (Madras, 1921).

—— *Outside the Right* (1963).

—— *Socialism Over Sixty Years: The Life of Jowett of Bradford* (1948).

Bullock, Alan, *The Life and Times of Ernest Bevin*, i (1960).

Busch, Eberhard, *Karl Barth: His Life From Letters and Autobiographical Texts* (translated by John Bowden) (1976).

Cadoux, Cecil J., *Christian Pacifism Re-examined* (1940).

—— *The Early Christian Church and the World* (1925).

Campbell Johnson, Alan, *Peace Offering* (1936).

Catchpool, E. St. John, *Candles in the Darkness* (1966).

Catlin, George, *For God's Sake, Go* (1972).

Ceadel, Martin, 'Interpreting East Fulham', in C. Cook and J. Ramsden (eds.), *By-Elections in British Politics* (1973).

—— 'The "King and Country" Debate, 1933: Student Politics, Pacifism, and the Dictators', *Historical Journal* 22 (1979).

—— 'Popular Fiction and the Next War, 1918–1939', in Frank Glover-smith (ed.), *Class, Culture and Social Change: a New View of the 1930s* (Brighton, 1980).

Clark, Ronald W., *Einstein: The Life and Times* (1973).

—— *The Life of Bertrand Russell* (1975).

Cockburn, Patricia, *The Years of 'The Week'* (1968).

Davie, Michael (ed.), *The Diaries of Evelyn Waugh* (1976).

Davies, George M. Ll., *Pilgrimage of Peace* (with an introduction by Charles Raven) (1950).

De Bunsen, Victoria, *Charles Roden Buxton: A Memoir* (1948).

De Ligt, Bart., *The Conquest of Violence: An Essay on War and Revolution* (English edn., with an introduction by Aldous Huxley) (1937).

Delisle Burns, Cecil, *War—and a changing civilisation* (1934).

—— *Civilisation: The Next Step* (1938).

Dell, Robert, *Germany Unmasked* (1934).

Dillistone, F. W., *Charles Raven: Naturalist, Historian, Theologian* (1975).

Dick Sheppard: By his Friends (1938).

Donoughue, Bernard, and Jones, G. W., *Herbert Morrison: Portrait of a Politician* (1973).

Duncan, Ronald, *All Men Are Islands: An Autobiography* (1964).

— *The Complete Pacifist* (1937).

— *How To Make Enemies: A Second Volume of Autobiography* (1968).

— *Journal of a Husbandman* (1944).

Elliott, W. H., *Undiscovered Ends* (1951).

Feinberg, Barry, and Kasritz, Ronald, *Bertrand Russell's America: His Translatlantic Travels and Writings*, i (1973).

Foot, Michael, *et al.*, *Young Oxford and War* (1934).

Fry, A. Ruth, *Victories Without Violence* (1930).

— *More Victories Without Violence* (1938).

Furbank, P. N., *E. M. Forster: A Life*, ii (1978).

Garnett, David, *The Flowers of the Forest* (1955).

Gilbert, Martin (ed.), *Plough My Own Furrow: The story of Lord Allen of Hurtwood as told through his writings and correspondence* (1965).

Gill, Eric, *Autobiography* (1940).

— *The Human Person and Society* (P.P.U., 1940).

— *Last Essays* (1942).

— *Money and Morals* (1934).

Goldring, Douglas, *Odd Man Out* (1935).

Gollancz, Victor, *More For Timothy* (1953).

— *Reminiscences of Affection* (1968).

Gooch, G. P. (ed.), *In Pursuit of Peace* (1933).

Graves, Robert, *Goodbye to all that* (1929).

Gray, A. Herbert, *Love: The One Solution* (1938).

Gregg, Richard B., *The Power of Non-Violence* (1935 edn.).

— *Training for Peace: A Programme for Peace Workers* (P.P.U., n.d. [1936]).

Halévy, Elie, *Imperialism and the Rise of Labour* (1951 edn.).

Hamilton, Mary Agnes, *Remembering My Good Friends* (1944).

Hardy, G. H., *Bertrand Russell and Trinity* (1942; facsimile edn., Cambridge, 1970).

Harrod, R. F., *The Prof.: A Personal Memoir of Lord Cherwell* (1959).

Heard, Gerald, *The Ascent of Humanity* (1929).

— *The Social Substance of Religion* (1931).

— *The Source of Civilisation* (1935).

— *The Third Morality* (1937).

Heppenstall, Rayner, *Four Absentees* (1960).

Hibbert, G. K. (ed.), *The New Pacifism* (1936).

Hobhouse, Stephen, *Forty Years and an Epilogue: An Autobiography (1881-1951)* (1951).

Holroyd, Michael, *Lytton Strachey: A Critical Biography*, i (1967).

Horsburgh, H. J. N., *Non-Violence and Aggression: A Study of Gandhi's Moral Equivalent of War* (1968).

Housman, Laurence (ed.), *What Can We Believe? Letters Exchanged Between Dick Sheppard and L.H.* (1939).

Howarth, T. E. B., *Cambridge Between The Wars* (1978).

Hughes, W. R., *Indomitable Friend: The Life of Corder Catchpool 1883-1952* (1957).

Huxley, Aldous, *After Many A Summer* (1939).

—— *Ends and Means: An Inquiry into the Nature of Ideals and into the Methods Employed for their Realisation* (1937).

—— *Eyeless in Gaza* (1936).

—— *What Are You Going To Do About It?* (P.P.U., 1936).

Hyams, Edward, *Few Men Are Liars* (P.P.U., 1937).

—— *The New Statesman: The History of its First Fifty Years* (1963).

Hynes, Samuel, *The Auden Generation* (1976).

Ingram, Kenneth, *The Defeat of War: Can Pacifism Achieve It?* (1939).

Jameson, Margaret Storm, (ed., anonymously) *The Challenge to Death* (1934).

—— *The End of this War* (P.E.N., 1941).

—— *Journey from the North: Autobiography*, 2 vols. (1969-70).

—— *No Time Like The Present* (1933).

Joad, C. E. M., *A Guide to Modern Wickedness* (1939).

—— *Journey Through The War Mind* (1940).

—— (ed.), *Manifesto: Being the Book of the Federation of Progressive Societies and Individuals* (1934).

—— *The Oxford Resolution* (1933).

—— *Pacifism and The Class War* (N.P.C. pamphlet No. 6, 1933).

—— *Under the Fifth Rib* (1932).

—— *What Fighting Means* (N.M.W.M., 1932).

—— *Why War?* (1939).

Johnston, Thomas, *Memories* (1952).

Koss, Stephen, *Nonconformity in Modern British Politics* (1975).

Lansbury, George, *My Quest For Peace* (1938).

—— *Why Pacifists Should Be Socialists* (*Fact*, No. 7, 15 Oct. 1937).

Lea, F. A., *The Life of John Middleton Murry* (1959).

Lewis, John, *The Case Against Pacifism* (n.d. [1940]).

—— *The Left Book Club* (1970).

Lindsay, A. D., *Pacifism as a Principle and Pacifism as a Dogma* (Burge Memorial Lecture, 1939).

Macaulay, Rose, *et al.*, *Let Us Honour Peace* (1937).

Macgregor, G. H. C., *The New Testament Basis of Pacifism* (1936).

—— *The Relevance of the Impossible: A Reply to Reinhold Niebuhr* (F.o.R., 1941).

MacKenzie, Norman and Jeanne, *The Time Traveller* (1973).

Macleod, George, *We Shall Rebuild: The Work of the Iona Community on mainland and on island* (Glasgow, n.d. [1945]).

Mannin, Ethel, *Brief Voices: A Writer's Story* (1959).

—— *Privileged Spectator: A Sequel to 'Confessions and Impressions'* (1939).

Manning, Leah, *A Life For Education* (1971).

Marquand, David, *Ramsay MacDonald* (1977).

Martin, Kingsley, *Editor: A Second Volume of Autobiography 1931–45* (1968).

—— 'The Pacifist's Dilemma Today', *Political Quarterly*, Apr.–June 1938, pp. 155–72.

Matthews, C. H. S., *Dick Sheppard: Man of Peace* (1948).

Mellanby, Keith, *Human Guinea Pigs* (1945).

Meynell, Francis, *My Lives* (1971).

Miller, Alexander, *Pacifism, Revolution and Community* (1939).

Milne, A. A., *Autobiography* (1939).

—— *Peace With Honour: An Inquiry into the War Convention* (1934; also 5th edn., 1935).

—— *War With Honour* (1940).

Morrison, Herbert, *An Autobiography* (1960).

Mowat, C. L., *Britain Between The Wars 1918–40* (1958).

Mumford, Philip S., *An Introduction to Pacifism* (P.P.U., 1937).

Murry, Colin Middleton, *One Hand Clapping: A Memoir of Childhood* (1975).

Murry, John Middleton, *Community Farm* (1952).

—— *The Necessity of Communism* (1932).

—— *The Necessity of Pacifism* (1937).

—— *The Pledge of Peace* (1938).

Murry, Mary Middleton, *To Keep Faith* (1959).

Nathan, Otto, and Norden, Heinz (eds.) *Einstein on Peace* (1963).

Nichols, Beverley, *All I Could Never Be: Some Recollections* (1949).

—— *Cry Havoc!* (1933).

—— *Failures: Three Plays* (1933).

—— *The Fool Hath Said* (1936).

—— *For Adults Only* (1932).

—— *Men Do Not Weep* (1941).

—— *News of England: A Country Without A Hero* (1938).

—— *The Star-Spangled Banner* (1928).

Norman, E. R., *Church and Society in England 1770–1970: A Historical Study* (Oxford, 1976).

Orchard, W. E., *From Faith to Faith: An Autobiography of Religious Development* (1933).

Orwell, Sonia, and Angus, Ian (eds.), *The Collected Essays, Journalism and Letters of George Orwell*, i and ii (Penguin edn., 1970).

Panichas, George, A., (ed.), *The Promise of Greatness: The War of 1914–1918* (1968).

Partridge, Frances, *A Pacifist's War* (1977).

Paul, Leslie, *Angry Young Man* (1951).

Paxton, William, *et al.*, *Dick Sheppard: An Apostle of Brotherhood* (1938).

Percy, Lord Eustace, *Some Memories* (1958).

Pethick-Lawrence, Lord, *Fate Has Been Kind* (n.d.[1943]).

P(lowman), D. L. (ed.), *Bridge Into The Future: Letters of Max Plowman* (1944).

Plowman, Max, *The Faith Called Pacifism* (1936).

—— *War and the Creative Impulse* (1919).

Ponsonby, Lord (Arthur), *Disarmament: A Discussion* (1932).

—— *Falsehood in Wartime* (1928).

—— *Life Here and Now: Conclusions Derived From An Examination of the Sense of Duration* (1936).

—— *Now Is The Time: An Appeal for Peace* (1925).

—— (*et al.*) *What Shall I Do About War?* (undated pamphlet of addresses delivered at the Guildhouse in the autumn of 1933).

Postgate, Raymond, *The Life Of George Lansbury* (1951).

Purcell, William, *Portrait of Soper: A Biography of the Reverend Lord Soper of Kingsway* (1972).

Raven, Charles E., *Alex Wood: The Man and His Message* (F.o.R., 1952).

—— *Is War Obsolete? A Study of the Conflicting Claims of Religion and Citizenship* (Halley Stewart lectures 1934) (1935).

—— *The Starting Point of Pacifism* (P.P.U., 1940).

—— *The Theological Basis of Christian Pacifism* (1952).

—— *War and the Christian* (1938).

Reynolds, Reginald A., *India, Gandhi, and World Peace* (n.d. [1931]).

—— *My Life and Crimes* (1956).

Richards, Edith Ryley, *Private View of a Public Man: The Life of Leyton Richards* (1950).

Richards, Leyton, *The Christian's Alternative to War: An Examination of Christian Pacifism* (1929).

—— *The Christian's Contribution to Peace: A Constructive Approach To International Relationships* (1935).

—— *Christian Pacifism After Two World Wars* (1948).

—— *The Crisis and World Peace* (S.C.M. Press Crisis Booklet No. 4, Dec. 1938).

Roberts, R. Ellis, *H. R. L. Sheppard: Life and Letters* (1942).

Roskill, Stephen, *Hankey: Man of Secrets*, iii (1974).

Royal Institute of International Affairs, *The Future of the League of Nations* (1936).

Royden, Maude, *A Threefold Cord* (1947).

Russell, Bertrand, *Autobiography*, i and ii (1967–8).

—— *Unpopular Essays* (1950).

—— *Which Way To Peace?* (1936).

Schwimmer, Rosika, and Lief, Alfred (eds.), *The Fight Against War* (1933).

Scott, Carolyn, *Dick Sheppard: A Biography* (1977).

Shaw, Bernard, *What I Really Wrote About The War* (1931 edn.).

Sheppard, H. R. L., *If I Were Dictator* (1935).

—— (ed.), *The Root of the Matter* (1937).

—— *We Say 'No': The Plain Man's Guide to Pacifism* (1935).

Shewring, Walter (ed.), *Letters of Eric Gill* (1947).
Simmons, Clifford (ed.), *The Objectors* (Isle of Man, 1965).
Simmons, Jim, *Soap-Box Evangelist* (Chichester, 1972).
Skidelsky, Robert, *Oswald Mosley* (1975).
Smith, Grover (ed.), *Letters of Aldous Huxley* (1969).
Soper, Donald, *Question Time On Tower Hill* (1935).
Speaight, Robert, *The Life of Eric Gill* (1966).
Sprigge, Elizabeth, *Sybil Thorndike Casson* (1971).
Swanwick, H. M., *Collective Insecurity* (1937).
—— *Frankenstein and His Monster* (W.I.L., 1934).
—— *I Have Been Young* (1935).
—— *New Wars For Old* (W.I.L., 1934).
Symons, Julian, *The Thirties: A Dream Revolved* (1960).
Tait, Katherine, *My Father Bertrand Russell* (1975).
Thomas, Gilbert, *Autobiography 1891-1946* (1946).
Thompson, Douglas, *Donald Soper: A Biography* (1971).
Thurtle, Ernest, *Time's Winged Chariot* (1945).
Townshend, Charles, *The British Campaign in Ireland 1919-21* (Oxford, 1975).
Tudur Jones, R., *Congregationalism in England 1662-1962* (1962).
Urwin, E. C., *Henry Carter, C.B.E.: A Memoir* (1955).
Ward, R. H. (anonymously), *H. R. L. Sheppard: A Note In Appreciation* (1937).
—— *Names and Natures* (1968).
—— (ed.) *Ten Peace Plays* (1938).
—— *What is Non-Violent Technique?* (Pacifist Publicity Unit, 1938).
Watt, W. M., *Can Christians Be Pacifists?* (S.C.M., 1937).
Weatherhead, Kingsley, *Leslie Weatherhead: A Personal Portrait* (1975).
Weatherhead, Leslie, *Thinking Aloud In Wartime* (1939).
Wellock, Wilfred, *India's Awakening* (1922).
—— *Off The Beaten Track: Adventures in the art of living* (Tanjore, 1961).
Wheeler-Bennett, John W., *The Disarmament Deadlock* (1934).
Wilkinson, Ellen, and Conze, Edward, *Why War? A Handbook for those who will take part in the Second World War* (n.d. [1934]).
Wilson, Roger, *Authority, Leadership and Concern: A Study in Motive and Administration in Quaker Relief Work* (1949).
Winter, J. M., *Socialism and the Challenge of War: Ideas and Politics in Britain 1912-18* (1974).
Wood, H. G., *Henry T. Hodgkin: A Memoir* (1957).
Woodward, E. L., *Short Journey* (1942).
Woolf, Leonard, *Downhill All The Way: An autobiography of the years 1919-1939* (1968).
Wrench, John Evelyn, *Francis Yeats-Brown 1886-1944* (1948).
Yeats-Brown, F., *Dogs of War!* (1934).

IV. SELECTED WORKS ON THE PEACE MOVEMENT.

Bainton, Roland H., *Christian Attitudes Toward War and Peace: An Historical Survey and Critical Re-Evaluation* (1961).

Barker, Rachel, 'Conscientious Objection in Great Britain, 1939-45' (Ph.D. Thesis, Cambridge, 1978).

Beales, A. C. F., *The History of Peace: A Short Account of the Organised Movement for International Peace* (1931).

Bell, Julian (ed.), *We Did Not Fight: 1914-18 Experiences of War Resisters* (1935).

Berkman, Joyce A., 'Pacifism in England 1914-39' (Ph.D. Thesis, Yale, 1967).

Birn, Donald S., 'The League of Nations Union and Collective Security', *Journal of Contemporary History*, 9(3) 1974, pp. 131-59.

Bisceglia, L. R., 'The Politics of a Peace Prize', *Journal of Contemporary History*, 7 (3/4) 1972, pp. 263-73.

—— 'Normal Angell and the "Pacifist" Muddle', *Bulletin of the Institute of Historical Research*, May 1972, p. 109.

Boulton, David, *Objection Overruled* (1967).

Bramsted, Ernest, 'Apostles of Collective Security: The L.N.U. and Its Functions', *Australian Journal of Politics and History*, 13 (3), 1967, pp. 347-64.

Brittain, Vera, *The Rebel Passion: A Short History of Some Pioneer Peace Makers* (1964).

Brock, Peter, *Pacifism in Europe to 1914* (Princeton, 1972).

—— *Pacifism in the United States: From the Colonial Era to the First World War* (Princeton, 1968).

—— *Twentieth-Century Pacifism* (New York, 1970).

Bussey, Gertrude, and Tims, Margaret, *Women's International League for Peace and Freedom 1915-65* (1965).

Buzan, Barry G., 'The British Peace Movement from 1919 to 1939' (Ph.D. (Econ.) Thesis, L.S.E., 1973).

Cain, Edward R., 'Conscientious Objection in France, Britain and the United States', *Comparative Politics*, 2(2), Jan. 1970, pp. 274-307.

Ceadel, Martin, 'Pacifism in Britain, 1931-1939' (D.Phil Thesis, Oxford, 1976).

Chamberlain, W. J., *Fighting for Peace: The Story of the War Resistance Movement* (n.d. [1928]).

Chatfield, Charles, *For Peace and Justice: Pacifism in America 1914-1941* (Knoxville, 1971).

Chickering, Roger, *Imperial Germany And A World Without War: The Peace Movement and German Society 1892-1914* (Princeton, 1975).

Driver, Christopher, *The Disarmers: A Study in Protest* (1964).

Field, G. C., *Pacifism and Conscientious Objection* (1945).

Glover, Jonathan, *Causing Death and Saving Lives* (Harmondsworth, 1977).

Graham, John W., *Conscription and Conscience: A History 1916-1919* (1922).

Hanak, H., 'The Union of Democratic Control During The First World War', *Bulletin of the Institute of Historical Research*, Nov. 1963, pp. 168–80.

Hayes, Denis, *Challenge of Conscience: The Story of the Conscientious Objectors of 1939–49* (1949).

—— *Conscription Conflict: The Conflict of Ideas in the Struggle for and against Military Conscription in Britain between 1901 and 1939* (1949).

Henderson, Gavin B., 'The Pacifists of the Fifties', *Journal of Modern History*, 9(3) 1937, pp. 314–41.

Hinsley, F. H., *Power and the Pursuit of Peace: Theory and Practice in the History of Relations Between States* (Cambridge, 1963).

Howard, Michael, *War and the Liberal Conscience* (1977).

Ingram, Kenneth, *Fifty Years of the National Peace Council 1908–58: A Short History* (N.P.C., 1958).

Jones, Goronwy J., *Wales and the Quest for Peace* (Cardiff, 1969).

Kyba, J. P., 'British Attitudes Toward Disarmament and Rearmament 1932–5' (Ph.D. Thesis, London, 1967).

X Livingstone, Adelaide, *The Peace Ballot* (1935).

Lukowitz, David, 'British Pacifists and appeasement: The Peace Pledge Union', *Journal of Contemporary History*, 9(1), Jan. 1974, pp. 115–27.

Martin, David A., *Pacifism: An Historical and Sociological Study* (1965).

Morris, A. J. A., *Radicalism Against War 1906–14* (1972).

Morrison, Sybil, *I Renounce War: The Story of the Peace Pledge Union* (1962).

Murray, Gilbert, 'The British People and the League of Nations', in P. Munch (ed.), *Les Origines et l'Œuvre de la Societé des Nations*, i (Copenhagen, 1923), pp. 189–209.

Nelson, John K., *The Peace Prophets: American Pacifist Thought 1919–41* (Chapel Hill, 1967).

Nuttall, Geoffrey, *Christian Pacifism in History* (Oxford, 1958).

Parkin, Frank, *Middle Class Radicalism: The Social Bases of the British Campaign for Nuclear Disarmament* (1968).

Patterson, David S., *Toward A Warless World: The Travail of the American Peace Movement 1887–1914* (Bloomington, 1976).

Paul, J. B., 'The Union of Democratic Control' (Review Article), *Australian Outlook*, 26(2) Aug. 1972, pp. 222–32.

Prasad, Devi, *Fifty Years of War Resistance: What Now?* (W.R.I., 1972).

Pugh, M. C., 'British Public Opinion and Collective Security 1926–1936', (Ph.D. Thesis, East Anglia, 1975).

Rae, John, *Conscience and Politics: The British Government and the Conscientious Objector to Military Service 1916–19* (1970).

Rempel, Richard A., 'The Dilemma of British Pacifists During World War II' (University Microfilms, Michigan, 1978)—not available in time to be discussed in this book.

Robbins, Keith, *The Abolition of War: The 'Peace Movement' in Britain 1914-1919* (Cardiff, 1976).

—— 'The Abolition of War: A Study in the Organisation and Ideology of the Peace Movement 1914-19' (D. Phil. Thesis, Oxford, 1964).

Ryan, Edward A., 'The Rejection of Military Service by the Early Christians', *Theological Studies*, xiii (1) Mar. 1952, pp. 1-32.

Swanwick, H. M., *Builders of Peace: Being Ten Years' History of the Union of Democratic Control* (1924).

Swartz, Marvin, *The Union of Democratic Control in British Politics during the First World War* (Oxford, 1971).

Thompson, J. A., 'Lord Cecil and the Pacifists in the League of Nations Union', *Historical Journal*, 20(4) 1977, pp. 949-59.

Tyrell, Alexander, 'Making the Millenium: the Mid-Nineteenth Century Peace Movement' *Historical Journal*, 21(1) 1978, pp. 75-96.

University Group on Defence Policy, *The Role of the Peace Movement in the 1930s* (pamphlet No. 1, Jan. 1959).

Waley, Daniel, *British Public Opinion and the Abyssinian War 1935-6* (1975).

Weinroth, Howard, 'British Pacifism 1906-16: A Study in the Ideology and Organisation of the British Peace Movement During The Early Years of the 20th Century' (Ph.D. Thesis, Cambridge, 1968).

Wilson, Bryan (ed.), *Patterns of Sectarianism: Organisation and Ideology in Social and Religious Movements* (1967).

Wiltz, John E., *In Search of Peace: The Senate Munitions Inquiry 1934-6* (Louisiana State University Press, 1969).

Wittner, Lawrence S., *Rebels Against War: The American Peace Movement 1941-1960* (1969).

Addendum: John Barnes, *Ahead of his Age: Bishop Barnes of Birmingham* (1979) appeared while this book was at the proof stage.

INDEX